THE EMINENT TRAGEDIAN
William Charles Macready

William Charles Macready as William Tell

Portrait by Henry Inman

THE EMINENT TRAGEDIAN

William Charles Macready

✧ ✧ ✧ ✧ ✧ ✧ ✧ ✧

Alan S. Downer

HARVARD UNIVERSITY PRESS

Cambridge, Massachusetts

1 9 6 6

My dear John,

Not every actor would be pleased to have a study of another actor dedicated to him, but I was first encouraged to make this gesture because of a long-ago discussion about your predecessors in the English theatre. You had been reading in Macready's *Diary* in preparation for a BBC broadcast commemorating his retirement, and you pretended to find certain similarities between yourself and the character revealed by those prickly volumes. But over the years, as I grew to know more of Macready as artist, as actor, director, and manager, I saw in his work the exacting precision, the just balancing of reason and imagination, the tireless perfectionism that characterize your own performances. Like you, he was a man of energy and mind working in a theatre that was frequently mindless and constantly on the point of exhaustion. That his art as well as his career can be recollected in some detail a century after he left the stage will, I hope, be of some comfort to you.

For it was another of your great predecessors, David Garrick, who gave succinct form to the actor's lament:

> Nor pen nor pencil can the actor save,
> The art, and artist, share one common grave.

If this were true, it would be a melancholy reward for a life of dedication, and indeed most pens and pencils in the past have produced volumes of gossip and anecdote creating, occasionally, a vivid picture of the man and his times, leaving little impression of his art. But stage history has in this century become a scholarly discipline, and theatre collections have ceased to be wax museums and freak shows and become laboratories for research. It is now possible to study the stage artist of the past with almost the security of the study of a poet's or a painter's work. The greater difficulty, of course, that confronts the stage historian is the necessity of reconstructing the work before he can discuss the artist.

Fortunately for the present study, Macready was perhaps the first English actor to be thoroughly "reported." Theatrical reviewing came into its own in the early part of the nineteenth century and column upon column was often lavished upon a single performance, describing it in detail and making minute comparisons with earlier performances. In addition, there is Macready's voluminous *Diary*, most often seen as the querulous chafing of an oversensitive egoist, but actually a precise account of an artist's development, from which can be derived a clear idea of his proposed goal and guiding principles. Because promptbooks had to be duplicated for touring engagements, half a hundred of these priceless production blueprints have turned up in both private and public collections. And since the telephone was not available to expedite communication, Macready wrote an untold number (I have seen over a thousand) of letters about business and art. Out of such materials I have tried to create a picture of the Eminent Tragedian as actor and director.

Inevitably, it is an impression, for it is one of the glories of the theatre that it is an art of the moment. The audience is present at the act of creation, the audience shares in the act of creation. And what is created belongs in its fullness only to that particular audience. Still, much can be recaptured, how much I have tried to indicate in the pastiche of Chapter 8. This reconstruction of Macready's *Macbeth* does not represent a record of an actual performance: it is assembled from dozens of different accounts set down at various times over a thirty-year period, as well as from three promptbooks, from drawings and letters. This hypothetical picture of a performance gains some justification from the fact that Macready early developed principles of acting and production to which he clung throughout his career. A consistent artist, he made always the same demands of himself.

I hope it is not presumptuous to believe that only a written account of a performance is truly representative: we have all heard recordings and seen films of the great actors of the past only to wonder at their acclaim. The camera does not see with the human eye, and the phonograph deprives the actor of his most powerful instrument. Even the sound film demands cinematic rather than theatrical technique. In this instance, at any rate, the verbal record has not been superseded in the progress of communications.

I have tried to write a book about an actor which you as an actor would respect, and which would convey to the general reader an understanding of a demanding and highly specialized profession. Macready's life has been recounted before, by William Archer and J. C. Trewin, and two editions of his *Diary* have made only too evident his character and personality. The biographical portion of this study, therefore, is controlled by my ultimate purpose: to show the man as Eminent Tragedian, and the artist as eminently Victorian. Macready was a man divided; he loved his art and despised the theatre where it must be practised. Had he trained for the bar he might have become, as Granville-Barker once told me, a Lord Chief Justice. But a combination of circumstances, all financial, kept him in the theatre. Fate having determined his profession, his own character forced him into a leading position, not just as an actor, but as manager and director. He became, in every sense of the word, the founder of modern theatre practice. Nearly every principle which we now accept—of design, lighting, directing, costuming, as well as the training of actors—he put consciously into practice during his two periods of management. I have tried to make some acknowledgment of our debt to him.

If, as Garrick wrote, much of the actor's art vanishes with him, the actor has taught himself to be content with the reward of an attentive and approving audience. I hope that this study may join similar studies in suggesting to the people of the theatre that their achievement has more permanence than they have perhaps supposed, and that, acting on this hint, they will take greater care of their own records, that the future may share, in some measure, the greatest experiences of this miraculous art.

Faithfully yours,
Alan Downer

Princeton, N.J.
February 1, 1966

ACKNOWLEDGMENTS

My interest in Macready began many years ago when the curator of the Theatre Collection at Harvard showed me transcripts of passages from his *Diaries* that by some unexplained means had escaped burning. To the late William Van Lennep, then, must go the first acknowledgment of my indebtedness. I could wish that I were as certain that I have included in the following list all those who have helped me along the way:

Helen Willard and Mary Reardon of the Harvard Theatre Collection; Marguerite McAneny of the William Seymour Theatre Collection, Princeton University; Dorothy Mason of the Folger Shakespeare Library; George Freedley and the staff of the Theatre Collection, New York Public Library; the Secretary of the Garrick Club, London; George Nash and the staff of the Gabrielle Enthoven Collection, Victoria and Albert Museum; the librarian of the British Drama League; the staff of the British Museum; Antonia J. Bunch, of the Guildhall Library.

The Macready family: the late Brigadier J. Macready; the late Mrs. Catherine Davidson; Mr. Anthony Macready; Mrs. Jay Preston; and in particular Mrs. Lisa Puckle, Langley Cottage, Pirbright, Surrey, W. C. Macready's granddaughter, for generously allowing access to family documents and answering impertinent questions with patience and frankness. Quotations from these documents are made with the permission of the heirs through Lisa Macready Puckle.

Professor Arthur Colby Sprague, who first introduced me to stage history and has been a source of constant encouragement; Professor Charles Shattuck of the University of Illinois, who should have written this book; Professor William G. B. Carson of Washington University, who sought answers to questions from his own unequaled knowledge of the St. Louis theatre; Professor Kurt Pinthus of Columbia University; Professor Gerald Eades Bentley, my Princeton colleague, who willingly served as a tryout audience.

Sybil Rosenfeld of the Society for Theatre Research (London), a human catalogue of British theatre collections, public and private; Professor J. Isaacs of the University of London, who allowed me access to his unparalleled collection of theatrical designs; Mr. and Mrs. Geoffrey Watkins of Sherborne; the late Sir St. Vincent Troubridge; the late Harley Granville-Barker.

The University Research Fund and the John E. Annan Memorial Fund of Princeton University for financial support.

Colleagues and friends and students during a decade who have listened with more patience or resignation than even friendship should demand.

Florence Downer, who over the years supplied equal amounts of criticism and encouragement, not always, I fear, received with equal grace.

A. S. D.

Contents

Illustrations

Frontispiece William Charles Macready as William Tell. Portrait
by Henry Inman. Reproduced by permission of the
Metropolitan Museum of Art, Rogers Fund, 1906

Following page 160

Text Illustrations

THE EMINENT TRAGEDIAN

William Charles Macready

Prologue

DRURY LANE, FEBRUARY 26, 1851

BY the middle of the nineteenth century, old Drury Lane was the last monument to two centuries of tradition in the English theatre. For four decades it had stood, in its latest phoenix-like resurrection, a huge dingy pile, with a pseudo-classical portico fronting on Brydges Street. Since rising from its own ashes in 1812, it had held and beheld terrors and wonders. Here the great romantic actor Edmund Kean had revealed the truths of Shakespeare by flashes of lightning; here, during the regime of Alfred Bunn, the National Drama had been blasphemed by the introduction of ballet girls and trained animal acts; here the texts of Shakespeare's plays were first heard without the ancient corruptions of Restoration improvers; here Monsieur Jullien had further insulted the National Drama by the importation of a company of French players in *The Count of Monte Cristo,* resulting in such an uproar of indignation as a London playhouse had rarely seen. Here, too, in 1847, Mademoiselle Jenny Lind made her English debut before the greatest audience ever assembled in a theatre—an audience that, for those who could afford higher prices, had bought every available reservation weeks in advance, and, for those who could not, had waited cheerfully in untold numbers—twenty, two hundred, four hundred—to be swept willy-nilly into the upper galleries.

But the crowd which had been gathering in Brydges Street since two o'clock on the bleak wintry afternoon of February 26, 1851, had not come to see the latest in sensational entertainments, to welcome or damn a renowned visitor from the continent, or even to encourage the rise of a new theatrical star. They were assembling, rather, for the farewell benefit, the "last time forever" performance of William Charles Macready, for thirty years the Eminent Tragedian of the English stage. And old playgoers with long memories declared that such a crush had never been known. The reserved seats in the stalls, boxes, and "slips"—the end galleries—had been bought up for days. The pit and gallery proper were unreserved, and for these "rush seats" the crowd waited, cheerfully whistling and shouting, or cursing and chaffing, hour after hour. And moment by moment it increased in size until Vinegar Yard and Little Russell Street were densely packed with those who had come to bid farewell to Macready, and with the crowd which had come to see the crowd.

An actor's farewell is always a public occasion. He is not merely a man, an artist, withdrawing from his profession. The nature of his profession makes him a kind of symbol. In his art and in his life the essence of his era is distilled, and his departure may signal the end of his era, or merely the passing of memory into history. Macready's farewell was both; but if it marked the end of the theatrical tradition established by the royal patents of Charles II, it celebrated the conscious beginning of a new idea of theatre.

Some of the older playgoers were doubtless aware that they were bidding farewell to an honorable tradition. Throughout his long career, the Eminent Tragedian had clung almost quixotically to his heritage. He believed in the legitimate drama when his fellows were largely deserting to catchpenny spectacles; he believed in the repertory system, when other managers were discovering the expediency of the long run; he believed in the stock company as a training ground for young actors and an ideal setting for the experienced. He was, as one critic remarked, the "last of the cocked hats."

But some of the younger men in the queue, like John Toole who was to become the first of the "modern" comedians, had come not to mourn the passing of a tradition but to honor a reformer. Macready had not been simply a traditionalist. With confidence in the dignity of his profession and in the importance of the drama as an art, he attempted reforms in management and production that only after the passing of a century can be fully evaluated. If his innovations seem to have given the cue, as he feared, to the worst excesses of the Charles Kean-Henry Irving school, a longer perspective clearly shows his anticipation of the basic reforms of the Duke of Saxe-Meiningen, of Antoine, of Stanislavsky, and of Granville-Barker.

The largest part of the mob around Drury, however, had not

waited four long hours either to hail a reformer, or to acknowledge the death of an era. They had come to see for the last time a *Macbeth* which was recognized to be the supreme creation of its chief actor, and to seal up forever a chest of memories: of the great days when Macready had played with Kemble and Kean and Young; of his comic-opera squabbles with "the Poet Bunn"; of his brilliant recreations of Shakespeare's major plays; and of the thousand private recollections that a memorable theatrical performance can revive. When the doors were opened at six o'clock, three thousand people poured into the vast barnlike interior, filled the boxes and stalls, the pit and gallery, and overflowed into the saloons and corridors. Outside, other thousands waited, to participate vicariously in the excitement.

After a century of increasingly decorous audiences, we can have little notion of the almost hysterical tension generated by Macready's farewell. At his first entrance, on the blasted heath, the whole house rose to its feet, waving hats and handkerchiefs, stamping, shouting, *yelling* its friendship in such a crescendo of excitement that George Henry Lewes, from his vantage point in the boxes, wondered whether the actor would be able to go on. But, when the audience had quieted to a deathlike silence, go on he did, giving such a performance of Macbeth as had never been seen, the spectators hanging on his every word. At the end, as Lewes reports, "when after a gallant fight . . . he fell pierced by Macduff's sword, this death, typical of the actor's death, this last look, this last act of the actor, struck every bosom with a sharp and sudden blow, loosening a tempest of tumultuous feeling such as made applause an ovation."[1] The uproar continued as one of the English Officers in Malcolm's army helped the fallen Scot to his feet and assisted him to his dressing room.

After a long interval, during which the audience had time to gain its second wind, Macready appeared again, alone on the great stage. His Scots armor he had changed for the plain black of an English gentleman, as emblematic of the occasion. Fifty-eight years old, he was of medium height, something under six feet, with a rather awkward carriage, a flat "Hibernian" face, large blue eyes, and graying hair clubbed in masses over his ears. His features were irregular—someone said that his face would have been the fortune of a comedian—a noble brow, steeply angled eyebrows, a small firm mouth that descended sharply at the corners, and a nose that was a composite, as a fellow player observed, of "Grecian, Milesian, and snub." True to his somewhat old-fashioned propriety, he carried a tall hat, and wore a pleated shirt with dignified standing collar and wrapped cravat. Many of the spectators noticed the black studs and crepe hatband, and recalled the recent tragic death of his beloved daughter Nina.

In the face of the thunderous reverberations of the renewed greetings of the spectators he stood, calm but sad. At length the ovation was hushed, and the actor began, in a quiet tone: "My last theatrical part is played, and, in accordance with long-established usage, I appear once more before you." He recalled that for thirty-five years he had been accorded the generous support of the London audience, cheering his onward progress and upholding him in "mortifying emergencies." Briefly he traced his career, alluding pointedly to the failure of his management of the National Theatres as the responsibility of those "whose duty it was, in virtue of the trust committed to them, themselves to have undertaken the task." But he found some satisfaction in the assurance he could draw from certain contemporary productions —he was here alluding to his protégé, Samuel Phelps—that the texts of Shakespeare were forever restored and the greatest care expended upon revivals of his works.

I have little more to say. By some the relation of an actor to his audience is considered slight and transient. I do not feel it so. The repeated manifestation, under circumstances personally affecting me, of your favorable sentiments towards me will live with life among my most grateful memories; and because I would not willingly abate one jot in your esteem, I retire with the belief of yet unfailing powers, rather than linger on the scene to set in contrast the feeble style of age with the more vigorous exertions of my better years. Words—at least such as I can command—are ineffectual to convey my thanks; you will believe I feel more than I give utterance to. With sentiments of the deepest gratitude I take my leave, bidding you, Ladies and Gentlemen, in my past professional capacity, with regret, a last farewell.[2]

It was a completely untheatrical speech, for Macready was no longer an actor. It was a speech of quiet dignity as befitted the Victorian gentleman. For a moment, at the end, his voice faltered and he wiped a tear from his eye, but the real demonstrations of sorrow came from the other side of the floats. Lady Pollock recalls, "The tears of his hearers flowed fast; and a voice from the gallery called out in lamentation, 'The last of the Mohicans!' Then arose a cheer loud and long, pausing for an instant, only to be renewed again and again with increasing power."[3] The crowd outside, hearing the shouts from within, echoed the cheers with their own. Macready bowed slowly, and left the stage. The audience continued to call for him, but he came no more.

❖ ❖ ❖ 1 ❖ ❖ ❖

The Profession

THE PROVINCIAL STAGE

O N NOVEMBER 26, 1794, the proprietors of the Theatre, New Street, Birmingham, issued a bill announcing its complete reconstruction and offering it for rent during the coming summer season.[1] For a provincial playhouse, it was not unimpressive: classically elegant on the exterior, it enclosed a stage almost fifty feet square and a horseshoe-shaped auditorium intended to seat two thousand spectators who would pay nightly some two hundred pounds at the box office.[2] The proprietors may be excused for not pointing out that, although the building faced the finest street in town, at its back was a slum so dark and threatening that the policemen walked it in threes. Nor did they remark that the New Theatre was a replacement for the old Theatre Royal which had been burned to the ground in 1792 by mob action.[3]

Almost at once the bill came to the attention of William McCready, an ambitious, ill-tempered, modestly talented Irishman who had been for nearly a decade a member of the company at Covent Garden in London. The son of a prosperous Dublin upholsterer, he had early rejected the family trade and enlisted in what he, along with generations of rogues and vagabonds, always termed the Profession. To the end of his days, in spite of ample evidence to the contrary, he maintained that the theatre conveyed the status of gentlemen on its professors; but by 1794 he could not shut his eyes to the fact that he was as much of a drudge and as little his own master in Covent Garden company as he would ever have been in the upholstery business.

His first years had been promising. After learning the rudiments of his new craft on the Irish country stages, he had been called to

Daly's company at the Smock Alley theatre in Dublin. Since he
could not at once aspire to leading roles he was not unpleased to
find himself cast in what might be called such Upper Utility parts
as Horatio. In 1785 Charles Macklin, the doyen of the British
stage, came to play a starring engagement with the company. He
was a crotchety and stubborn old man who insisted that every
actor, however locally important, submit to his direction, and he
was pleased to find young Mr. McCready amenable to instruction.
He informed the young man that the proprietor of the Liverpool
and Manchester theatres was in search of someone to play "Gentlemen Fops and Tragedy" and hinted that this might be a step
toward London.[4]

Confident of success, McCready submitted an application and
was accepted as a member of the Liverpool-Manchester company.
Here he fell in love with Christina Ann Birch, whose rank as an
actress was on a level with his own, but whose family background
was composed of clergymen and surgeons and was untainted by
trade. Perhaps dazzled by the lady's charms, perhaps preoccupied
by the necessity of learning a new repertory, he does not seem to
have noticed that Gentlemen Fops and Tragedy did not fall to
his lot, but only more Horatios: Trueman in *George Barnwell,*
Pylades in *The Distressed Mother.* Nor is he likely to have complained when he was cast as Faulkland to the Julia of Miss Birch
in *The Rivals.* They were married in June 1786, and in September
of that year, through the continuing good offices of Macklin, transferred to London where Christina seems to have settled down
without regret as a housewife and mother, and William looked
forward to a steady ascent through the actors' hierarchy at Covent
Garden.

By 1795, when William was fifty and his wife thirty, they could
look back upon their years in London with a sense of equal
industry though not perhaps of equal achievement. Christina had
produced five children, of whom three had survived. William had
made a good beginning in the Horatio-line, playing during his
first season Norfolk to Holman's Richard III, Gratiano to Macklin's Shylock, Sir Walter Blunt in *1 Henry IV,* Fenton in *The
Merry Wives of Windsor.* There were signs of a better future as
he was permitted to exchange Horatio for Laertes and to try his
hand at Paris. Nine years later, however, he had advanced no
further than Malcolm in *Macbeth,* Tybalt in *Romeo,* and Edmund
in *Lear,* and his critical acclaim seems to have been limited to the
fact that he was always letter perfect. While in an overworked and
under-rehearsed company of repertory players this may well have

been a mark of distinction, the restless, middle-aged actor was confronted with the fact that he had been standing still for some years. He had twice tried his hand at playwriting, but *The Irishman in London* and *The Banknote,* while serviceable afterpieces, were only adaptations of older plays and added little to his position or his income. And in addition to himself and his wife there were Olivia (born 1791), William Charles (born 1793), and Letitia Margaret (born 1794) to be provided for.

It was characteristic of William McCready to seek security in speculation; and the kind of insecurity that was the inevitable result of speculation was to haunt his more famous son throughout his own career. Equipped with little more than ambition and responsibilities, William McCready undertook the management of a summer company at the New Theatre in Birmingham, offering the proprietors £500 and half the season's profits.[5] It is just possible that he knew more of the problems he would confront and the resources that were available to him than history has recorded. In his opening announcement, addressed to the "Ladies and Gentlemen of Birmingham and its Vicinage," the new manager "respectfully pledges himself to have a succession of the most capital Performers on the London stage during the Summer;—for he will only presume to solicit encouragement from the Public so long as his Exertions shall prove that it is his greatest Ambition to merit their Favour and Protection."[6]

Experienced readers of old playbills will recognize in the style and vocabulary of the announcement that "Manager's English" whose pompous words and billowing promises had little relation to what could be expected of the performances. But subsequent events prove that McCready was quite sincere both in determining to seek the patronage of Ladies and Gentlemen (rather than the denizens of the darksome slums) and in promising the best stars the metropolitan theatres had to offer. Thus, as a fledgling manager, it may have been to his advantage not to have advanced too far in his own career as a player, and it was certainly to his advantage to be known to his superiors as both teachable and accurate. At any rate, he never seems to have wanted for friends within the acting profession who were willing to lend luster to his company during their provincial tours or on off nights in London and, what is more important, to supply him with copies of successful new plays while their initial reputations were still warm.

At the end of his first summer in Birmingham William McCready returned to London, not much richer perhaps, but a demonstrated success. It could have done his small store of patience little good to find that he was expected to continue in the same line of Walking Gentlemen[7] as in previous seasons, even undergoing a demotion from Malcolm (who has at least one scene to himself) to Ross, who does little but fetch and carry. One more season of such work, and another successful summer in Birmingham, and he was prepared to quarrel with his London masters. Ostensibly the dispute was over salary, but the nineteenth century was the age of the self-made man and McCready, advancing from artisan to theatre manager, anticipates the upward movement of a whole class, epitomized in the progress of his son from theatre manager to country gentleman. It was not so much personal ambition as the spirit of the times that impelled the father to reject the status of servant, first to a master upholsterer and then to a master of players, and to become himself a master; and it was a source of constant annoyance to his son that he must maintain the fiction that he—the first actor of the day and director of the National Theatre—was the "public's humble servant." Humility does not come naturally to the actor, but in the early years of the nineteenth century it was an inert element in the human organism generally. Encouraged by financial success, however limited, and by the experience of being king, over however small a domain, McCready resigned his place at Covent Garden, dabbled briefly in the management of a small London theatre, and returned thankfully and optimistically to Birmingham.

For a while his optimism was justified. The stars came and audiences responded. Sarah Siddons, first lady of the stage, was a regular visitor, along with Thomas King, who had originated the role of Sir Peter Teazle, and William T. Lewis, the genteel comedian. These were established stars from the last decades of the eighteenth-century theatre, but McCready was alert for novelty also. He engaged William Henry West Betty, the sensational "Young Roscius" who played Shakespearean heroes at the age of twelve, and Edmund Kean, still a provincial aspirant. But a recent study of the promptbooks surviving from his regime proves that his managerial wisdom did not stop with the obvious but chancy attractiveness of touring stars. These promptbooks indicate an attention to details of scenic design, of lighting effects, and of stage business quite unexpected in even the better provincial theatres.[8]

The modern theatregoer has become so accustomed to high standards of physical production that he is for the most part unaware of the mechanics of staging. Yet it is not to be supposed that the "Theatre Royal, Huffington," where Vincent Crummles and the Hinfant Genius or the Fotheringay might appear for a few miserably attended nights, was only the imaginative creation of a distinguished caricaturist. In dedicating *Nicholas Nickleby* to McCready's son, Charles Dickens was perhaps indicating his awareness of the difference between Crummles and the Birmingham manager and at the same time his awareness of the small and not quite accidental gap which set apart the Theatre Royal, Birmingham and the Theatre Royal, Huffington.

All provincial theatres, of course, professed to model themselves after the parent or National Theatres of London, Drury Lane and Covent Garden. Barn or palace of Thespis, each was gilded with all the pomp and promise the imagination and vocabulary of the manager could devise. They were staffed by resident companies, each member of which had been hired to fill a special line of business: juvenile hero, heavy father, character comedian, or "Gentlemen Fops and Tragedy." It was not uncommon for the actors to be engaged by mail, sight unseen, through a London agent like William Kenneth. A good many managers, however, industriously cultivating their own gardens, found it more economical to raise a stock company than to import one.

A glance at the Robertsons, who played towns in the north of England, will help to establish by contrast the originality of McCready. The Robertsons were a company of better-than-average reputation and would produce a playwright who is often credited with a major contribution to the reform of the British stage. But every member of the company had a double function, before and behind the curtain, so that whatever succeeded during performance must have been the result of lucky accident or the most rigid conventionalism. A young actor, just down from London, was summoned to his first morning "rehearsal" with the company:

"Mrs. Robertson!" called the Prompter.

"Mrs. Robertson is looking out the checks. Read for her," grimly remarked Mr. Robertson.

"Gabble-gabble," commenced the Prompter—"gabble! Now, sir, that's your cue: On you come from behind the centre arch."

"Where will the arch be?"

"Where will the arch be, Casson?" inquired the Prompter.

"Second grooves," replied the master-carpenter.

"It will be a drawing-room. Here is a chair; there a table," continued the Prompter.

"But I don't see either the one or the other," I replied.

"No, but you will at night."

"Shall I?"

"Oh, yes! it will be all right at night . . ."

"Gabble gabble—squeak [continues the prompter]. Cross to right, then to left and up centre. Mind you give Mrs. Robertson the stage: she wants plenty of elbow-room. Now, Mr. Rogers, if you please."

Mr. Rogers . . . sits upon me, warns me to give him the stage and keep my eye on him, and begins to gabble and growl. I respond to the best of my ability.[9]

It will be all right at night. Those sad and hopeful words formed the principal tenet of the actor's creed in theatres more ancient than Mr. Robertson's and they are not unheard today. The provincial reviewers never wearied of pointing out just how far from all right the performances were. Actors, of whom there were never enough, were seized by illness or (as the critics openly hinted) by the bailiffs, or by the anodyne of the bottle, and their substitutes were forced to read their roles from playbooks.[10] Rant was substituted for eloquence, squinting and face-making for dramatic expression. Rehearsals were perfunctory, there was little time for study, and characterization rarely penetrated beyond the most obvious stereotypes. One old stager, instructing a novice in the ways of his art, explained that he made it a point to remember only whether the character was young or old, angry or pleased in each scene; and boasted that he had studied his profession in one comprehensive rule, laid down for him by an Irish prompter: "Get on the stage when you see they want you; get them off, and then get yourself off." When he had been entreated to be very particular, he had sometimes condescended to write out his part after this fashion: "Go on—blow up Jenkins—make love to Miss Tompkins—kick Alfieri when he enters, tip him a sentiment about a strong arm and good heart, and cut."[11]

Occasionally invention failed, even the feeble invention that might keep the play moving in the general direction intended by the author. The actor then, since the idea of teamwork was un-dreamed of, would rattle off whatever conventional tags stumbled into his memory, "Go to, thou weariest me. Take this well-filled purse, furnish thyself with richer habiliments, and join me at my mansion straight," and exit, leaving his fellow to get out as best he could.[12]

The actors lived in a ragged half-world, desperately pretending not to see the real while hopelessly failing to create the illusory. And, although playbills were forever promising new scenery, machines, and dresses, the physical production was almost certain

to present that half-world to the eye, assuming that it, too, would
be all right at night. But the willing suspension of disbelief came
easier on the stage side than on the auditorium side of the floats;
critics *would be* seeing:

Like the performers, the scenes are miserably deficient in number; and
night after night are we doomed to witness the same round of ruined
canvas. There is one scene which seems to be a particular favorite:
we allude to the one with a portrait intended for Shakespeare, we
suppose, on one side, and some thickheaded old codger, we know not
who, on the other; and be the scene of action where it may, Venice or
Windsor, Rome or London, you are sure to see Shakespeare and his
friend *tete-a-tete*.[13]

Sometimes the audiences rose in protest. In Ipswich, for instance, the art lovers, goaded beyond endurance by the incompetence of the artists, began pitching pennies at the performers they
most disliked, and the local critic became so virulent in his attacks
that he was forced to attend the scene of his duties accompanied
by twenty stout mercenaries. Nonetheless, one of the players, as
courageous as incompetent, sat next to the critic in the audience
and set upon him before he could appraise the evening's exhibits.
In the ensuing riot, the theatre was pretty well destroyed.[14]

Such theatrical riots were fairly frequent in those days, and the
auditoriums were accommodatingly flimsy; a satisfying amount
of destruction could be accomplished with very little effort on the
part of the anguished devotees of Thespis. It was as a result of
such a riot, in fact, that the old Theatre Royal in Birmingham
had been burned to the ground in 1792.

But once William McCready was installed as manager in Birmingham, and wherever else he later chose to preside, there were
no riots growing out of the playgoers' resentment at the play-
producer's incompetence. Eccentric and old-fashioned he might
be, but William McCready had firm standards and was a stern
taskmaster. He drew up, printed, and distributed to his astonished
players a set of regulations,[15] with frequent references to the
practice of the London theatres, instructing the actors in the
behavior expected of them before and behind the curtain. They
learned that they would be subject to a fine if they refused an
assigned part, if they were unwilling to take part in processions
and choruses, if they went into the front of the house in costume,
if they altered their costumes without the consent of the manager.
The occasions cited for penalties and the amounts assigned (from
a guinea for refusing a part to ten shillings for neglecting to appear

in a procession) indicate McCready's determination that his performances should be properly conducted.

But more astonishing to the actors and perhaps more important for the satisfaction of the spectators was an equally firm set of rules for rehearsal. The manager promised that ample notice—by the end of the evening's performance—would be given of the pieces to be rehearsed the next morning. After that, the actor was on his own. Since several plays would be run through, performers of the first piece were allowed ten minutes' grace; after that the fines were relentless: a shilling for missing the first scene and sixpence for each succeeding scene. If the actor were not "reasonably perfect" in his lines at the end of a rehearsal period, he forfeited five shillings. And if he was so careless of the serious business of the morning as to appear on the stage while someone else's scene was in rehearsal, sixpence was deducted from his salary. Similar fines were imposed on actors who failed to carry into performance the instructions of the rehearsal, if they could not remember when or where to make an entrance or exit, if they were visible in the wings, if they introduced unrehearsed bits of business.

Elaborate as the system of fines was, McCready was strict almost to crankiness in applying it. In a certain scene, two hapless players, Darley and Garthwaite, had been directed to wear their hats. Garthwaite remembered, but Darley forgot, and both were fined: Darley for his bad memory, and Garthwaite for his bad taste in wearing his hat and so exposing his companion to the audience. This anecdote was often repeated to prove that McCready fulfilled the requirements for eccentricity to become the "character" necessary to make his place in the late eighteenth-century pantheon. Yet his purpose, in opposition to the catch-as-catch-can, all-right-at-night theatre of his time, is both plain and honorable.[16]

To the purveyor of theatrical anecdotes, the manager was indeed well equipped with eccentricities. The actor Alexander Pope once attempted to arrange some stage business to suit himself while appearing as guest with the Birmingham company. McCready stood it as long as he could, and then roundly announced, "Look ye, sir, you may be the only Pope in the profession, but you are not infallible." Pope replied in kind, forgetting the manager's Irish background, "With your leave, Mr. McCready, I would rather change characters and represent Henry the Eighth who was the first English Monarch to cast off Papal authority." "Bad luck to the heretic," cried the manager. "But Pope or Potentate, sir, I am the Apostle of the Faith *here*, and my word must be respected while I hold the keys of the treasury." Pope rightly interpreted this as a hint that his engagement would be a short one.

McCready was not one to keep his affairs or his opinions to himself. Walking down the street he would sputter all his troubles aloud; those who were in his disfavor could thus learn his reactions to their conduct, and his general business problems were broadcast for all to hear. He would groan audibly whenever he discovered a well-filled house at a performance, explaining (to the air) that he had no way of checking the attendance and so was certain to be cheated by the money takers. Correspondence he read and sometimes answered in the street. Some years after his London success, Edmund Kean offered to play an engagement in Birmingham for half the nightly receipts. "Mighty grand that!" exclaimed McCready, marching down the sidewalk. "Sure his Little Highness forgets when I redeemed his wardrobe and paid his lodgings to enable him to join us at Birmingham. To the divil I pitch the ingrate!" and Kean's letter sailed into the gutter.[17]

As a manager, McCready was true to the principles of the late eighteenth-century theatre in which he grew up. Since he had been discovered by Macklin, he professed a quite natural admiration for the old actor, and for Henderson, Holman, and John Philip Kemble, who had been the bright stars of the London stage during his decade there. They were all, with the possible exception of Macklin, actors in the grand style which had succeeded the rather tricksy naturalism of Garrick, "brick and mortar" actors, theatrical analogues of the neoclassic formalism of Burke and Reynolds and Johnson. His taste in plays also ran to the neoclassic, to Lee and Sothern and Otway and the improved versions of Shakespeare. It is true that he yielded to the growing taste for the romantic and produced more and more of the melodramas and historical spectacles which were the earliest dramatic manifestations of that new spirit. But his only comment on the acting of Edmund Kean, not perhaps uncolored by his resentment at the romantic artist's economic realism, was, "It's very poor!"[18]

Like a true stroller, he was incorrigibly optimistic; his son calls him Micawber. Something would always turn up: a famous actor suddenly at liberty, a large benefit in the next town, or the next town but one, or the town after that. But his violent temper and his stubbornness were amplified by his conviction that the manager must be a dictator—or, in the terminology of the modern stage, a regisseur. "A theatre," his son observed, "is like a little kingdom, shut out from intimacy and sympathy with the little world around it."[19] The Profession was a world of its own and actors, rejected by the world of commerce and society, and generally scorned by the other professions, were forced to live apart, ignoring the world that ignored them, concerned only with their nightly performance and their daily bread. Thus, when the audience did not come and bread began to vanish, they could only fall to quarreling among themselves about the loss of their attractiveness or the failure of public taste. Of the failure of crops in an agricultural community, or at this particular time of the effect of the industrial revolution on the whole society, they were dangerously ignorant.

At times this failure to see beyond the curtain could reach heroic proportions. McCready once insisted on going through with a scheduled performance on the night that a civic fête had been decreed to celebrate the Allied victory over Napoleon. In vain was he told that no one could be expected to attend a theatre when such a free show was available. The performance began with two boys in the gallery, and one man in the pit. His son sat in a box so that there might be an audience in all parts of the house. Young William stuck it out through two scenes and then went for a walk through town to enjoy the illumination. When he returned the play had just concluded, and the man in the pit had left. But the boys in the gallery, though obviously bored, remained in their seats until the musicians struck up the music to introduce the farce. At this one of them leaned over the railing and cried out in exhaustion, "Oh, dang it, give over." Since there was now an empty house, the manager was forced to "give over" and the company was free to go out to enjoy the sights.[20]

This determination not to disappoint the audience was honorable enough and conventional enough, but it does not mark the shrewd businessman any more than do the temper and eccentricity that were part of McCready's character. In Birmingham, by close attention to the business of management during a period of reasonable prosperity, he succeeded well. By 1807 his annual rent and the proprietor's share of his nightly receipts had paid off the entire cost of reconstruction. According to provincial custom, he had taken his company to play short seasons in nearby communities, thus establishing a "circuit." Perhaps as a result of his success, the proprietors doubled the annual rental. McCready promptly resigned his management.[21]

No doubt resentment had something to do with his action, but ambition was the sterner stuff in his decision. For some years his companies had been playing on the outskirts of Manchester, and now he had news of a new theatre under construction there. With total irrationality, McCready rented the unfinished building for £1600 and set about acquiring funds to complete the decorations and equip the stage.[22] Through the good offices of Mrs. Siddons, he was introduced to an Irish fencing master named Galindo, who agreed to invest £3500 in the project, subject to immediate repayment if the theatre should fail. But failure was not yet a part of the McCready lexicon; without, apparently, glancing at the newspapers or inquiring into the conditions of trade, industry, and agriculture, he assumed an impossible burden.

The theatre opened for a summer season on June 29, 1807, but it did not prosper. The local critic, apparently from personal spite, attacked the actors violently, though McCready had assembled a respectable company and augmented it with visits by Mrs. Siddons, Young Roscius, Elliston, and Munden. The journalist further criticized the manager for insisting upon playing leads in "the whole round of the drama," although the evidence seems quite to the contrary.[23] But it was not the critic, it was not the manager, it was not the company that was to be blamed for thin houses. In the summer of 1807 the price of wheat rose from 86 shillings to 106 shillings. The poor rate increased from 24 to 40 thousand pounds and a rapid diminution in exports began to be worrisome to the few people who noticed such things. One such declared in a newspaper that "The present prospect of the industrial classes of people in every branch of business is gloomy beyond that of any former period."[24] And although the theatre always addressed itself to the "Ladies and Gentlemen" of its community, it was the industrial classes, the "operative" classes, that filled the galleries and made the difference between profit and loss. And it became increasingly plain that loss was to be the destiny of McCready's Manchester venture. By December 7, 1808, the theatre was offering a performance of *John Bull* for the benefit of the local "Soup Charities." Yet neither McCready nor his son nor any subsequent historian seems to have been aware of the implications of what the moving finger had written on the playbill for the benefit. The manager's partner, Galindo, however, was aware of imminent failure. He defaulted on the remaining installments of his investment and demanded immediate repayment of the money already advanced. Within a year the theatre was offering benefits for the distressed manager rather than the community, but the situation could not be saved.[25] In November 1809 William McCready was bankrupt and facing debtor's prison.

One of McCready's eccentricities as provincial manager had been his refusal to recruit the members of his growing family to save the expense of hiring London performers. His wife rarely appeared on the provincial stage, and then apparently only in an emergency. No actor on the Birmingham circuit could complain, like the walking gentleman in Crummles' company, that he had been held back by family conceit. Indeed the McCready children seem to have been kept away from the very theatre building itself as much as possible.

William Charles Macready[26] was only two when his father* made his first venture in Birmingham. He had been thrust into a day-school as soon as he began to get underfoot, and his childhood and boyhood were henceforth, as he says, "all school." Not that these schools were in all respects preferable to the vulgarity of theatrical life in training up the innocent mind; his earliest day-schools seem to have been run according to the educational system of endless punishment and bad food instituted by Mr. Squeers at Dotheboys Hall. Only in summer vacations was he free to observe his father's establishment, although he was inevitably involved in such school plays as the masters, not very willingly, permitted the students to get up. In 1803 at the age of ten he was shipped off to Rugby with his "library"—an abridgment of Plutarch, Tooke's *Pantheon,* a compendium of mythology, Pope's translation of Homer, a history of Ireland, and *Mentor's Letters to Youth,*† a somewhat formidable juvenile reading list.

Two things must have determined the choice of such a school for the provincial manager's son. The curriculum, designed for future public men, seemed as useless as possible for the stage, and William Birch, a cousin of Mrs. McCready, was a member of the tutorial staff.

Rugboeian education was very much of the old school: solid, stolid, making no concession to juvenile psychology or natural interests. Long hours in the classroom were spent in absorbing the Greek and Roman classics, in writing Latin, in practicing mathematics. Of modern literature there was only Milton, and discussion and creative activities were half a century in the future. Speeches and "declamations" were insisted upon, but only as the practical exercise permitted embryo statesmen and divines.[27] Yet this rigorous and restricted curriculum so formed or coincided with young Macready's taste that the English theatre of the mid-nineteenth century was to be directly affected by it.

---

* The elder McCready chose to spell the family name with the simple "Mc" while William Charles, his son, invariably employed "Mac." Their preferences have been respected in this study as a means of distinguishing between the two men. There seems, incidentally, to be no disagreement about the proper pronunciation of the name; it is always "Mac-*reed*-y."

† *Mentor's Letters to Youth* is unidentifiable, but *Mentor: Moral Conduct of Youth* (London, 1802) probably is the work cited.

William Birch, Macready's cousin, was not the best-loved of the Rugby tutors, but to be loved was not yet a pedagogic goal. He was reported to have a fist "like a sledgehammer, which he pretty freely made use of," and the public school rooms generally were sprinkled with broken switches at the end of the day.[28] Yet Birch was the first to sense Macready's true calling. In 1808 he sent this glowing—if somewhat apprehensive—report back to the Birmingham theatre:

Your eldest son improves in everything and I think will make a very fine man, to whatever he may turn his abilities. I cannot omit (though I don't know whether you will thank me) expressing my admiration of his wonderful talent for acting and speaking. Such a combination of fine figure, expression, countenance, elegance and propriety of action, modulation of voice, and most complete power of representation I have formed an idea of, perhaps, but have never before met with; and that is the sense of every one who has heard him. I know this rare talent may be turned to good account in the Church or at the Bar; it is valuable everywhere. Whatever is your intention I will second it, and if you determine to send him to Oxford next summer I will endeavour to prepare the way.[29]

Birch knew that the elder McCready had taken a stubborn resolution that young William should not become an actor. But the boy's talents were not hidden from others of his teachers. In the occasional amateur theatricals he had played—without any sense of humiliation—such females as Dame Ashfield and Mrs. Brulgruddery. In these he achieved such success that the worried headmaster, Dr. Henry Inglis, once took him aside and inquired what profession his father had in mind for him. Macready said that he was intended for the law.

"Had you not thought of your father's profession?" [Inglis asked.]
"No, sir."
"Should you not like it?"
"No, sir, I should wish to go to the bar."
"Are you quite certain you should not wish to go on the stage?"
"Quite certain, sir," [said Macready firmly.] "I very much dislike it, and the thought of it."[30]

This was to be William Charles Macready's professed attitude through life. If it can be justified in the light of his later experiences, it is difficult to see how he could have arrived at it this early. No doubt his father had something to do with it. Although the elder McCready always held that acting was a gentleman's profession, he recognized that it was not generally regarded as such by society. If this was the age of the self-made man, it was the age of the snob also, and thus the ambitious manager had determined that William Charles should become a lawyer, just as he had decided that his younger son Edward (born 1798) should enter the army. But Rugby itself must have been an influence. If William Charles had taken some pleasure in his vacation glimpses of the tinseled glamor of the stage, he had the more personally gratifying experience of making a place for himself and even advancing among the gentlemen's sons at his school. But he was sufficiently sure of his future and of his own tastes to publicly declare his aversion to seeking greatness in his father's profession.

And almost at once it was thrust upon him.

In the winter of 1808, young William returned from Rugby to Manchester for what he meant to be a brief vacation. But a family friend, a lady—the ladies were always to be his conscience and his cross—took him firmly in hand, informed him of his father's difficulties, that funds were lacking to pay the debts of the theatre, to say nothing of the school expenses. This was a blow indeed, for he had thought of going to Oxford before studying for the bar, but the very strong sense of responsibility which was the most prominent trait of his character manifested itself at once. Not only must he free his father of further educational costs, he would take positive action in relieving him of the burden of his debt. He very much disliked the stage, but there was only one immediate resource open to him. And thus the stage life of William Charles Macready began.

The elder McCready did not yield at once. He protested that it was "the wish of his life" to see his son at the bar, and he must have been aware that a course of reading in the Greek and Latin classics, in philosophy, rhetoric, and aesthetics was hardly substantial preparation for the rough-and-tumble chanciness of provincial theatrical life. But the son was firm and necessity was adamant. The manager submitted to the conscientious resignation of the elder son, taking some comfort from the possibility that his younger son Edward might continue his studies.

As for William Charles, at the age of sixteen he embarked upon his newly chosen profession with no misgivings, snatching such moments as he could to read classic authors between lessons in fencing and memorizing the juvenile leading roles in standard drama. He had the sure instincts of a player; even at Rugby he had felt "an inward elation in marking, as I slowly rose up [to recite an oration from Livy], the deep and instant hush that went through the whole assembly." There was nothing to suggest to him, except perhaps the precariousness of his father's financial status, that he had taken an irrevocable step into a way of life which was to be a constant torment to him.

The disastrous Manchester season dragged on to its disastrous end, William Charles continuing his studies as best he could, and absorbing much of his father's taste and principles in the art. John Fawcett, a visiting star, observing the young man's struggles and perhaps, as a metropolitan actor, realizing that the manager's ideas were somewhat out of date, suggested to the boy that he should observe the practice of the best actors of the time and learn to fence from the best masters, and implemented the suggestion with an invitation to spend some weeks in London as his guest.

Before this could be done, William Charles must go on to Newcastle with the Manchester company to supervise their two months' summer season at that town. The elder McCready remained behind, to settle his Manchester affairs as best he could, undertaking various stratagems to avoid imprisonment for debt, selling all the equipment he had purchased for the theatre and persuading some relatives to put up £1000 security. Even his household furniture in Birmingham was disposed of, leaving him homeless and destitute but free. The Newcastle season seems not to have increased the company stores, though it was not sufficiently bad to discourage further operations. As William Charles left his first theatrical command to go to London, his father took over the company for a season in Leicester.

THE METROPOLITAN STAGE

Young Macready's introduction to the London theatre was prophetic: he was at once confronted by an audience determined to show the managers who was whose "humble servant." He arrived on September 19, 1809, the day after the opening of the new Covent Garden theatre, rebuilt after the destruction of the old by fire. John Philip Kemble was the manager, and George Frederick Cooke, Charles Mayne Young, Charles Kemble, and such comedians as Munden, Fawcett, Emery, and Liston were in the company. The venture promised well, and to meet the expenses of the new theatre and the excellent company Kemble and the board of managers had increased the price of each ticket by a shilling. The public, less supine than the audiences of our day, responded with vigor. For months the theatre was the scene of a continuous riot, of howling, catcalling, parades, and fisticuffs. Banners were unfurled from the balconies proclaiming the determination of the spectators to get back the old prices. The management imported prizefighters to quell the disturbance. The rioters responded by remaining away until half-price, that curious system whereby a spectator might be admitted for the last two acts of a play and the afterpiece at reduced admission. The riots lasted for sixty-six nights and ended in a compromise, the general admission price being lowered, the boxes remaining at the management's price.[31] The whole affair was an ample illustration of just how far the drama's patrons would go in those days in establishing the theatre's laws.

In the meantime, Macready was learning much by observation, for the performances—which continued throughout the din— might just as well have been pantomimes. The new theatre itself must have made an impression upon him. However respectable the Theatre Royal, Birmingham, it was only a provincial theatre with consequent limitations. Covent Garden had been planned by John Kemble as the shrine of the National Drama. It was an impressive pile.

The architecture of the shrine, like that of the Birmingham theatre, was classical, but on a much grander scale, an attempt on the part of the Profession to manufacture a dignity and respectability denied it by society. The outer walls were decorated in bas-relief, Athena and the inevitable Muses, Dionysos, Sophocles, Shakespeare, and—a tribute to the manager and his illustrious sister, Mrs. Siddons—Lady Macbeth and her husband. The main entrance, under a portico of massive columns, opened into a grand hall with white-veined marble walls, red porphyry pillars, and a stone staircase leading to the grand saloon. This was a promenade behind the first tier of boxes, sixty feet in length with refreshment bars at either end, scarlet-covered sofas along the walls, more porphyry pillars and rows of classical statues in plaster. There was a similar saloon for the upper tiers of boxes, and a simpler one for the galleries. These saloons and the persons admitted to them were a constant source of irritation to the defenders and opponents of the stage as a "national pastime," and Macready could not have failed to notice the controversy and its causes. But the artistic direction of a theatre rather than the control of public prostitution was his immediate concern. And Covent Garden was an excellent theatre, both in the possibilities it so clearly presented and in Kemble's failure to exploit them.

To a more dedicated newcomer to the profession than young Macready, the vast cavern of the auditorium, which seated about 2800 spectators, would have been awesome. On three sides of the pit were three tiers of boxes painted white with gold and pink ornamentation and illuminated with glass lamps which required 270 wax candles nightly. The third tier of boxes, source of such fretful argument, were let by the season and each was equipped with a small private anteroom, "which fancy can fill with profligacy unseen." Still higher up were the galleries, 86 feet from the stage.

But dedicated or not, the visitor noted with admiration the stage and its appointments. It was spacious and well equipped. The apron, slowly to be abandoned as the staging became increasingly realistic, extended over twelve feet into the auditorium. Behind this stood the proscenium arch, a gilded frame 38 feet 8 inches wide, 36 feet 9 inches high, draped with gold-fringed curtains and bearing the motto *Veluti in Speculum,* as conventional in precept as it was disregarded in practice. The stage itself was 68 feet deep and 42 feet 6 inches wide. It was lighted by 300 patent wax and oil lamps. Experienced professional men pronounced it as nearly perfect as a stage might be.[32]

Yet Kemble's productions left much to be desired. For all his scholarship and ambition, he still inclined to the older tradition of careless staging. Like Garrick, he was an actor first, a producer second. And Garrick's productions had been notoriously haphazard. The older playgoers could recall "the miserable pairs of flats that used to clap together on even the stage trodden by Mr. Garrick; architecture without selection or propriety; a hall, a castle, or a chamber; or a cut wood of which all the verdure seemed to have been washed away." When Kemble became manager of Drury in 1785, "nearly everything, as to correctness, was to be done." Kemble, like Macready, came of an acting family and had been educated somewhat more thoroughly than was the professional custom. Consequently he displayed his learning by writing essays on Shakespeare, producing the works with some care, and wilfully slashing and rearranging the texts to suit his own purposes. Contemporary critics seem to feel that he was more interested in processions than anything else—and surely these provide the readiest opportunity for a display of stage technique—and even Boaden, to whom Kemble was only a little less than Shakespeare if not much more than God, unconsciously recognizes this in his comment on *Henry VIII*:

The processions in which this play particularly abounds, afforded great scope for the knowledge of ancient habits and manners which Mr. Kemble had acquired; and that study of the picturesque, by which Shakespeare himself, quite as much as any other quality transcended all other writers for the stage. Mr. Kemble arranged these exhibitions with punctilious exactness; and having himself to sustain a character not very much occupied in the play [Wolsey], he gave his attention, when it was needed throughout; until all raw material was worked into the smoothness of graceful habit. He had employed his pen, too, in alterations.

Kemble's idea of correctness may be gathered from the list of scenes new-designed and painted by William Capon for general use at his earlier theatre. First Capon provided six chamber wings, "for general use in our old English plays," studied from actual remains. Next, three drops: a view of New Palace Yard, Westminster, in 1793, the ancient palace yard of Westminster in the fifteenth century, and the Tower of London for *Richard III*. Finally there were two large pairs of wings to go with the Palace drop, and six sets of wings depicting ancient English streets, "combinations of genuine remains." It will be noted that although the artist and Kemble were both proud of the historical and architectural accuracy of their setting, in only one instance was a particular play consulted in the design.[33] Scenes were still changed in full view of the audience, and tables and chairs pulled on and off with huge ropes.[34]

In the matter of costume, too, Kemble was more interested in picturesqueness than in accuracy. His Hamlet was in the style of Van Dyck, his Othello appeared in a full set of British regimentals, and he allowed one of the witches in *Macbeth* to present herself in a fancy hat, powdered hair, rouge, point lace, and fine linen. His most recent biographer, well over a century away from the spell which operated on Boaden, concludes that as a producer Kemble was a failure.[35] He intended well; but his research was that of an antiquary rather than of artist, and his attention to the minutiae of production was directed mainly to spectacle, to processions, where the effect would be grandiose and startling. He was interested only in preparing big effects; the lesser moments were either eliminated or left to take care of themselves. The actor, the star-actor, is the thing.

When the scenes are first drawn on, or the roller ascends, the work exhibited is considered a few moments as a work of art; the persons who move before it then engross the attention; at their exit it is raised or drawn off, and is speedily forgotten, or seen with indifference the second time.

The setting has, that is, no integral relation with the whole work The real interest lies in the actor or actress:

When we have such a being as Mrs. Siddons before us in Lady Macbeth, what signifies the order or disorder of the picture of a castle behind her, or whether the shadows lie upwards or downwards on the mould-ings of a midnight apartment? It is to the terror of her eye; it is to the vehement and commanding sweep of her action; it is to the perfection of her voice that I am a captive, and I must pity the man who, not being the painter of the canvas, is at leisure to inquire how it is executed.

Boaden went so far as to prefer the painted scene of battle, with the prompter and his assistants shouting behind it, to the affecta-tion of reality which brought supers on the stage to create bustle and confusion while two anonymous champions fought it out on the apron to the terror of the orchestra.[36] But Boaden like his idol had his aesthetic roots in the eighteenth century. For him the generalized antique was sufficiently true; it was no more than the necessary background. The actor performed against it, not in it. Only in the poetry and fiction of the romantic revival was environ-ment an organic element; the theatre, as always, was the last by whom the contemporary was tried.

Kemble's failure to lead public taste, or to reflect fully the ro-mantic spirit of his times, was perhaps less obvious to the observer from the provincial theatre since the rival theatre, Drury Lane, was in ashes and its company was camping out at the Lyceum. But if their performances were forgivably makeshift, at least the actors at the Lyceum could be heard, and Macready listened with attention to such distinguished comedians as Dorothy Jordan and Charles Mathews. Although he had himself but little instinct and few talents for comedy, Mrs. Jordan was to be one of the dominant influences on the formation of his style and technique.

In London, also, Macready made his first acquaintance with authors, a relationship which he was to maintain and develop throughout his stage career and his social life. To an ambitious actor, the playwright was second only to the manager in ensuring his progress. To have a personal vehicle, a star part especially de-signed for his talents, was a necessity in a profession that prospered by dividing its efforts between metropolitan repertory and starring engagements in the provinces.

That such necessity was very much in his mind is indicated by the authors Macready chose or chanced to meet. They were the-atrical journeymen, Frederick Reynolds and Thomas Morton, who had demonstrated their ability to write to order, if not to write for posterity. Somewhat less fortunately he was introduced to Theodore Hook, then the patcher-up of unremembered trifles, farces, melodramas, musical pieces, but soon to be the editor of *John Bull,* a libelous scandal-sheet in the Tory interest. At least once Hook's poisoned pen would pierce Macready's thin defenses and cause him loudly proclaimed anguish. It would never be possible for him to distinguish a direct attack on his status as an actor from an indirect attack on the politics of his friends and associates.

That, however, was for the future. At the moment he found satisfaction in his acceptance by the famous and successful. But always his eye was upon business. He took daily fencing lessons from Henry Angelo to develop grace and flexibility and power, observed a demonstration of gas as a new method of illumination, and listened to the general opinion that it would never be of much use. Five years later it was to be installed in the legitimate theatres as the first major advance in the mechanics of production since the inventions of De Loutherbourg, Garrick's designer.

Young Macready had gone to London with some idea of discovering the best that the British theatre had to offer. However, aside from its greater resources in physical equipment and acting talent, the London stage had little to show him that he had not seen in Birmingham. His earliest memories of the stage, recorded in his *Reminiscences,* are of Tom King still playing the role of Lord Ogleby which he had created in *The Clandestine Marriage,* and of the "grand deportment and beauty of Mrs. Siddons." The same style of eccentric comedy and heroic tragedy still held the stage in London, which had not yet been electrified by the romantic and revolutionary style of Edmund Kean. And if the settings were less battered and had some occasional reference to the style or period of the play they were intended to grace, they were still far from possessing that propriety which would only become general after Macready himself had led the way. In fact, Macready seems to have gone back to the provinces with no very high estimate of the London theatre, and he was in no hurry to return to it in a professional capacity.

His sole concern—he would hardly have dignified it as his ambition—was to re-establish the family business. And he was at once presented with a situation that was to haunt him through his life, to make him almost pathologically conscious of the precariousness of the profession in which he was trapped, and fanatically dedicated to the security of himself and his family. His first duty on his return from London was to accompany his father to the house of the Manchester sheriff's officer to whom he was to surrender himself. The stubborn old Irishman, after fifty years of making his way upwards, proprietor of theatres, director of com-

panies, king of his small world, was destitute. There were bills
unpaid, a family without support, a theatrical company without
a head. When the boy looked upon his father, a prisoner unable to
act, unable to meet any of his responsibilities, he broke down and
wept. The prisoner's response was typical. After a moment's
struggle with his emotions he declared that he could stand anything but pity and ordered William Charles to go away if he could
not control himself. Since William Charles remained with his
father until he was actually led off to jail the next morning, it must
be assumed that he regained command of himself, but the moment
was never forgotten as the opening scene of his theatrical career.

The two had much to discuss. There was no question now of the
boy's commencing actor and making the family fortunes. He must
rather, with no experience and few examples, undertake the management of what remained of the McCready company in Chester.
He must learn to handle with authority and justice a group of
older and more practiced professionals, many of whom were in
active mutiny. He must search the standard repertory of the theatre for popular plays and invent attractive novelties. He must put
a bold front to the public and to the players. Perhaps only a very
young and theatrically ignorant man could have faced the prospect,
even with the heavy heart to which William Charles admitted.

From the first he took a firm hand; he would be Caesar or
nothing, a principle to which he clung throughout his professional
life. The actors seem to have taken his determination with good
grace; perhaps they saw that it was the quality which could pull
them out of their difficulties. At any rate, they addressed him
henceforth as "Mr. William," they responded to his call for greater
discipline at rehearsals and more careful performances, and were
justified when two politicians, Lord Grosvenor and Mr. Egerton,
"bespoke" to crowded houses. A bespeak was a kind of command
performance. The manager was permitted to announce in his bills
that the King, the Governor, the Commander of the local garri-
son, or some other figure with publicity value had requested the
production of a favorite play, and would be present on the evening
of its presentation. Depending on the attraction of the public
figure, the house that night would be more or less crowded beyond
its usual attendance. In London, Queen Victoria's commands were
to bring such crushes in the pit that dignity, clothing, and sometimes life was lost. In the provinces, the bespeaks were often as
dismally thin as the regular nights of performing. But Mr. William
had a native astuteness about publicity. His two bespeakers were
political rivals in Chester and the adherents of each saw to it that
the box-office record was a happy one. This combination of in-

genuity and generalship enabled the fledgling manager to leave Chester after two months with his accounts settled, the reputation of the Macreadys as theatrical proprietors re-established, and with three of the best actors of the company pledged to join with the best actors of the Leicester company for a major effort at recouping all the elder McCready's losses during the approaching two-month season at Newcastle.

But if discipline, industry, and ingenuity could produce prosperity, the end of a season and a change of theatres meant that the struggle must begin again and from the bottom. With the three actors and a five-pound note, Mr. William left Chester on Christmas Eve of 1809 for the long journey to Newcastle by coach. In the cold and the snow the miles passed slowly, and it was not until noon of the next day that they stopped for dinner at an inn at Brough on the border of Westmoreland. Here their purse was lightened by the necessity of paying a portion of the five-pound note to the post boy who had brought them the last stage of their trip. But when the boy attempted to change the bill into cash, the landlord declared it to be counterfeit and further, that the roads were so bad he would not let them continue their journey with fewer than four horses, at a considerable added expense. Not only would it cost them more than they intended to reach their destination, but even what money they had was useless. With this stunning announcement, the landlord left the premises, satisfied that the stricken players had been finally stopped. But he reckoned without the determination of actors to get on with the show whatever the cost. Macready's own watch having been pawned in Chester, those of his three companions were produced by threat or persuasion. The landlord was resummoned and treated to some of Mr. William's best Rugboeian eloquence, asserting the respectability of the group. The landlord held out for the four horses, Mr. William for change for his five-pound note. As a compromise the landlord changed the note and advanced three pounds on the watches, and the actors hired the specified team. This effort, and the funds thus obtained, carried them to Durham where they were well known. Here they spent the night and continued on to Newcastle the next day. By such transactions was the young man introduced into what his father insisted was the "gentlemanly" profession of manager, through debtor's prison and pawn shops, confronted with wayward actors, rapacious creditors, suspicious landlords, and inefficient subordinates. At Newcastle further enlightenment awaited him.

Encouraged by his success at Chester, Mr. Williams applied his principles of production to a vastly better theatre and a vastly better company. The standard offerings, *Hamlet, Othello, Venice Preserved,* were played through to good houses, largely because of the popularity of Conway, the leading man. New plays, such as *The Foundling of the Forest,* were got up with new scenery and costumes under Mr. William's "most careful superintendence," and had a run. It is well to be cautious in interpreting "new scenery and dresses." As must be fairly evident, provincial scenery was at best perfunctory, a backdrop or two and a set of wings, and very often the "new scenery" was newly unearthed from the cellar. Still, *The Foundling of the Forest* "was an attraction for many nights," and the season in general was so successful that three pounds a week were sent to the elder McCready "in his melancholy duress." It was evident that conscientiousness was an asset in a theatrical manager: an important lesson to be learned by any tyro, but one which it was difficult to exemplify in the country.

Mr. William's success was not merely financial or artistic. To his surprise—since to doubt it had never entered his head—provincial society condescended to notice him. Some of the respectable ladies of Newscastle invited him to tea and dropped a plain hint that other respectable citizens would be glad of his acquaintance if they could be sure that he was select in his associates. It had not, apparently, occurred to Macready that respectable citizens would deny him their acquaintance; he considered himself a gentleman, and his schoolmates had accepted him at once. But the Misses Headley, his monitors, were firm in their conviction that a signal honor was being paid to the integrity of this young man, in spite of his profession. Their point was perhaps emphasized when a drunken officer, whom he had ordered removed from the theatre, challenged him to a duel, and then refused to meet him on the apparently acceptable excuse that he was not a gentleman. The admonition of the Misses Headley, spoken in time, opened his eyes to the actor's position in society and saved him from the dissipation which, he declares, "might have induced habits destructive of ability and reputation." Many a later associate of Macready's could also thank them that he was kept strictly in his place, behind the footlights, and was never permitted to enter his manager's family circle.

By the end of the Newcastle season, reputation and financial credit firmly established, Macready was happy to welcome back his father, released from prison with a certificate of bankruptcy. His managerial responsibilities were over and he could now devote himself to preparation for the anonymous but fateful moment which was the traditional beginning of every actor's career.

$\diamond$ $\diamond$ $\diamond$ **2** $\diamond$ $\diamond$ $\diamond$

Steps to the Temple

BIRMINGHAM

On Thursday Evening, June 7 will be presented the
Tragedy of
ROMEO AND JULIET
(Written by Shakespeare)
The Part of Romeo by a *Young Gentleman*
(Being his First Appearance on any Stage)
Friar Lawrence, Mr. Harley; and Juliet by Mrs. Young.
In Act I. *A GRAND MASQUERADE*
In Act V. *THE SOLEMN DIRGE*

S O READS, in part, the playbill with which William McCready
announced the debut of his son at the start of the summer
season in Birmingham in 1810. The anonymity, the ostentatious
lack of fanfare, was by theatrical tradition calculated to allow an
unsuccessful debutant to retire to some other profession without
the taint of the stage upon him. On the other hand, it did nothing
to stifle the curiosity on which the public arts prosper.

Conventional as the announcement was, Macready's preparation for the role and the rise and fall of his spirits during the rehearsal period established a pattern peculiar to himself which was
to be repeated with nearly every part he undertook through his
long career. Unlike the old stagers who would settle for an approximation of the author's words and the most casual concession
to the "business" of the play, he got by heart every last detail, not
only of his lines, but of his positions on the stage, the gestures he
was to make, the intonations to use in reading, the feelings he was
to represent. On Sundays, when the theatre was deserted, he would
lock himself in and pace the stage, acting his character over and

over and reciting his speeches until he was quite worn out in body and voice. Though he at first approached Romeo with some confidence, he soon found himself doubting his abilities, crying out in the midst of a private rehearsal, "I cannot do it." But his Juliet encouraged him, and his father varied his "That will not do," with an occasional, "Very great improvement." Encouragement and practice, however, were never sufficient to give him a sense of security; he was —as ever in the future—seized with stage fright at the sight of the playbills posted in the street, an emotion which lasted well after his first entrance upon the stage. Only the response of his audience could release him. His own memory of the debut is vivid:

There was a mist before my eyes. I seemed to see nothing of the dazzling scene before me, and for some time I was like an automaton moving in certain defined limits. I went mechanically through the variations in which I had drilled myself, and it was not until the plaudits of the audience awoke me from the kind of waking dream in which I seemed to be moving, that I gained my self-possession, and really entered into the spirit of the character and, I may say, felt the passion, I was to represent. Every round of applause acted like inspiration on me: I "trod on air," became another being, or a happier self.

And as he saw the curtain fall, full of the enthusiasm of the novice and with the applause of an audience for the first time ringing in his ears, he cried, "I feel as if I should like to act it all over again."[1]

His success was unquestioned. Following a review in *Aris's Birmingham Gazette* which had "no hesitation in predicting his future fame and prosperity," came a repetition of Romeo and a first appearance as Lothair, the young hero of Monk Lewis' *Adelgitha,* a modern claptrap. For the second performance of this play, on the sixteenth of June, the "young gentleman" emerged on the bills as "Mr. William McCready"; the open secret need no longer be kept. He appeared occasionally throughout the rest of June and July, and finally on July 27 had the pleasure of attaching this announcement to the evening's bill for *The Exile* and *Tom Thumb:*

Mr. WILLIAM MCCREADY, with gratitude to a liberal Public for the fostering Encouragement and cheering Applause bestowed on his *first Dramatic Efforts,* laments that his other Engagements will not admit of his appearing here *This Season* After Monday next, July 30, on which Evening will be presented the historical Play of

GEORGE BARNWELL

His debut safely behind him, Macready settled down to the task of becoming a leading provincial actor. He seems to have had no ambitions beyond the family circuit, and was content to take such instruction and such parts as his father decreed. Since the manager was convinced that a portrait exhibited in galleries and shop windows was excellent publicity, the young Romeo was sent to London to "stand" for his portrait in character to Samuel deWilde. William had some misgivings about this, and the process was so often repeated that on his London debut at least one soured playgoer greeted him as an overfamiliar face.[2] DeWilde's painting of Macready as Romeo, often reproduced, may have had some publicity value, but Macready expressly states that it was an artistic distortion of his own interpretation of the character, which explains the discrepancy between the "chubby-faced boy" of the portrait and the all too plain fact of the actor's face.

Yet there is in the portrait something more than a hint of a style totally unlike that traditionally associated with the "Macready school" of acting. At the edge of a misty English forest, young Romeo, in a costume vaguely reminiscent of the Italian Renaissance, stands gazing upwards, sweeping the greensward with the plumed hat in his left hand, his right arm in fourth position *en haut,* his left leg in a *battement dégagé.*[3] This may be taken to represent the instruction of the elder McCready who was, according to F. C. Weymss, an excellent master. "I learned more," says the American actor and manager, "during my short stay in his company, of the practical part of my profession, than any two years of past experience had afforded me. He was a strict disciplinarian— one of the best instructors of acting I ever met."[4] Macready said many years later that his father's ideas of acting were somewhat old-fashioned and "stagey," founded on his admiration of Henderson, Kemble, and Macklin.[5]

In their own time and by their own audiences, the style of Kemble and Henderson was considered natural. It is the customary difficulty in studying the history of acting that *every* great actor is described as natural by critics who subscribe to the same theory of imitation, for the definition of nature varies as widely on the stage as it does in the criticism of poetry. Henderson, whom Macready came to think of as "stagey," was felt to be almost too natural by Boaden: in contrast to the reading of the other relicts of Garrick's school, Henderson's declamation employed undertones and was less "upon the level." Yet Macready's description of him suggests a rigid formality which ill suits with Boaden's epithet, "unheroic."[6]

Of this early training, Macready says he had much to unlearn.

But one precept he carried with him to the date of his retirement. His father repeated to him Charles Macklin's customary address to his fellow actors at a rehearsal: "Look at me, sir, look at me! Keep your eye fixed on me when I am speaking to you! Attention is always fixed; if you take your eye from me you rob the audience of my effects, and you rob me of their applause!" This was intended as the First and Great Commandment for a theatre of star actors, and as such it continues in force today. But within the principle of focus there is the germ of realistic illusion, of which Macready was to become one of the earliest advocates when he became himself an instructor of players.

The roles in which he presented himself to the public were also of his father's choosing. Most of them were from the standard drama, Barnwell, Lothair, Norval, Zanga (*The Revenge*), Orestes (*The Distressed Mother*), Alexander the Great. There were a few Shakespearean parts: in addition to Romeo he played Hamlet, Posthumus, Richard III, Antony, Hotspur, and Leontes; and there were a few "modern" parts: Rolla, Frederic *(Lover's Vows)*, Cheveril *(The Deserted Daughter)*, Wilford *(The Iron Chest)*, and Octavian *(The Mountaineers)*. All told, in just over five years in the provinces, he was to play eighty-two characters.[7] If this seems a busy apprenticeship, it was no more remarkable than that of any beginning actor in his situation.

In his *Reminiscences*, Macready is modest about his achievements in the Shakespearean plays. All his characterizations he seems to say, were tentative, first sketches merely for his later interpretations. At Newcastle in 1812, momentarily asserting his independence of his father's repertory, he tried to restore a forgotten play of the master's to the stage. *Richard II* had not, he believed, been produced since Shakespeare's time; even the busy hands of the eighteenth-century improvers had not been able to make it attractive. Macready saw to it that all the resources of the country theatre were employed in the production, and he was gratified by a kindly reception from the audiences. But the success of the play in Newcastle was not repeated elsewhere. Macready was to make several attempts in the course of his career to give *Richard II* a permanent place in the repertory, but even in his final season the play was foredoomed. He concluded finally that the characters lack "purpose and will."[8]—a good Victorian reason, at the least.

If the play seems a strange one for a young actor to fix on for experimentation, it should be noted that the central character, both as poet and poseur, is given almost unequaled opportunities to exploit his voice. From the beginning, Macready's voice was his

principal asset, but it would be many years before he would learn
to use it as an actor. His first London critics recognized the quality
of the instrument; it was "full, clear, soft, and powerful," said
Leigh Hunt,[9] and Hazlitt thought it not sweeter than Kean's, but
yet "the finest and most heroical on the stage." But it was Hazlitt
also who put his finger on the young actor's failure to make the
most of his equipment; some years after Macready's London debut,
the critic was to recall "that mere melodious declamation which
he used to deal out, sentence after sentence, like a machine turning
ivory balls."[10] Macready had made his first mark, after all, in
schoolroom declamations, and his father had thrust him into one
declamatory role after another. Not until he could see Edmund
Kean at the height of his powers would he receive the hint that
would be developed into his own distinctive delivery.

There were frequent criticisms, too, of the passionate violence
of his action and gestures, perhaps emphasized by the monotony of
his declamation. Considered historically, this violence may have
been the desperate attempt of inexperience to kindle a spark of
theatrical fire in the damp ashes of the late Augustan dramatic
repertory. A journalist in Bath, remarking that he is "too boister-
ous," rather kindly adds that this is a general fault of young
actors.[11] But if his violence and bursts of passion seemed to the
critics to lack the control of the highest art, there is ample evidence
that they were most attractive to audiences. Perhaps at this stage
in his development Macready was responding unconsciously to the
time-spirit, as the realism of Fielding was succeeded by the sheer
fury of *The Monk* before giving way to the comparative restraint
of the nineteenth-century novel.

The quality, the degree, of intensity of gesture and movement
was the first element of his acting style to be subjected to the
process of unlearning. After his retirement he recalled his motives
and his method in a long letter to Lady Pollack:

There was a time when my action was redundant—when I was taught
to attempt to imitate in gesture the action I might be relating, or to
figure out some idea of the images of my speech. How was I made
sensible of this offense against good taste? I very soon had misgivings
suggested by my own observation of actual life. These became confirmed by marking how sparingly, and therefore how effectively, Mrs.
Siddons had recourse to gesticulation. In the beginning of one of the
chapters of "Peregrine Pickle" is the description of an actor (who must
have been Quin) in Zanga, elaborately accompanying by gesture the
narration of Alonzo's emotions on discovering and reading a letter:
the absurdity is so apparent that I could not be blind to it, and applied

the criticism to myself in various situations, which might have tempted me to something like the same extravagance. A line in the opening of one of the Cantos of Dante—I do not immediately remember it—made a deep impression on me in suggesting to me the dignity of repose; and so a theory became gradually formed in my mind, which was practically demonstrated to me to be a correct one, when I saw Talma act, whose every movement was a subject for the sculptor's or the painter's study. Well, as my opinions were thus undergoing a transition, my practice moved in the same direction, and I adopted all the modes I could devise to acquire the power of exciting myself into the wildest emotions of passion, coercing my limbs to perfect stillness. I would lie down on the floor, or stand straight against a wall, or get my arms within a bandage, and, so pinioned, or confined, repeat the most violent passages of Othello, Lear, Hamlet, Macbeth, or whatever would require most energy and emotion; I would speak the most passionate bursts of rage under the supposed constraint of *whispering them* in the ear of him or her to whom they were addressed, thus keeping both voice and gesture in subjection to the real impulse of feeling. . . . I was obliged also to have frequent recourse to the looking-glass, and had two or three large ones in my room to reflect to myself each view of the posture I might have fallen into, besides being under the necessity of acting the passion close to a glass to restrain the tendency to exaggerate its expression—which was the most difficult of all—to repress the ready frown, and keep the features, perhaps I should say the muscles of the face, undisturbed, whilst intense passion would speak from the eye alone.[12]

In addition to the study and exercises of his art, the novice had much to learn of the strategy of his profession. He had to learn that he could not force his own tastes, formed by the Rugby curriculum of classical literature and philosophy, on a public that paid for its preferences. The present rage was for the equestrian drama, and the elder McCready engaged a troupe of horses from Covent Garden to perform in such melodramas as *Bluebeard* and *Timour the Tartar*. When the company moved on from Birmingham to Newcastle, nothing would do but the equestrians must be engaged there, also. William Charles tried hard to argue on the score of taste, but his father would not hear of any such nonsense. And as it turned out he was right. What audience, provincial or metropolitan, could resist the varied temptations announced in the Newcastle playbill for *Bluebeard* on February 25, 1812?

The most Beautiful and Wonderful Exhibition ever beheld on a provincial Stage . . . The Scenery includes:
ABOMELIQUE'S PALACE. Erected upon Arches, thrown over a Moat, with a Stupendous Drawbridge, &c—attacked by the Spahis, in which scene are beheld THE CAVALRY FORDING THE MOAT—

THE BREAKING OF THE DRAWBRIDGE on which the Combatants are engaged, who are precipitated into the Water—THE ASCENT OF THE CAVALRY UP THE BROKEN BRIDGE, &c. as on the Preceding Evenings of Representation.

But to Attempt an Exact Description of the Scenes in which the
HORSES
Are concerned would be impossible: The Feats of these Wonderful Animals, who are beheld in the various Situations of an Engagement, And even in the Agonies of Death, must be seen to be Credited. Among them are:
     The Beautiful White Horse, ADONIS, late his Majesty's property;
And the BLACK CHARGER
TAKEN FROM THE FRENCH GENERAL, MARSHALL LE FEBVRE, IN SPAIN

A few performances of the hippodramas and the manager was safe from debt, relatively speaking, for many years. It was perhaps with an ironic glance at both his son and his audience that he produced in the next year Massinger's *Roman Actor,* with the descriptive statement, "Tending to elucidate the real Purposes for which the Stage was first erected."[13]

These, too, were the burgeoning years of the romantic revival, which for the general public meant the appearance of the poetical romances of Walter Scott. Hack playwrights pounced upon them as soon as they were published, as a later generation was to pounce upon his novels, and turned them into plays with music, that is, melodramas. In March 1811, the Newcastle theatre was offering *The Knight of Snowdoun, or Roderick Vich Alpine!* with "The part of the Highland Warrior by Mr. WILLIAM MCCREADY," a foretaste of one of his great metropolitan successes. Three years later, the Scott drama of the season was *Marmion,* and the bill was careful to indicate its authenticity: "The language is entirely selected from Walter Scott's celebrated Poem, with the Exception of the few common Place Sentences necessary to the conduct of the Fable."[14] If the playwright was a hack, at least he had no illusions about the quality of his own contribution.

Further, Macready learned the vital secret of making a benefit. To every actor, in the provinces or the metropolis, a benefit was the most important night of the season. It was the night when he was entitled to the full box-office receipts after certain fixed charges had been set aside, and it frequently was his one opportunity to acquire a few pounds for future necessities. On such occasions, anything that would attract a ticket-buyer was considered legitimate: tragedians acted comedy, comedians played Hamlet, variety acts were added to the program, and performances often lasted six hours or more. When benefits succeeded, the star of the evening might look forward to a few days or weeks of good meals, or a new pair of shoes, or a much-needed addition to his wardrobe. When they failed, the actor was confronted with both humiliation and starvation—and, given the nature of actors, it is difficult to say which consequence was the more disastrous.

The benefit system drove pride, dignity, and artistic integrity out of the theatre. Leading actors could be found selling tickets from door to door, or sending passes to friends in the hope of receiving a contribution in excess of the admission price. The following notice, from a Newcastle playbill, May 1, 1811, epitomizes the fate of the leading players on a provincial circuit:

For the Benefit of Mrs. CLIFFORD. *"Hope is the Nurse of Life."* Led on by that Idea, and impelled by other Motives, Mrs. CLIFFORD ventures once more to advertise an Evening's Entertainment for her Benefit: and relying on the well-known clemency of a British Public, trusts she will not be deemed forward or intrusive in submitting to the Consideration of the Ladies and Gentlemen of Newcastle, the following Circumstances:—In forming an Agreement, each Performer receives a Weekly Stipend for the Advantage of their Aid; but the chief Emolument and gratifying Compensation for their exertions through a Season in the Service of the Public, which every Actor anxiously looks up to as a Token of Public Favor and Esteem, is the Profits of an Evening dedicated to their Benefit, the Failure of which must be severely felt as a Loss of Time, Interest and Reputation. Having gone through an extensive and varied Line of Business for two Seasons in the Town of Newcastle, in the former of which she had the Misfortune to experience a total Failure on her Night, Mrs. CLIFFORD, having laid before the Public the Statement of her Situation, with every Deference earnestly solicits that Support it will ever be her principal Object to gain, and her greatest Study to deserve.

Mrs. Clifford offered her public Joanna Baillie's tragedy, *The Family Legend,* a melodrama, *Ella Rosenberg,* and a farce, *Matrimony.* Whether the program or the lady's humble urgency produced a "bumper," the records do not show. But the situation is eloquent evidence of the precarious relationship between the player and the playgoer, between the player and prosperity.

Benefit-making, then, placed the actor without possible ambiguity as the hireling fool of the public, and for Macready it was to become the distasteful reminder of a distasteful fact. Many years after his London debut he wrote to a fellow-player, "Benefits make beggars of the best of us, and therefore I must follow in the train."[15] Since they were also his best opportunity of achieving financial independence, he early devoted himself to perfecting the art of arranging a benefit that could not fail to attract. The secret, of course, was a combination of quantity and novelty, with very little regard for quality. For instance, Macready's benefit on December 19, 1811, began with a revival of Hughes' old tragedy *The Siege of Damascus,* whose novelty was Macready's first appearance as Phocyas. This was followed by an entr'acte specialty which was perhaps a strange choice for an actor who was to take so strong a stand on the purposes of the theatre:

Mr. Wilson, a performer on the high wire was announced to walk from the STAGE to the PIT and BACK again, wheeling a real BARROW and supporting a BOY at the same Time. Likewise a WHIMSICAL DANCE, with two BOYS suspended to his Feet.— Throw a SOMERSET ten Feet high, Playing the Tamborine at the same Time: with several other astonishing FEATS.

Mr. Wilson was succeeded by Mrs. Stewart singing, "Come tarry a while with me," and the evening concluded with Macready as Puff in *The Critic,* a role which had become a conventional comic resort for tragedians. For his Newcastle benefit in 1815 the novelty attraction was Sieur Sanches, who exhibited "his Wonderful Antipodean Power" by walking head downwards over the stage. To assert his own sense of propriety, even on a benefit night, Macready performed the leading role of *Henry V,* after the antipodean demonstration.

The regular succession of touring stars who joined the company at intervals provided Macready with many objects of study. He had an opportunity to compare their styles and to act in secondary roles opposite the greatest players of the day—Mrs. Siddons, Miss Jordan, Holman, Young, Miss O'Neill, and others—and the memories of them in his *Reminiscences* are vivid portraits of these stars in action. That he was a man of promise was evident to them all; they seem to have gone out of their way to praise him and give him advice, all of which he listened to and much of which he followed religiously. He observed that Dorothy Jordan, the incarnation of the comic muse (which Macready was not, nor ever was to be), was not the carefree spirit in rehearsal that she appeared in performance. He remarked as he watched her at work "how minute and how particular her directions were; nor would she be satisfied, till by repetition she had seen the business executed exactly to her wish. The moving picture, the very life of the scene was perfect in her mind, and she transferred it in all its earnestness to every movement on the stage."[16] After he had spoken his first line in the rehearsal, Mrs. Jordan started with surprise, and exclaimed, "Very well indeed, sir!" As his father had impressed Macklin, so Macready impressed the visiting stars with his diligence and application. He was later to learn that it was not a common experience for the splendid stroller.

Perhaps because she was primarily a comic actress, Mrs. Jordan had little use for the formal, poetical, or declamatory reading of dramatic verse. "The lines are all good verse," she once complained to a fellow player, "but why *scan* them all the time you are speaking them." To counteract a tendency to declaim, she recommended writing out the dialogue as if it were prose and studying the copy rather than the original.[17] It is difficult to estimate how much influence this suggestion may have had upon the development of Macready's "domestic" manner; however, there exists a partial copy of the role of Othello in prose, in Macready's hand. Since there is no punctuation whatsoever in the copy, it may have been made originally as a mnemonic device. But that it was later used for the study of the part cannot be questioned since it is annotated with comments and directions to himself in Greek and Latin and the marks for emphasis, pause, and modulation that appear in all his working copies.

The performer who most impressed him, and remained his ideal throughout his stage life, was Sarah Siddons. It is hard to describe the awe in which she was held by the whole of the English theatre, on both sides of the curtain, at the turn of the century. Actors admired and feared her, for she was a martinet and a miser in her professional engagements; but for the spectators she was the incarnation of Tragedy, standing, as Hazlitt said, "with [her] feet upon the earth, and [her] head raised above the skies, weeping tears and blood."[18] Her love of money would persuade her to make several ill-advised reappearances after her official retirement, and the spectacle of greatness in decay making itself a motley to the view was to haunt Macready almost as much as the vision of his own father in debtor's prison.

When she came to the Newcastle company in 1812, however, she had not lost the Siddons terror or the Siddons magic. The very thought of standing by the side of the Tragic Muse hung over the young actor as he memorized the role of Beverley in *The Gamester* that he might be perfect at the first rehearsal. He could not have spent his time more prudently. Mrs. Siddons, who was then 47, looked upon her nineteen-year-old husband, made a pleasant joke about age, and proceeded to give him his instructions. He followed these so explicitly in performance that she condescended to prompt him, kindly, when he forgot a line and cried out "Bravo" at one of his points from her observation post in the wings.

From the study of her performances of Lady Randolph in *Douglas,* and Mrs. Beverley, Macready believed he was able to identify the one great excellence that set her apart from all other tragic actresses. "This," he wrote, "was the unity of design, the just relation of all parts to the whole, that made us forget the actress in the character she assumed."[19] At Rugby, Hugh Blair's *Lectures on Rhetoric* had taught him that unity was the key to the beautiful in art; Mrs. Siddons demonstrated its possibility in her own craft; and throughout his career, both as actor and manager, unity in performance was to be his goal.

Mrs. Siddons had other counsel for him also. At the end of her engagement she summoned him to her dressing room for a few words of advice. "You are in the right way," she told him, "but remember what I say, study, study, study, and do not marry till you are thirty." In her twenties, as a rising actress, she had had to cope with the distractions of a husband and young children and had found them a constant impediment to the practice of her art. "Beware of that," she concluded. "Keep your mind on your art, do not remit your study and you are sure to succeed."[20]

The first part of the advice was simple enough for him to follow. Macready was a born student and perfectionist. But the second must have been adhered to with considerable difficulty. Throughout his stage life Macready was troubled by his attraction for the opposite sex. His leading ladies were forever falling in love with him and making what he felt were indiscreet revelations of their passion. And in his youth, with the general looseness of the times added to the habitual looseness of the profession, his enthusiasm and romantic nature exposed him to temptation on every side. Nor did his position as leading actor and son of the manager make him less interesting.

Mrs. Siddons may have been making more than a generalization when she told him to avoid marriage until he was thirty. For some years the elder McCready had employed as a minor member of his company Sarah Garrick, the neglected wife of a nephew of the great David. She was nine years older than Mr. William and, although he is properly reticent about her character and her charms, it is plain that he was increasingly attracted to her. Mrs. Siddons, then, may have been addressing herself to the particular occasion, and the advice of so great and so successful an artist had its effect. Henceforth the business of being an actor was his exclusive preoccupation, though he was not so unsentimental as to completely abandon his early sweetheart. In later years he was to come to her rescue with careful advice and, whenever he was in a position to do so, to give employment to her daughter, who acted under the name of Miss Murray.[21]

And so the years of apprenticeship rolled by, guided by his father, by his own observation, and by the new conviction that he would reach a higher degree in his art if he thought more of it and less of himself. To proposals from other managers he turned a deaf ear: his apparent aim was to take over the family business when the time came. The circuit was extended. From Newcastle the Macreadys moved on to invade Scotland. At Glasgow Mr. William made his bow in *Hamlet* and was received with murmurs of approbation from the two knots of critical playgoers who regularly sat at the corners of the stage and passed judgment on performances in progress. But the going was not always smooth, and the ups and downs of fortune, constantly repeated, were proving too much for the disposition of his father. His Irish temper, notorious even among Irish tempers, broke forth, and Mr. William suddenly discovered that he too had a temper, a discovery he was later to credit as the source of most of the misery of his life.

The subject of the family quarrel is only hinted at in the *Reminiscences,* but it would not be surprising if there were some question of Mr. William's usurping his father's authority. Whatever the cause, relations between them were from that moment strained and they took to living in separate lodgings, although continuing to work together in the interests of the circuit. But there were recurrent outbreaks of temper and disputes over matters of management and production, until the young man felt he could no longer remain in the "embarrassing position," in which his father's obstinacy had placed him. Casting about for a course of action, he remembered William Dimond.

Dimond was the author of a number of successful melodramas and the manager of the theatre in Bath. The elder McCready had his opinion of "the Bath man" and it must have been a source of added bitterness to him to learn that his son had applied to him for a position. But in 1812 Dimond had invited Mr. William to take an engagement in Bath as a stepping stone to London, and it was to him, quite naturally, that the young actor turned.

On the twenty-ninth of December, 1814[22] Macready opened as Romeo in the Theatre Royal, Bath, and the days of his apprenticeship were over.

BATH AND GLASGOW

He had yet much to learn. Having moved from the family circle, he was no longer the manager's son, the crown prince of the company, or the pet of the circuit. Editors of local newspapers could no longer be expected to treat him with the friendly enthusiasm which was the due of every citizen and subscriber. From the Bath critics he first learned the truth about his ugly face: "an everlasting bar" to his success was the decree of one dimidiate Aristotle.[23] On the whole his reception was favorable, the public attended, Romeo was several times repeated, and ladies were overcome by his performance of Beverley in *The Gamester*. This was their fashionable reaction to any highly emotional performance, but it was not without its value in publicity. The Reverend John Genest, who had retired to Bath for his health and became a kind of theatrical Beau Brummel, pointed out that Dimond had paid Macready the compliment of casting Romeo to the best advantage, and had opened a new pantomime on the same night to ensure him a good house. The pantomime, he further remarks, was completely successful. Genest had taken a strong dislike to the new star, and the last volume of his monumental *Account of the English Stage* contains a number of uncomplimentary judgments, some based on Genest's own observation and some selected from an ample scrapbook of unfavorable newspaper clippings which he assiduously collected.[24]

Macready's engagement with Dimond seems to have been tentative, its length depending upon the enthusiasm of the public. Neither actor nor manager had cause for complaint. The playbill for Macready's fourth appearance, January 5, 1815, a repetition of Romeo, announced that he had "upon Tuesday night, again crowded the Theatre at an early hour, his extraordinary attraction and popularity increasing with each successive performance." Lest this be written off as a mere demonstration of the puff direct, the manager added, *"No Orders or Free Admission during Mr. Macready's Performance,"* a trustworthy indication that his audiences were indeed overflowing. The engagement was extended, in fact, to the eighteenth of February, and included appearances at Bristol, a part of the Bath circuit. Macready ran through the round of his characters, Barnwell and Hotspur and Orestes and the rest, gave two performances of Richard II (to bad houses, as Genest is quick to note),[25] and left with a promise to return next season on more favorable terms.

His Bristol appearances on the first of February had been announced as *"Previous to his departure from Bath for the Metropolis."* It was the expected thing that a promising young actor would use Bath as a way station for London. And indeed, as soon as accounts of the new star's success had reached Henry Harris, the acting manager of Covent Garden, he had despatched his assistant, John Fawcett, to Bath to observe and negotiate.[26] Macready, however, received Fawcett's proposals coolly. He was not, even with his almost instant success in the provinces, so in love with his profession that he would rush into a London engagement. Always in the front of his consciousness was the admonition of the Misses Headley: he might be received in society, might attain the status of gentleman. All that was necessary, apparently, was sufficient money to maintain the estate and appurtenances, and this his good beginning on the circuits seemed to promise. He sent Fawcett back to Harris with his terms: he would only accept an engagement for a period of years at a high salary; he would not surrender a known good for an unknowable future.

Fawcett must have given Harris an impressive account of Macready's talents to balance the uncompromising terms. Harris announced that he was willing to meet them and voluntarily gave up his privilege of breaking the contract after a year's trial. It was his obligation, as manager of a National Theatre, to see that the best talent in the profession was presented to his audiences (an attitude that Macready was to inherit along with the managership) and he was not disposed to haggle over the price (an attitude that Macready was most decidedly to reject).

Before the agreement could be concluded, however, the elder McCready got wind of it. Although young William was a star in his own right, to his father he was still the son of a great provincial manager, an actor shaped by his hands. He at once assumed direction of the negotiations, without inquiring what his son had proposed, and suggested to Fawcett that Covent Garden offer an experimental engagement of half a dozen nights at £20 a night. If William were successful, the engagement would be made permanent. This, of course, being more favorable to Harris, was the offer that was finally made, but Macready was not tempted. He rejected the proposal, and set out for the metropolis of the north, Glasgow.

Here the wisdom of his decision was made clear to him. Although he was a rapidly rising provincial actor with a reasonably secure reputation, his Glasgow engagement was overshadowed by the anticipation of the first appearance in that city of Edmund Kean, who was reputed to command a salary of £100 nightly.

These were Kean's years. He had taken London by storm; every actor, old or new, was compared with him and found wanting. The same comparison would have awaited Macready at his Covent Garden debut and, until the enthusiasm had somewhat abated, he would have stood but little chance of getting a fair hearing; after six nights he would have been forced back to the provinces with a diminished reputation. As it was, he found himself an untarnished country star and his receipts were satisfactory even in the face of metropolitan competition.

During the Glasgow engagement it was necessary to find a substitute at short notice for one of the children in *The Hunter of the Alps*. By chance Kitty Atkins, the pretty, nine-year-old daughter of the scene painter, was selected. Her fright, or the brief time allowed for preparation, caused her to be imperfect in her lines, and the young visiting star read her a lecture on professional responsibility. Kitty dissolved in tears. The situation was prophetic, for Kitty was his future wife and this was only the first of many hortatory encounters. But Macready was not yet thirty, and he went on to his first engagement in Dublin free in heart and heavier in pocket, leaving the child behind him to improve as best she might.

In his *Reminiscences* Macready writes at some length about the Dublin audience. It was notorious for its unruliness until its interest or sympathy was aroused, at which point its glowing sympathy allowed the actor to experience the full triumph of his art. The gallery would inform the actor, in the friendliest fashion, if his shirt-tail chanced to slip its confinement, would cheer local favorites above London stars, and, when roused by a burst of passion or a touch of nature, "no assembly could watch more intently, with more discriminating taste, or more lavish applause."[27] It was the kind of audience to provoke an actor to the top of his bent, and it confirmed Macready's principle of acting, *always to be in earnest,* as no earlier experience had. The result was further success and more money in the bank (he was receiving £50 a week). For his benefit, he made another attempt at *Richard II*, but without success. He could hardly have demonstrated his faith more strongly than in selecting the play for so financially crucial a performance as a benefit. It failed him, and his duty was plain; he gave up Richard for forty years.

From Dublin, Macready returned to England and a summer of alternate brief engagements and intermittent vacationing with his family. However, he found himself increasingly in disagreement with his father. In matters of theatre management the two were equally dictatorial, their ideas and tempers were in constant conflict. The elder McCready further had both an attraction and a weakness for the ladies. Macready's mother had died when he was ten, and his affection for her memory as well as his horror of irregularity of any sort increased his resentment against his father.[28] Nor could he have taken very kindly his father's interference in the Covent Garden engagement.

After this summer, Macready made no pretense of living with "his family," but began an independent life socially and professionally. He could not, of course, cut himself off completely. His sister Letitia became his housekeeper and confidante, and he continued to act as London agent for his father. Nor was he permitted to dissociate himself from his father's sexual irregularities. As Macready grew in fame and possessions, he became the natural target of constant applications for money or work from brothers and sisters whose necessity may have been as legitimate as their relationship was not. The situation was distasteful, both morally and economically, but after deep searching of his conscience and his banker's account, Macready usually ended by honoring the necessity and denying the relationship.

LONDON

The winter season in Bath turned out to be "a dull one," for a reason which Macready could not recall. It is very possible that the dullness may have been due to the general depression instead of the expected period of prosperity following the victory at Waterloo—but as usual such matters seem never to have occurred to Macready in computing the reasons for success or failure in any engagement. The dismal science had not yet made inroads upon the popular mind. But the actor managed to profit by his bad houses, using such performances as a lesson, a kind of public rehearsal, to try experiments and gauge reactions. He was vastly pleased with the success of such experiments, not knowing, of course, that Genest was jotting after his name as Benedick on the bills, "very bad," and after his Duke Aranza in Tobin's *Honeymoon,* "he spoke one serious speech well, but was very bad on the whole."[29] The innocent actor, in fact, declares that his performance of Benedick won him friends.

In spite of Genest and the dull season, Macready continued to be attractive to the London managers. This time, an overture came from Drury Lane, then operated by a committee which included Lord Byron. Without Macready's knowledge, some of his friends at Rugby had brought pressure to bear on the committee, largely through the Reverend J. Noel, a cousin of Byron's. The Reverend Mr. Noel, who seems to have been as suspicious of the theatre as he was ignorant of the character of his titled cousin, declared that, in addition to all his accomplishments as an actor, Mr. Macready was a very moral man. "Ha!" said Byron, "I suppose he asks five pounds a week more for his morality." But whatever the commodity and whatever the value, the Drury Lane committee decided that it could not meet Macready's price and the definite offer was not made. Instead, the management of Covent Garden, through John Fawcett, renewed the negotiations of the previous year. "Come to us next year," Fawcett wrote, "for one year, two years, three years, or for life. The article shall be made as you please, only don't be exorbitant." And he pointed out, what must have been most impressive to the young actor, "Kean seems likely to be more in your way at Drury Lane than Young would be at Covent Garden. All your best parts you might act with us and not trespass upon anybody."[30]

This was a tempting offer and Macready resolved to make the most of it. He wrote to Harris indicating his interest and stipulating for certain characters and business. "Mr. Harris's answer," he wrote many years later, "showed me at once the unreasonableness of my desire, and the impossibility of granting it.—His reply was— 'Do you think I pay you a sum of money to be idle, or not to make the most I can of your talent? If you bound me by all the parchment in the world, to give you a line of business, and the town *chose to prefer* Mr. A or Mr. B. I *must* put them into it:—in the same way, if *you* carry the town with you, how can I put a person of less pretentions or less favour with the public—*to my own injury*—before them?' "[31] The reasonableness of Harris' reply seems to have persuaded the young actor that his future was in safe hands, although the negotiations stretched over a period of months, during his entire engagement in Bath and a subsequent one in Dublin. In his *Reminiscences* Macready explains his delaying tactics:

A London engagement, the crowning object of every player's ambition, was to me, in its uncertain issue, a trial that I shrank from, and which I would certainly have deferred if by opportunity of practise elsewhere, for instance at Edinburgh, Liverpool, Norwich, York &c., I could have maintained my income and further matured my powers. The hazard was great. The cast must be a decisive one: one on which my life's future must depend, and in which the great talents of those already in secure possession of the public favour seemed to leave me little room for success. But no alternative presented itself: the irrevocable step must needs be taken.[32]

To an actor of a more happy-go-lucky disposition than Macready's, the terms he exacted would hardly have occasioned such misgivings: £16 a week for the first two years, £17 a week for the next two, and £18 for the fifth. But in his determination to put security first and in his fear of losing what position he had already attained, there is an inkling of the passion which was later to rule his life, to accumulate as quickly as possible and retire from a profession which was to become increasingly distasteful. Indeed, during his thirteen-week engagement in Dublin, he had settled down with the avowed intention "by a very ascetic regimen . . . 'to increase my store', a duty to which I had not been hitherto sufficiently attentive."[33] No doubt he was strengthened in his determination by his observation of the experience of John Philip Kemble. Lack of money had forced Kemble to linger on the stage after both his talents and attractiveness had worn out. Dublin received him with inattention and empty seats, and Macready may at that time have formed the resolution which he was happily to carry out, to retire while at the height of his powers.

Six years of provincial strolling had taught Macready that audiences might suddenly desert even the actors whom they had received with enthusiasm. He was becoming aware, too, that styles of acting are subject to the whims of the times. Kemble's obviously was out of favor; Kean's was all the rage. His own style was as yet unformed, and there was no anticipating the reaction of a London audience. To be sure, he was not going to compete with Kean in his own theatre, Drury Lane, yet the profession generally trusted the rumor that a group of Kean's followers, who called themselves the Wolves, had banded together to hunt out of the metropolis anyone who ventured to contest Kean's position. As it happened, Kean and his Wolves were no hindrance to Macready, yet the time was to come when another popular idol and his supporters were very nearly to cost him his life.

For the moment, Kean's popularity did Macready only this disservice, that he was not able to open in London in a part which displayed all his abilities. Rather, for safety's sake, the manager determined to display him as Orestes in *The Distressed Mother*, an outmoded neoclassic tragedy adapted by Ambrose Phillips from Racine's *Andromaque*. It was the kind of role admirably suited to the style of John Philip Kemble, and the cool reception of that old stager by the Dublin audience did little to increase the confidence of the debutant. But the agreement was made and there was no turning back.

COVENT GARDEN

On the sixteenth of September, 1816, the playbills of Covent Garden announced the debut that night of Mr. Macready, "(*From the Theatre Royal, Dublin*) being his first appearance in London." Macready had spent the morning in the theatre, inspecting his dressing room, going through a careful rehearsal, and becoming apprehensive at the vast size of the auditorium. The management had made the usual generous proffer of an unlimited number of passes for friends of the debutant, but this only reminded him that he had no friends to call upon for support. He was quite alone, at the mercy of the critics and the Wolves, and discouragement and doubt were foremost in his thoughts. After dinner he lay down to compose himself as best he could and concentrate upon his character until the early hour when he must report at the theatre, since the performance was to begin at seven o'clock. Once there he dressed in silence, hearing the call-boy's "Overture on, sir!" with a shudder, and awaiting the rap that summoned him for his entrance. It came almost at once and he stepped forth, with what possession he could muster, but with the awful feeling of stage-fright that always awaited him, "The same agitation, and effort to master it, the dazzled vision, the short, quick breath, the dry palate, the throbbing of the heart." In the wings he found Abbot, the Pylades of the evening, a completely competent and thoroughly second-rate actor. Grasping Abbot's hand, he dashed on the stage, shouting his opening line and experiencing for the first time the applause of a London audience.

It was a considerable audience. Row upon row they stretched away beyond the floats, unknown, indistinguishable, but not unfriendly. Kean was there, in a box, applauding generously, and the critics, the silent professionals preparing their journalistic opinions, the vociferous amateurs pronouncing damnation or triumph on the spot. After a few awkward moments at the beginning, during which there was a suggestion of a titter in the front of the pit, a burst of passion—"Oh, Ye Gods! give me Hermione or let me die!" —brought down the house, and the subsequent development of the character through a series of rants and mad scenes left the audience cheering and applauding long after the final curtain had fallen. It was a trying debut, both because of the antique mode of the play, and the vagaries of casting which gave the sorrowing Andromache to Mrs. Glover, one of the best of English comic actresses. But it was the more a personal triumph for Macready. Manager Harris recognized this in his congratulatory speech:

"Well, my boy, you have done capitally; and if you can carry a play along with such a cast, I don't know what you cannot do."[34]

As for the professional critics, the *Times* decreed that neither Young nor Charles Kemble had anything to fear from the young star, the *Globe* found him a "man of mind," and the *News* began with a left-handed salute: "Mr. Macready is the plainest and most awkwardly-made man that ever trod the stage, but he is an actor whom in some respects we prefer to Mr. Kean."[35] William Hazlitt, arbiter of the stage and disciple of Kean, wrote at length of the debut in the *Examiner*:

A Mr. MACREADY appeared at this Theatre on Monday and Friday in the character of *Orestes* in the *Distressed Mother,* a bad play for the display of his powers, in which however he succeeded in making a decidedly favourable impression on the audience. His voice is powerful in the highest degree, and at the same time possesses great harmony and modulation. His face is not equally calculated for the stage. He declaims better than any body we have lately heard. He is accused of being violent and wanting pathos. Neither of these objections is true. His manner of delivering the first speeches in this play was admirable, and the want of increasing interest afterwards was the fault of the author, rather than the actor. The fine suppressed tone in which he assented to Pyrrhus's command to convey the message to *Hermione* was a test of his variety of power, and brought down repeated acclamations from the house. We do not lay much stress on his mad-scene, though that was very good in its kind, for mad-scenes do not occur very often and when they do had in general better be omitted. We have not the slightest hesitation in saying, that Mr. MACREADY is by far the best tragic actor that has come out in our remembrance, with the exception of Mr. KEAN. We however heartily wish him well out of this character of *Orestes* . . . We think it wrong in any actor of great merit (which we hold Mr. MACREADY to be) to come out in an ambiguous character to salve his reputation. An actor is like a man who throws himself from the top of a steeple by a rope. He should chuse the highest steeple he can find, that if he does not succeed in coming safe to the ground, he may break his neck at once, and so put himself and the spectators out of further pain.[36]

Macready came away from his first night with some credit, then. But if Orestes had done him no damage, it could do the box office little good. And his next role, Mentevole in *The Italian Lover,* selected with equal caution, was likewise unattractive. There was nothing for it but to make a bold stroke for an attraction, and Harris announced that Macready and Charles Young would alternate the roles of Othello and Iago. This was an old theatrical dodge, always sure to arouse interest, since there was the possibility that the performance might turn into a cockfight. If it had, the victory should have gone easily to Young, an actor of several years' experience in playing the great roles before a metropolitan audience. Macready had rarely played Othello in the country, Iago he had never even studied. But the roles must be played. In something like ten days, he prepared an interpretation of the Moor; five days later he appeared as Iago—it could not be called an interpretation since he had barely time to learn the words of the part. But Charles Young was a cold and dignified man who depended largely upon the music of his voice to hold the attention of his audience. He was unwilling to put forth the physical exertion demanded in a contest for individual superiority; Macready, unprepared as he was, could literally act circles around him. "Young in Othello," said Hazlitt, "was like a great humming-top and Macready in Iago like a mischievous boy whipping him." On the other hand, the romantic critic found Macready's Othello too effeminate; he behaved as if he were in a drawing room, and allowed pathos to creep into his voice as he said, "Othello's occupation's gone."[37] But for the *Times* the performance removed any doubts it might have had as to Macready's capacity in the higher walks of his profession.[38] All in all, though unready, Macready did himself no discredit in his first Shakespearean attempts in the metropolis.

Henry Harris had been honest with him when he declared that it was to his own interest to make the most of his performers. He had tried Macready in two leads, he had tried him with Young in a classic. Now he announced in the bills for October 25, "Mr. MACREADY will shortly appear in a Principal Character in a NEW forthcoming DRAMA." This was, of all unlikely things, the role of Gambia in the musical play *The Slave*, first performed on November 12. Macready describes the character as "Placed in situations of strong interest, with highflown sentiments and occasional bursts of passion."[39] Genest's description is "a compound of despicable clap-traps from beginning to end."[40] The script had been patched together by Thomas Morton, hack playwright of Covent Garden, who joined parts of Mrs. Behn's *Oroonoko,* an old play which first approached slavery from a humanitarian basis, and parts of *Pizarro,* a sensational German melodrama, and shifted the locale to Surinam, whose slave trade was a matter of considerable contemporary interest. The music was written by Henry Bishop and sung by Kitty Stephens and John Sinclair, with low comic scenes played to the hilt by Emery and Liston. With such a combination of talents and such a mixture of attractive themes—

comedy, romance, music, melodrama, and sentiment—the play could not fail, and indeed was performed some thirty-three times in the course of the season.

In spite of the manager's efforts, Macready was not altogether happy. The competition at Covent Garden was stronger than he had been led to expect. Charles Young and Charles Kemble usurped the most attractive of the leading roles in spite of Fawcett's promise; John Kemble returned to play the round of his favorite parts before retiring from the stage; and the comic and musical companies were exceptionally strong. But in the true manner of his old school, Macready selected a motto from Seneca, *Inveniet viam, aut faciet,* and settled down to make the best of what was beginning to seem a poor bargain.

It was the Kean fever that most intrigued and distressed him. He went frequently to see the little man play during his own free nights and was only partially convinced. The enthusiasm of the audiences at Drury Lane confirmed his impression that the style of Kean was often offensive to his own aesthetic sense. With Kean's Sir Edward Mortimer in *The Iron Chest* he had no quarrel. His reading was "flowing, discriminating, and most impressive." His pantomime and his pauses were full of meaning. His transitions— the frenzy of the recital of his crime climaxed at "I stabbed him to the heart!" followed by a pause as if the vision suddenly presented itself to him, a lowering of the voice, a slowing of the tempo, "And my oppressor rolled lifeless at my foot"—were a significant contrast to the measured declamation of Kemble which rose and fell in waves.[41]

But in *Oroonoko* Kean's worst characteristics as an actor emerged. He underlined the violence and crudity of the horrors, altered lines for bathetic effect and generally comported himself in an inartistic manner. A quarter of a century later Macready was to recall Kean's "exaggerated attitude" and "distortion of Countenance" as "melodramatic . . . blots upon the bright genius of a superlatively great actor, and which were never—*never*—to be detected in Mrs. Siddons, in Talma, in Kemble, or in Miss O'Neill."[42]

But the public cry was for more Kean, and when Henry Harris heard of an obscure country actor who, from appearance and manner, might be the little giant's brother he hastened to offer him an engagement. This was perilously close to the last straw for Macready, though as it turned out he had little to fear. The new recruit was Junius Brutus Booth, later to be a star of the American stage and founder of a famous acting family. At this moment, however, he was but an imitator, and not a very experienced one, of the romantic manner of the idol of the theatregoers. On February 12, 1817, he gave a performance of *Richard III* at Covent Garden which was almost a mirror of that being offered at Drury Lane. It was successful enough to be repeated on the following night and to make him confident that he could extract a larger salary from the manager than he had been promised. The manager appeared to haggle and Booth withdrew from his engagement.

At this point, his great original approached Booth with a suspiciously generous offer to join the ranks of Drury. Booth, as flattered as he was naive, jumped at the salary of £10 a week and found himself on February 20 playing Iago to the Othello of his master. Kean acted him off the stage. "There were improvements," said the *Times*, "in Kean's acting of which we did not think the tragedian's art had been susceptible."[43] By the time the curtain had fallen, Booth was no longer naive. Although the performance was announced for repetition the next day but one, he sent a note to the Drury Lane management saying that he had been taken ill and was forced to leave town. This was followed by a letter declining to appear again at Drury: "since he could not appear in his own characters," he was returning to Covent Garden. With obvious malice, the whole story, with documents, was published openly in the Drury Lane playbills.

The outcome was visible from afar. The public had been "insulted" by one of its "humble servants." On the evening of the twenty-fifth, when Booth made his reappearance as Richard, Covent Garden was crowded and tense. Howls of rage filled the air at his first entrance and continued with increasing fury as the injured public (abetted perhaps by the Wolves) took its revenge. The riot continued for several nights, until audiences tired of paying money to hear themselves roar. All this tumult should have been music to Macready's ears, for Booth would have been a serious rival in his own company, but the management was determined to make the most of their bargain and continued to push the pseudo-Kean, letting him play Sir Edward Mortimer and Posthumus. He aroused Macready's aesthetic disgust by squeezing a spongeful of rose-pink in his mouth during the dying spasms of Sir Giles Overreach. And several times Macready was forced to play secondary parts to Booth's leads, though in each instance Booth seems to have come off with something less than a triumph. *The Theatrical Inquisitor* may have salved Macready's injured feelings with its comments on the performance of *The Curfew,* March 27, 1817:

Mr. Macready surprised us by his brilliant embodiment of *Robert,* which he rendered the most conspicuous undertaking of the evening. This gentleman was honoured by the most cordial reception, and appeared to feel encouragement like the Ox in Horace, who galloped over the field with his *foenum in cornu.* Such assiduity, zeal, and distinction, were justly united; and the government of Mr. Macready's feelings, under the exclusion from the capital part to which his claims were so decisive, does equal honour to his forbearance and urbanity. It is true, indeed, that slender reasons were left for regret, in the superior applause by which his subordinate endeavours were attended.

Again, in a new play by Dimond, *The Conquest of Tarranto,* the leading role was given to Booth and to Macready fell, in spite of his willingness to pay a forfeit to give it up, "one of the meanest, most despicable villains that a romancer's invention ever teemed with."[44] Bitter throughout the rehearsal period, and sick at heart the night of the performance, Macready nonetheless managed to steal the climactic scene from the star with his intense portrayal of a traitor shuddering under the exposure of his guilt. This scene saved the piece from damnation and, according to the *Morning Herald,* Macready's acting was the principal ingredient in the success of the scene. Booth was disposed of, but Macready's triumph proved a bitter cup to him.

The Conquest of Tarranto ran its brief career in six performances through the month of April, and the company was soon summoned for rehearsals of the next new play. It was the custom of those days for the actors to gather in the greenroom, a sort of parlor and waiting room between the stage and the dressing rooms, to hear the play read through by its author. The playwright on this occasion was Richard Lalor Shiel, a struggling Irish barrister who had turned to providing vehicles for the talents of his countrywoman, Eliza O'Neill. As he commenced reading *The Apostate,* the actors exchanged their usual glances of amusement and misgiving, for Shiel was no exception to the general rule that authors are poor readers. But they were soon enthralled with the plot, a monstrous and horrible tale. It is the story of Hemaya, a Moor, who wishes to marry Florinda, a Christian. To win her he becomes a Christian himself, forsaking his Moorish brethren for his white bride—who had already been betrothed to Pescara, the villainous governor of Granada. Pescara immediately embarks on an elaborate program of revenge. He taunts Hemaya, who replies with noble scorn:

> The frown of fortune could not make me base
> The smile of fortune could not make thee noble.

To which Pescara:

> My birth:—confusion—
> And must I ever feel the reptile crawl,
> And see it pointed at?—what if I rush,
> And with a blow strike life from out his heart?
> No—no! my dagger is my last resource.

That final line may be taken as Pescara's motto. When Hemaya provokes him to action, he draws back just in time, crying:

> I might have slain him, and a single blow
> Had burst the complicated toils I weave.

These complicated toils involve, among other things, persuading the hero to incite a revolt of the Moors which leads him to defeat, capture, and the Inquisition. Florinda escapes from Pescara, only to be returned to see her lover placed upon the rack. She agrees to wed Pescara to save Hemaya, takes poison, and dies. Pescara's villainy is exposed, and Hemaya, finding himself in the impossible position of being alive just before the final curtain, stabs himself.

Pescara is typical of the screaming, cursing, gigantic villains of the early nineteenth-century pseudo-Jacobean tragedies. No simple revenge will do for him; he must plot diabolically to undo his victim in some new and untried manner. It does not signify if half a city must be destroyed to catch that victim as long as the means are sufficiently complex. And Macready left the greenroom with the speeches of Pescara clutched in his unwilling fist.

But he must be in earnest, and he must make a way if none presented itself. He worked conscientiously at the hated role, made the most of the irony and the bursts of passion, and shared the general success of the production. At least no one could say that his face was not suited to the character. Ludwig Tieck, the German playwright and dramatic critic who happened to be in the audience, said more: "This villain was admirably represented, and was indeed so vehement, truthful, and powerful a personation, that for the first time since my arrival in England I felt myself reminded of the best days of German acting."[45]

Macready had been experimenting with a new technique which may account for some of the high praise bestowed on the melodramatic monsters he was called upon to play. Almost from his London debut, critics had been calling his attention to his excessive violence. The *Atheneum* described him as giving way "to sheer passion until it almost chokes utterance"[46] and Charles Young had warned him that half his energy and fire would be more than sufficient for a successful performance.[47] These com-

ments were not wasted, and while he was rehearsing *Adelgitha*
(1818) finally took shape in his mind as the principle of repressed
force. "The truth had become manifest to me," he explained,
"that, as passion is weakness, the real sense of power is best expressed by a collected and calm demeanour."[48] This repression, of
course, was a matter of degree. To audiences accustomed to the
full-throated violence of melodramatic villainy, Macready sometimes appeared dull; to Bernard Shaw's father, a generation later,
he was like a mad bull.[49] But the principle is clear. As Macready
was to advise a young player, "Confine your excitement to your
mind, and leave your muscles to take care of themselves!"[50]

The success of Pescara unfortunately typed him in the eyes of
the manager and threatened to do so with his audience. His first
new role in the next season was Dumont, a ruined merchant, in
The Father and His Children by Frederick Reynolds. Its plot,
bald and melodramatic, involved the pathetic situation of a father
who must commit a robbery to keep his brood from starving.
Dumont was one of a succession of such parts, deriving from the
Germanic school of Kotzebue and *The Stranger,* each of which
became more distasteful to him. *The Castle of Paluzzi* (May 27,
1818) found him as the villain in a play which was announced as
dramatizing *"some of the interesting facts in a recent Trial on
the Continent,"* and which involved a murder, the only witness
to which was an inmate of a brothel. Here the *Theatrical Inquisitor* found him somewhat wanting. He "seemed to think the
part beneath his powers, and that it was not worth his while to
give himself any trouble, and consequently was a feeble representative of the character."[51] Macready's own judgment bears
this out. The role was, he says, "The lees of the distasteful cup."[52]

The third season found him still occupied with villains.
Adelgitha, which he had played with great success in the country,
was to be revived. But with a difference: in the country he had
been Lothair, the hero; in London he was to play Michael Ducas,
the villain. He resented the change, loudly, but to no avail; the
repulsive character was his and old John Fawcett said to him,
with some wisdom, "Why, William, you grumble at every part
that is given you, and you succeed in them all! Set to work at this,
and, though it is rather an odious gentleman, you may make
something of him by hard study."[53] Macready never needed to be
told twice to study, and the repugnant Ducas brought him added
acclaim. The *Literary Gazette* roundly declared, "Macready, in
Michael Ducas, as in fact in all he undertakes, displays talents
not surpassed by any performer on the metropolitan stage. His

powers are truly terrible; and, with the exception of Talma, we know but one other with whom to compare him. If Kean had his voice and person: or he had Kean's face, what an Actor there would be!"[54] Macready could take comfort in being rated always against Kean, against the best, rather than against Charles Kemble, or Young, or any other members of his own company. But neither the general critical estimate nor the gradual development of his own individual style of acting could save Macready from his villains.

When Maturin's *Fredolfo* was to be presented, the actors were sure that it would fail. Three of the characters were villains, a bad, a worse, and a worst. Macready's part was Wallenberg, the worst. And for once the actors were right in their estimate of a play's success.

Although a minor event, neither critics nor performers were able to forget the first and only performance of *Fredolfo*. Maturin, who had a not inconsiderable reputation as an author of Gothic tales of terror, had apparently determined to "sting the [theatrical] public into a sense of his power." The characters he assembled were depraved beyond imagination, "ruffians of the Byronic school, loaded with all the dark vices, but displaying none of the grand and rugged genius, which distinguishes the originals." So violent was the action and so gratuitous the horror that the audience, which seemed to recognize a kind of parody of Shiel and Kotzebue, was disposed to laugh until the climax, an action so "thoroughly unEnglish" that the play's damnation was complete. It was, of course, Macready's responsibility to perform the act, and the effect was burned into his memory:

The play passed (May 12, 1819) with little applause and occasional disapprobation to the last scene, the interior of a cathedral, at the altar of which Wallenberg had secured Urilda (Miss O'Neill), and threatened Adelmar, her lover (Charles Kemble), who with his band had burst in to her rescue, with her instant death unless he surrendered his sword. In the agony of his despair Adelmar on his knees gave his weapon into the hands of Wallenberg, who plunged it directly into his bosom, upon which the pit got up with a perfect yell of indignation, such as, I fancy, was never before heard in a theatre. Not another syllable was audible. The curtain fell in a tumult of opposition, and 'Fredolfo' was never acted again.[55]

It is hardly to be wondered that a man of Macready's tastes and education should seriously question the wisdom of remaining on the stage. The London venture was not turning out as he had hoped, the other actors were secure in their places, the new roles which fell to his lot were unsatisfactory. Since he had followed Mrs. Siddons's caution against marriage, he had no responsibilities except to himself. His old schoolfellows were encouraging him to believe that he could readily progress to a degree at Oxford, and one even offered to advance the necessary money. He began to think seriously of retirement from the stage and entrance into the Church. This, however, was a commitment not to be lightly assumed, and in the meantime there came an event which put an end to any ideas of escape. His brother Edward was in need of money for advancement in the army and Macready's sense of duty drove him to accept the profferred educational loan, give the money to his brother, and resign himself to his unhappy profession.

In the ensuing year, also, the elder McCready was once more in financial difficulties. He had lost the Newcastle theatre and was determined to try his fortunes in Bristol. William Charles took advantage of the Lenten off nights at Covent Garden to go down to Bristol with a fellow actor, Daniel Terry, and give the theatre a grand opening. The occasion was celebrated by a playbill couched in the provincial manager's most persuasive terms:

To trace out the causes of the Drama's reduction in Bristol, from the high state of favour and repute in which it once flourished, would be as fruitless as laborious. The fact is sufficiently ascertained to justify this preliminary appeal to such as may desire the enjoyment of a well-regulated Theatre.

The Manager, solicitous to let no occasion slip of redeeming his pledge to use every exertion in bringing forward THE FIRST POSSIBLE ENTERTAINMENT that can be procured, has the gratification of informing the Ladies and Gentlemen of Bristol and its Vicinity, that, having obtained permission from the Covent Garden Proprietor, he is enabled to open the Theatre with the United Talents of

M R .   M A C R E A D Y

and

M R .   T E R R Y

From the Theatre-Royal, Covent Garden[56]

The outcome was prosperous. William McCready lived out his days as the respected head of the Bristol theatre, married one of his actresses, and bequeathed to his descendants a title so secure that it outlasted the century.

There were further demands upon the young actor. His friends were as great a responsibility to him as his family. To his early love Sarah Garrick, now widowed, who was in theatrical difficulties in Liverpool, he wrote:

How are you circumstanced for money?—If you are yourself unable, I will endeavour to supply you with sufficient for your journey to London, as I think it is very necessary that you should see your late Husband's agent—If there is anything else I can do for you, or George & Sarah [her children], or for your Brother let me know: & be assured my best exertions shall be theirs . . . —Can I assist your Brother in procuring an engagement, do you think?—At Glasgow I could recommend him strongly.—He would not be compatible with my father, or I could do that directly for him:—but I could get letters to Edinb. (I should not like to write them myself)—if there is anything else that I can do, pray point it out to me.—*What do you intend to do with George?*—pray let me know your views and wishes with respect to your family, as *perhaps* it may be in my power to promote them essentially. —I am very, very happy to hear that Sarah grows a very sweet girl, although she does so much dislike me—I cannot bring myself to return her aversion, or if I had ever thought unkindly of her, should NOW forget it.—I hope sincerely that you NEVER *let her go behind the scenes of the Theatre:* if you would keep her from thence:—nothing but vice is to be inculcated THERE. For Gods sake, let her hold herself far above anything so low and bad.[57]

So many virtuous acts could not, in the tradition of the theatre, but be rewarded. Shortly after Macready resigned himself to his profession for his brother's sake, the Covent Garden management acquired Pocock's musical adaptation of Walter Scott's *Rob Roy Macgregor.* It was a well-made little patchwork with plenty of highland songs and thoroughly pasteboard characters. Nor was the central figure all that Macready had dreamed of as his proper sphere. But Rob Roy was at least a positive character exhibiting pathos, humor, and heroism. Perhaps best of all, from his standards, Rob Roy was not a villain but a romantic outlaw, who could cry out when accused by the supposedly honest Rashleigh Osbaldistone, "If you know what I am, you know likewise what usage made me what I am; and whatever you may think, I would not change with the proudest of the oppressors that have driven me to take the heather brush for shelter." [II, 1.]

The effect of this sort of sentiment on the middle-class audience and on the literary men of the year 1818 is readily foreseen. After attending the performance, Barry Cornwall published a poetical tribute to the

> buoyant air, a passionate tone
> That breathes about thee, and lights up thine eye
> With fire and freedom; it becomes thee well.[58]

Charles Lloyd, the friend of Lamb who had spent four years in a condition diagnosed as "melancholia," was taken to see the play. At the moment when Rob Roy, overcome with emotion, openly weeps, Lloyd broke down, wept, and was restored to his senses. He too rushed to print an ode to "Gifted Macready."[59] In this one role in a minor musical piece Macready discovered two sources of his unique attraction in later years, the power of sensibility and the appeal for the rights of man. The play was not too far off which, uniting these appeals in a tragic setting, would lend them magnitude.

But before that play arrived in the post, there were other trials to undergo. There were more villains, of course: Amurath, the renegade in Shiel's *Bellamira* (April 22, 1818), Glenalvon in a revival of *Douglas* (June 2, 1818), Dumont in a revival of *Jane Shore* (November 9, 1818), and Ludovico in Shiel's adapted *Evadne* (February 10, 1819). On Macready's performance of the first of these monsters, the *Literary Gazette* commented:

for the bad and stormy passions he has not, in our opinion, a superior upon the stage; and if an equal, only one. His very glare was malignity; and it is remarkable of this performer, that in the most potent delineation of a deep and diabolical nature, he does not o'erstep the line, but is invariably probable as well as powerful.[60]

There were attempts at Shakespeare: for the benefit of Farley on June 16, 1818, he played Hotspur in one act of *Henry IV* on a bill which included an act from each of five Shakespearean plays; for the benefit of Miss Sally Booth on June 30, 1818, he undertook Posthumus to her Imogen; but benefits were largely ignored by the critics and the performances are significant in that such occasions were the only chance he was given to test his real powers.

The Covent Garden season of 1819–20, which was to thrust Macready into the first rank of which he dreamed, began with rumblings of disaster. The company had been sadly depleted by the resignation of Charles Young, by the absence (to be made permanent by marriage) of Miss O'Neill, by the illness of the great comedian Liston. To Charles Kemble fell such roles as Macbeth, for which he was ill suited, while Macready came forth as Joseph Surface, which only grim determination to succeed would convert into a minor success of later years, but which at the moment failed to attract. The electrifying O'Neill had been replaced by the stodgy wife of Alfred Bunn, the stage manager. This, in face of a company at Drury Lane which was unparalleled in comic power and promised a reappearance of Kean, drove manager Harris to declare that he frequently wondered in the morning whether he should not shoot himself before night. He tried expedients. Macready was brought out to modest acclaim in Henry V, in Othello, in Rolla. A debutant named Amherst attempted the title role in Lee's outmoded *Alexander the Great* to the derision of a diminished audience. Desperate measures were called for, and Harris decided that Macready should challenge Kean on his own ground.

The character was to be Cibber's version of Richard III, Kean's greatest personal success, and the diamond test of a romantic actor. Macready shrank from it for his usual reasons: it would be a risk to the popularity he had already gained, there was little time for the study he would require for a major attempt, the play was threadbare—and he had an aversion to the "improved text." Harris cut him short by announcing the performance and Macready had no choice but to "undergo the ordeal." He studied, and not only Cibber but history and Shakespeare's text, basing his interpretation on what he found in these sources rather than on the "sententious and stagy" lines of Cibber. His endeavor was not to make points—that is, to bring the house down by an electrifying delivery of some thrilling line: "Off with his head—so much for Buckingham!"—but to render "the hypocrisy of the man deceptive and persuasive in its earnestness, . . . presenting him in the execution of his will as acting with lightning-like rapidity."

On October 25, 1819, the audience, anticipating a major triumph or a major catastrophe, jammed the theatre to the beams and greeted the contender on his entrance with a round of applause, which, if intended to cheer, only served to unsettle him. But Macready extended himself to the uttermost and the audience frequently interrupted, as was customary, with plaudits and cheers, and finally, after the murder of the children in the tower, leaped to its feet, waving hats and handkerchiefs in a tumult of approval which was repeated over and over at the end of every scene until his last and greatest exertion, the death of Richard, sealed his triumph:

His combat was savagely ferocious, and his death terrible;—when he lay expiring upon the ground, and speech had failed him, the fiendish glare with which he regarded his victorious foe, gave to his eyes a resemblance to coals of fire fading into white cold cinders; for the gaze became dull and unmeaning; the eye-lid quivered and dropped—and the tyrant was no more. In a death scene our tragedian never fails.[61]

The boundless enthusiasm of the spectators even prevented the usual formal announcement of the repetition of the play. They would have Macready back. As one of the spectators scrawled on his program as a memento of that exciting night:

Macready was the first actor who went before the curtain at the conclusion of a piece to take what is termed in theatrical parlance "The call;"—he done it after the last act of Richard the third at Covent Garden Theatre on the 25th of October 1819, from that evening the custom was adopted.[62]

The anonymous historian is not quite accurate. Kean had returned for calls occasionally at Drury Lane. But Macready was certainly the first at Covent Garden, and though he later found the practice reprehensible and annoying, he was also more than a little upset if the audience did not summon him, and promptly, and before any of the other players. He rightly interpreted the call as a barometer of popularity, if not of critical acumen.

The press echoed the audience.[63] The *Chronicle* commented on his originality, his endurance (Richards were apt to fail vocally in the final scenes because of the excessive demands of the earlier big moments);[64] the *Times* felt it a performance which "could only result from a great histrionic talent, combined with physical and mental energy"; the *Courier* heard in his voice the matchless sway of Siddons; the *Literary Gazette* found him admirable "to the full meaning of that very lofty word." Only one critic, Leigh Hunt, had the temerity openly to compare him with the man whose rival he had plainly become. Macready's Richard, he declared, was livelier and more animal than Kean's:

At the same time when we compare Mr. MACREADY with Mr. Kean, it is to be recollected that MR. KEAN first gave the living stage that example of a natural style of acting, on which Mr. MACREADY has founded his new rank in the theatrical world. Nor must we omit, that the latter falls into some defects, which the former is never betrayed into; and those too of a description inconsistent with the general style of his performance. We allude to some over-soft and pathetic tones toward the conclusion of the part, where *Richard* is undergoing remorse of conscience. *Richard* might lament and even be pathetic; but he would certainly never whine, or deal in anything approaching to the lack-a-daisical. . . .

We certainly never saw the gayer part of *Richard* to such advantage. His very step in the more sanguine scenes had a princely gaiety of self-possession; and seemed to walk off to the music of his approaching triumph.[65]

The result was all that Harris or Macready could have hoped for. Covent Garden was re-established, Drury Lane acknowledged the strength of the competition by restaging Kean's Richard, learned comparisons of the two interpretations of the corrupt text were somewhat foolishly drawn up, and the expected ballad appeared proclaiming that the new Richard III ought really to be called *Richard the First*.[66] *Coriolanus* was rushed on, though with painstaking care on Macready's part, and rode the crest of popularity. Barry Cornwall announced in a sonnet that he now stood "Distinct among the genius of the land."[67]

Nothing would do but Harris must anticipate Kean with a revival of Tate's version of *King Lear*. At this Macready balked. As he said, "It would not have been consistent with the principles I held in respect to my art to venture . . . the grandest and most affecting of the Great Master's creations without time to search out the clearest conception of his intentions, and perfect myself in the most elaborately studied execution of them."[68] Edmund, the villain, he was willing to assume, and the unsquelchable Booth had no hesitation in undertaking the mad king. In spite of Harris' proclamation that Booth's triumph "surpassed those sanguine expectations of success which might be formed of the most favoured Actor, in the present day,"[69] the revival spent itself in three nights, while Macready went on with undiminished reputation for twenty-four nights as Henri Quatre in the title role of a new musical romance by Henry Bishop.

It was in April of 1820 that he received a letter from an old acquaintance, John Tait, the Glasgow publisher, urging him to read a new play by an unknown author. The manuscript arrived one midafternoon and Macready, prompted by some whispering of fate, put other business aside to read it through: *Virginius*, by James Sheridan Knowles. As he reached the last page he was in such a state of excitement that, throwing caution to the winds, he very nearly accepted the play on the spot. His instinct did not betray him. This was the play which was to bring wide fame and fortune both to himself and to the author. When he had collected himself, he reread the manuscript and, in "sober certainty" of the justness of his first impression, he committed himself to paper.

✧ ✧ ✧ 3 ✧ ✧ ✧

The Eminent Tragedian

Virginius

JAMES SHERIDAN KNOWLES was the first of many literary men who would follow Macready into the theatre. Most of them professed only their friendship and their desire to serve the actor and his great end of restoring the drama to the pre-eminence it had held in the Elizabethan era. Some who began with such disinterested motives were diverted by hunger or the applause of friends to an interest in their own success at the box office. Neither motive was calculated to produce work of enduring merit: the plays were shaped to the special talents of the actor, if not in first draft, certainly by first performance. And it was standard procedure for the actor to reshape them with his own pen, guided by the advice of a sort of cabinet of literary friends. The product was a series of vehicles, few of which survived Macready's retirement, hack-written or custom-tailored, and singularly revealing of the star's peculiar talents and the taste of his audiences.

Not all of the Macready playwrights have been forgotten as literary men: Bulwer-Lytton, Robert Browning, Charles Dickens, Barry Cornwall. And some, like Sergeant Talfourd, are remembered for non-literary achievements. But many, like T. J. Searle and Westland Marston, were literary hacks, "naturally fast in pace, and brilliant in action," as Thackeray defined them, but suitable only to the short, commercial runs.

Of these hacks Knowles was first in time and stature. He managed to deceive even the best of the contemporary critics, and audiences responded to his tragedies with the enthusiasm usually reserved for spectacle, opera, and melodramas starring trained horses, dogs, and monkeys. It is a testimony to Macready's sense

of time and taste that he recognized the possibilities for success
in the work of an unknown playwright. It is typical of him that
he should at once begin to suggest alterations and improvements.

Although his first letter to Knowles does not seem to have survived, Knowles' reply permits the inference that the actor had
summoned his classical critical sense to temper his first enthusiasm.
His objections were to matters of diction, to words that lacked the
dignity of tragedy. Verbal insensitivity is perhaps the most obvious
of Knowles' poetic flaws, not surprising in a period dominated by
the subject matter and techniques of the Elizabethan drama as
anthologized by Charles Lamb[1] and the reforms of the language of
poetry instituted by Wordsworth and his followers.

Knowles, overjoyed at receiving a friendly hearing from the
metropolitan star, rushed to reply to his objections:

I have but a few minutes—I should say moments—to write. All your
suggestions I have attended to: I believe so, and if I have not, I fully
proposed to attend to them, except so far as the word "squeak" is
concerned: that word I know not how to lose, for want of a fit substitute—*the smallest possible sound*. Find out a term, and make the
alteration yourself; or if you cannot, and still wish an alteration, do
what you like, I don't care about it, I merely submit the matter to
you. Oh, I have forgotten the word "cheer"; what shall I do also in
the way of finding a substitute for that word?

I cannot stop to write another line. . . .

Make any alterations you like in any part of the play, and I shall
be obliged to you.[2]

Macready must have thought that he had got hold of a rather
odd fish, but the letter was characteristic of its writer. Knowles
was at the moment an impoverished schoolmaster, an Irishman
of great sentimentality, a writer of some facility and some crabbed-
ness. Between him and Macready there was to develop a friendship, fitful and romantic, and ultimately destroyed by jealousy
and bad temper. Knowles' heart was on his sleeve; he was, like
many of his poetical race, intemperate, impractical, very much
the sort of Irishman that Boucicault used to like to portray. In
the midst of the tightest pinches of fortune, he could look upon
his large brood and remind his wife that they were "rich in these."
Openly entangled with an actress, he could ingenuously rest his
claim to fame on his portraits of innocent and spirited maidens;
to a lady who thanked him for his generous estimate of her sex,
he replied, "God bless you. I painted them as I found them."[3]
And his industry was amazing. He had written *Virginius* in three
months while teaching thirteen hours a day. Small wonder that

he "cannot stop to write another line" to the actor who has befriended him.

Next day, however, he finds an interval to write again and at greater length, revealing more of what an actor expected a playwright to do with his work:

Surely you must think me the oddest fellow in the world to write such a letter as that I despatched yesterday. The truth is that I had not time to write; and yet to forward the copy without acknowledging your kind—most kind epistle was quite impossible—I am sure it must have been a most incoherent composition; but if you have gathered from it the idea that you have been the means of making me very happy—stranger to you as I am—you have done what I wished you to do.

I think I have attended to all your hints—and I attended to them because I was convinced of their propriety and not out of empty complement [sic]—except what referred to the two words—squeak and cheer. My confidence with respect to the propriety of retaining the 1st term is unqualified—'twould be dishonest with me not to say so— for I feel a conviction that were I the most highly bred man upon the earth, being placed in the situation in which Virginius uses it, it is just the word that I should use—Observe however, that I state this, because my vocabulary does not at present furnish me with any word half so eligible—but hang a word—if you and your friends are against me, out with it—I am not fastidious about twenty words—much less one [Across this is written "What do you think of Squeal"]. As to the other term—I don't like it—and shall be very grateful if you will substitute one for it—or change the construction so as to omit it.

I thought it best to give Virginius an entrance in that scene of the 3d act which you recommended me to alter. You know he will have changed his dress—and the thing will be more effective—I speak with submission to a master of effect.

Now my Dear Mr. McCready, don't stand upon any formality with me—cut out what you like. I leave the management of the thing in your hands—if they will be so kind as not to decline the trouble. . . .

Of one thing I am satisfied—if you have read the play a 3d time, you will find other corrections necessary—Now once for all will you make them yourself, & not wait for the result of a communication to me—

Now my Dear Sir, attend to what I say—and at your own good judgement give decision—I know not your party or whether you have any party—but Mr. William Hazlitt—of the Surrey Institution—is one of my earliest and best esteemed friends. He was a young man, and I, a boy, when we 1st became acquainted—I was then passionately fond of scribbling—not much to the satisfaction of my family, who would have been better pleased at seeing me occupied with more solid pursuits—and to Hazlitt I used to take delight in showing my attempts for he applauded and encouraged me—whatsoever ideas I have of late I owe to him—indeed he is the parent of my style—little honor as it may do him—for he used to take pains in pointing out to me what was well done & what was ill done—and would recite to me passages from great poets & show me wherein the beauties that he directed my attention to peculiarly consisted—beside all which he was my own kind and steady friend—Now my Dear Sir, I could wish that the piece should be seen by my friend—should it be represented before its publication—This is all—Judge for me, if you will be so kind. . . . What a bundle of business has been put into your hands that you dreamt not of three weeks ago![4]

Macready, apparently sure that he had a good thing, minded not in the least the bundle of business that he found on his hands. He hunted out Bryan Waller Proctor, then well known as the poet "Barry Cornwall," who promised to provide an epilogue and to get John Hamilton Reynolds, the friend of Keats, to write a prologue. He arranged for the sale of the copyright to the publisher Ridgeway after being rejected by John Murray. He bargained with manager Harris and got excellent terms for the author—£400 for twenty nights—£100 better than was customary. Finally, he undertook the staging of the play at the request of Fawcett, teaching Maria Foote, who was to be the heroine, how to be effectively simple, directing the rest of the cast so zealously that there was muttering behind his back, and annotating his own script in Latin, Greek, and Italian that those players who "chummed" with him in the common dressing room might not misunderstand the devices and observations that were intended only to excite his own feelings.[5]

The night of trial was May 17, 1820. All did not at first go well. Charles Kemble, happily cast as the brave and honorable young lover, Icilius, was so hoarse that he could not be heard. There may have been some misgivings in an audience which had been taught to expect blood and rant in its modern tragedies when the prologue announced:

> To-night, no idle nondescript lays waste
> The fairy and yet placid bower of taste:
> No story, piled with dark and cumbrous fate,
> And words, that stagger under their own weight;
> But one of silent grandeur—simply said,
> As though it were awaken'd from the dead!
> It is a tale—made beautiful by years;—
> Of pure, old Roman sorrow—old in tears!
> And those you shed o'er it in childhood may
> Still fall—and fall—for sweet Virginia!

There may have been some disappointment at the not wholly unexpected appearance of the same old stock settings which had served for *Julius Caesar,* and *Cato,* and *Coriolanus,* and the same familiar Roman costumes (except Macready's—he provided his own). But such misgivings were soon forgotten in the interest of the story, for Knowles had caught in his sad tale of Virginia and the Liberation of Rome the spirit of the new age.

If the first scene with its sneers at the citizenry and political corruption is reminiscent of other plays of ancient Rome, the second is pure English domesticity. Virginius, the noble centurion, learns that his daughter is in love with Icilius. He thereupon takes time off from the business of war and state to "quizz" her in a genteel manner, and the resultant maidenly confusion would have been decorous and characteristic in Amelia Sedley. In the next scene, Virginius gives her to her lover:

> My daughter truly filial—both in word
> And act—yet even more in act than word;
> And—for the man who hopes to win her hand—
> A virgin, from whose lips a soul as pure
> Exhales, as e'er responded to the blessing
> Breathed in a parent's kiss.

Overcome with emotion, the tears streaming down his cheeks, the father bestows his beloved daughter on the man of her heart, and the audience weeps with him, filled with right-minded sensibility.

There is a villain in the piece, of course, a black and unmitigated one, the tyrant Appius. Virginius and Icilius being engaged in a military campaign, Appius casts his eye upon Virginia and desires her. By the laws of Rome and romantic tragedy, it is impossible for him to undertake his wooing directly, and he plots that his client Claudius shall claim the girl as a slave taken from him in infancy by Virginius. Warned of the infernal toils, the father explodes in thundering wrath, but is bound to undergo the trial of the law. Folding his daughter to him, he cries,

> So thou art Claudius' slave? And if thou art,
> I'm surely not thy father! Blister'd villain!
> You have warn'd our neighbors, have you not, to attend
> As witnesses? To be sure you have! A fool
> To ask the question. Dragg'd along the streets too!
> 'Twas very kind in him to go himself
> And fetch thee—such an honour should not pass
> Without acknowledgement. I shall return it
> In full! In full!

At this point Virginius reaches a climax of heroic wrath. Virginia, however, begs "Dear father, be advised—Will you not father?' and his wrath is dissipated in a moment of domestic tenderness. With a sudden shift of tone and volume, he says,

> I never saw you look so like your mother
> In all my life!
> Virginia. You'll be advised, dear father?
> Virginius. It was her soul—her soul, that play'd just then
> About the features of her child, and lit them
> Into the likeness of her own.

In performance the shift of tone was unexpected, revolutionary, and completely successful. It revealed the essential humanity of Virginius, translated the situation into terms which the average bourgeois playgoer could readily assimilate, into feelings which he could share. Later critics, looking at the whole history of English tragedy, might say with William Archer that this was undignified, dismal, stodgy,[6] but for the large class of Englishmen who were already in 1820 becoming "Victorians," domestic sensibility was your only wear.

Immediately upon this "domestic touch" comes the climactic scene of the play, the trial. After the perjured word of a slave woman has been produced as the villain's evidence, Virginius is called upon to speak. Bringing his daughter forward, he launches into his defense, a speech typical of both Knowles and the period in its sentiments, and its unfortunate attempt to elevate the domestic into "poetry."

> Is this the daughter of a slave? I know
> 'Tis not with men, as shrubs and trees, that by
> The shoot you know the rank and order of
> The stem. Yet who from such a stem would look
> For such a shoot? My witnesses are these—
> The relatives and friends of Numitoria,
> Who saw her, at Virginia's birth, sustain
> The burden which a mother bears, nor feels
> The weight, with longing for the sight of it!
> Here are the ears that listen'd to her sighs
> In nature's hour of labour, which subsides
> In the embrace of joy!—the hands, that when
> The day first look'd upon the infant's face,
> And never look'd so pleased, help'd her up to it,
> And thank'd the gods for her, and pray'd them send
> Blessing on blessing on her.—Here, the eyes
> That saw her lying at the generous

And sympathetic fount, that at her cry
Sent forth a stream of liquid living pearl
To cherish her enamell'd veins. The lie
Is most abortive then, that takes the flower—
The very flower our bed connubial grew—
To prove its barrenness!

Appius, of course, is not convinced; Virginius' supporters, including Icilius, are driven out of the Forum by soldiers. Whereupon
follows a stage direction which must be unique in the annals of
romantic tragedy:

*Virginius, perfectly at a loss what to do, looks anxiously around the
Forum; at length his eye falls on a butcher's stall with a knife upon it.*

It is difficult to imagine a romantic hero in a crisis of the action
"perfectly at a loss what to do," but this was to be a man whom
the audience could recognize. Seizing the knife, he plunges it into
his daughter, still wrapped in his embrace, his countenance plainly
telling the agony of his soul. To one observer the next moment was
absolutely unforgettable. "He plunges the weapon in her breast,
and with the reeking blade, uplifted towards Appius, in a burst of
frantic energy, devotes him to the eternal gods, then rushes with
the strength of a legion through the amazed soldiery that bar his

Virginius, Act IV, from Scharf's *Recollections*

progress."[7] Pathos, fury, Roman nobility and parental domesticity, pride and devotion—these feelings intensely mingled had been displayed, and the audience was utterly overcome.

A final act is devoted to the revenge of Virginius as, driven out of his wits, he hounds Appius to his death. The actual killing is not shown—the two men exit struggling—but as the stage carpenters drew open the flats upon the next scene the audience was nearly overpowered by the "Ugolino look" of the maniac father crouched over the dead body of the tyrant, the grasp of the vulture on its prey, not knowing that it had ceased to live.[8] A moment later, his friends are with him, thrusting upon him the little urn that contains the ashes of Virginia, and a flicker of recognition returns to him as he sobs out her name and falls on Icilius's neck. This display of grief stunned the spectators momentarily into silence, but they soon were recalled to themselves and applauded so violently as almost to deafen the actors. There was no question that Macready had acquired a great new role, and that Knowles had contributed a play to the standard repertory which would be acted for many years to come.

It is easy to laugh at *Virginius;* nor could a fellow playwright's accolade, "our modern Shakespeare,"[9] do Knowles much good with a future generation. But seen in context, in the light of its day and next to the monstrosities of Shiel and the other practicing dramatists, and the blundering failures of the great romantic poets, *Virginius* acquires a respectability at least historical. With some allowance for party prejudice and friendship, the comments of Hazlitt may be taken as an honest estimate:

Virginius is a good play:—we repeat it. It is a real tragedy: a sound historical painting. Mr. Knowles has taken the facts as he found them, and expressed the feelings that could naturally arise out of the occasion. Strange to say, in this age of poetical egotism, the author in writing his play, has been thinking of Virginius and his daughter, more than of himself! . . . Besides the merit of Virginius as a literary composition, it is admirably adapted to the stage. It presents a succession of pictures. We might suppose each scene almost to be copied from a beautiful bas relief, or to have formed a group on some antique vase. . . . But it is a speaking, a living picture we are called upon to witness. These figures so strikingly, so simply, so harmoniously combined, start into life and action, and breathe forth words, the soul of passion—inflamed with anger, or melting with tenderness. . . .

We have seen plays that produced much more tumultuous applause; none scarcely that excited more sincere sympathy. There were no clap-traps, no sentiments that were the understood signals for making a violent uproar; but we heard everyone near us express heartfelt and unqualified approbation; and tears more precious supplied the place of loud huzzas. . . . Mr. Macready's Virginius is his best and most faultless performance . . . and Miss Foote was "the freeborn Roman maid," with a little bit, a delightful little bit, of the English schoolgirl in her acting.[10]

There were, quite literally, no objections to the new play and nothing stood in the way of its complete success, neither the hoarseness of Kemble, the novelty of the playwright's manner, nor that offensive "squeak" which had so bothered Macready upon first reading. To the end of his countless performances of the part, when the mad Virginius is threatening Appius in the dungeon, Macready found himself crying:

> Attempt that noise
> Again, and I will stop that vent, that not
> A squeak shall pass it,

and no member of the audience ever suspected the pains it cost him to utter the undignified word.

With the successful production of *Virginius,* Macready acquired the final property necessary for his security as a leading actor: a personal vehicle which would permit him to accumulate both money and acclaim. But the play had a greater importance for his career than he perhaps recognized at the time. After ten years of application in the profession he had never intended to profess, he suddenly stood forth as an original actor with a style of his own.

THE MACREADY STYLE

So far as uniqueness is possible in the theatre Macready's style was unique, and its characteristics were apparent to the mass audience as well as to the higher critics. Although he instructed his fellow actors during rehearsals, the older established performers like Charles Kemble of course clung to their own methods, but, as the seasons went by and Macready became more and more the leader of his profession, younger actors were to adopt his style and critics were able to speak, as critics delight in doing, of his "school" of acting. It was Macready's first contribution to the theatre of his time, and it became part of the heritage of the theatre that succeeded him; refined by science and psychology, it underlies the whole tradition of naturalism, of Stanislavsky and his heirs.

The faults of his early training, obscured in the provinces, had been clearly revealed by his first performances in London. To some extent he had recognized that the style preferred by his father was stagey and old-fashioned, but he had tried to correct this by substituting sheer violence for classical posturing. Sudden bursts of passion made his speech completely unintelligible, while on the other hand the "level" passages were delivered with a monotonous alternation of rise and fall. But his virtues were also evident: he was industrious and observant, he desired to learn and was willing to study. And the melody and power of his voice were recognized even by the critics who were least favorable to him.

His observation of other actors and their effect on audiences was, of course, immeasurably valuable to him. His *Reminiscences* record his sensitivity to style and its consequences. The early chapters contain frequent references to the staginess of his father's friends. Later, Macready's criticisms continue to be directed against those actors who seem to him artificial: William Farren, who, in addition to being a thorn in his managerial flesh, was "harsh as a crabstick . . . a man speaking points *at* an audience all through the play"; actors of German opera, "the same un-natural gesticulation and redundant holding up of arms and beating of breasts" common to all opera acting; and, unexpectedly, Rachel. French acting in general he did not like. It was conventional, all mannerism; "it resembles figures in relief, no background, and almost all in single figures, scarcely any grouping, no grand composition: this sort of individual effect may be good for the artist, but not for the illusion of a play." That is, the performance lacked unity. Rachel had insufficient variety and was lacking in both tenderness and grandeur. As a result her passionate scenes wanted relief, and degenerated into scolding; she was "too cat-like in the spitting out of her reproaches."[11] His admiration he reserved for Fanny Stirling, then rising into prominence as a supremely natural performer. He found her "freshness and truth of tone" unequaled among actresses. And among the opera stars he found reason to praise Mme. Schroeder-Devrient, who alone was able to abandon herself to her feelings—to identify herself with her character—in a way that Macready could genuinely approve; her performance, he wrote, was "as tender, animated, passionate, and enthusiastic as acting in an opera could be."[12] His ideal actor, then, avoids mere violence, redundancy, artificiality, and formalism, and aims at variety, naturalness, and self-abandonment. It is no coincidence, of course, that the faults were Macready's own early faults, the virtues those toward which he constantly strove.

It has already been suggested that the secret of variety was revealed to him by his observation of Edmund Kean in such a play as *The Iron Chest*. As early as 1819, Hazlitt was commenting on the influence. After noting that Macready's Coriolanus no longer displayed his former monotony of declamation, he suggests that the experimenting actor has perhaps gone too far in the other direction: "He is also apt to be too sudden and theatrical in his contrasts, from a loud utterance to a low one; nor must it be concealed that his finest touch of all, where he literally casts in Aufidius's teeth the scornful word BOY! was toned and gestured too obviously, however unintentionally, in the manner of MR. KEAN."[13] Reading the criticism, Macready might have dismissed it as Hazlitt's notorious idolatry of Kean, but it is certainly true that the first piece of Kean's business that Macready records in his *Reminiscences*—Richard III staring at his withered arm and then beating it back in disgust—business which he first observed in the company of his father in his provincial days, he inserted ("however unintentionally") in his own performance.[14]

Within a year or two of Hazlitt's criticism of Coriolanus, Macready, through constant study and practice, had developed Kean's trick of contrasting tones and tempos into an intellectual instrument for revealing the subtlest involutions of Shakespearean verse. As a first step he acquired a trick of his own, a device still known to actors as the "Macready pause." In part this was a slowing down of the reading of speeches to give the effect of a man thinking, particularly in the soliloquies, where Macready was often praised for making one thought seem the natural consequence of its predecessor, and as often blamed for what appeared to the critics eccentric deviations from the punctuation of the received text. In larger part, the Macready pause was a deliberate halting to allow a climactic effect to register on the audience, or, as he put it, a discrimination made palpable to and impressed on an audience. The pausing led to certain accusations of sententiousness (*The Spectator* said that he played Joseph Surface like an undertaker), and at Bristol he was once driven almost to homicide by a prompter who persisted in throwing him a cue whenever he paused for effect. But the pause became one of the most distinctive aspects of his style, one suited both to the enormous size of the theatres in which he had to play and to the interpretation which his audiences were disposed to put upon the word natural. *"Time, time and discrimination,"* he wrote, *"but time insures discrimination."*[15]

By discrimination Macready appears to mean the thoughtful relationship of succeeding ideas, a revelation of the meaning rather than the mere performance of the text. The contrasts he was able to produce were sometimes very striking, and sometimes only theatrical. Certainly an illumination of the author's text was his transition in the closet scene of *Hamlet* upon the appearance of his father's ghost, "where he broke from the most intense and passionate indignation to the lost and bewildered air, and with a voice of unearthly horror and tones of strange awe, tremblingly addressed the spirit."[16] The reasoning behind the *Hamlet* transition is clear. To some of his others there were objections. Of *The Fatal Dowry* a critic complained, with false humility: "We cannot comprehend the meaning of some of his extraordinary sinkings and transitions of voice. They may be very fine and very sublime; but we confess that the refinements are much too sublimated for the grosser atmosphere of our 'groundling' taste."[17] It may be that the critic was looking for more than Macready intended, since he seems occasionally to have used the transition as an artistic device to give "relish and effect." He himself criticized Mrs. Sharpe's Constance in *King John* as being too much on a level, lacking contrast and variety to make it vivid. To a good many spectators, however, this was a mere mannerism, as artificial as the school which he was superseding. He would, as far as they could see, suddenly break off "whilst the highest pitch of declamation is still vibrating on the ear," and fall into the "deepest sub-colloquial whisper."[18]

But when the transition was appropriate and the meaning apparent, as in the *Hamlet* scene, Macready was able to make a point far superior to the clap-trapping points of his predecessors. In his interpretation of *King John* such a contrast was at the very center of his conception of the character and the production as a whole:

The transition from the chivalric hero to the criminal was artfully managed, both by the actor and the manager. A gloom, which came in sudden contrast to the previous bustle of the drama, seemed to usher in the conversation between John and Hubert. A change had come over the play. It was a forboding look that John cast on Arthur, the tongue faltered as the horrible mission was intrusted to Hubert. For a moment the countenance of the king beamed as he said "Good Hubert," but the gloom returned when he said "Throw thine eye on yonder boy." That he did not look Hubert in the face when he pronounced 'death' was a fine conception.[19]

If, as was widely believed at the time, Macready had adopted the vocal transition from Kean in the beginning, he had enlarged it from a personal device almost to a theory of staging, as Kean could never have done. Indeed, according to Westland Marston, it became second nature to the actor and was carried over into his everyday conversation.[20]

In addition to variety, Macready strove for "naturalness" in his style, and these sudden transitions in voice were a part of what is probably his most original contribution to the technique of acting for nineteenth-century audiences. His colloquialisms, or "touches of nature," were inseparable from the style and the man, and are indeed the most Victorian aspect of his art. They, at any rate, were selected by *The Spectator* as the keystone of his performance:

If we say that *naturalness* (an ugly but a useful word) is at the basis of all Mr. Macready's impersonations, we do not conceive we shall widely err. To seize on an emotion, to make it perfectly comprehensible to every capacity, to familiarize the creations of the dramatist to the spectator, rather than to hold them in a state of august elevation, seems to be his constant aim.[21]

That this was in fact his aim is clear from various entries in his *Diary:* the Rosencranz-Guildenstern scenes in a *Hamlet* performance were earnest and real "ad homines"; every line must be tested by "a natural standard"; a Macbeth was good because of a "manly colloquial tone," a Lear bad because of a "crude, fictitious voice."[22] The appearance of the colloquial in his first great original success, *Virginius,* was due to the nature of the playwright. Macready simply applied his new-found transitions to the part. This combination produced the new effect of the touch of nature, which carried home "to the business and bosoms of men"[23] the reality of the sufferings of the patrician in a way that Kemble and *Cato* had totally failed to do. This must have impressed on Macready the value of his discovery. As late as 1833 he was continuing to work on it: "I find the good effect of that natural manly tone of dialogue, with which I must endeavour to improve the colloquial groundwork of my acting."[24] It was generally recognized then by his critics, by his successors, and by Macready himself that the domestication of acting was to be his principal contribution to the spirit of his time.

A somewhat impressionable provincial critic in Birmingham, after waiting several days to regain his composure, began an enthusiastic review of a performance of *Virginius* by pointing out that the two first acts were a "beautiful display of the sternness of the Patrician opposed to the feelings of the Father."[25] An Irish critic, coming from the same type of performance, merely accused him of dryness.[26] These extreme reactions from two critics show the novelty of the path Macready was treading in anticipating what his own age would define as natural. The comment of the first critic also points to the most frequently noted of his domestic touches—the feelings of a father. As Prospero, he emphasized the moral dignity and goodness of the character, and his fatherly care for Miranda.[27] The *Examiner* sums up his revision of *Werner* by saying that "Byron makes us think only of the *theft of a purse;* Macready of *the love of a father,*" and illustrates this with a description of the concluding scene:

the greatest effect is produced, we think, where *Ulric* being charged with murder, the father twines round his son in one last passionate embrace. We see that that affection is for life and death—in shame, in honour, and through the darkness of the grave. His latest effort is to falter forth a prayer of entreaty for *Ulric*—but his lips only move in silence, till a sudden crying sob breaks from them to proclaim that his heart has broken.[28]

Perhaps the last place that a contemporary audience had been led to expect the feelings of a father was in *King Lear,* but when Macready first undertook the role in 1833, without sacrificing the monolithic grandeur of the primitive king, the magnificence of his rage, or the tempestuousness of his madness, he contrived to remind the audience that it was witnessing the sorrows of a real man, like themselves, to make them feel emotionally for Lear as they would for Joe Gargery or Little Nell. At the end of the great curse, at the lines "How sharper than a serpent's tooth it is / To have a thankless child," his voice so shifted from wrath to agony that—and here you have the Victorian critic also feeling like a father—the audience almost excused the malediction. More pity was evoked at Macready's hiding his face on the arm of Goneril as he said

> I'll go with thee.
> Thy fifty yet doth double five-and-twenty,
> And thou art twice her love.

"A noble conception of shame," approved the *Examiner.* The Fool was treated with parental tenderness, as was Lucius, Brutus' boy attendant in *Julius Caesar,* and Seyton in *Macbeth.*[29]

A second domestic touch, strongly marked in Macready's own

character and one to which he resorted whenever opportunity was given, was the love of home. Bulwer's *Lady of Lyons* seems today absurd in concept and attitude. It was equally absurd that Macready should play Claude Melnotte, an aspiring young peasant, a part totally unsuited to his physique or his age. Yet we have the word of George Henry Lewes, who saw him in his last years on the stage, "None of the young men whom I have seen play Claude Melnotte had the youthfulness of Macready in that part; you lost all sense of his sixty years in the fervour and resilient buoyancy of his manner; and when he paced up and down before the footlights describing to the charming Pauline . . . the home where love should be, his voice, look, and bearing had an indescribable effect."[30] To parental tenderness add love of home and kindness to the less fortunate and you have surely a model of the Victorian gentleman as he saw himself. Unfavorable critics could attack the effect as sentimental pathos, complain that the colloquial tone "jars sadly with the passion[s] that the previous passage delivered with the intensest energy, have excited,"[31] or remind him that the tragic heroes must be invested with artificial dignity to maintain the *"beau ideal* in poetry as in sculpture."[32] Like the transitions, colloquialism became so much a part of him that it was difficult to distinguish, at times, when he was acting. During a rehearsal of *Virginius* in a country theatre, Macready gave his cue: "Do you wait for me to lead Virginia in, or will you do it?" and was somewhat startled to hear, instead of the reply Icilius should give: "Why, really, my dear sir, I don't care; just as you do it in London."[33]

To increase the naturalness of his acting, Macready was careful to introduce as much familiar detail as was consistent with ideal presentation. His personations were full of "minute, fine, subtle touches" traced by the *Theatrical Journal* to the German influence which "has pervaded our literature since the commencement of the nineteenth century."[34] As an example of the general type of truth and sincerity which characterized his acting, it was pointed out that when he had to read or write a letter on the stage he did it, instead of performing some conventional symbol for the act like mumbling or scribbling. To further contribute to the reality of the senate scene in *Othello* he played with his back to the audience,[35] and in directing a modern comedy forced the players to perform within the setting, back of the proscenium arch, instead of on the projecting apron of the stage, their traditional, unrealistic acting area.[36]

Naturalism was not yet the gospel either of literature or the theatre, but its first formulations could have been made from Macready's practice as an actor. Fifty years after Macready's retirement, Stanislavsky, who was to be the leader of the school of naturalistic acting, called upon Chekhov for additional aid in developing the characterization of Lopakhin in *The Cherry Orchard.* He received a long letter from the avowed naturalistic playwright describing how the character looked, what he wore, his habitual posture, gesture, and movement.[37] So when John Forster appealed to Macready for help in an amateur performance of *Everyman in his Humour,* he got from the actor a precise description of the costume and properties for Kitely, the character he was to play, and directions as to how they were to be worn and used.

—Kitely should always wear his keys.—
—His hair is cropped—see print.
—The girdle is the cord round his waist . . .
The sword of Kitely is a *real* Toledo—just such a one as such a respectable gentleman would have worn. . . . But you had better look at T. Gresham's statue or print—or ask my sister to show it you the 2nd Vol. of costumes in my *dressing room,* in wh. you will see the habit of an *English merchant* in Elizabeth's reign, which will give you all information. The hook is for his keys—a large bunch;—his watch should be on a small *fob* on the R. side. [illegible] the pouch, or large external pocket, could be for his handkerchief or purse &c— two small straps with swivel hooks sewn on the dress on the L side under the girdle, to which he appends his sword. . . . He should wear his sword—or put it on—in the Counting-house scene with Cash, and of course through the remainder of the play—i.e. in every scene except his first.—He draws it as he interposes between the brawlers in his warehouse and [illegible] not sheath it again—or if he does, he must draw it again before he goes out with Cash to *search.*—He then sheathes it in the next scene, when he finds his search is fruitless.— Anything you have to ask, ask freely.—Perhaps it would [be] very good, if in *his (K's)* 2nd scene his sword, hat & gloves were lying together on the table, and he were to hook on his sword, as he takes it with his gloves &c—on the stage.—*I could turn that to account.*[38]

While naturalistic acting puts considerable stress on such externals of costume and the manner of handling properties, it also stresses an inner realism of feeling, employing what Stanislavsky was to call emotional memory. This too is clearly anticipated in Macready's practice. He was just such an earnest, home-loving, devoted father as he delighted to portray on the stage. And the emotions of his private life were the tools of his public performance. In his annotated copy of Blair's *Lectures on Rhetoric and Belles-Lettres* he marked especially the passage describing how Quintillian set before his own imagination " 'Phantasiae' or 'Visiones', strong pictures of the distresses or indignities which he had suffered." In the margin, Macready wrote, "in my own art, I have constantly resorted to this method in order to excite the different emotions of anger, pity, love, terror or any anguish more strongly within myself."[39] Evidences of this practice and its effects are abundant. When Virginius gives his daughter to her betrothed the image of his own wife and daughter came into his mind: "I spoke from my soul—the tears came from my heart."[40] During a performance of *The School for Scandal* he was discomforted by Mrs. Glover's natural reading of her question: "Bye the bye, I hope 'tis not true that your brother is also ruined"; his thoughts turned to "his own brother Major Macready."[41] He told Lady Pollock that he credited his successful playing of the scenes with the Ghost in *Hamlet* to his ability to recollect a youthful dream in which he saw the ghost of a friend.[42] The tears and the emotion, recollected as it were almost in tranquility but at any rate at will, were real tears and real emotion, neither symbols nor stage conventions. Macready, to perform to his own satisfaction, must *be* the thing he represented.

At least it was his often repeated belief that he did not act well if he had not identified himself with his character. He is a remarkable example of the celebrated and rather foolish paradox of the actor, that he must surrender himself to the part while remaining as far as possible a conscious artist. Dr. Johnson once declared that if an actor really believed himself to be Richard III, he deserved to be hanged whenever he played the part. And one school of actors is frank in admitting that the whole of their art consists of standing outside themselves and keeping a critical eye upon every move. To this school, Macready did not, and did not profess to, belong.

His *Diaries* are full of self-recriminations at having been so carried away in certain parts that he cursed audibly at his fictional opponents. As Virginius he came so close to choking the villain in reality that on one occasion his fellow actor added to his costume a velvet collar stuck full of tiny steel pins. When Macready questioned the appropriateness of the decoration, he was informed by the lesser player, "Acting . . . is but feigning. I am not a gladiator or a wrestler, sir, and I set some value upon my windpipe."[43] But acting was more than feigning to the Eminent Tragedian, or he believed that it was. "My acting tonight was coarse and crude," runs a typical entry, "no identification of myself with the scene."[44]

It did not take much to destroy this identification: a cold audience ("if they do not abandon themselves to the actor's powers his magic becomes ineffectual"), a crepe beard which threatened to come loose, the imminent death of the King ("The state of suspense in which I was kept to the very moment of the beginning of the play so agitated me that when I went on the stage I was weaker than I often am when I finish a character"), the overcrowding of the pit, overhasty preparation, an unfamiliar costume ("in two important points it did not fit"), a crying child.[45]

He was forever finding justification for his principle in the acting of his models. Miss O'Neill, who he felt was superior to Rachel, seemed to him a remarkable instance of self-abandonment in acting. "She was an entirely modest woman; yet in acting with her I have been nearly smothered by her kisses."[46] He quoted with approval a French playwright's eulogy of Talma: "Il n'est point acteur . . . il vit chaque jour pendant deux heures de la vie du personnage qu'il représente,"[47] and whenever time permitted he followed Talma's practice of preparation for a performance, dressing early to possess himself more with the feeling of his character. He wrote:

My long experience of the stage has convinced me of the necessity of keeping, on the day of exhibition, the mind as intent as possible on the subject of the actor's portraiture, even to the very moment of his entrance on the scene. He meditates himself, as it were, into the very thought and feeling of the person he is about to represent: enwrapt in the idea of the personage he assumes, he moves, and looks, and bears himself as the Roman or the Dane, and thus almost identifies himself with the creature of his imagination. It is not difficult to produce individual effects *ad libitum,* which will of course have their full estimation with the run of audiences; but I cannot conceive the representation of character without this preliminary preparation, or some such mental process.[48]

Joseph Jefferson remembered that Macready began to assume his character the moment he entered the theatre. He would remain in his dressing room, incommunicado, absorbing himself in his part, with his dresser posted outside the door to open it a moment before the time for the actor's appearance on the stage.[49] "I cannot act Macbeth without *being Macbeth,*" Macready declared, and constantly echoed the anxious question of Schroeder: "Ai-je bien joué le rôle? Ai-je été le personnage?"[50]

Lady Pollock points out that to Macready the characters of a play, at least of a Shakespearean play, were real. She recalls that his daughter Katie once was driven to laughter by the solemn way in which her father declared that a certain action of Antonio, in the *Merchant*, was very kind. He seemed, she said, to think Antonio was alive. "And so he is to me," Macready replied, "So are they all. Who is alive if they are not?"[51] Nor, he maintained, could an actor of bad morals express by mere intellectual means the nobler emotions with which he had no sympathy.[52] The corollary, that a good man could hardly act a villain, he met by pointing out that the good man, having conquered temptations, would of course know them as well as the morally corrupt. Judging from his own practice, he felt it necessary for the actor to have in his memory certain images the recollection of which would enable him to produce the effects demanded by his role. By identification and recollection he could thus make his portrayal "the very thing, the reality."[53]

On the other hand, his search for "the very thing, the reality," could not lead him to the naturalism of Chekhov or the Moscow Art Theatre. His plays and playwrights were still those of the romantic revival and their successors and their Elizabethan models. However he might talk about the effect of subdued power, he was no apostle of the repressed force which was to become the major tenet of a later age. At the end of *Werner*, he emitted a yell of agonized despair that made the audience shrink back in their seats.[54] Sheridan Knowles, who as a playwright brought colloquialism to nineteenth-century tragedy, nonetheless has the highest praise for Macready's moments of passionate abandonment:

Mr. Macready excels in passages of tender emotion, but he absolutely transcends himself in those of high and impetuous feeling. You see the passion flashing in his eye and flaming on his cheek, and you hear it in the thunder of his voice—the finest voice upon the stage. Here he never thinks of his delivery, but gives his utterance the rein, and lets it bound along with all the freedom of wild and headlong nature.[55]

It is something of a tribute to Macready's artistry that he could deceive so close an observer into the impression that at such moments "he never thinks of his delivery." For Macready's scenes of passion and apparent self-abandonment differed from those of many of his contemporaries chiefly by the careful control and preparation that preceded them. There was not in his finished style the alternation of bursts of volcanic power with level stretches that could barely hold the attention of an audience. At every moment he tried to hold the entire character in view, to maintain that unity of design which he thought the great distinction of Mrs. Siddons. When Charles Buller, the M. P., once suggested that his acting in the scene following the murder of Duncan was too strong, Macready was "not quite satisfied," although he usually listened eagerly to the criticism of his friends. Buller, it appeared, had entered the theatre at just that point in the play and therefore had not seen the careful preparation and building toward that particular moment.[56] Macready's attitude is evident in his own analysis of another performance of Macbeth:

The general tone of the character was lofty, manly, or indeed as it should be, heroic, that of one living to command. The whole view of the character was constantly in sight: the grief, the care, the doubt was not that of a weak person, but of a strong mind and a strong man.[57]

Wholeness or unity of design was one of the most frequently praised aspects of Macready's acting. It was a feature which grew in attractiveness as the years passed. Early audiences were more pleased with the startling truths which Kean would occasionally reveal. Later audiences learned to admire the perfect finish of Macready's successful performances and to agree with the *Monthly Magazine*'s critic that only he could seize on "all those minute traits which circumstances impart to an individual—to form a correct outline, and to fill up with those diversities, brought into complete harmony."[58]

In the study and rehearsal of a part, Macready searched for character traits which an audience would recognize as natural, and by the skillful use of pause, transition, and colloquialism strove to convey the poet's meaning to the general. "The highest reach of the player's art," he once wrote, is "to fathom the depths of character, to trace its latent motives, to feel its finest quiverings of emotion, to comprehend the thoughts that are hidden under words, and thus possess oneself of the actual mind of the individual man."[59] When Macready came to London, an actor's success depended upon his original "points," and audiences looked only for them. By the time of Macready's retirement the modern system of acting, with its emphasis upon unity of design, was firmly established. If this was due in part to the spirit of the age, it was due in larger part to Macready's example and practice.

THE MACREADY PLAYS

Within ten years of his debut, Macready had developed a style of acting that was distinguishably his own and had discovered a new playwright whose work could be precisely adjusted to that style. He was now an established commodity in the theatrical market: the style was his trademark and the "Macready School" was soon to become a brand name. The next two decades would be devoted to exploiting the commodity, to refining and developing his art as an actor, and to establishing himself in the non-theatrical circles of social and literary London into which he was drawn by instinct, training, and principle. But he could only achieve a secure place as a private gentleman by maintaining a secure place as the humble servant of the public. Occasionally he recognized the irony of his position; more often he fretted over the bitterness of necessity. Still, though he might grumble in his lodgings and complain to his diary, he was never one to shirk his duty, and success had brought certain compensations.

As first player of Covent Garden Theatre and creator of a role of first importance, Macready could now go to the country circuits with assurance that no metropolitan actor could outdraw him. The summer of 1820 found him playing *Virginius* in Dublin, where Shiel paid him the ultimate compliment: "nothing . . . like it since Mrs. Siddons"; and *Virginius* in Liverpool, where his Virginia was a lady who had considerable talent in playing aged mothers;[60] and *Virginius* in Aberdeen, where his Virginia was rather strikingly to his taste. To begin with, she came to rehearsal an hour early; she was earnest. In the second place,

She was dressed in a closely-fitting tartan frock, which showed off to advantage the perfect symmetry of her sylph-like figure. Just developing into womanhood, her age would have been guessed more, but she had not quite reached fifteen. She might have been Virginia. . . . There was a native grace in her deportment and every movement, and never were innocence and sensibility more sweetly personified than in her mild look and speaking eyes streaming with unbidden tears;[61]

she was a womanly woman. And in the third place, she had a story. Her father and mother were old troupers of almost no talent, totally dependent upon her for support; she was dutiful. "There is a girl here," he wrote to his sister Letty, "quite a child— who plays Virginia, I think if anything better than Miss Foote, which I thought impossible. She astonished me by her extreme nature and feeling. As abler critics would say—there it is!"[62]

There was, however, more in the young Virginia than "abler critics" could recognize. Macready soon discovered that she was Kitty Atkins, the child he had scolded into tears some seasons before in *The Hunter of the Alps,* and that he was taking a strong parental interest in her well-being. He gave liberally of advice and direction, wished "that her public career might expose her to no immodest advances to disturb the serenity or sully the purity of her unspotted mind,"[63] and parted from her with the gift of the handsomest shawl he could find in Perth. All in all, it was a summer of great happiness, repeating his winter triumphs, winning new laurels, and making inroads on a young lady's heart. He was, after all, in his twenty-eighth year.

His fifth Covent Garden season began in the autumn with a repetition of the triumphs of the spring. For new parts in the standard repertory, Macready was directed to prepare himself as Iachimo in *Cymbeline* and as Zanga in Young's old tragedy *The Revenge*. In neither did he make much impression on the audience, but fortunately there were some original roles awaiting him during the season which kept his reputation untarnished. The first of these was *Wallace*, a clap-trap put together by C. E. Walker in the hope that he might earn enough money to attend Oxford. Such an aim, coupled with a prominent leading role, could hardly fail to arouse Macready's enthusiasm, and Harris was persuaded to produce the play on the fourteenth of November, 1820. *Wallace*, a watered version of the romantic melodrama of the type of Home's more, and more deservedly, famous *Douglas*, is "simple and direct," in the words of an early reviewer—"bald" might be a better term. In the climactic incident the villain confronts the heroine with the choice of her husband's life, or her own dishonor. Mrs. Bunn, playing the heroine, did what she could to express in the single word "no!" both love of husband and love of virtue, but even the favorable critic observed that this was a trick which "would have demanded the potent sorcery of a Siddons."[64] The piece was no *Virginius*, obviously, but it would serve until a better came along. In the meantime, matters domestic and social kept him pleasantly distracted.

During the engagement Macready had received from Mr. Atkins, father of the fascinating Kitty, a letter requesting assistance in securing a position for his daughter. The young actor, prompted by what feelings he refused to admit to himself, immediately wrote at length to his own father, then managing a season at the Whitehaven theatre.

How are you off for women?—What is your rate of salary?—and are your weekly payments regular at present?—I wish to recommend to you, if these things sort, a girl of more promise than any thing I have seen through the country—Her Father—a d——d hick—what Ned Tighe might say—never mind—and her mother a *female hick*—or hickess:— but she can deliver messages very well and can "make up a show"—and

the Sire can paint *very fairly* indeed.—The girl is *remarkably clever*—
let her act Rosalie Somers or Virginia and screw me strait! or strike
me ugly! if she will not astonish you!—She is moreover a good as well
as clever girl and I certainly expect to see her stand high in her
profession. . . .

The Father (I forgot to mention his name—allow me to introduce
Mr. Atkins to you) is only fit on the stage to deliver messages, conspire
against states and perhaps when not very heavy to take the government
of Venice in his hands, but he is a *very fair painter* indeed. . . . The
girl is a prize.—and one increasing in value—very young, but that, her
greatest fault, she is mending of.—Could you give the Girl £2—the
Father 1:5:0 & the mother 15s? You will MUCH OBLIGE me by considering of this. . . . The Girl "sings a little, & dances a little"—but does not
"swigg the flowing can"—Can you do anything for me?[65]

The elder Macready, overwhelmed by such conviction and quite
certainly not suspecting its cause, hired the Atkins family *in toto*
and set them to work respectively, as his son had suggested, in
mobs, in the scene dock, and—for her debut on January 10, 1821,
—as the leading lady in *Virginius*. The arrangement lasted for
two untroubled years.

More immediately, Macready was establishing himself in the
world outside the theatre. If he could not yet aspire to the company of ladies and gentlemen of society, he knew how to make
himself agreeable in literary circles. Thackeray in *Pendennis* has
painted the artistic world of the Regency as a Bohemia, but it
was respectability itself compared with the tawdry irregularity of
the Profession. And Macready managed to see to it that his few
associates were, for the most part, drawn from the group of gentleman amateurs whose incomes were assured by other sources and
wrote for the theatre with a kind of Renaissance *sprezzatura*. Even
among the more Bohemian professionals he moved with careful
dignity, as if to confer the respectability he sought. "I have been
indulged with a classical conference with Macready," wrote
Charles Lamb, the passive verb being at once ironic and revealing.
And Henry Crabbe Robinson noted that there was "nothing of
the buffoon in him."[66]

It was during this period that he became firm friends with
Thomas Noon Talfourd, poet, lawyer, and critic, the very model
of a gentleman-amateur. Talfourd was almost exactly Macready's
age and had made his poetical debut in 1811, the year after
Macready had first presented himself to the public. But the poet
was never required to depend on the public for his livelihood.

Whenever he wished he might resort to complete anonymity or to the legal security of poems "printed for private circulation only." Like Macready, he had begun as an imitator of eighteenth-century conventions, but had come under the influence of the romantic revival. In his capacity as literary critic for *The New Monthly Magazine* he had, in fact, been one of the earliest to recognize the special and lasting contributions of Wordsworth to the English poetic repertory. As a lawyer he was more sound than brilliant, detached rather than emotionally involved in his cases. During the opening speech of an opposing advocate, he would amuse himself by "rapidly turning it into verse, and writing the verses on the blank leaves of his Brief."[67] While this facility was much admired by his colleagues of the Bar, it was not calculated to create an impressive record of legal victories. On the other hand, it assured him a place among the poets whom he admired. He was literary executor for Charles Lamb, and when cases involving literary property came into court he was a logical contender. Moxon chose him as advocate when he was prosecuted for the publication of *Queen Mab*, and Macready, with mingled feelings, had occasion to employ his services.

Another of the lawyer-poets was Bryan Waller Procter. A friend of Lamb and Leigh Hunt, he was a contributor to the *Literary Gazette*, and more of a Bohemian than Talfourd. If Talfourd's home life was irregular, it was from indifference: there were complaints about uncooked food appearing on the dinner table, and cats sharing the chairs of the host and hostess.[68] Procter's life was irregular through amiability. Eager in his friendships, a vigorous proponent of new talent, he wined and fed a large circle of literary acquaintances to such an extent that he was often in the financial difficulties Macready deplored in his theatrical associates.

The friendship of such men as Lamb, Talfourd, and Procter gave Macready the prestige and companionship he desired, but, especially in the case of the latter two, it was an unending source of trouble. He got into the habit of consulting them in artistic matters, reading new plays for their judgment, anxiously awaiting their comments on his performances. They, in turn, were eager to assist him by providing him with new roles which might increase his security and add to their own incomes. Yet where he would trust them to amend other men's work, he was constantly doubtful of their own efforts. While he encouraged their contributions, he was troubled by the conviction that he must correct their deficient knowledge of the stage. He thus became a collaborator, sometimes unacknowledged, in the creation of a theatrical repertory that has properly been called "The Macready Plays."

For example, in 1820 Procter found himself in need of funds to compensate for his habitual hospitality, and suggested that he supply Macready with a new role. Like many another poet he could persuade himself that it was necessary merely to compose a great scene; the rest would arrange itself. With typical off-handedness, he presented the actor with a completely finished second act, but no beginning or ending. Macready recognized the "dramatic power and interest" of the fragment and urged the poet to write further. This produced a first act, but no third, fourth, or fifth, since Procter could not decide on a plot, although he did have a notion of the sort of catastrophe he wanted. After several false starts, the poet demanded that Macready suggest a line of action. This the actor was not loath to do, drafting the situation and suggesting "in familiar words" the content of the dialogue. Procter, naturally, was not satisfied; he was no playwright and his momentary inspiration was obviously leading him into a good deal of drudgery. He tried to put off the task by consulting Shiel, hoping that the more experienced playwright would pronounce the whole venture impossible. Shiel, however, declared that Macready's plan was the best Procter could hope for, and so the wearying process of hacking out scene after scene according to blueprint went on to the completion of the tragedy, *Mirandola*.

This is quite plainly not the way dramatic masterpieces get written, and *Mirandola* is no masterpiece. But in a day when the ablest writers were unwilling to subject themselves to the severe restraints imposed by the conventions of the theatre, or when they believed (in direct contradiction of their attitude toward other forms of art) that only imitations of the Elizabethan tragic writers were worth undertaking, it was the only way that the works of others than hacks could survive exposure on the stage. It is not to be wondered at if, in the confusion, Macready's sure sense of the theatre somewhat overpowered his sense of the integrity of a work of art.

Mirandola had a successful run of six nights and brought Procter £300 in addition to performance fees. As for the actor, his role won him more of the kind of acclaim so necessary to him, the acclaim which not merely kept him at the top but distinguished him from his greatest rivals. Perhaps his intimate acquaintance with a character which he had practically constructed in every detail for himself may have presented his unique style in a clearer light, or perhaps a succession of original characters since *Virginius* had served to emphasize his singularities.

Macready was next emboldened to an experiment, tentative but prophetic of one of his most important contributions to the stage. For over a century the plays of Shakespeare, to which all men of the theatre professed reverence, had been produced by them in the mutilated versions of Colley Cibber, Nahum Tate, and others of the post-Restoration "improvers." During the same period, scholars and editors had labored to establish the true texts of the plays, but they were openly ignored by the producers. Given a choice, it was inevitable that Macready should align himself with the scholars. And in the flush of his success, he determined to do something about the acting version of *Richard III*, Cibber's firmly established "improved text."

Although other radical performers had from time to time played with the notion, the idea of a return to Shakespeare was directly suggested by an office clerk who submitted to the theatre a purification of Cibber. This text was so much like Cibber's that Macready decided to see how much of the original could be restored without bewildering an audience. "The absolute necessity of introducing passages from Henry VI, illustrating part of Richard's character, must, it is thought, be allowed, as Richard III is but the superstructure, of which the foundation is laid in the two previous Plays," he explained in the preface to the printed text.[69] The lamentations of Margaret are ruthlessly curtailed, "under the apprehension that the cause of her grief, being so very remote, would prevent the audience from commiserating or sympathizing with its expression." The preface includes also some high-toned disparagement of Cibber, while expressing a desire not "to detract . . . the just praise of having formed a very clever Play from his great materials," and presents a statistical table of what has been accomplished by the new editor:

Cibber's Play consists of more than....................1990 lines
Of which Cibber's own composition amounts nearly to....1100
Leaving of Shakespeare about......................... 900
In very many of which Cibber has made alterations.
The play as now printed consists of..................1960 lines
Of which are Cibber's not more than.................. 200 lines
Making an acquisition of about....................... 860 lines
of Shakespeare.

Macready's system of arithmetic is not so much faulty as indicative of the patchwork nature of the piece. For example, Act I, scene 2 of his revised revision concludes with this (added) soliloquy of Gloucester.

So far my fortune keeps an upward course [*3.H.VI.*5.3,1]
And yet I do but dream on sovreignty;—[*ibid.*, 3.2,134. altered by Cibber]
First I must marry Warwick's youngest daughter [*RIII*, I.1,153 altered]
What though I kill'd her husband and her father?⎤
The readiest way to make the wench amends   ⎥
Is—to become her husband and her father;—   ⎥
The which will I:—not all so much for love,   ⎬ [*RIII*, I.1, 154–159]
As for another secret close intent,   ⎥
By marrying her which I must reach unto:—   ⎦
I'll play the orator as well as Nestor, [*3.H.VI* III.2, 188–189]
Deceive more slily than Ulysses could—
Can I do this, and cannot get a crown? [*3.H.VI* III.2, 194–195]
Tut! were it further off, I'd pluck it down!

The better part of wisdom encourages the retention of the better part of Cibber; no actor will willingly forego, even for Shakespeare, "Off with his head!—so much for Buckingham!" But some of the worst of Cibber is also retained. For Shakespeare's

> Methinks the King has not that pleas'd alacrity
> Nor cheer of mind that he was wont to have,

is substituted Cibber's

> The King, methinks, looks sad: did you observe
> The strangeness of his altered countenance,

—sinking with a vengeance.

But, for all the patchwork result, Macready's revision had a purpose. The play was, as he saw it, a character-portrait of Richard, and he knew Richard well from his study not only of Shakespeare but of the possible historical sources available to the playwright. In his preface he quotes from Sir Thomas More's *History of Richard III*, to prove that Cibber has distorted the character of the king by making him "moody, and wanton in his mischiefs, stopping to sneer at every object, past which Shakespeare hurries him with a contemptuous indifference," while ignoring what seems to be his most prominent characteristic, "alacritie and mirth of mind." To bring out this vivacity was Macready's purpose; if he did not succeed at once—the adaptation was given only two performances

—he held fast to his intention. Richard was to become one of his great roles.

Macready's first five years in London had been a period of steady progress. He had started as near the top as the caution of the managers would permit, his conscientious attention to business had enabled him to make much of characters which might have left a lesser man in obscurity, the critics had been for the most part friendly, and he had been fortunate in hitting the temper of the public. By gentlemanly behavior and intelligence he had won a circle of acquaintances outside the theatre in the world of literature and art which was to stand him in good stead when his days of management arrived. And he was in an excellent position to bargain respecting the renewal of his contract with Covent Garden.

Henry Harris was amenable to Macready's terms. He agreed that the actor was a valued asset and should receive the "highest salary given in the theatre." That is, Macready's salary would be equal to the highest paid any other performer. Charles Young, returning from a season at Drury Lane, had been engaged at £20 a week; that was to be Macready's salary also, although it was verbally agreed between the manager and the actor, with Reynolds as a witness, that "if any regular performer in the theatre should receive more than that sum, my payment should be immediately raised to the same amount." This was the kind of gentleman's agreement in which Macready would obviously like to trust implicitly. That it was broken in most ungentlemanly fashion may have been the basis of the actor's firm future belief that no gentlemen were to be found in the theatrical profession, and was certainly the cause of the extended haggling over terms which every future manager had to suffer from him.

The next two seasons at Covent Garden were a sad contrast for Macready with his first five. Young's return deprived him of the first claim on all new leading characters, and he was forced to play mainly those which he had already made his own, Virginius, Gambia, Rob Roy, and Romeo. Henry Harris withdrew from the post of manager and Charles Kemble, who had acquired his brother John's share in the property in addition to his own, succeeded to the commanding position over the two minor proprietors, Willet and Forbes. These two, although they had little to say, were to hear a great deal, almost at once, from Macready, who was naturally jealous of such eminence as he had attained, and naturally fearful of Charles Kemble as a manager who could not be wholly disinterested in maintaining the rights of other actors.

The bad feeling between manager and actor reached a crisis over the most delicate subject in any actor's engagement—a benefit. Macready had persuaded Kean, from Drury Lane, to appear on his night and was anticipating a bumper. Charles Kemble, from policy of one sort or another, revived an ancient regulation that no performer from the other theatre might appear at Covent Garden. Macready complained to Fawcett, the stage manager, to no avail. He presented himself to the committee—Kemble, Willett, and Forbes—and was, so he thought, curtly handled. He then addressed the "disinterested" two of the committee through the post in his most infuriatingly distant manner. The long letter is typical of the increasingly fretful state of his mind in matters which affected his professional standing and his purse:

To—Forbes and Willett, Esqres.
Gentlemen
   The peculiar circumstances under which I labour compell me to address you thus and as business alone can be the cause of my intrusion I beg leave without further preface to submit it to your attention.
   My engagement in Covent Garden Theatre was contracted with a gentleman whose interest in his performers' good or ill success was regulated by concern for the establishment only. My subsequent transference to the present Committee has materially altered my situation: it is not that I am at all jealous or distrustful of your intentions towards me but as it is impossible to ascertain immediately the precise limits of an actor's various claims, I am warranted, I trust, in assuming that you, in consequence, are silent in the question or [of?] vindication of my right, and thus my fortunes are surrendered to the single sway of an actor, whose aspirations to supremacy in his profession must render my reputation but of secondary moment to him, while he who has the motive, is also armed with the power to molest and distress me.
   It is in consequence of gross injustice that I appeal from the answer of Mr. C. Kemble to yourselves, and through you to any other gentlemen who may have a voice in the direction of the Covent Garden Theatre,—whom I earnestly request to scrutinize this matter and on whom I rely for the redress of my grievances.
   Whether or not I have served the Theatre beyond my bond of agreement since the accession of the Committee to the management I must appeal to yourselves or to Mr. Fawcett.—In the hope of remunerating myself for those advantages I relinquished when at the urgent representation of the Committee I consented to remain in London and perform Daran, Surface and Prospero, not one of which I had the least right to do,—I had, guided by the precedents of former years—(viz: Mr. Russell of Drury-Lane Theatre, Mr. Farren of C. G. T.—Miss Stephens, Madame Catalani, Madame Vestris, &c) prevailed on Mr.

Kean to act for my benefit,—*but at the close of the season* within a *week of the nomination of the benefits,* I am informed that a rule is made or revived, which precludes me from participating in this most important advantage.

Gentlemen, I submit to you my appeal against the creation of this new, or enforcement of this old law, whichever Mr. C. Kemble chooses to call it, at the *present time.*—When I signed my engagement there was no such law in existence, for, if ever made, its frequent infraction by the Managers was a virtual rescission.—It is with confidence in your honor, and in your promises of good faith and justice, that I enquire of you, if you intend to authorize an action like this?—if it is not monstrous, that a manager having profited by the exertions of a player during a whole season should attempt to frame, or revise laws *at the end of that season,* to come between the performer and the emolument he has been reasonably anticipating and earning by a season's services?—

. . . I have stated fairly to you, gentlemen, the ground of my complaint, and I trust I shall not need to urge more in the assertion of my claims.—My elevation I cannot expect should be in Mr. C. Kemble's interest; but if he be permitted to exercise his influence without control over the course of a contemporary actor, the Committee may expect to see him the single support of the Covent Garden stage, as no gentleman of talent or feeling can brook so irrational and partial an autocracy. . . .[70]

The same complaints of autocracy were to be raised against Macready during his own managership, and with as little effect as his present cries against "Mr. C. Kemble." The Committee took Kemble's side and Macready was forced to accept the services of Charles Young for his benefit.

It is to the credit of both parties that neither Young nor Macready seems to have allowed professional jealousies to interfere with their duties to each other as first actors. For Young's benefit, Macready undertook the part of Hubert in *King John* and made an exact point of placing himself on the stage in their climactic scene so as "to give prominence" to Young's effects. In return Young played Iago to Macready's Othello and seems to have done nothing to detract from the younger player's clear triumph. For the benefit of two minor players, Miss Gibbs and Mr. Yates, the two stars joined forces in *The Merchant of Venice,* Young as Shylock and Macready as Antonio, for the first and last time. Then Macready embarked upon a summer and fall tour of the continent, industriously visiting each point of cultural interest from the tomb of Juliet to Herculaneum. He returned to London in November to discover that Elliston, the Drury Lane manager, had succeeded in luring away Young, Liston, and Miss Stephens from Kemble, leaving Covent Garden a feeble company indeed: a desert, to use Macready's term.

The harvest of the year was as barren as the prospect. Between Kemble and Macready there was increasing bickering and friction. The managerial committee was so desperately penny-pinching (in the face of Elliston's openhandedness at Drury Lane) that there was little hope of recruiting outstanding talent to fill up the gaps caused by the secessions. What Macready felt to be Shiel's best play, *The Huguenot,* was foredoomed to failure because of inevitable miscasting, and Mary Russell Mitford's respectable tragedy of *Julian* met the same fate: "the Covent Garden company was no longer equal to the support of plays containing several characters."

Miss Mitford's published correspondence relating to this play casts further light on the general attitude of the dramatists of the day. Not only was she lacking in theatrical experience, she was also without a sense of dramatic purpose. In her mind a play must be a vehicle for its actors and nothing more: it could have no artistic integrity of its own. Asking a friend to suggest a plot, she stipulates, "It should have *two* prominent male parts—and I should prefer an Italian story in the fourteenth, fifteenth, sixteenth, or seventeenth century, as affording most scope, and being less liable to blame for any deviation from truth in the plot than any well known incident in the greater states."[71] In a later letter she is more explicit about the *two* prominent male roles: a "fine and splendid character, the real hero for Macready, and some gallant-spirited youth, who may seem the hero, for Mr. Kemble."[72] In October 1822, she writes that she has been twice to London to consult with Mr. Kemble about the production of her play, but that nothing can be settled until Mr. Macready returns from "his Italian tourification." And she adds with a wisdom that would do credit to greater experience, "nothing, I believe, is certain in a theatre till the curtain is fairly drawn up and let down."[73]

Kemble was disposed to put off the production as long as possible. Macready was set to training Miss F. H. Kelley to take the place of Miss O'Neill, an arduous and ultimately fruitless task. He was instructed to prepare himself in Cardinal Wolsey and King John and he was kept on the rack about *Julian.* Further, he had suspicions that certain members of the company were being paid salaries larger than his, and had been directed to conceal the fact from him. On February 15, he exploded in a letter to the Committee, scribbled in white heat and the third person from the box-office of the theatre:

Mr. Macready informs the Committee of Management that he does not think eight days sufficient to study one of Shakespeare's characters, if his mind were completely free, at least it is his practice to study something beyond the *words* of a part.—Harrassed and irritated as he is by the suspence in which he is kept—and nervous and ill as he has been made by the conduct of the Committee, he CANNOT undertake the character of King John for Monday sennight!—if it should be his misfortune to have any concern with them so long as the following Monday, he will endeavour to be ready in the part, but neither his spirit nor his power of mind are, under their conduct, what they have been, and to them and to them alone is attributable the nervous state, in which he has been for some time.

Mr. Macready desires to know of the Committee why his name, whilst he has the misery of belonging to this Theatre, is omitted in the Play Bills for Cardinal Wolsey—and why they will suffer their agents to disgrace them by breaking a promise, given at least ten times, of the performance of Macbeth as a recompense for undertaking Wolsey?[74]

King John was scheduled, no doubt, to enable Kemble to appear as Faulconbridge, a role for which he was pre-eminently suited, and Macbeth was denied Macready because the dominant member of the committee had aspirations toward that character too. But Macready did not give up *Julian*. Later in February Miss Mitford wrote: "Macready will drive the matter on. It is odd enough that I and this zealous friend of mine have never met! He is just such another soul of fire as Haydon—highly educated, and a man of great literary acquirements—consorting entirely with poets and young men of talent. Indeed it is to his knowledge of my friend Mr. Talfourd that I owe the first introduction of my plays to his notice."[75] *Julian* was finally staged on March 15, and was repeated eight times, a moderate success. Apparently Macready, having "collaborated" on *Mirandola,* offered the same kind of advice to Miss Mitford but found it less acceptable. The resultant conflict, not wholly on aesthetic grounds, led the playwright to a final shrewd observation on her leading man:

That Macready likes me I know; but I have perhaps suffered even more from his injustice and prejudice and jealousy than from the angry attacks of the Kembles. Do not misunderstand me: our connection is merely that of actor and author; but his literary jealousy, his suspicion and mistrust have really the character of passion. And yet he is a most ardent and devoted friend; and it seems ungrateful in me to say so much.[76]

The irritations continued. The death of John Philip Kemble forced Charles to withdraw from a prospective performance of

Hamlet for the benefit of the Western Philanthropic Institution, and the officers approached Macready as a substitute. His remarks upon the occasion, about calling on the Commander-in-Chief when the Corporal fails in his duty, and the announcement that he had "condescended" to play Hamlet for charity returned to plague him not many years later. The success of the Christmas pantomime led the management (as was customary) to prohibit the writing of orders, i.e. free admissions, by members of the company, and Macready was obliged to confess as much to Mrs. Munden, wife of the great comedian. However, "you are well aware," he added, "how illiberal a thing is management, and therefore I need no further apology."[77] And his health was troubling him. The increasing labor of rehearsal, study, and occasional provincial tours caused him to complain of rheumatism in his shoulder, and more than one performance had to be canceled because of illness.

The upshot of two seasons of unpleasantness was a pamphlet against Kemble brought out by Macready, setting forth his injuries, and a series of fruitless conferences and attempts at arbitration conducted for Macready by his friend Talfourd. But all came to naught. The Committee of Management quite clearly had no intention of keeping to the terms of the agreement which Henry Harris had most explicitly conveyed to them, and Macready had no choice but to withdraw from the Covent Garden company, resolutely turning his back on the theatre which had been his London home and the setting of his metropolitan history, and betake himself to the country.

Almost at once, the world brightened. Kitty Atkins, who had moved on with her family to the theatre in Dublin, had been a constant correspondent and Macready, without realizing it, had become more and more deeply involved with her career and her private life. When he heard that her father and brother had been drowned at sea, he thought of her alone and unprotected in the theatre—and found himself declaring his feelings in an unequivocal manner. Kitty replied in kind and their engagement was sealed, by mail. In the fall, Kitty returned to England to meet her future relatives, in particular Macready's sister Letty, who had for some years presided over his household and who had not been as blind as her brother to the true state of his heart. The eager young man was somewhat disconcerted at the first meeting between the two women: not a word was exchanged and Letty's countenance expressed disappointment and revulsion. Matters were not improved when, arriving at their hotel, Letty took to her room and spent the afternoon weeping on her bed. Her brother reasoned with her as best he might and finally coaxed from her the admission that he had no choice but to go through with his plighted word, but that he had better postpone the marriage for a while until Kitty, who was henceforth to be called Catherine, had been educated to a level consonant with her future station as the wife of William Macready. Surprisingly enough, Catherine consented, and the marriage was postponed for a year while she submitted herself to the tutelage of Letty and her groom-to-be, who spent many a happy hour interleaving and annotating texts of philosophy[78] and art for her instruction. Macready was not wholly without appreciation of Catherine's position. The name he attaches to her at this period is Griselda.

The second turn of events during the summer was the opening of negotiations with Elliston for an engagement at Drury Lane. Robert William Elliston was a florid and extravagant man, one of the great uniques of the period. As actor and manager he had created a legend for himself; nimble of tongue, whimsical of action, careless of both money and detail, he was a wholly theatrical man. Fresh from his Covent Garden misfortunes, Macready responded to his offers with a most precise statement of the terms which he expected. Financially, Elliston was generous—£20 a night—but there were other matters to be considered, since both Young and Kean were leading tragedians at Drury. On September 8 Macready sent Elliston's deputy, Reynolds, his proposals:

To the points of your letter on Drury:—you know the cause of my disagreement with Covent-Garden; money I value as little as most men, and I hoped to have demonstrated that by the *"nominal"* proposition. ... This then is my view of the engagement———

"Mr. Elliston to give me £20 per night for thirty nights—the thirty nights to be divided into two periods, each not to exceed ten weeks— the first commencing October thirteenth—the next at Easter:—in the event of Mr. Elliston desiring to add ten more nights to this agreement, he is to receive my clear benefit."—If this be understood, all is said about *time* and *money*.

I should include Hamlet among the *Single* parts, in which indeed I should prefer opening.

My plays with Kean, we must previously *agree upon.*—You must see the absolute necessity of so doing:—I DREAD the thought of a misunderstanding—my mind had literally been shaken by the torture in which I was kept all last winter—no more of that. Let me come to you free and strong-hearted, unchecked by any disquieting jealousy or apprehension: let me come with the resolution of doing all I can, but in the case of Kean let me know especially what it is I am to do, & let me say distinctly *I will do it*—not to deceive Elliston, nor lose my own peace of mind in contesting unexpected requisitions. I want to pull strongly and cordially with you, if I am in your boat, and this is the only way to be sure of doing so.

Ergo—what plays are we to do together?—in J. Caesar *anything*— in Henry the same—but of course Caesar first.—What else have you to offer?—out with it, that I may say yes or no.—I will not say, no, if I can possibly say, yes. Write by return so comprehensively, that my answer may be *final*, as you must know I have others pending your letters.

You say nothing about Gracchus—I cannot ask Elliston to *pledge* himself to any thing of the kind, but I should like to know, if he holds it in his contemplation. I have seen it since your last and I tell you, *it is sterling.*[79]

Reynolds replied that the statement was "candid and fair," and wrote to Elliston about Macready's characters:

as to Hamlet, as Young played it, you could not well refuse him,—& really in your present state, you must not stand on ceremony—as to Kean, I told him, if we waited for his answer, or arrival, or sentiments as to the parts, we might wait for ever [;] that after Macready's fair proposal as to *Henry 8th* & *Julius Caesar* Kean must play with him or have the worst of it. I have told him I have no doubt you will not press him to play in any plays with Kean, where he will sink in public estimation. Now pray write to him and nail the bargain.[80]

On the sixteenth of September, Macready wrote to Elliston directly, assuring him "If my feelings are said to be warm, they are equally so in friendly as in hostile bearings." His main worry is, of course, what parts he is to play with Kean. Again he suggests *Caesar,* and adds *King John* and *Venice Preserved. Henry VIII* he "should not like to try until the *very last thing,* as I am not so confident about it." Iago and Iachimo he will not undertake unless Kean gives "a perfectly satisfactory equivalent" in another play. Finally, he suggests, though not very seriously, that Kean might alternate Macduff and Macbeth with him.[81]

In his letter to Reynolds, Macready had pointed out that other offers were awaiting his decision, depending upon the Drury Lane contract. Evidently he was quite prepared to turn his back upon London completely, if he could not get the sort of engagement he wanted, and reap a harvest in the country. Among the provincial managers proffering contracts was Alfred Bunn, at the moment director of the fortunes of the Birmingham Theatre Royal, and soon to be Elliston's stage manager at Drury Lane.

In the light of future events, a hastily scrawled and frequently illegible epistle which Macready directed to him in the midst of the Drury negotiations is of curious interest. Macready had played several weeks in Birmingham in July, sharing stellar parts with Mrs. Bunn and, apparently, leaving an order for a new pair of breeches to be purchased for him by the manager. Here is the letter, as much of it as is still decipherable, a glimpse of a rare side of its author's character:

> You gentlemen of Drury, who live at home at ease
> Ah little do you think of daggers[82] such as these
> Who keep one all the morning at the Theatre rehearsing
> And at night are so d—d bad they set one always cursing
> > So the day
> > Wears away
> > And no letter to the Po———

—st Office.—This is the fact, though in the dress of fiction—I am harried out of my soul—in addition have been exceedingly drunk, and in consequence exceedingly ill—or you should have received this on the day I write it.—Besides I have had letters to write to Elliston and Reynolds, and have now some claims, which I put by for you, you rogue.—Why you must have sent Kemble to London as joyous as an unkicked fidler—you "let him depart and crowns for convoy put into his purse"!—What a swindle!—a regular DO—done and done—By heavens, you cannot think how it has amused me.—*I suppose he returns next season!!!!!!* Of course I am not in mourning at the poor figure they cut in Brandon's affair—I could quote instances of that man's zeal for them IN MY OWN CASE, that would effectually silence some of their charges, but GIVE THEM ROPE, if they do not swing I will give up my trade of soothsayer, and say that the breeches are good.— Breeches they are not—being, as Tristram Shandy says, simple pantaloons—but you had no right to interfere with them—"What is the matter with them?"—the matter indeed?—why the straps are all wrong and pull so tight across the mystery of my podex, that in a week I shall not have as much skin there, as would make you a travelling cap. Poor Claremont is gone then at last!—What will the glass in the green-room do without him.—That is bad economy I think—they are not worth much but they do not take much—I wish you could have got *Old* Grimaldi—and then you would have settled them I think—I do not know yet whether I go to you, everything is concluded, but I wish to have a veto in the case of parts in our double plays—without which I cannot go—the very apprehension or possibility of annoyance would almost drive me mad, so much am I shook by my season of suffering at Covent Garden with that d—d Committee.—I cannot come to London at all events before Oct. 13th—If I could come to do good, I should like to be at Drury, but you know I am never confident about myself, and therefore I leave all to the Ruler of chances.—I hope to God it is not true that Miss Stephens goes to the other house.—Sinclair is the only thing I think that Elliston has to fear, if he should break down, Drury must go up. . . . You say nothing to me of my kind and valued friend Cope—how is he? but you will tell me this and all other matters at Liverpool—that is—if Elliston does not *shy* at my request, which he will not do, if he can confide in my integrity, and means me fairly (as I think he does) himself.—There is no news for you—my summer has been, *thank God, very* good on the whole. There is a pewter pot, which would do admirably as a urine-receiver, indeed it was made for the purpose, that I could get for fourteen pence. Shall I send it to you for your benefit?—or to hold C. Kemble and his attraction?—Can I do anything for you in the coal-trade here?—You most immense fellow!—Remember me most kindly to your wife & tell her I wish I could give her a [illegible]. Adieu—Immensity!

Your's while his own W.C.M.[83]

All matters were at last settled to the satisfaction of both parties, and on the thirteenth of October, 1823, Macready appeared as Virginius at Drury Lane, on the same bill with a "horse piece," *The Cataract of the Ganges,* which had caused Elliston and Reynolds almost as much worry as the engagement of their new star. But he carried his public with him, and his success was instant in spite of the unfamiliarity of the theatre, and a typical Ellis-tonian lack of attention to the proper handling of backstage affairs. "A thousand pair of eyes from the pit alone was directed to his entry," reports *The Literary Gazette,* "and he met with a reception of loud and tumultuous applause, which lasted for some minutes. The change of scene, which had evidently agitated him, and this cheering manifestation of public feeling, seemed to excite his energies in no common degree, and we never witnessed a finer performance of the part."[84] He played successively Rolla, Hamlet, Macbeth, and Leontes in a company which included Wallack, Munden, Terry, Mrs. Glover, Mrs. Bunn, and Mrs. W. West.

But the auspicious beginning was never exceeded during his first two seasons at Drury. No new play of any stature came his way, Kean was obviously afraid to try a fall with him, and, while he lost no popularity, he made no progress from the position he already held. Knowles' *Caius Gracchus,* by which he had set some store, proved to be a dull political play with the usual Roman mob being pulled hither and yon with that wonderful unanimity which Mr. Puff celebrates. Macready had been attracted to it by a number of rhetorical speeches in praise of liberty, that notable Roman theatrical virtue, and he attributes its early withdrawal to the influence of Elliston's new stage-manager Bunn, whose wife made no impression at all in the leading female role. Whether this is an instance of Bunn's roguery or his immensity, he does not specify.

He began to notice, too, a distinct party of opposition in the newspapers. At first he was inclined to set this down as a cabal organized by Covent Garden, but the attacks were too general and too long-continuing to be attributed to so ephemeral a cause. Throughout his life Macready was plagued by certain journals and journalists who for one reason or another took exception to his claims to gentility, to stardom. Many of them were inspired by professional jealousy, by the injured feelings of rejected playwrights—and Macready was by no means the only actor publicly pilloried in the daily press. An actor was as fair game as a politician, and the early nineteenth-century journalist was a master of vituperation, as Macready was to find out.

Between engagements at Drury, Macready made use of his time to play his favorite characters in provincial theatres. The date of his marriage was approaching, and to his aesthetic sensitiveness was added a new apprehension regarding his bank account which increased his jealousy. From Dublin, February 4, 1824, he wrote to his father:

"The taste and judgement of the Dublin people" well displayed themselves on the first night of Julius Caesar by receiving me with a moderate round of applause and CHEERING Mr. Warde! until you would have thought their throats were lacerated.—I am sure any Englishman in the Town must have been equally disgusted with their want of manners and utter barbarism.—I was determined to shame the b—g—ds, & I did—for I *showed up* their "wooden god" in most unequivocal contrast—He never will be looked on as a first rate again here, I think!—The American boy is very bad, they tell me.—You will have to give me several pounds to make up deficient *hundreds*—So much for Dublin!—the worst engagement I have ever made. . . . PRAY TELL ME, what sort of an actor Butler really is—is he not a man of genius? Is he as good as myself?[85]

The actor's life at best is hardly one of ease, and Macready, driven as he was by a sense of duty and necessity, was literally wearing himself out, traveling back and forth across England and Scotland, making excursions to Ireland, rehearsing with the resident company all day and playing until a late hour in the evening, sleeping little and worrying much. On June 24, 1824, he took time off to be married to Catherine Atkins, who had completed her period of trial under Letty. The fact was announced to his father in a letter dated June 15:

In about a week or very little more I shall be united to a lady, whom you have known (although I believe she is somewhat changed from her you will recollect)—perhaps you have more than once suspected what important reasons prevented me before from disclosing that Miss Atkins has long been in possession of my affections, & now I have the pleasure of informing you, that she is the lady of my love, whom all my friends, that know her, concur in thinking I am acting most wisely and *really* prudently in seeking as my wife.—We shall see you at Swansea. Letty accompanies us, & is very partial to my future wife. . . . Do not talk to me about *money*—I might have had a girl with upwards of £40,000, but could I buy *happiness* with it?[86]

It was widely rumored in the newspapers of the day that Macready might have married the daughter of a noble earl. Earlier biographers have been inclined to question the lady's existence, but the final sentence of the letter quoted seems to indicate that some competition for Griselda was at least in the background. And the fact is reiterated in Macready's first letter to his father in his new role of husband (combined with his old one, of course, of aspiring actor):

Weston-super-Mare
June 30, 1824

My dear Sir,

You would scarcely have expected sooner a reply to your last favour, as I left on Monday last, & since then I have really been too happy, *much too happy* to think of business, or anything but the immediate cause of my felicity. I am not well versed in worldly wisdom, perhaps not well enough—but I think I have consulted a better kind of prudence in promising for myself feelings of delight and contentment, that I never before experienced, and which, in my fondest dreams of joy, I had not ventured to anticipate. To a newly-married person, I shall be told everything looks unusually cheerful, and nature seems to dress herself in her brightest colors, but I do not think my prospects of felicity are likely to terminate with the first rapture of happiness, and I do confidently look for, from the amiable disposition and engaging manners of my wife, a consoling friend in sorrow, and a promoter of my pleasure in serener moments. What have I to desire that I do not possess?—I am young, that is: I am not old—God has been ever good to me—I will strive to deserve his bounty, and perhaps it will still be continued—I am happy—UNSPEAKABLY HAPPY—what could I be more?—what would you wish me more?—I might have married £40,000 —I declined it—I knew I could not purchase the blessing of mutual affection, and in that *I am now blessed.*—Surely herein I have falsified no hope that I ever yet held out.

I shall be able to be with you at Swansea Monday 19th July, & I think I can stay with you nearly a fortnight, so as not to play *every night*. . . .[87]

So the honeymoon was combined with business, an uninter-
rupted series of engagements throughout the summer and fall in
Ireland and England until the opening of his second season at
Drury Lane on November 15, 1824. Again he went through by
now standard characters, Macbeth, Leontes, John, and Wolsey,
and prepared for the first novelty, Shiel's adaptation of Massinger's
old tragedy, *The Fatal Dowry*. Since this is but one of many adaptations from the Jacobean drama to appear in what would seem to
be the unpropitious surroundings of the pre-Victorian theatre, it
will be profitable to hearken to the words of the prologue as
spoken by Macready on the opening night, January 7, 1825. The
prologue first regrets that Massinger should have been the "poet
of an elder age":

> Oh! had he sung in these our chaster days,
> And sought from your applause his meed of praise,
> Nothing, that should not be, would then have been,
> Pure every stain, untarnished every scene!
> Nor we, as now, had laboured to remove
> Thoughts, that your nicer taste could ne'er approve.

Yet there was a precious jewel hidden in the dirt:

> The nervous diction, the harmonious ease,
> The patriot zeal, the passion's tender glow,
> And all the power of art without the show.

Milton, we are reminded, drew (copiously) from the crystal waters
of Massinger:

> Then let not Rowe's Fair Penitent—a tale
> Drawn feebly from our great original,
> With laboured phrase and specious eloquence,
> Usurp the place of Nature, Truth, and Sense;
> If but the copy can applause command,
> Approve the earlier and the master hand:
> True taste at once and Massinger restore,
> "And give the Stage one classic drama more."[88]

We may be permitted to wonder that the Macready who so despised Nahum Tate and Colley Cibber could read such lines
without choking. Actually, Jacobean violence purged of certain
Jacobean diction proved highly popular with nineteenth-century
audiences, and *The Fatal Dowry* was on the way to becoming a
hit when Macready was seized with the consequences of his overwork. Macready says he was taken with an inflammation of the
diaphragm, though the newspapers reported it variously as a bilious

attack and rheumatic fever. Whatever the name, the attack was serious, so serious that the newpapers (and Macready) despaired of his life. The run of *The Fatal Dowry* was effectively stopped and, when his health was restored, Kean and Miss Foote had taken all the attention of the town by the lurid scandal of their divorce trials and there was no interest in the purely dramatic attraction which Macready could offer.

Fortunately, the indefatigable Knowles was at hand with a new play, *William Tell*. In its original form it had all the faults of Knowles' style and few of the virtues: it was shapeless, strung-out, and crabbed. However, as Macready notes, Knowles had "less of the tenacity of authorship than most writers,"[89] and listened readily to suggestions from the star for whom the vehicle was being constructed. The play was reshaped and rushed into rehearsal, for Elliston's treasury, as usual, was desperately in need of the attraction of a novelty. For Macready it was a period of considerable trial. His health was not good, he assumed the responsibility of staging the new play, and he was continually at work with the author putting it into playable shape. Consequently, he had barely time to learn his own lines—and Knowles' style is sufficiently peculiar to present some obstacles to the quickest "study." On the morning of the day before the first performance, when the fifth act was finally being rehearsed, Macready walked off the stage, declaring that he was imperfect, that the production was unready, and should not be opened as announced. Elliston sent after him, but the messenger returned, having found Macready in bed, with the declaration that nothing would induce him to act Tell the following night. The bluntness of the reply was modified in a letter the next day. After admitting that he had twice before, in *The Winter's Tale* and *Gracchus*, permitted Elliston to persuade him to go on though not thoroughly prepared, Macready declares that the state of his health forbids him "to yield to your necessities." Knowles had been making difficulties, suggesting that the play might not go on, and deserting him at the last to carry on alone, and now Elliston sends to tell him that he must play the part on the announced date, or not at all. To this he can say:

If you will give me back my strength and health, I will do it. I am truly, truly sorry that I cannot; and since my engagement must be of little or no value to you without a novelty, I do not desire to take your money, or occupy your nights, unless I fully answer your demands on my exertions.

Unprepared and imperfect as we are I am OBLIGED to say, I cannot (although I would if I could) play it to-night. In declaring this, to show you that I wish only justice, I also state that I will, without a murmur, abandon my engagement, and even my benefit night, the only *chance* I look to for meeting the expenses of my coming and staying here, rather than that you should be able, for one moment, to impute to me selfish or sinister motives.[90]

Elliston lost no time in setting out for Macready's home, only to meet him on his way to the theatre, whereupon the manager gave a brilliant characterization of The Friend in Need and Macready was, as he says "importuned and, I may truly say, worried into running the hazard of its performance, trusting to momentary impulse for much of my effect (a very dangerous reliance)," and even, during the moments he was not actually on stage, learning the words of the concluding scene.[91]

The audience was delighted and the reviewers were favorable. "It is evident," wrote one of them, "that Mr. Knowles has read Schiller's piece." This both Knowles and later critics were prone to deny, for there is little resemblance in plot, beyond the "necessary scene," between the two plays. In the matter of tone and style, however, the early reviewer makes some shrewd comparisons. "Mr. Knowles as a dramatist, has some of the faults and some of the merits which distinguish the German school. He mingles tragedy and farce—terror and buffoonery—he enters into domestic details which are natural, but utterly ignoble—he turns history into dialogue with great force and truth, and commands every now and then some admirable touches of dramatic instinct and strong feeling."[92] The strongest points of the play, of course, are the speeches on liberty and the skillful, if a trifle obvious, way Knowles manages to turn all the catastrophes upon a domestic point.

William Tell was first produced at Drury Lane on May 11, 1825, with Mrs. Bunn as Emma and Clara Fisher, the child prodigy, as Albert. The principal role was well suited to Macready's style: even Genest was moved to record that he was "much and deservedly applauded,"[93] and T. Hall began a sonnet to him with the words,

> Rave on wild monarch of the storm, I love
> To hear thee vent thy fury.[94]

The eleven performances of *Tell* which brought his engagement to a close were a satisfactory ending to a season that had promised very little.

Macready had now reached the highest rank in his profession in England. Wherever he played, country or city, he claimed and received top salary and top billing as "That Eminent Tragedian,

Mr. Macready." To a young and ambitious man in a century whose keyword was Progress this must have looked very much like standing still. But there was still another world to conquer. The American theatre had been supplied almost exclusively with British talent since the pre-Revolutionary days of Tony Aston and his fellow strollers. And although the crossing of the Atlantic was tedious and still perilous, a reigning British star who was willing to undertake it could be reasonably sure of a warm welcome and a considerable addition to his fame and fortune. Edmund Kean had made the trip twice, once triumphantly and once almost fatally, his sharp tongue having cut the supersensitive Americans to the quick.

On July 22, 1826, Macready went to Liverpool to sign an agreement with Stephen Price, manager of the Park Theatre in New York, and called by Francis Wemyss "Star-giver General to the American Theater."[95] Macready was somewhat uneasy at the manager's unwillingness to commit himself to written terms, though he was demanding £50 a night, over twice what Elliston had paid him at Drury. He was further convinced that the manager was no gentleman, but a mere speculator, with no knowledge of dramatic literature or the art of the stage. With such gamblers and men of business, however, it was the artist's fate to deal. The contract was signed and preparations for the voyage begun.

A few commitments remained to be played off in the country theatres before his departure; after a performance of *Hamlet*, August 21, 1826, at Birmingham, he took an "unaffected and affecting" leave of his earliest friends, only to find in the morning that a robber had broken into the box office and stolen the receipts, and that the whole thing was to do over. "It is a knock-down blow," he wrote his father,[96] but he undertook to play Virginius three nights later as an extra performance, thus making up his own loss and insuring that the company would receive their weekly salary. On the second of September he embarked for New York, bearing with him the good wishes of the Birmingham players and their assurance that his "truly liberal and disinterested conduct towards the head of the establishment of which we are members has excited in us all so warm a feeling of admiration and esteem," that they desired to express their gratitude and best wishes for prosperity and safety. "We honour the motives," their letter read, "which have induced you to act as you have done on the present occasion, and we feel grateful to you, not only for this individual instance of your kindness, but for supporting by your example, both in public and in private life, the respectability of a profession which has been too much degraded by many who ought to have sustained its credit and character." Sweet words indeed to have ringing in his ears as he set forth on a twenty-five-day trip across the Atlantic.

There were other words from members of his profession which would have pleased him less. On October 18, 1826, Covent Garden presented *The Green Room,* a new farce by James Kenney,[97] in which a poet, whose marriage to the manager's daughter depends upon the success of his play, resorts to a series of tricks to prevent the leading man, Mr. Starling, from upsetting his plans. The role of Starling was filled by the celebrated Irish comedian Tyrone Power and there was no question that, whatever Kenney's intentions, the characterization was a cruel thrust at Macready. He is represented as unfeeling, heartless, and unprincipled; he refuses to wear the costume always alloted to the role he is rehearsing, declaring haughtily that, "If I can't have a better, I won't play the part"—a wilful failure to understand Macready's insistence upon propriety of costume. As the principal Tragedian he thinks it his right to have a comedy entirely to himself, and makes lachrymose demands that his character be made "more comic."

One of the tricks played upon the "leading man" exposes his pretensions to taste and poetic power. A gentleman is introduced to him as a critic who has written a play and Starling is immediately most graciously eager to help him. The gentleman presents him with a quire of blank paper tied with a red tape. During the rehearsals, this "play" is frequently referred to and Starling makes a considerable display of his critical judgments on the plot, the beauties of the dialogue, and so forth. He is finally, of course, forced into opening the manuscript to demonstrate a point and is crushingly exposed. "We hope," wrote the critic of *The New Monthly Magazine* for November 1826, "that the supposed resemblance is merely accidental; for the imitation of manner and voice is certainly, if designed, very imperfect; and the attempt would be peculiarly unfair in the absence of the party from England." Another critic, however, has no doubts either as to the intention of the playwright or the justness of his strictures:

Whether all this will be peculiarly pleasant to Macready may be doubted; but if he deserves the lesson, we can see no objection to its being given. We have much respect for the ability which the stage requires, and we have much for the personal qualities and private conduct of some of the players; but we have nothing but dislike and censure for the affectations with which some bloated and self-conceited individuals of the stage are unhesitatingly charged. Caprice in an actor is impertinence. The pretence to superiority, or dictation in their intercourse with writers, deserves the severest contempt; the jealousy which refuses to bear not merely a rival but a "brother near the throne," is silly; and the perpetual refusal of parts, under the idea that they are not worthy of the high abilities and transcendant fame of [actors who would not] in a better day of stage, have been suffered to do more than carry a message or a mantle in a melo-drama, is altogether insolent and insufferable![98]

As the most unkindest cut, the role of the poet who triumphs over the caprices of Mr. Starling was filled in high glee by Mr. C. Kemble.

The Splendid Stroller

THE CONQUEST OF TWO WORLDS

FROM the first, Macready was eager to like America. It was still, in 1826, a foreign land to an Englishman, to be "done" as conscientiously as the cathedrals of Italy or the wild beauties of rural Wales. And so the actor arrived in New York on the twenty-seventh of September, with wife and sister, intent not only on making more money in a few months than England could possibly yield him, but also on observing "the government of the country, its society, the manners of its citizens, and its scenes of grandeur and beauty, so unlike what we had left behind in our own dear land."[1]

New York City was a curious mixture of the urbane and the crude. Trim three-story houses standing in long rows along the principal streets suddenly yielded to the intrusion of a crazy wooden shack. Uptown, around the City Hall, there were side-walks of large oblong blocks and the streets were well-kept, the cobble-pavement being sprinkled regularly from great barrel-laden carts, yet the side streets were still largely hard earth (or mud, depending on the weather), tree-lined but without lamps save those provided by the householders or merchants. The streets were filled with sweepers with faggot brooms, water-sellers, dealers in lottery tickets, ladies and gentlemen on horseback. Glass-enclosed omnibuses and horse-drawn coaches rumbled over the stones without regard for pedestrians; ladies jumped to the sidewalks to avoid being splashed by passing vehicles or tripped by the pigs constantly rooting in the gutters.

If this seemed a trifle primitive after London, there were compensations. Letters of introduction brought him the acquaintance of David Colden, lawyer and statesman, and T. A. Emmett, the Irish exile who had become a leader of the Bar. They lost no time in establishing him in the city's aristocratic and literary circles, and providing information about the American way of life, a subject of increasing concern to the visitor. It was after watching Emmett hold a jury spellbound with his oratory at the courtroom in the City Hall that Macready and his friends passed the figure of Aaron Burr, "a mysterious shadow of unrepented evil."[2] At another time, he watched with much delight and amazement two brick houses being moved to new foundations. With Captain Basil Hall—whose estimate of America was scarcely as favorable as his own—Macready made an overnight excursion into New Jersey to visit the falls of the Passaic, the geologic peculiarities of which he carefully noted, together with the flora and fauna of the vicinity. During this, as on his future trips to America, he diligently revealed that curiosity which for Matthew Arnold was a characteristic of the gentleman of culture.

New Yorkers had, in the meantime, been prepared for his arrival and first performances by the accepted form of theatrical puffery, a character sketch in *The New York Mirror and Ladies Literary Gazette,* where he is dignified as William C. Macready O. E., B. F.* After a lengthy transcript of his farewell address to the audience in Birmingham on the night the box office was rifled, the article quotes a summary by an English correspondent of the actor's career to date:

Mr. William C. Macready, who has for the last five or six years been, as a general actor, in the front line of his profession, and in his own peculiar walk decidedly at the head of it, is now about thirty-three years of age. . . . It is a curious fact, that he has given birth to a distinct species of tragic composition, and that to his talents the reputation and success of the principal tragic authors of the day are to be ascribed. William Tell, Damon, Gracchus, Wallace, Mirandola, and all Shield's [sic] and Miss Milford's [sic] tragedies, were written expressly for him; and until it was represented by Macready, the tragedy of Virginius, and its gifted author, were entirely unknown (IV, 85–86).

On October 2, Macready opened in his favorite role of Virginius at the Park Theatre, across from the City Hall. The debut was in

* If the precise meaning of these initials is obscure, their general intention is clear enough. The publicity value of even a nonexistent title or honor has been demonstrated by the long line of "Kentucky Colonels."

every way auspicious; the large auditorium was crammed with spectators who overflowed into the lobby and stood on tiptoe to catch a glimpse of the latest importation. Although the actor was struck by a kind of apathy in the audience—they did not respond as readily as those at home—by close attention to business he was able to kindle them into the kind of excitement that convinced him he had performed well, and the play ended to the typical American accolade of applause reinforced by the rattling of canes against the seats. The newspapers were friendly, the *Times* reporting with satisfaction that there was not a seat in box or pit but might have been filled twice over to see a tragedian who united "with talents of uncommon eminence, an unspotted private character."[3]

This clear allusion to the distinctly spotted character of Edmund Kean, the last great visitor from the English theatre, did not prevent the more judicious critics from passing well-tempered judgements. At the end of the first week, during which Macready had performed *Virginius, Macbeth,* and *Damon and Pythias,* the critic of *The Albion* wrote:

In the general summary of Mr. Macready's acting we confess that we have seen many passages performed more to our liking by others. The flashes of Kean's genius make us dizzy with the intensity of their blaze —the fine and commanding figure of Cooper may charm us, and the graceful movements of Conway please us; but we have never sat out a whole play with more real gratification than we have done with Mr. Macready.[4]

Macready was to make many complaints about American audiences and actors and critics. It is well to notice that, during his initial appearances in New York, an American critic was the first to comment not on his "original points," not on how this bit of Macready's business compared with that bit of Kean's or Thomas Cooper's, but on the *wholeness* of his interpretation. For this, the necessity for unity, the concern for the total performance, was to be his great contribution to the progress of his art.

Professionally the New World brought him only kudos and money; Macready intended to repeat the familiar pattern of a tour of the English provinces. Throughout the month he played at the Park every second or third night his established repertory, Damon, Tell, Macbeth, Hamlet, with Coriolanus for his benefit on the twenty-third. His principal competition was from the once despised imitator of Kean, Junius Brutus Booth, who had turned up in America some five years before and who was playing a round of

Shakespearean parts at the Chatham Theatre. Since Macready does not mention him in his *Reminiscences,* it is clear that no harm was done to his receipts either by Booth's reputation, which was growing, or by the fact that they were often playing the same characters, a common if somewhat cutthroat practice in the profession.

On the night of his benefit, there was a different kind of competition: the opening of the New York Theatre in the Bowery, "a low quarter of the city."[5] The company was a remarkable one, in terms of the future history of the American stage. It included Conway, who had been a member of the elder McCready's troupe, and two native actors, George Barrett and Edwin Forrest. Of these, Forrest's is a name of ominous significance in Macready's biography, and the Englishman's comments on his future American rival are shrewd and accurate. As Mark Antony, "his figure was good, though perhaps a little too heavy; his face might be considered handsome, his voice excellent; he was gifted with extraordinary strength of limb, to which he omitted no opportunity of giving prominence. He had received only the commonest education, but in the reading of the text he showed discernment and good sense of an intellect much upon the level of that of Conway; but he had more energy, and was altogether distinguished by powers that under proper direction might be productive of great effect."[6] In Macready's own role of *William Tell,* "His performance was marked by vehemence and rude force that told upon his hearers; but of pathos in the affecting interview with his son there was not the slightest touch, and it was evident that he had not rightly understood some passages in his text."* Macready concluded that he was a young actor of great promise, a promise which was never likely to be realized by reason of the blinding enthusiasm which he aroused in his supporters. These were the "Bowery b'hoys," who attended the low-priced theatres and were recklessly devoted to the thunder of Forrest's voice and the rippling of his muscles;

* The judicious critic of *The Albion* wrote of Forrest on April 14, 1827: "He is a great favourite with the Bowery people, and his talents are of an order that should make him a favourite anywhere. We are afraid, however, that he is disinclined to that laborious and incessant study without which no actor can reach the summit of his profession. His personal and intellectual endowments fit him for the very highest rank, but unless he is content to devote all his time and all his faculties to the art, he may rest assured he will never reach that rank. . . . The greatest blemish of Forrest's acting is its unnecessary and extravagant vehemence. It is out of all keeping." It is curious that this closely parallels, in idea and phrasing, Macready's judgment on Forrest as recorded in his *Reminiscences* (I, 320). Forrest was later to accuse his English rival, without justification, of collusion with the London press. This agreement between Macready and an *American* critic could have been made into a more devastating weapon: the haughty Englishman and the unpatriotic journalist uniting to deflect the rise of native genius.

furthermore, Forrest was an American, and among the middle and lower classes of the country there was at that time developing a spirit of Jingoism and resentment against foreigners of which Macready was to feel the full force two decades later.

For the moment, however, America was friendly to him, his first engagement in New York was prosperous, and he moved on to Boston where he opened at the Federal Street Theatre as Virginius on the thirtieth of October. Here for two weeks he repeated his standard roles and his earnest sightseeing, and made the acquaintance of the first citizens of the community. A brief engagement in Baltimore preceded his second series of appearances in New York, where he added King John, Pierre (in *Venice Preserved*), and Henry V to his repertory and £500 to his stores. On January 10, 1827, he moved on to the Chestnut Street Theatre in Philadelphia, returning to the Park once more on the seventh of February, with *The Fatal Dowry* and *2 Henry IV* as novelties, and contributed his services as Cassius to a special benefit for Conway. A brief repeat season in Boston preceded a fourth engagement in New York, where he added Gracchus, Othello, and Wolsey, and undertook a performance of Virginius the night after Forrest had appeared in the character at the Bowery. On the twenty-sixth of March he was again in Philadelphia as Othello, and two days later he was playing *The Stranger* opposite the Mrs. Haller of Mrs. Wood, the Countess of Mrs. Jefferson, and the Steinfort of F. C. Wemyss, one of the few men of the American theatre who seems to have had a genuine admiration for Macready's talents. After various engagements in the east, including an appearance in Albany and a trip to the wilds of the Niagara, Macready wound up his first American tour with a fifth season at the Park, beginning with Hamlet on the twenty-fifth of May, and concluding with Macbeth on the fourth of June.

He had good reason to be satisfied with the expedition. At £50 a night he had amassed a considerable sum; he had observed closely the customs and antiquities and the natural wonders of the New World. He had been freely received by men of the best society without prejudices against his profession, and he had noted that the cost of a gentleman's living was remarkably low. Altogether his impressions of America were favorable and it may have been during this early tour that the idea of eventually retiring to this land of excellent promise first occurred to him.

Certainly his reception in England was a contrast to provoke thought. From £50 a night, he was forced to return to his former salary of £20. And although the audience which greeted him as

Macbeth in his first appearance at Drury in two years, on the night of November 12, was "most respectable" and welcomed him "most warmly," the house was by no means crowded. Nor had the condition of the national theatres improved during his absence. Stephen Price (who was now "speculating" in English theatrical properties) was a manager to remind the homecoming actor of the unhappiest days of his struggle to achieve first rank. On the twenty-eighth of January, 1828, Macready found himself creating the role of Ribemont in *Edward the Black Prince,* patched up by Reynolds from Beaumont and Fletcher's *Philaster, Bonduca,* and *The Two Noble Kinsmen.* Two performances sufficed for this enormity, which an apologist for Price called "a most beautiful performance."[7] The apologist continues, "Mr. Price has never trammelled the genius of any artist at his theatre, by a paltry consideration of expense, and to this, perhaps, may be attributed the lead that Drury Lane has this season taken in every department of the drama, tragedy excepted. There Covent Garden 'held despotic sway.' Macready, Wallack, and Cooper, talented as they are, could not withstand the powerful rivalry of the phalanxy of talent engaged at Covent Garden. Kean, Warde, Young, and C. Kemble, formed a tragic company that probably never will be surpassed at any theatre."[8] Actually, Kean was a sick man, Young about to retire, Kemble no tragedian, and Warde not much of an actor of any sort. It was thus the more apparent that Macready failed to attract the Londoners. During the season he played but twenty-four times, and made frequent excursions to the country. At Norwich, where he played the week of March 18, 1828, he was greeted, according to an actor's diary, by houses that were variously "good" and "great."[9] But on his return to London, Price bought off his contract, paying him for sixteen nights rather than permitting him to perform. This tale, though set down in malice by Alfred Bunn,[10] seems unfortunately to be true. Because of ill health, or overwork, or, as he said of Master Betty, "by becoming used-up in the frequent repetition of the same characters,"[11] something had happened to Macready in his two years away from Drury.

His enemies on the newspapers, too, were hard at work against him. The critic for *The Age,* always of the opposition, seized upon Kean's first appearance in *Virginius* as an opportunity for an unkind comparison, especially unkind since Kean was then in the last stages of his decline, with a failing mind and only occasional glimmerings of the greatness that had made him the leading actor of his time. In sharp contrast to the general attacks on Kean's performance, *The Age* reported on December 26:

KEAN played *Virginius* for the first time, on Monday last, and played it like himself with a striking originality of genius in every point. He was perfect in the text of his author; and far, very far above *Macready* in his conception of the part. His delivery of certain passages, abounding with pathos of a delicate, deep, and phrenzied character, in that clear, expressive, and poetical undertone, which is peculiar to the actor, was above all praise, and left all competition in the race for fame behind him. If there was any want of perfection in the representation, it arose from stature, and perhaps he might have suffered somewhat by comparison in dignity; but the attitude of his bold and energetic mind rose superior to the natural advantages of his predecessor in the part.

Macready's disappointment, if he felt any, was soon to be mitigated. In August 1827, the actor Abbot was appointed manager of the Théâtre Favart in Paris and scheduled a season of English plays, with a resident company of English actors and such visiting stars as Charles Kemble, Kean, Maria Foote, Harriet Smithson, Mme. Vestris, Young, Macready, Liston, and Daniel Terry. The consequences of this venture, which was wholly commercial in intent, could hardly have been foreseen. Opening with *The Rivals* on September 6, 1827, the English company attracted enthusiastic audiences from the highest literary and social circles and fanned into full flame the sparks of revolt which had been dimly glowing in the wings of the French theatre. For a hundred years the stage in France had been in the rigid clutches of classical tragedy performed in a cold and formal style. Outside of melodrama and opera, the art of the scene painter and stage manager was practically unknown. The drama had been effectively separated from life, with only an occasional genius like Talma to vitalize it and give it present meaning. Thus the critic A. Duval comments on death scenes, a specialty of the romantic English tragedians: "In France, the actor dies with great decorum; the hero strikes himself and announces, 'I die!' In England, the hero strikes himself or is struck, and then is a quarter of an hour in dying. Before he expires, he treats us to all that is most painful: *le tétanos, le râle de l'agonie et le rire sardonique.*" He praises Mlle. Bourgoin for weeping "as the English actors do, without concern for costume or make-up, for dabbing the eye with a handkerchief would scarcely soften the heart of a Turk, however disposed to be gallant."[12]

The French theatre, too, had never quite known what to do with Shakespeare. Voltaire's attitude, that he was a barbarian, was perhaps more extreme than that of the average playgoer of the early nineteenth century, but nevertheless, if *Macbeth* made its appearance in Paris, it was apt to be in the form of a speaking pantomime with transformations, flying animals, and plenty of red fire. *Hamlet* was produced as a ballet with a grand denouement in hell, *Othello* as a "pantomimic spectacle, mixed with dialogue and ballet."[13] The effects of the English invasion on both the reputation of Shakespeare and the future development not only of the French stage but of the English were most curious.

Nearly all the French critics were immediately converted. The first offerings of the English company revealed Liston as Bob Acres in *The Rivals* and Charles Kemble as Hamlet. Alexandre Dumas, Victor Hugo, and Alfred deVigny discovered at once the kind of romantic fervor they had sought to impart to their own writings; flesh-and-blood passions on the stage, real men and women, not classical personifications. And in "la belle Smidson" the French audience found a new idol. Actually Harriet Smithson was an Irish actress with a thick brogue who had counted for little in London, but she capitvated those whose ears were not very finely tuned to English speech and who may, in fact, have heard more music in her distortions than in the fine clarity of Kemble's reading.

Macready made his first appearance with this company on April 7, doubtless expecting very little in the way of response, since his friends of the press had been up to their familiar tricks. The Paris Correspondent of the *Theatrical Observer* reported:

[I]nstead of appearing as *Virginius* or *Tell,* which he has made his own, he persists, it seems, in commencing with *Macbeth,* and our good-natured Paris critics have already selected every line of censure which their London brethren have bestowed on his performance of the "ambitious Thane"—merely, they say, to give the public time to "*Think* before they *pay*"—the fact is, they are angry at Macready's preceding Kean, about whom there is great anxiety; they are afraid he'll die before they see him; his name is in everybody's mouth as the "*only Shakespearean.*" (April 7, 1828)

Macbeth was produced under difficulties. The Favart was the home of the Italian Opera, and such scenery as was available was better suited to the romantic extravagances of the south than the barren plains and draughty palaces of Shakespeare's north. The Scotch heath in the production was a dusty corner of a grand-opera forest where Macbeth's small army ranged itself like a "chorus of Tancred's knights." The dagger scene was played in a comic-opera palace, the witches performed without their customary music (but excited laughter anyway from some neoclassicists in the audience who cried out during the brewing of the potion, "Oh, mon Dieu! quel mélange!"),[14] and the final engagement between the armies was represented by four men. In spite of this, one critic declared, "The tragedy of *Macbeth* produced an almost unheard of emotional reaction."

On the sixteenth of April, after a repetition of Macbeth, Macready gave the Parisians a taste of his Virginius, leading the critics to remark that if the performance of the former was a "succès d'estime," that of the latter was a "succès d'enthusiasme." Wrote the critic of *La Reunion*, "Who would have thought that this man, to whom nature has denied everything—voice, carriage, and looks—could attain to the heights of our Talma, to whom she gave everything? . . . Never has an actor so completely effaced his own personality to give reality to his characterization: never have such terrible emotions so expressed themselves in the countenance of a man as to pass into the hearts of his audience; the illusion was complete, and almost painful." The critic was embarrassed to find himself weeping, and there was one moment when he was not able even to look at the stage. Magnin, in the *Globe,* praised Macready's diction for its naturalness, its freedom from sing-song. *Le Mentor* was startled at its own unwillingness to criticize him for his boldness in occasionally turning his face away from the audience; everything was made to contribute to "la verité de l'action."[15]

A pioneer is not without honor. . . . To be sure, the London critics had gradually accepted Macready as an actor of the first rank, but always they compared him with Kean or Kemble, or their own particular favorite. But in countries where the older acting style had remained fixed audiences had seen none of the tentative steps in the direction of realism. In America the leaders of the stage had come for the most part from the English school of John Kemble. As for French acting, Macready himself characterized it as sculpturesque with little attempt at grouping, or unified composition[16] which might be advantageous for the star but hardly for the total realization of the play. Set against such a tradition, or the conservative American rhetorical style, the fully developed art of Macready could hardly fail to attract attention, favorable or unfavorable.

Edward Macready, who had accompanied his brother to Paris principally to visit the gambling houses, was present at the *Virginius* performance and was caught up in the general enthusiasm. Next morning he wrote to Catherine in London:

I never saw such effects produced in a theatre as those of the betrothing of Virginia and the return of Virginius to reason. You may conceive these in some degree when you learn that the exclamation—Ah! C'est Talma! was repeatedly extorted from a French audience. . . .

A lady who sat behind me last night was in one continual murmur of Ah! Que c'est beau,—Ah! son visage! C'est la nature, during the home scenes, but at the murder her head dropped and after a pause she said from the middle of a sob, 'Ça me fait du mal'—I turned and saw her pretty hand on her heart and again heard 'Ça me fait du mal' as she rose and went sobbing home.[17]

Tributes poured in from all sides, and firm friendships were cemented between the actor and his French admirers, the leaders of the romantic movement. The final testimonial of success was the presentation of a burlesque of *Virginius* at the Variétées, with Odry as Macready in a wig so frizzled that he could not enter between the scenes, and wearing a centurion's costume over English leather breeches and polished boots.[18]

At the end of the month, Macready retired for a time to London to give place to the much-expected Kean, but Kean's decayed performances only served to increase the enthusiasm for his predecessor, and Macready was soon back for a second engagement which extended from the twenty-third of June to the twenty-fifth of July. He opened in the popular *Virginius,* played *William Tell* and *Hamlet* with, apparently for the first time in Paris, the scene of the "fossoyeurs." The French were not pleased with his Hamlet, which emphasized too much, they thought, "the Sentimental Aspect."[19] They preferred Charles Kemble's version, the tragedy not of passion but of thought. Despite the heat of the season, however, he continued to draw audiences for Tell and Virginius. "The monde," he wrote to his friend and adviser, H. P. Smith, "is in the country . . . though the residue here still Talma me. . . ."[20]

Not all the "monde" was in the country. Louise, Queen of the Belgians, in a charming letter to her father, the Duc d'Orléans, indicates the wide interest in Macready's performances:

Je me suis forte amusée hier bien cher Papa, Macready a joué [*William Tell*] à merveille; peut être avec moins de naturel que dans Virginius, mais avec autant de talent—il a été fort applaudi et avec raison. Master Webster, son élève, enfant de 14 à 15 ans, a très bien rempli aussi, le rôle du fils du Tell. Guessler [*sic*] et les autres acteurs, étaient en revanche bien ridicules. Cependant je suis sûre que la pièce Vous ferait beaucoup de plaisir à voir. J'ai bien regretté que vous n'y fussiez point hier. . . . Maintenant, que ma curiosité a été satisfaite au sujet de Guillaume Tell, je ne désire plus que voir jouer à Macready, Coriolan. Ce rôle était le triomphe de J. Kemble, il est son imitateur, et l'on dit que c'est aussi un de ces plus beaux rôles.[21]

After his performance of Othello on July 21, a crowd of young admirers—contravening a strict ordinance forbidding performers from taking curtain calls—bore him through the orchestra on their shoulders to the apron of the stage where he received a triumphant ovation and a crown of laurel.[22]

A French critic summed up the national estimate of Macready and his fellows thus:

Of the three tragedians, Charles Kemble, Edmund Kean, and Macready, who share the applause of the English public, Macready is the one whom we prefer. It is he who appears to us to possess in the highest degree the secret of speaking to the soul, and the gift of creating emotion; it is he who approximates most nearly to our taste, by being natural without vulgarity, and elegant without affectation. He is occasionally chargeable with action a little too formal, with attitudes a little too academical; and also with exclamations too much prolonged, and, consequently without effect . . . but these are faults which may easily be corrected. . . . He has already had the courage to reform a manner which had been very successful, but which did not satisfy the purity of his taste.[23]

The effects of this season of English acting were far-reaching. Edward had predicted to Catherine that Macready's domestic scenes would "give a bias to French dramatic literature." The French actors studied well the lessons of realism and freedom of action and gesture, and then improved on their masters. In the early twenties Hazlitt had found Macready at times undignified; now the French were greeting him as astoundingly real. In a few years, French actors of the "new school" were to give the English an exhibition of naturalistic acting so compelling that their audiences began calling Macready stagey and unnatural. The complete reversal of the French technique of playwriting and acting, given such an impetus by the Paris season of the "comédiens d'Outre-Manche," was to lead to the English playwriting reforms of Tom Robertson, who superseded the school of Knowles in England, and to the concurrent acting reforms of the Prince of Wales's Theatre company which effectively ended the "school" of Macready.[24]

After his return from Paris, Macready devoted two years to the provinces. True, his friend on *The Age* announced in November that he had been playing at Sheffield to very indifferent audiences: "he is at present in town, expecting an offer from one of the large theatres,"[25] but there is no indication that negotiations were under way, or that he had any intention of giving up the country for the time being. There is little to report of these campaigns. Houses varied from decent to wretchedly thin—at Portsmouth he "carried on" to an audience only a few souls larger than that which his father had quixotically entertained on the night of the Waterloo illumination. At Stratford, on the twenty-ninth of January, 1829, he played for his own benefit, in the Shakespearean Theatre. The choice of the play is significant—the good citizens of the Bard's home town chose to see *William Tell*.

ELM PLACE

The compensation for the trials of his profession, as he confided over and over to his diaries, was his home and his expanding family. Catherine had accompanied him to New York; it was to be her last journey of any consequence. If the actor was required to undergo the hardships of vagabondage, the gentleman's wife was to pursue a life of quiet domesticity in a household as stable and as far from the theatres as her husband could afford. Always before his mind's eye was the moment when he could turn his back on public life and retire to the country to raise his own food and give himself over to the "studies and 'lettered ease' " which he hoped were more congenial to his disposition.[26]

On his return from America he had installed his wife and sister in a rented house in Pinner Wood, some fifteen miles from the London theatre district. In 1830, with his first-born in prospect, he leased Elm Place, a nine-acre farm in Elstree, which was to be the family residence for seven years. Never, after a vexing tour of the provinces or a trying three-day engagement in London, does he fail to record the joy in his heart as he stepped from the stagecoach and invited the innocence of the country to wash away the "vulgarity, heartlessness, and quackery" of the great world.[27]

He worked as hard at his role of country gentleman as ever he had at Virginius. He cultivated rural pastimes, archery, rowing on his "reservoir," walking in his gardens and fields. He inspected his crops and supervised the cutting of his hay; he walked three miles to Edgware to purchase plants, and gave many an unregretted hour to trowel and hoe. He personally oversaw the purchase of a cow and kept as strict account of her periodic freshening as of his professional income. He acquired a brace of wolfhounds to accompany him along country lanes and, regrettably, managed to strangle one to death with an ill-chosen tidbit.

It was somewhat more difficult to pursue the studies and the lettered ease of which he dreamed. The regular debut of a new Macready every year or two—Christina in 1830, William in 1832,

Catherine in 1835, and Edward in 1836 were born at Elm Place—imposed new and welcome responsibilities. His principal object was henceforth educating and providing for his children; the accumulation of money acquired a new sanctity, the effort to establish himself in good society a greater selflessness. If he bargained for the last shilling with a hard-pressed manager, it was to assure a competence for his "blessed babies"; if he bitterly resented the slowness of his Elstree neighbors to accept him as a social equal, it was always in the light of the future of his family. Thus the practice of his profession became at once more odious and more necessary. He must study, he must go forward, he must be still in earnest.

Meanwhile he resumed the study of classic authors to prepare himself for the education of his sons, romped with the children, heard them in their lessons, or set them new lessons when dissatisfied with the assignments of their teachers. He was a demanding if not downright stern parent, and his infant pupils were not infrequently treated to the same condemnations for inaccuracy or inattention that were the lot of his fellow actors. Yet there is no doubt that he was a loving father: he was as forgiving when Nina kept him from his work by falling asleep in his arms as he was pained at the necessity of punishing her. "Thank God," he wrote, "my doting affection for these dear children does not, nor ever shall, make me guilty of such injustice to them as to spare my own feelings at the expense of their future, perhaps their eternal welfare."[28]

Toward his wife, whom he might have preferred to worship with the ardor of young Romeo, he felt himself forced into the role of Mrs. Beeton combined with Henry Higgins. When business took him from home his daily letters to his "heart's darling," his "ever blessed love," are full of instruction. She must remember to have the winter's wood stored and the fences repaired, she must rise at seven when daylight comes at six-thirty, she must enforce punctuality on the household. She must write in her diary with the "simple intention of keeping an account with yourself of the good and evil that you *do, think,* or *receive.* If you make it with reference to another's supervision, you are certain to deceive yourself."[29] He reproves her for the emotional diction of her own letters to him and urges her to continue her studies of Locke and Bacon. He reads or "jumps through" the works that may fall into her hands to keep her from anything that might debase "the holy forms of young inspiration." He would have her an ornament of that society to which he aspired, she must learn "good sense (which is good breeding),"[30] to ask questions if necessary, but to be silent unless she has something to say. And in spite of her emotional nature, her easily awakened jealousy, her chronic ill health, and the time consumed in child-bearing, Catherine was one of his successes. She was intelligent if not intellectual, well read, sympathetic with his desire to escape from the theatre, but unquestioning in support of any course he chose, and her devotion caused even so contrary-minded a female as Jane Carlyle to confess to Macready: "If I had not loved you for your own sake, as I have done since the first time you ever spoke to me, in your grave true voice, I should still have cherished a life-long interest in you for the sake of that dear, sweet, loving woman, for whom you were a sort of Divinity on Earth, and whose friendship for me gave me some of the very happiest hours I ever enjoyed in my life!"[31]

On his side, Macready was not unwilling to interrupt his serious business to answer household demands. He shopped for dress-goods in Dublin, searched the Birmingham factories for trinkets (but hesitated to make a purchase: "Thinking it better to leave her the means of buying them, than perhaps the necessity of seeking the means by selling them"),[32] bought preserves and whiskey, interviewed nursemaids in London, and responded graciously to the emergency of a leaky roof in the kitchen.

Fortunately for Macready there was one member of his home circle who never seemed to intrude on his time, who could be trusted to anticipate difficulties, and to assume responsibilities. Sister Letitia was his faithful lieutenant and female counterpart. His standards, principles, purposes were hers, and her devotion was as unshakable as Catherine's. She shared in all decisions, domestic and artistic, that came before the family council. She accompanied him to London on the important business of purchasing a barouche; it was to her ministration that he entrusted an aching head before studying a new play, it was to her hands that he entrusted the yearly accounts. And if his wife's jealousy was easily aroused, may it not have been due to the fixed presence of this too-capable image of her husband? There is perhaps an indication of how matters stood in Macready's farewell on departing for a tour in 1833: "Kissed my darling babes in the nursery, and taking leave of Letitia, also of my wife . . ." Letitia for her part was not without a trace of spite as the marriage-bed proved more and more fruitful.[33]

But Macready was a man with two families, the one of his own begetting and that of his father's. It has already been noted that William senior was more than casual about domestic relations, and, long before his death in 1829, the son who had grudgingly followed his father's profession, ungrudgingly, for the most part, assumed his father's responsibilities. For his brother Edward he had made the initial sacrifice of his own chosen career: he never ceased to interest himself in Edward's affairs, seeking to purchase his military promotion with the same earnestness that he strove to develop his character. To another sister, Ellen, he made a yearly allowance, and endeavored to ignore her unwelcome, if well-meaning, attempts to transmit compliments and gossip. He was conscientious in assisting his relatives in Ireland when opportunity forced itself upon him, he gave generous assistance to his stepmother and her children. He even, and with what pain is evident, called on one of his father's mistresses in Birmingham "as a duty to humanity."[34]

When in London, and less frequently in the provincial cities, he found time to cultivate and enlarge his circle of non-theatrical acquaintances. In this Talfourd was of particular service, for he delighted in knowing everybody and bringing about introductions. It was at Talfourd's that Macready spent his first evening with John Forster, although they had met at Kean's funeral in May 1833. And after the new friends walked home together, Macready wrote in his journal, "he appears to be quite an enthusiast; I like him."

So firm and rash a declaration from Macready is rare enough to warrant quotation, but Forster could, on occasion, make himself extraordinarily agreeable. Almost twenty years Macready's junior, he was a prominent figure in London journalism, theatrical critic of the weekly *Examiner*, essayist and historian. But his constant ambition, as his biographer says, was to know "everyone worth knowing."[35] To that end he lived much in society and in the clubs, listening, approving, advising, and keeping his eyes open for young men who promised well. He was not, however, a toady or time-server. He was a man of strong and forcefully expressed opinions, and quite without tact. His pen could crush as well as caress, and he was sufficiently egotistical and thin-skinned to make his criticism frequently suspect.

From the hour of his evening walk from Talfourd's, Forster was to make himself indispensable to Macready. He sought out plays and attended rehearsals; he undertook contractual negotiations, supported him in the *Examiner*, kept him informed on theatrical affairs; he stood beside him during his later domestic tragedies. There were, of course, periods when neither could bring himself to recognize the other, when Macready would be full of doubts as to Forster's loyalty and Forster would silently sulk in the Garrick Club. But there was between them an affection as deep as their emotions were quick.

Such was the private life of the Eminent Tragedian. The thirteen miles of highway between the national theatres and Elstree were his route from Vanity Fair to the Heavenly City. And eventually and on occasion Elm Place became the gentleman's abode he envisioned. He was accepted by his neighbors, who deigned to overlook his occupation; he is able to write of many a pleasant supper party, with claret in the summer house; and to declare that although an actor's life "is in direct hostility with regularity of every kind . . . at home I am a chronometer of exactness."[36] Macready, of course, had to recognize that the road which led him to "the glory of the grass, the splendour of the flower" must inevitably lead him back to the "gilt bedaubed guards, the plumed women, the tumult of spectators."[37] If the sight of the Elstree hills brought joy to the homecomer's spirit, no less precious—for its pathetic interest—was the last sight of his wife and children, one, two, three, and finally four, waving farewell to their eminent breadwinner.

The thirteen miles to London passed profitably in study, or in irritated perusal of the newspapers. For his country tours he often used his own carriage, which allowed ample room for his costume and property trunks, his case of books, and his special traveling pillow. Letitia had once suggested that he might rest better in the uncertain accommodations along his route if he were to take a portable bed, but this he vetoed, recollecting with a shudder the interested query of an Italian lady passenger when once he had included a bed in his luggage: "Are you amorous, sir?"[38]

SUR PLACE

The provincial theatres were a constant threat to his health as well as his equanimity. They were dirty and drafty and he was forced to conduct rehearsals in his greatcoat. When he was scheduled to perform daily, and especially in preparation for the Macready plays, he would drill the resident actors until midafternoon, write letters until evening, and then struggle to carry with him "a company as deficient in the words allotted them as in the knowledge of how they should be spoken."[39] But constant rehearsal and his own energetic performances could not compensate for the conditions of provincial production. One night in Exeter he found that the manager had cast the company's "old woman" as his

romantic lead; two nights later the villain of the play fell out of
his throne, dead drunk. In the first instance Macready resolved to
"cut out all my tenderness in order to leave her, if I can, all the
laugh to herself";[40] in the second, an unrehearsed substitute was
hurriedly thrust on, book in hand, to finish the play. But it is not
to be thought that the touring star bore these crosses in silence, or
confined his complaints to his diary or his daily letters to Catherine. The malefactors were publicly berated—sometimes in
the midst of performances—and in language inherited from his
father.

Occasionally an actor with a real or fancied grievance would
protest, much to Macready's surprise, for he was always surprised
at delusions of grandeur in others. Miss Kenneth, for example, had
a long record of caviling on the ninth part of a hair. In 1826 in
Manchester, where she had been engaged to replace Mrs. McGibbon, certain of Mrs. McGibbon's fans protested. Miss Kenneth
promptly rushed into print with accusations, most unreasonable
considering the circumstances, against the manager who had
employed her.[41] Macready knew her, her untruthfulness, and her
"foul mouth" of old, yet he seems to have been quite unprepared
for her behavior when he encountered her during a Dublin
season in 1830. In the company was Mary Amelia Huddart, a
rising young actress of "rather lurid beauty" and considerable
power, whose career was later to be bound up with Macready's.
With the view of increasing the effectiveness of his performances,
he cast Miss Huddart whenever possible opposite him. To this
Miss Kenneth took offense, thanking him, with whatever approach
to a prima donna's irony she could summon, for "depriving her
of her business." Macready professed ignorance, and she replied
that both the Irish proprietor, Calcraft, and Alfred Bunn, his
manager, had confirmed Macready's insistence on Miss Huddart's
services. He denied the charge, of course, satisfied that Miss Kenneth had spoken "to gratify her own vanity and spleen," and
forgot the matter, but Miss Kenneth did not forget.[42] Her foul
mouth was prepared to cause him greater distress on his next visit
to Dublin.

Despite such annoyances Macready devoted the two years after
his return from Paris almost exclusively to the provincial theatres.
He was aware of the injury it might do him, "goading an exhausted
frame and voice and mind. How can anything but ill habits result
from such abuse of one's powers?"[43] But he was also aware of a
steadily increasing account at his banker's, and that, if he played
with such wretches, at least he was not one of them. After con-

cluding a particularly difficult series of performances at Wisbeach, he rose next morning and from his hotel watched the resident company prepare to move on by canal to the next town in their circuit. "The fly-boat," he reported to Catherine, "which two horses drag along at the rate of 4 miles an hour, was loading opposite my window, whilst I was dressing. The entrails of the Theatre were disgorged, but by a very slow process, into the boat. The actors were variously occupied, some sitting on the cabin roof, indifferent to the gaze of about 30 curious or theatrical spectators, others watching a trunk, bag, or basket of provender—some reading, some lounging, one walking apart from the rest; I immediately said to myself, 'That's the first Tragedy!' and so it was. I could not help thinking that a life like this might have been my lot. Great God! How ungrateful am I (yet devoutly wishing to be grateful) to murmur at the few crossings of my will, which are so easy to endure, if I would but duly exercise thought and patience!"[44]

During these two years of strolling he added nothing of importance to his repertory except an experimental production of Lord Byron's *Werner*, which he seems to have tried first at Bristol, January 25, 1830. During a brief rest at home, he wrote to his solicitor, John L. Greaves, a letter which tells much of his state of mind and body during this comparatively static period. He had been experiencing bad weather and consequently bad houses. "My general health," he goes on, "barring what a very excitable temperament and an abandonment to exertion in my profession takes out of me, is not to be complained of." Although he restrains himself as to diet and drink when away from home, eating brown bread and taking not more than two glasses of wine daily, his natural instincts are those of an epicurean, not an abstainer. "I find much, very much of my own character reflected in that surprising specimen of Shakespeare's power of individualizing, *Jaques* in As You Like It—who has grown into a moralizer from his experience of the unsatisfactory nature of sensual enjoyments etc." After discussing the possibility of retirement—which creeps into nearly all his letters during this period—he suggests that Greaves read Harriet Lee's original tale of *Werner*. "It is superior to the play—a powerful picture of human weakness, its crime and virtue."[45] Some years later when Miss Lee expressed her pleasure in his interpretation of the role, he wrote her that he had had frequent recourse, back of Byron's text, to her work, "so rich in instances of the most intimate knowledge of the human heart and of the most profound observations on its workings."[46]

London got its first sight of Macready's version of *Werner* during an engagement at Drury Lane which commenced October 18, 1830. The patent houses had now entered upon the dog-days of their long history. The licenses for the exclusive performance of legitimate drama in London, created by Charles II and bestowed on Killigrew and Davenant as men competent to direct theatres, had passed for a century and a half through more or less competent, generally professional, hands. But by the third decade of the nineteenth century the original patents, through insolvency and catastrophe, had been broken up into shares and were held by committees of management. This theatrical absentee-landlordism increased the dangers not only of insolvency but of artistic catastrophe. The committees were interested in rent money, without a manager's concern for creating a company, a repertory, an audience, or an actor-manager's responsibility to his art or his reputation. Consequently the national theatres fell into the hands of a succession of speculators who, with one exception, followed one another into oblivion like rental agents for once noble mansions now subdivided into shoddy tenements.

At the time of Macready's reappearance in London, Alexander Lee was the acting manager for Captain Polhill at Drury Lane. Only after a fervent reading by the star player was he persuaded to allow him to step out of his customary roles; he certainly did not recognize in *Werner* a permanent addition to the Macready plays. But for the actor it was the only important event of the season.

The piece is a curious choice from Byron's dramatic work, an ill-written, dull, pseudo-Germanic story of crime and punishment, the only play of Byron's without a single poetic line, as Lady Pollock said.[47] Byron, of course, had made his usual disclaimer: "The whole is neither intended, nor in any shape adapted, for the stage,"[48] but there is little question that he would have been pleased by its success, if a little startled by Macready's treatment. In Byron's play, Werner is the assumed name of Sigendorf, an outlaw who finds himself, by coincidence, in a decayed castle where his principal enemy, Stralenheim, is spending the night. In revenge, and to provide means for flight, Werner robs Stralenheim of his purse. He is forced to reveal himself to his son, Ulric, who has appeared, also coincidentally, in Stralenheim's company. Ulric, determined to conceal his father's dishonor, kills Stralenheim, without revealing his action to Werner, allowing the Hungarian Gabor to take the blame for the murder. Werner now becomes Count Sigendorf. Almost at once Gabor appears to accuse

Ulric of the murder. Ulric, well-accustomed to the method by now, offers to kill him to silence him, but his father finally comes to realize the endless nature of evil, and dies horrified at his own past and his son's heritage.

The whole piece is conducted in the baldest kind of prosaic poetry with occasional sinkings into involved similes, and with generous lashings of the sardonic. It seems at times almost a burlesque of the domestic romantic melodrama made popular by Kotzebue, and "the Illustrious Goethe" to whom it was dedicated must have shuddered as he turned the pages. Macready's achievement as a playwright and actor is the more remarkable in the face of this uncompromisingly bad play.

Not that Macready was able to remake it into a classic. *Werner* is in no danger of being revived today or at any future time. But by a liberal use of the shears and by the introduction of long passages of new dialogue culled whenever possible from Miss Lee's original tale, Macready created a genuine play of character where only a play of rather hackneyed situation had before existed. "In truth," said the *Spectator* on December 18, 1830, "it was a dangerous experiment to represent a tragedy, the passion of which turns upon the point of petty larceny!"

The season was otherwise undistinguished. A limping translation of *Hernani,* called in English *The Pledge, or Castilian Honor* occupied him for eight nights, and *Alfred the Great,* one of Knowles' most crabbed tragedies, for fifteen. At his benefit he offered the public a monster bill combining *Coriolanus, The Critic,* and *Bluebeard,* the first employing the services of Miss Huddart, who was beginning to realize the promise Macready saw in her, and the last "Mr. Cooke's magnificent Stud of Horse." The benefit, whether the major attraction was Macready or the horses, netted £176.

The next season he was again at Drury, still under the speculative aegis of Captain Polhill, playing what nights a season of successful spectacles (involving in one instance a boa-constrictor and an elephant) left open to him. Werner, Hamlet, Richard III, and Macbeth were among his roles, together with Scroope in T. J. Serle's *The Merchant of London.* Serle was a capable hack who was to become Macready's general factotum. In the present drama, however, his services were negligible. It opened on April 26, 1832, and on the first of May a bill appeared with a note proclaiming that "unanimous call for its repetition by the fashionable and crowded Audience induce the Management to announce it for performance EVERY EVENING . . . until further notice." On the fifth of May, Macready noted in his diary that the *Merchant* was attended by a "wretched house," and with the ninth performance its tale was told. Since Alfred Bunn was now acting manager of the theatre, it would seem that the announcement was one of his early essays in a craft of which he became past master. For his own benefit on the fourteenth of May, Macready got together another exhausting bill consisting of *The Winter's Tale,* an interlude of songs by John Braham and Mme. de Meric, Garrick's cutting of *Catherine and Petruchio,* and the farce of *The Waterman.* And on the thirtieth he journeyed to Covent Garden for the first time in nine years, to play the Ghost to the Hamlet of Charles Young, who was taking his farewell of the stage. The *Spectator* was pleased with the gesture but not with the result:

MACREADY's Ghost was not ghostly: he spoke not in a sepulchral but a tender tone; and the part in his hands lost power by a too nice attention—a too refined care of his diction. He nursed and fondled every word, as no ghost should with the morning air under his nose.[49]

The following summer was spent in study and rest at Elm Place, preparing for the season to come. Its commencement was not auspicious. To begin with, there was the part of Colberg in Serle's *House of Colberg,* done with after four performances. A revival of *Every Man in His Humour* was repeated only once, although Kitely should have been a part cut to Macready's measure. Then on November 6 he discovered that two days earlier he had been announced to play Iago with Edmund Kean. This, the dream of some years ago, now only made him angry. Kean was, of course, in the very last stages of decline and Macready had nothing to fear from him, but he attended a performance of Kean's *Hamlet* to reassure himself. He even surrendered his weekly holiday with his family to study his role. "It is worth the sacrifice," he wrote to Catherine, "of pleasure and feeling, if I can set myself in a strong position with the public, and if I cannot, at least to make as good a defensive battle as possible."[50]

On the twenty-second he reported for rehearsal, but went through it without the appearance of his former great rival. Finally, on the twenty-sixth, Kean came to rehearse, and in the evening they played together for the first time. The results were about what might have been expected: Kean resorted to foolish tricks to keep Macready from making his effects and Macready's nervousness prevented him from doing himself justice in a part for which he was thoroughly suited. At the conclusion of the performance, according to Bunn, Macready bounced into his office in a rage, declared that he would play no more with an actor who upstaged him, demanding "and pray what is the—next play you expect me to appear in—with that—low man?" Bunn, the happy go-between, carried the inquiry to Kean whom he found in his dressing room removing make-up with one hand and downing brandy with the other. Kean's reply was characteristically blunt, "How the——should I know what the——plays in?"[51]

Although the playbill for the first performance announced that on the Thursday Macready would appear as Othello to Kean's Iago, the alternation never took place. Instead, on the eleventh of December the bill equivocated:

Mr. Kean and Mr. Macready having on their fifth appearance together in Shakespeare's tragedy of *Othello,* attracted one of the most crowded audiences ever in the theatre, and their performance having been hailed with the loudest acclamations, they will repeat their celebrated parts of Othello and Iago on Thursday next; and will shortly afterwards alternate their respective characters.

Bunn's reckless technique as puff-maker was successful, and Macready was apparently resigned. On the tenth he noted in his *Diary* that he "Acted well when Kean did not interfere with me," and he even took some interest in the state of Kean's health. On the twenty-eighth he observed that the failing actor was quite strong on his legs and in his voice. But at least once during the series of performances Kean gave out, and Cooper was forced to take over Othello. On February 8, the two stars made their final appearance together, and Macready gave what he felt was one of his best performances. Three months later, he escorted the corpse of Kean to its grave and solemnly shook the hand of young Charles Kean who was destined to assume his father's place in Macready's disesteem.

During this season Macready's *Diaries* begin to be full of complaints about the conduct of Alfred Bunn. As Polhill's acting manager, he of course had full control of the business of the theatre; decisions as to repertory, engagements, advertisements, all rested with him. Macready's contract gave him £30 a week with, at the same time, leave to take a country engagement during Lent. This was a customary arrangement since the London theatres were still prohibited from performing dramas on certain nights during that season. A star actor customarily turned this enforced vacation to account by accepting a provincial engagement, thus materially increasing his income without relinquishing his position in the London theatre. On the fifth of January, 1833, the actor made a proposal to manage the Bristol and Bath theatres for a short season during the Lenten hiatus. But Bunn, not unnaturally, thought his own interests came first and was continually reluctant to set a date when Macready might consider himself free to go elsewhere, and this first managerial venture died unborn. Instead he undertook a brief acting tour, opening in Dublin.

Here he was once again in company with Miss Huddart, who played opposite him in *Tell, Macbeth,* and other plays, and related a tale which much displeased him. Miss Kenneth, now married to F——, had industriously circulated a tale that Macready had paid her "serious attention."[52] It is hard to say, judging from his often remarked ugliness, the rigid propriety of his behavior, and his irascible manner during rehearsals, wherein lay Macready's fascination for the young ladies of his profession. He was now forty years of age, but the attraction seemed to increase as he grew older. It was a situation that never failed to dismay him, though he was sometimes capable of joking about it. "What a fine fellow I must be," he wrote Catherine after a lady had betrayed her esteem. "Philander Macready. I think I shall put out an advertisement 'To be let on advantageous terms—a young gentleman, elegantly furnished. None but women desirous of being superlatively happy need apply. Grey hairs and other fixtures to be taken at a valuation.' "[53] Miss Kenneth was perhaps merely making trouble as she had during the last Dublin season, though her pique at the time might be set down to the coldness with which Macready received her attentions. And now Miss Huddart was clearly smitten with him.

Unfortunately for her, Macready was a devoted husband and she was not a womanly woman. Accompanying her and the Dublin manager to the port whence he would leave for England, he dined with them at a small inn and afterwards noted in his *Diary,* "How disenchanting in the female character is the manifestation of relish for the pleasures of the table!"[54] When he and Miss Huddart arrived in Manchester where they were to continue their engagement, he carefully put her into a cab and set out on foot to his own rooms. But by the end of the engagement, during which he had occasion to see Miss Huddart privately to give her advice and instruction, he notes with some relief that he is set free from a temptation.

"B—N *vs.* M———Y"

After a month of performances in the country, Macready returned to London to discover with some apprehension that Bunn had succeeded Polhill as lessee of Drury Lane. In the long line of directors of the English-speaking theatre from Philip Henslowe to the Shuberts, none was more consistently deplored than Alfred Bunn. Like most managers, his eye was glued to the main chance, and it was his misfortune that the public taste had become so vitiated (only in part through his own efforts) that spectacle, opera, claptrap farce, and melodrama were required to keep a theatre open. The English, he declared with some justice, "are an untheatrical people, and consequently when we support those establishments, it is not through any love of the art or profession practised within them, but from extraneous excitement held out to us as a temptation to enter them."[55]

The *Theatrical Times* calls him "the presiding genius of dramatic humbug, the great incarnation of managerial quackery," and sums up his career in these frank sentences:

His early *professional* (?) career was marked by nothing beyond an aptness for mimicry, which induced himself and friends to imagine he possessed abilities for the Stage and its direction; he married some time since, Miss Margaret Agnes Somerville, the actress, and shortly after that event took upon himself the management of the Birmingham Theatre. He was after this one of the seven managers of Drury Lane, and has intermitently [sic] figured as an author(?) and lessee ever since. He has continued during this career to enact such superlatively indecorous antics within the hallowed precincts of the temple of Melpomene, as threatened to restore the British drama to the enviable position it held in the time of Alleyn, the contemporary of Shakespeare, who occupied the post of bear-keeper to James I., in those enlightened days when it had to struggle for dignity and pre-eminence against its ursine competitors.[56]

Bunn's managerial practices were of the sort now accepted as normal by theatregoers throughout the world. Who is so foolish as to believe theatre "news"? But in the early days of the nineteenth century it was not wholly ethical to send such a communication as the following to the editor of a respectable newspaper:

DRURY LANE THEATRE. Crowded houses continue to witness *The Daughter of St. Mark* & the Pantomime—notwithstanding which, other novelties have been put into preparation, on Mr. Bunn's return from Berlin.

Drury Lane
Sunday

Dear Sir,
    I shall feel much obliged by getting the above in tomorrow's Herald

Always your obt
A. Bunn[57]

The classical plays, as far as he was concerned, could take care of themselves. Like Elliston, he was given to personal display and resounding rhetoric and he was happy to seek a public that would concur with his tastes. Macready was not alone in repudiating the result. Edward Fitzgerald describes a performance of *Macbeth* with "such a set of dirty ragamuffins as . . . could not disgrace any country barn. . . . The theatre is bare beyond anything I ever saw: and one begins to hope that it has touched the bottom of its badness, and will rise again."[58]

As an author, the talent so coyly questioned by the *Theatrical Times,* Bunn restricted himself largely to adaptations and to providing the librettos for such famous musical dramas as *The Bohemian Girl.* Bunn's librettos and lyrics are no worse than the average, but the average, of course, is not high. The *Theatrical Times* describes his lyrics as "the twaddle that any lack-a-daisical young gentleman might scribble in the albums of a feminine sentimentalist," and a poem dedicated to him by *Punch* was to assign him his Homeric epithet:

> Oh! to a book-stall quickly run,
> A dictionary get;
> And very likely, Poet Bunn,
> You may be happy yet.

"The man that can sacrifice the genius of Shakespeare," concludes the *Times,* "to the twang of a harpsichord, the turn of a note, or the pedal movement of a denuded danseuse, is necessarily supposed not to possess any very lofty status of classicality or intellectual and moral worth."

With these sentiments Macready would be in hearty concurrence. He confided in his *Diaries,* when informed that the erstwhile Rogue, the erstwhile Immensity, was now lessee of Drury Lane, "I know him to be destitute of honesty and honor, and from Mr. Reynolds' communication to-day he is evidently doubletongued; my policy is *Silence and Vigilance;* I can do without him, and must not yield to his schemes."[59]

These schemes involved an immediate reduction of the actors' yearly salaries, or by some other means obtaining financial terms more advantageous to the establishment. With this Macready would, of course, have nothing to do. He had labored long to establish his position, to attain his present rate of payment, and his sole ambition was to accumulate toward an early retirement. Silence and vigilance were his words—if Bunn attempted to refuse him just recompense, there was always Covent Garden, then in search of a lessee. John Cooper, the actor, and Frederick Reynolds, the theatrical writer and handyman, were urgent that Macready should undertake management, but he was reluctant, deciding to wait upon Bunn's first move. Other actors, frightened by the hint that Bunn's first move might be to become lessee at Covent Garden as well as Drury, added their pleas. But Macready was not yet ready, or driven, to so rash a course. On May 17 Reynolds wrote to inform him of what the profession had dreaded, that Alfred Bunn had outdone his old master, Elliston, the Great Lessee, and was now manager of both Drury Lane and Covent Garden. The unhappy event ushered in the age of the greatest artistic depression the English drama was to know.

On the first of June, while Macready was performing in Birmingham, the first blow fell. Cooper told him that Bunn had issued the expected manifesto on maximum salaries. The new manager was firmly convinced that high salaries had been the ruin of his predecessors and intended to return to the £20 a week offered by Henry Harris during Macready's early seasons in London. Although the actor had previously determined to take whatever came with calmness, the news destroyed his performance and gave him a sleepless night. However, Bunn later assured him that the manifesto did not apply to him, and in a conversation on the twelfth of June "seemed anxious to accede to all my proposals." After some confusion on both sides, the agreement was signed: £30 a week for two hundred consecutive nights, play or no play, the actor's services to be given wholly to the Drury Lane company, unless he chose to perform at Covent Garden.

Much of Macready's irritability and apprehensiveness in these preliminary skirmishes may have been due to his recognition that his career was perilously near a Center of Indifference. In several years of labor he had added only one new character to his permanent repertory. He must have novelty to continue to progress, to attract audiences. But not a novelty born of the taste and talent of Poet Bunn. So, in spite of the manager's reassuring behavior, Macready spent his summer in the never-ending search for new plays or new characters with which to add novelty to his attraction. In 1831 he had made an agreement with Knowles to adapt Beaumont and Fletcher's *Maid's Tragedy* for the nineteenth-century audience. A good part of the work was to be done by Macready, Knowles writing three scenes on speculation of receiving half the profits. The manager of that season, Captain Polhill, had rejected the manuscript, but now Macready pulled it out of his files and, since the author's fees from its performance would be a considerable addition to his income, set to work to make it acceptable to Bunn. He considered, for the fourth time, the possibilities of making Byron's *Sardanapalus* into an effective stage-play, and leafed through Voltaire and Massinger. Bunn was anxious to add *Lear* to his repertory, and the actor embarked on a systematic study of the role. On July 28 he wrote in his *Diaries:*

I have begun more seriously this month to apply to the study of my profession, impelled by the necessity which the present state of the drama creates. I do not feel that I have the talent to recall attention to art from which the amusement cannot be drawn but by an exertion of the intellect. The age is too indolent in part, and in part too highly cultivated. But while I see the desperate condition to which, at this late period of my life, my profession is reduced, I am not thereby inclined to let my spirits sink under the disheartening prospect. To do my best is still my duty to myself and to my children, and *I will do it.* I will contend while there is ground to stand on—even with neglect, the bitterest antagonist, and I will try to merit honours, if I cannot obtain them.

And with such desperate resolution he opened one of the unhappiest periods of his professional life.

The infelicities began at once.

While on a brief round of country appearances, he saw in *The Globe* newspaper that Bunn had announced him as Prospero for opening night. As far as the manager was concerned, *The Tempest* was a perfectly "legitimate" play and Prospero a proper role for his distinguished tragedian. But it was the Davenant-Dryden Prospero, a mere shadow of the Shakespearean original—and Macready could only sputter to himself. To fan his discontent he recollected that Bunn had cheated him of £200 during an engagement in Dublin, pleading insufficient receipts. But when he broached the subject of the debt, Bunn evaded neatly by pointing out that provincial managers—and he mentioned the elder McCready—were often "unfortunate." Two weeks later Bunn sent him the role of Ford in *The Merry Wives of Windsor* with instructions to prepare himself in it. Such a command decision, imposed without consulting the eminent tragedian, increased his rage; he composed a furious note to Cooper, the acting manager, thought twice and sent a substitute which coldly pointed out that he had never played the part. Having done so much, he sat down to read Ford through, and discovered to his surprise that he "did not dislike it." Shortly thereafter, on October 11, he wrote to his friend Gaspey, editor of the *Sunday Times,* "I am going to try if I can make anything of Ford:—I ought, but do not feel certain of myself."[60]

The season began well, with good houses. The company was inferior, the leading actress being a Mrs. Sloman, from the provinces, who failed to live up to her reputation (largely created by Bunn). Macready found her artificial and vulgar; her Belvidera in *Venice Preserved* was mere rant; her Mrs. Haller in *The Stranger* lacked imagination, feeling, and grace. She was of the old school of formal "tum-ti-tum" which Macready had abandoned, and she made little or no impression on London audiences. Yet she had the impudence—or the innocence—to thank Macready for his support. But he notes it was Bunn's tactic, however bad the performers, to cry "Send them on!" like old Thornton's "They must go forward!"[61] and Macready was forced to take a silent revenge. When he went to bed at Elm Place, he smiled to hear "Mrs. Sloman" lowing goodnight from his barn.

The irritations continued, the causes being sometimes obscured in the *Diary* by Macready's tendency to insert epithet instead of explanation. The part of Osmond in *The Castle Spectre* was sent him—"ugh! . trash!" is his first comment. After a rehearsal of *The Winter's Tale,* he discovered that no costume had been provided for him. The reworking of *The Maid's Tragedy,* now called *The Bridal,* was returned, without comment, by an underling of the manager's. "Mr. Bunn appears to be in a Malay humour, ready to run amok—pitiful wretch!"[62] *The Merry Wives* was postponed and *Antony and Cleopatra* substituted at the last moment. This was the final insult to his sense of responsibility to his art. As of November first, Macready decided to hold no more converse with the lessee, "he is such a blackguard, and so out of the pole of respectability," but to conduct his business through John Cooper—unfortunate Mr. Cooper!—the stage manager.[63] This mended matters very little.

During the run of the revival of *Antony and Cleopatra* the two opponents crossed swords over a question of the actor's health. On November 18 Macready became ill with a cold and soon developed such a hoarseness that Cooper sent for Bunn and advised him to postpone the opening. Bunn was rather suspicious of the illness, perhaps because Macready had been reluctant about undertaking the role. He offered to "shut up the theatre," but not to substitute another play. Macready furnished him thereupon with his doctor's certificate ordering him not to play for several days. Bunn gave him two days, and on the twenty-first *Antony* was performed with an ailing leading man, ridiculously insufficient rehearsal, and a haphazard production. Macready now proposed to Bunn, *via* Cooper, that "if he would for the next fortnight limit my performances to three nights per week I would try to go on without impeding the business"—if not, he would be guided by his doctor. The manager's only reply was "Is Mr. Macready disposed to give up half his salary for that fortnight?"[64]

Macready's reaction was to attempt to resign his engagement with a forfeit, to which Bunn replied "in a friendly tone," refusing to give up the engagement and promising to consult his wishes in the future. "All this," declares Macready, "is mere froth, and the froth of a venomed dog, too; he has been mighty in his promises before, and they have only been means of alluring me to cajolement. Henceforth *I put no trust in him whatever.*"

Bunn was now determined that Macready should be given a part which he could not cavil at, even though it should primarily serve the manager's purposes. Earlier in the season Macready had been contemplating the possibilities of *Sardanapalus;* Bunn now proposed a production with a grand spectacular conflagration scene. And Macready was silenced. His only complaint, and he kept it to himself, was that the play was injudiciously cut; but he fell to studying it, after checking with the original to see just what had happened. The arrangement was by Frederick Reynolds, an old hand at this sort of carpentry, and, as far as Bunn was concerned, it was thoroughly satisfactory. "It was admirably arranged by him," he says; "and it is no easy task to reduce so much radiance into one focus, that should dazzle, but should not blind."

For a month Macready studied the part in silence, finding that it did not grow upon him, that it was heavy; in the meantime playing a variety of roles, and fretting over the conduct of the "blackguard" Bunn and his "sottish" assistants. On the fourth of January, 1834, however, he seems to have made a kind of New-Year resolution:

The necessity of rising still in my profession, and of gaining suffrages to my reputation, presented itself so strongly to my mind, that I determined, contrary to my original intention, of offering such benefit as my advice could yield towards the play *Sardanapalus* and of doing my best to make the play successful, which notwithstanding I have hope of effecting.

He immediately set to work to cut and revise Reynolds' work and took the opportunity on January 7 of offering suggestions at rehearsal. This effectively stopped proceedings. Stage Manager Cooper could not understand him, being, as Macready says, "as capable of directing the mise-en-scène of a play as a man devoid of information, industry, genius, or talent may be supposed to be." Finally Bunn, determined to be conciliatory (or perhaps recognizing that Macready had a genuine talent for this sort of thing), turned the manuscript over to him and told him to alter it as he pleased.

After some further days of work, the approaching Easter holidays required the entire attention of the theatre to be concentrated on the traditional pantomime and *Sardanapalus* dropped temporarily from sight. Macready had time now to devote himself to several projects of his own: to consult with various actors about the possibility of "elevating the profession"—that is, assuming management of a theatre; and to erect a memorial to Mrs. Siddons in Westminster Abbey, a scheme to which he was passionately devoted. He heard of Fanny Kemble's success in America, but explained it on the grounds of her retirement and approaching marriage to an American. He took considerable delight in recording scandalous gossip about Charles Kean and his co-star Ellen Tree (which several editors of the *Diaries* have not seen fit to reprint, although a theatrical paper of the time openly demanded to be told why she did not *"become his sleeping partner"*).[65] Forced to call at Bunn's home on business, he was annoyed to notice the "Turkey carpet, damask curtains, liqueurs and cake on the sideboard, easy chairs," luxuries which he felt had been purchased at his expense, that is to say, out of the moneys owing him from the past. Bunn further entertained him with witticisms about Knowles, referring to one of his plays as *The Blind Bugger of Bethnal Green;* and declared that his endeavor at the present time was to get his theatrical venture established as a going concern, and *then* he would give "the drama" its chance. *"Yes!!!"* is all Macready had to say.[66]

Early in March he was in Dublin on his Lenten round of provincial engagements. Miss Huddart was at once at hand to soothe spirits troubled by his professional difficulties and his growing conviction that the cause of the drama was hopeless. On the seventh of March he sat the whole evening with her, and hastens to justify either his waste of time or the possibility of compromising himself. "I was so low-spirited that nothing but the presence of female society could soothe my fretful state of mind." And a few days later, "It is a sort of repose to my mind and spirits to lounge away a few hours in the society of an agreeable woman." The effect of female society is demonstrated in the cool tone of a letter to Cooper dated the same day, March 9:

In reply to your favour of the 4th inst. communicating to me Mr. Bunn's wish to produce Sardanapalus on Easter Monday, I have little observation to offer, and question my right to intrude any. The attempt to produce a tragedy, in which the principals rehearse for the first time together on the morning of representation, and in which one of them has never seen a scene set, a supernumerary placed, nor the dress and properties he is to use, we can only suppose justified in Mr. Bunn's mind by some dependant arrangements, which he does not think himself called upon to disclose.—I have no wish to interpose objection, which the letter of my engagement would not fully warrant, and therefore make up my mind to do the best I can under the circumstances. . . .
Respecting the substitution of Richard III on Easter Monday (as about to be recommended by you) my own interest and reputation being therein involved, I beg to state, that as I have not done the part in London these two years and a half, I should not *look at* nor *think of anything* else, until I had played it, in which case Sardanapalus *must* wait.—that I could not act [Richard] without two rehearsals—nor without proper dresses; the one made for me having gone the round of the Theatre on every occasion since; I should certainly require a refitting in the character, the expense of which I am sure its production would not repay.[67]

His intention in this letter, he confided to his *Diary,* was "not to let Mr. Bunn have an opportunity of saying I thwart him; if he wishes to ruin the little chance belonging to *Sardanapalus,* I do not feel that I have the right to stop him; at any rate it is not worth a contest."
In the meantime, Bunn's plans for his production of *Sardanapalus* had been suddenly altered by a letter from Paris signed by Charlotte Mardyn, an actress of some decades past who had flamed into notoriety when she was (falsely) credited with causing the rupture between Byron and his wife. Miss Mardyn assured the manager that she had received the part of Myrrha *viva voce* from the author's own lips, and that Byron had always wished "that the Greek girl's sandals should be worn by *me.*"[68] In the face of such ready-made publicity Bunn could not be expected to hesitate. Ellen Tree, who was to have played Myrrha, was relieved of her assignment and the new casting was announced. Its effect upon Macready could be anticipated. "The nasty motives," he wrote April 3, "which actuate Bunn in thus presenting to the public a woman, who with youth and beauty to arrest attention was never

able to retain it, merely because some suspicion may be circulated of her connexion with Lord Byron, only confirms the disgusting character of the man. His ignorance of the drama, his utter disregard of its interests and respectability, his wish to attract a house by any empirical advertisement, however disgraceful, are so undeniable, that one passes by him and his actions, as we would the most offensive nuisance which the negligence of the police has overlooked." And certainly the upshot of the present affair more than justified Macready's judgment. In response to a series of inquiries about dates of arrival in England, and times of rehearsal, Bunn received from "Miss Mardyn" reports of illness, equivocations, and postponements until he decided that he was the victim of a hoax perpetrated (for a reason unspecified) by William Dimond, who was pursuing a dissolute career in Paris. On the seventh of April, when Macready reported to rehearse *Sardanapalus,* Bunn showed him the letters and confessed that he suspected a humbug. Macready asked him what he would do if Miss Mardyn should appear and proved unpresentable. Bunn's answer was typical: "Kick her arse, and send her back again!"

When Miss Mardyn's final letter arrived during rehearsal on April 9, begging that the performance be no longer delayed on her account, Bunn was in something of a quandary. Ellen Tree declared that since the part had been peremptorily taken from her she would not resume it. "Punch has no feelings," was Bunn's happy quotation as he sent for her and declared that she had no choice but to act. Macready, witnessing the whole affair with distant disapproval, advised her to take the part and she submitted. After two rehearsals only, *Sardanapalus* made its appearance, a prospect that would horrify any modern actor even more than it horrified Macready, who had taken the final attitude, as he declared in a letter to Cooper, "If Mr. Bunn chooses to play *Sardanapalus* . . . he does it at his own risk—I shall not attempt to expostulate upon the proceeding."[69] *Sardanapalus* justified all of Bunn's machinations. Largely because of the spectacular final conflagration, it was performed twenty-three times to good houses, and to the intense boredom of its leading man.

The boredom was apparently not communicated to the audience, but the more critical sympathized with him. The diarist Crabbe Robinson comments, "Macready is most unfitted to represent the indolent voluptuary—he is a man of rigid earnestness of character in his features and air. Though he threw off a good deal of his nature, he could not qualify himself for the part by art; but the character itself is not in nature, it is a mere apology for certain habits and feelings which with egoistic speculation Lord Byron wished to present to the public."[70]

Macready now began to look forward to his benefit, for which he had exacted, as he thought, specific commitments from Bunn, and which was important to him this year not only for the profit it might bring him but because it was to be his first metropolitan performance of *King Lear.* There were, of course, immediate difficulties with the manager, and, since Macready writes of them at length, we are permitted to see how complicated a matter the making of a benefit had become. As the expenses would be £200 or more for the evening, it was necessary to attract a crowded house to realize a maximum profit, and benefit-building was an art which Macready had perfected over the years. With all the resources of Covent Garden *and* Drury Lane at his command, the present benefit, including his initial Lear, should be an unparalleled triumph. But there was always Bunn to reckon with.

The actor wished the Covent Garden ballet to perform. Bunn refused on the grounds that they were needed in that theatre. Then he conceded that Macready might have them between the acts of *Lear,* an offer which the tragedian found "unintelligible." Carlotta Grisi, the ballerina, was available between 7:30 and 8:45, "which if she brought me £500 I would not accept," since this would also be an interruption in the play. Benefit or no benefit, *Lear* was to be the feature of the program. Braham was engaged to sing, but H. Phillips, his reliable accompanist, was engaged elsewhere. The worries mounted, along with the conviction that Bunn was not playing him fair. Once he nearly resigned his benefit, but Bunn gave ground and on the twenty-third of May, Macready performed *Lear* to a crowded and enthusiastic house, which was afterwards regaled by Braham and by the comic opera of *The Lord of the Manor.* Bunn, in an apparent attempt to demonstrate his good will, even informed Macready that he had made a point of asking Westmacott, editor of *The Age,* to "be civil" to the performance, a statement which Macready records without comment.

During the summer and fall of 1834 Macready confined his appearances to the country while negotiations for the renewal of his contract with Bunn were going on. Bunn had acquired some new and cheaper, and perhaps more tractable, talent in Vandenhoff and Denvil, steady second-raters, and his offer to Macready— whatever it may have been—was unacceptable. Macready therefore made the best of his time in the country, experimenting with a play, making contacts with authors, and venturing for the first time into the manager's chair.

In Dublin he supervised the first performance of his long-considered adaptation, *The Bridal*. The conditions for its production, except in that it took place far from the London critics, were hardly ideal. Calcraft, the manager, was careless and unbusinesslike; many of the actors were unfitted for their roles. In desperation, Macready took Miss Allison aside and drilled her in the role of Aspatia, but the next day he was unable to remain in his seat at the prompt table, she was "so ineffective." The only other actress in the company who could be assigned the role proved to be a slow study, and *The Bridal* went on with Miss Allison, Macready conducting the rehearsals in a progressively worsening temper. On the day of performance, he discovered that the scene plot he had so carefully drawn up had been discarded, that a set he had intended for Act II was used for Act I, and that the scenes provided were shabby and ill-matched. Needless to say, he gave his first reading of Melantius in a distraught frame of mind, forgetting his opening lines, and failing to arouse the wild enthusiasm he had hoped from the audience. But the play went well enough and was reviewed in a friendly fashion by the local newspapers, which Macready lost no time in sending to Bunn.

In Dublin, he seized the chance to become better acquainted with Edward Bulwer, who was making a considerable reputation for himself as a novelist. He asked him directly to write a play for him; Bulwer replied that he had already tried his hand in the form, that he had written a play on the death of Cromwell but, for some reason, claimed to have lost most of it. The two men were friends at once, and remained so for many years, their friendship ripening into an artistic partnership of considerable importance to each. But at the moment Bulwer had no play for him, and Macready had to be content with a tragedy called *The Provost of Bruges*, by George W. Lovell, which he read with "interest, emotion, and pleasure." His first impression of the play was most favorable, though of course he was unwilling to trust a first impression.

When he arrived home on December 28, he sent for Lovell and went through the manuscript with him scene by scene, suggesting changes and rendering a "candid opinion on the merits of his play." Lovell listened attentively to all his mentor had to say and assented readily to every proposal. The result, produced in the following season, was one of the more respectable plays of the half century.

Macready continued on his tour, playing variously at Lincoln, Boston, and other stations on Robertson's circuit. At Louth, on

November 29, Mr. Robertson discovered how much of his father the actor had in him. The theatre was a converted courtroom, "not the worst" Macready had seen. When he had finished dressing in the magistrate's chambers, he went out to find Robertson looking solemn. That could mean only one thing. " 'Bad house?' 'Bad, Sir, there's no one!' 'What, nobody at all?' 'Not a soul, sir—except the Warden's party in the boxes.' 'What the d——l! Not one person in the pit or gallery?' 'Oh, yes. There are one or two.' 'Are there five?' 'Oh, yes, five.' 'Then go on; we have no right to give ourselves airs, if the people do not choose to come and see us; go on at once!!" And on they went, and Macready never acted Virginius better in his life.

While still in Dublin, Macready had signed an agreement with a provincial manager named Woulds to manage in partnership a short winter season at the theatres in Bath and Bristol. It was neither an important nor a happy speculation, but its brief history gives a miniature picture of Macready the manager, a picture which needs only magnifying to suggest his later direction of the two National theatres. He was indefatigable in hiring stars and arranging for attractive programs. He even sent to Bunn for permission to use certain material in his possession, and to employ Ellen Tree and William Farren. Nor was he backward in announcing what he had to offer. The playbills (worthy of Bunn) began:

A COMBINATION OF TALENT *without precedent in this or any theatre out of the Metropolis, and at present defying competition on the part of the London Theatres.*

From Macready's point of view, the statement was no exaggeration. If Maria Lovell, and E. F. Saville, and such players as Stuart and Munro had their equals in London, what metropolitan theatre could advertise Macready?

He did his earnest best to make the venture successful. He played the round of his favorite roles, got up spectacular afterpieces like John Kemble's *Lodoiska;* rehearsed the standard plays with care, restaging them according to his own ideas; fretted over the imperfectness of the actors; was disturbed when the audience received Saville's ranting and Stuart's face-making as enthusiastically as his own acting "in the best taste." Almost at once, too, he began to regret his commitment to Woulds. By January 7, 1835, he was convinced that the attempt was a "mistake-blunder-folly." He would give £300 to be released. Though Woulds reported a satisfactory balance at the end of the first week, and an old gentleman talked reasonably about the next season making up present losses, he vowed firmly, "If they catch me in this hateful occupation again may all its worst consequences fall on me!"[71] The end of the second week was equally promising, the box-sheet, which recorded advance reservations, was an omen of future success, and the house on the fifteenth was good. But his heightened hopes took a tumble, on the seventeenth, when he overheard a woman saying to the ticket-seller that Macready and Dowton might be good actors but she wanted something entertaining for children: "When will *Aladdin* be done?"[72] And as the days went on and the houses fell off, his temper grew worse, his associates more vicious. "The connection with this theatre in Bath," he wrote on March second, "seems to have brought back my mind to its former littleness; I feel disgusted with the beings in connection with me and ashamed of myself." He was convinced that he was "paying everybody concerned, even to that *sot*, Mr. Woulds," by his own unrequited labor. His first try as a manager was a failure, and he had no choice, though many misgivings, but to sign an agreement for the following season at Drury Lane with Alfred Bunn.

In spite of Bunn's objections, he held out for his own terms, £30 a week for not more than four nights of performances, half the proceeds of a benefit, *The Bridal* to be produced at the usual rates, and a three-week vacation during Lent. Bunn's chief protest was that the actor insisted on being subject to no fine or forfeit, an "outrageous stipulation" he called it. "The natural question," he wrote later, "arising out of a perusal of this precious document, is, why was a person making such stipulations, engaged? He would come on no other terms; if therefore he was not engaged, there would be an outcry upon the town! if he was, the 'outcry' would be, as it was, all the manager's."[73] If this is not a very convincing explanation of Bunn's yielding to Macready's "outrageous stipulation" there is another and possibly better one. Bunn had signally failed in operating the two theatres together. Covent Garden was no longer under his control. He must once more be heedful of competition; the Vandenhoffs and Denvils would be poor ammunition to use if Macready were to go to the other house. As for *The Bridal*, when he told Macready that the play seemed to be the actor's particular pet, he got the frank answer, "No; that I wished to make it a means of remuneration without loading the theatre with additional salary, and I only regarded it as additional to my income."[74] *The Provost of Bruges* was to be produced, and *Ion* (a new play written for Macready by Talfourd) would be considered. Ellen Tree and Mrs. Yates were available for leading roles and Miss Huddart, whom Macready had urged upon Bunn, would therefore not be required. The arrangements seemed to be favorable to Macready, if he could be sure of Bunn's keeping to them. But he undertook the engagement with reluctance, and with a curious foreboding. It was "the season which will decide my fortune." Apparently he felt he would be able to retire if all went well, but he was ill at ease.

The opening night, October first, went badly. He tried, perhaps too hard, to perform Macbeth in his best manner, but the result was told him when his three closest friends, Talfourd, Forster, and Wallace, came round to his dressing room at the close with never a word of congratulation. He was desperate. "The stake of my future life was upon it, for speedy profit, or, perhaps, poverty, and it is lost!" His nights were sleepless. Over-conscious of himself, he rehearsed badly, was nervous in performance, and spent the weekend in misery with a dejected wife and a weeping sister. But the papers were surprisingly kind; he took new resolution, and on the Monday Wallace made a point of congratulating him on his performance of Jaques. The consequence was that, confidence regained, he so carried the audience with him in a repetition of *Macbeth* that Talfourd declared he had "never seen me finer, if indeed I had ever played it so well."[75]

Mr. Bunn, determined to keep the respect of the critics who were concerned about the legitimate drama as well as of the popular audiences who were interested only in display, announced grandiloquently in his bills:

The public is respectfully requested to take notice, that notwithstanding the immense success of the grand military spectacle of Cavaliers and Roundheads, and without any regard to the great expense incurred in its production, the lessee has made arrangement for its performance as an afterpiece, in order that there may be no impediment to the continuous representation of the standard works of the British Stage.[76]

As further proof of his honest intentions, he insisted on a performance of *Othello* on the twenty-first of October (although Macready was unwilling to undertake it at such short notice) and received this accolade from the *Times:*

It appears from the manner in which the various characters were allotted, that it was the intention of the manager to bring all his resources to bear upon this representation. One marked proof of this was that the part of Emilia was filled by Miss Ellen Tree.[77]

It was apparently one of Macready's finest performances, and Bunn marked it for frequent repetition until *The Siege of*

Rochelle, an opera by Balfe, swept all before it, and *Othello* and Bunn's pretensions to legitimacy disappeared together.

The manager now suggested that Macready take the leading male role in *The Jewess,* an operatic spectacle which was to be the next offering of the theatre. But Macready declined it as melodramatic, and the part was assigned to Vandenhoff who, until that time, had had to content himself with secondary leads. *The Jewess* was first performed on November 16, in combination with the sixteenth representation of *The Siege of Rochelle.* "Mr. Vandenhoff," commented the *Times,* on the twenty-third, "plays the part of Eleazer so infinitely better than we supposed him capable of playing any part, that the public have reason, not to regret, but to rejoice, that Mr. Macready was so mistaken as to suppose the character unworthy the exercise of his capabilities, which, though generally, of far greater compass than Mr. Vandenhoff's would we think, have failed to make the Jew, in his person, half as effective as Mr. Vandenhoff makes it."[78] The two spectacles appear continuously in the bills until December 26, when *The Siege* was played for the forty-ninth time, *The Jewess* for the thirty-fourth, and the annual Christmas pantomime, *Dick Whittington,* was added for good measure. The performance began at 6:30 in the evening and concluded at one the next morning.

At first Macready was not unappreciative of Bunn's achievement. *"The Jewess,"* he wrote "is the most gorgeous pageant I have ever seen on an English stage—beyond all reach of comparison. The acting was up to the spectacle mark of old times, when I have seen Terry, Wallack, etc." But by the twenty-first of November he begins to be a-weary of the sun and longs for the footlights. Musing over his situation, he feels the peculiarity of being interdicted from appearances during the greater part of the season "and all the hopes of profit from new characters, upon the strength of which I made this engagement, utterly falsified." By January he had made up his mind that he must continue upon the stage for five years longer and then try America. In the meantime, though Bunn was paying him a weekly salary for remaining idle, he accepted an engagement in Bristol.

Returning to London on the twenty-ninth of January, Macready received a note from Cooper informing him that, since he had not presented himself to perform the task, "I undertook to read the Tragedy of *The Bridal* [to the actors] myself, and have now to inform you that it will positively be produced on Tuesday next, and rehearsed every morning at 12 o'clock until that day."[79] Next day, Cooper came in person to report that the first rehearsal had been completed, that Ellen Tree had been cast as Aspatia, and Mrs. Sloman as Evadne. He, Cooper, thought the play shocking, and James Warde, a fellow actor, concurred, and Ellen Tree would, he was sure, have thrown the part of Evadne in his face had it been offered her. But Macready heard nothing beyond the name of Mrs. Sloman, on which Bunn, who was certainly unhappy over his bargain to produce *The Bridal,* may have calculated. In reply to the actor's demand for compensation for the violation of the agreement that he was to be consulted in the casting of the piece, Cooper declared, "I am instructed to offer £33 6s 8d, and to withdraw the play." This Macready indignantly scorned, and the unhappy Cooper was forced to continue, "Well, then, I am desired to ask you upon whose authority you went to Bristol." This was, naturally, too much for the exasperated actor. "Upon my own!" he cried, and informed Cooper that the question was a gross impertinence. The interview ended with harsh words on both sides.

Next day came a letter from Cooper demanding to know when Macready would be ready to appear in *The Provost of Bruges.* Bunn was apparently determined to get the Macready plays over in a hurry. But the actor was not to be hurried; he would inform Cooper in two or three days when he expected to be ready. In the meantime, his salary for the past week had not been paid and he desired it might be immediately.

Cooper's answer was not calculated to make matters smoother:

By absenting yourself without any permission (from Saturday Jany 16th to Wednesday Jany 27th,) when your services were required, & could not be used owing to such absence, you violated your engagement with Mr. Bunn, who, as some slight compensation, ordered your salary to be stopped for that period of one week, & a half—but if you are disposed to render your best assistance to the management in a more harmonious manner than your recent correspondence would lead him to believe, Mr. Bunn will have great pleasure in remitting this stoppage.[80]

Macready's written reply to this was so abrupt that Cooper came in person with a conciliatory offer from Bunn, and a reasonable complaint about having to do all the manager's "dirty work."

Macready resumed his engagement on February 3, as Othello, the first legitimate play at Drury in three months, and began intensive rehearsals of *The Provost of Bruges,* performed for the first time on the tenth. Lovell's play is a good one, although based on a typical dramatic absurdity. The law of Bruges decrees that any person marrying the child of a serf becomes himself a serf.

At the time of the action, the law has conveniently fallen into neglect and the serf Bertulfe has risen to the post of confidential advisor to the Earl of Flanders. Bertulfe, Macready's character, is a truly heroic figure:

> Regard him as he is!
> Think of the arm that saved the state in war—
> The wisdom that has sway'd its peaceful councils.
> View the proud step that spurns the lowly earth,—
> The untam'd eye, whose fire no years can quench;—
> Hark to the voice, whose music wraps the soul.

This heroic figure has a daughter Constance to whom he is devoted, after the manner of *Virginius*. There is something very pleasant in her lover's description of her:

> Beauty to shame young love's most fervent dream,—
> Virtue, to form a saint, and reign in heaven,—
> With just enough earth to keep her a woman!

There is, too, *Virginius*-like, a villain Thancmar, who succeeds in evoking the old law at a critical point in the development of the love plot, thus thwarting the lovers and causing the suicide of Bertulfe. It is not much of a story, thus baldly synopsized, but, considered in its dramatic form, it seldom fails to hold the attention and in several scenes is poignant and exciting.

The play seemed at first to be attaining its deserved success; audiences liked it; newspapers were laudatory, and Forster, Talfourd, and Macready's new friend Robert Browning complimented him highly on his performance, while remaining somewhat reserved about the play itself. On the twentieth came a note from Bunn declaring that he must withdraw *The Provost* if the author's terms were not reduced—Macready having stipulated that Lovell should receive £20 a night. Lovell, with an author's eagerness to keep his child alive, proposed to cut the royalty in half which, since this was also the figure Bunn had in mind, was agreed to. On the eighth night Bunn withdrew the play, although Lovell was willing to allow it to be performed gratuitously. Bunn's reason was that it was losing money and he gave figures to show that it never earned the expenses of £220 a night. According to Macready, Bunn wanted the *Provost* costumes for a new spectacle, *Chevy Chase*.

Without prejudice in favor of Macready, it would seem that his explanation is the correct one. This was Bunn's year for spectacle —*The Jewess* was still drawing houses, Auber's *Bronze Horse* was a new operatic success, and the "grand chivalric entertainment" of

Chevy Chase might well run forever. On the other hand, he was paying Macready a weekly salary for infrequent and ill-attended appearances. Operating on the theory, well-grounded in the light of audience behavior, that anything would sell if the quantity or the price was right, he decided to try a combination of tragedy and spectacle, with the tragic portion of the bill occupying a secondary position as the afterpiece. Not only was Macready announced to play *William Tell* as an afterpiece to Malibran in *Zampa*, but Cooper, planning his own benefit, was emboldened to request him to perform *2 Henry IV* as an afterpiece. Macready denied Cooper out of hand, but the performance of *Tell* had already been announced. To this indignity, therefore, he submitted with reluctance:

The proceeding is unjustifiable and without precedent in all my experience—I ought not even conditionally to agree to it, and *only upon a direct guarantee that it shall not recur during my engagement, will I consent for this night,* merely to prevent further embarrassment.

If Mr. Bunn gives through you such an undertaking, I will attend the performance;—if not, *I positively decline appearing.*[81]

The "undertaking" Bunn gave, though not without reluctance, and Macready went through with the odious task, taking particular pains with his role, and was both gratified and surprised to discover that the audience did not leave until the very end and that those who remained after the fall of the curtain summoned him back for a call and cheered him enthusiastically.

Macready next had difficulties with his manager over the subject of his benefit. He had determined upon a first performance of *Ion* with Ellen Tree as the leading woman, and had requested Cooper to play Ctesiphon. Using the argument that Macready had refused him, Cooper refused—and Bunn backed him up. The state of Bunn's mind is revealed by a note scrawled on the back of a communication from Macready to Cooper. "Pray do not trouble me," he begins, "with any more of Mr. Macready's long-winded letters." He admits that stars have always been permitted to refuse to play on benefit nights, but he feels that this should be reformed, on "principle." He further exonerates Cooper from blame for refusing to play for "one who refused to play his best part for you." And he adds gratuitously that if Macready refuses to play his principal characters at half-price he is considering a plan to "reduce the prices on the 'off' nights of Malibran, and play him through his range of business."[82]

The final conflict began when Bunn, who knew only too well what he was doing, appended a notice to the playbill for April 27: "*On Friday,* the Three First Acts of RICHARD III. Duke of Glo'ster, Mr. Macready, with the First Act of CHEVY CHASE. And THE JEWESS." He justified himself later by declaring that his sole aim was to diversify the program and keep within reasonable time limits, and justly pointed out that Macready himself had, on his benefit nights, produced "scraps" of Shakespeare, one act of *2 Henry IV* for instance, and had combined *Rob Roy* and *Henry V*, and *The Lord of the Manor* and *Lear.* On Macready's side it should be said that things were permitted on a benefit that neither audiences nor actors would tolerate in regular performances, that to be given a portion of a play to act was as great an insult as to be forced into an afterpiece, and (perhaps strongest argument of all) Macready's Richard was as notoriously deficient in the first three acts as it was a triumphant success in the last two.

Macready was at first inclined to go on and ask the audience whether they would have the mutilated play, or the complete version—but his contract seemed to leave him no choice but to submit. Next he thought of resigning his engagement, but as that meant forfeiting £250, he decided against it. During the rehearsals even those actors who had suffered from his tempestuous demands for perfection expressed indignation at Bunn's behavior, and his old enemy, Charles Kemble, called it a scandalous and insulting procedure.

On the twenty-ninth of April, the day of the performance, Macready was still wretched and undecided in his mind. His pride as an actor and his spirit as an artist revolted against performing in mutilated Shakespeare, but there seemed nothing he could do. He tortured his way through a rehearsal, hearkened to commisseration on every side, and tried to concentrate, without much success, on the part of Richard. The performance, was, of course, not good,—"tetchy and unhappy, [I] pushed through the part in a sort of desperate way as well as I could."[83]

At the end of the third act, leaving the stage filled with feelings of shame, anger, and desperation, he began to make his way back to his dressing room. In this unhappy frame of mind he passed the door of Bunn's office, and in a fit of temper, threw it open. The manager was sitting at his desk checking bills, previous (he piously affirmed) to their payment the following morning. Without thought of the consequences, and overcome at last by the family temper which had hounded him all his life, Macready rushed upon his tormentor, crying "You damned scoundrel! How dare you use me in this manner!" The manager jumped up to meet him and received a back-handed slap on the face. Under a second blow Bunn went down with a black eye and a sprained ankle (he was accustomed to write, he explains quaintly, with his leg twined around his chair), bedaubed with blood, lamp oil, and ink, and with Richard III on top of him. "On my naturally inquiring if he meant to murder me, and on his replying in the affirmative," wrote Bunn, "I made a struggle for it."[84] It was over in a moment. Bunn threw off the actor, seized him by the collar, wrestled him about the room, and forced him down on the sofa where he got Macready's little finger into his mouth and bit it. Then he screamed "Murder" loudly enough to summon the prompter, a scene-painter, and the call boy. The contestants were hauled apart without much difficulty, and Macready was hustled off to his room where his friends removed him from the theatre, and took him home for a cup of tea and such words of cheer as he, suffering agonies of shame, would listen to.

They were scarcely out of the theatre before Bunn summoned a physician, a surgeon, and a lawyer, and sent a policeman for his assailant, but too late.[85] For three weeks the manager ostentatiously kept to his quarters, appearing at rehearsals at the end of that time with equal ostentation on a pair of crutches. Macready, for his part, was in the tortures of self-abasement. The terms which he formerly reserved for his enemies and rivals in his *Diary*, he now applied to himself. Reading by accident Johnson's *Life of Savage*, he was horrified by the thought that he might have murdered Bunn, though from all accounts Bunn seems to have been more than holding his own when they were interrupted. Going about his business he took a coach that he might not have to look pedestrians in the eye. Even in his own club, the Garrick, he did not venture to speak to anyone who did not address him first. He was sickened by placards for *The Age* newspaper, which read: "Great fight. B--n and M------y." "The fair fame of a life," he wrote, "has been sullied by a moment's want of self-command." He could hope only that his sons, reading his *Diary*, might take warning by his weakness and *"Keep their passions under due restraint—the* first means of happiness, the best worldly effect of wisdom."

Macready's sensitivity to the rules of gentlemanly conduct more than paid for his rash act. And he discovered to his relief that his valued friends did not turn from him, but rather drew closer. The press, except for the scandal sheets, was generously silent; strangers

went out of their way to encourage him. Almost at once, Osbaldiston, the manager of Covent Garden, offered an engagement
which Macready was not too far gone in misery to bargain over,
while Bunn wrote that he considered Macready's Drury Lane
engagement *"cancelled and determined"* by the *"attempt to assas-
sinate"* him. Meeting Kemble in the Garrick Club, Macready
drew him to one side and delivered himself of a formal speech of
thanks for his attitude towards "this unfortunate affair." Upon
Kemble's replying that he had ever cherished friendly feelings
towards Macready, they both drew off their gloves and shook hands
on the spot. It was a highly emotional scene, which Macready
promptly had misgivings about—he feared he had "acted on
impulse in a matter that should have been only deliberated on"—
but since he was now to be a fellow-player with Kemble, it was
just as well that they should commence friends.

On May 11, 1836, Macready began his brief engagement at
Covent Garden with *Macbeth*. As he made his entrance, over the
rustic bridge on the blasted heath, the whole audience rose to its
feet, cheering, and waving hats and handkerchiefs in the air. The
acclamation was so loud and prolonged, in fact, that it rather upset
him in the early moments of his portrayal, but the obviously
friendly nature of the reception soon provoked him to do his
best; he made his "points," and felt that he had never been so
real or "altogether better." The fall of the curtain was the signal
for another tumult from the audience, who plainly intended to
show the actor that they were on his side. After some confusion,
he came before them with a curtain speech, the composition of
which had cost him some soul-searching in the preceding days.
"Ladies and gentlemen," he began,

Under ordinary circumstances I should receive the manifestation of
your kindness with silent acknowledgement; but I cannot disguise from
myself the fact that the circumstances which have led to my engagement
at this theatre, after an absence of many years, are uppermost in your
minds. Into these circumstances I will not enter further than by two
general observations: first, that I was subjected in cold blood, from
motives which I will not characterize, to a series of studied and annoying and mortifying provocations, personal and professional. The
second, that, suffering under these accumulated provocations, I was
betrayed, in a moment of unguarded passion, into an intemperate and
imprudent act, for which I feel, and shall never cease to feel, the
deepest and most poignant self-reproach and regret. It is to you, ladies
and gentlemen, and to myself, that I owe this declaration, and I make
it with an unaffected sincerity. To liberal and generous minds, I think,
I need say no more. I cannot resist thanking you.[86]

AN END TO STROLLING

The matter did not, of course, end there. Bunn's suit for damages, which Macready refused to contest, ended in an award of £150 to the plaintiff. The trial was of intense interest to the theatrical population of London, who crowded the courtroom and the lobby outside to hear Bunn's lawyer, Thesiger, summon the evidence for premeditation and Talfourd's witty and eloquent defense (would a man undertake a premeditated assassination while encumbered with the hump of Richard III?). Although the actor was quite prepared for a verdict of £1000 against him, he had soon sufficiently separated his sense of guilt from his instinct of acquisitiveness to such a point that his friend Talfourd became in his eyes first a man who lacked the moral courage to defend him, then a clog hung by destiny around his fortunes, and finally a poor, pitiful creature. Thesiger fared worse. Although Macready's sense of shame had caused him to order Talfourd to make no defense, he was deeply injured when Mr. Thesiger said openly in court the very things he was privately accusing himself of. Thesiger is referred to throughout the *Diaries* in the most uncomplimentary terms, and he becomes at last a synonym for blackguard. A year does not pass without reference to the "day of wrath" and the misery he still felt in remembering it, but his behavior over Bunn's suit for damages is an illustration of that combination, not entirely peculiar to Macready, of high moral principles and a low boiling point.

In the course of his Covent Garden engagement he was to perform Talfourd's *Ion* for his benefit on May 26. The play had been on his mind for several years, he had worked it over with care in anticipation of its eventual production. A somewhat stiff classical tragedy, he considerably quickened its tempo by skillful cutting, simplified and made more direct the frequent obscurities of the plot, and carefully eliminated every reference to the youth of his own character. "Macready played *Ion* admirably," said the critic for the *News and Sunday Herald* on May 29. "His appearance is not indeed sufficiently juvenile, but his acting amply atoned for this physical disqualification." The role of the orphan who single-handed triumphs over tyranny and oppression was, of course, simply *William Tell* in a chlamys, and well suited to the Macready style. In his curtain speech, an indulgence which was becoming habitual, he thanked his audience and hinted that "This might be perhaps the last new play" in which he would appear before them.

This was the first overt announcement of his long and secretly cherished plans for retirement, although rumors to that effect had been circulating for some time. He was happy to hear cries of "No, no!" from the assembly. He was made even happier by a supper celebrating the event at the Talfourds' home, where he met Wordsworth, Landor, the painter Clarkson Stanfield, young Robert Browning, and Ellen Tree—the leading lady who shared in the triumph of *Ion*—a company which so elevated his spirits that he was even able to pass a joking word to Miss Mitford, another member of the party.

During this brief engagement, too, he played for the first time with Helen Faucit, who was destined to be closely associated with his future career and to cause him many unhappy moments through her more than professional attachment to him. She was the daughter of an actress who had deserted her husband to become the mistress of William Farren, but although Miss Faucit's childhood was spent in a decidedly irregular menage she was to become the very ideal of the Victorian woman "as a representation of wifely devotion, virginal grace, and moral worth."[87] Her "uncle," Percy Farren, seems to have been the first to recognize her talent, and it was he, rather than his more famous brother, who devoted himself to training her as an actress, William contenting himself with plaguing any manager who engaged his "stepdaughter."

She was not yet twenty when she first appeared with Macready in *The Stranger*, and she found him at his most gallant, refusing to go on for "the call" without taking her with him. Next she assumed the role of Clemanth in *Ion*, which had been taken by Ellen Tree for the première only. As a substitute, Miss Faucit was unsatisfactory; Macready wrote that he did not like her, she wanted heart. Of the many rash judgments which he committed to the privacy of his *Diary*, none was further from the truth. The young actress had a diary of her own, in which she recorded her impressions of the actors she observed with "dear Mr. Percy Farren." Of Macready in *The Provost of Bruges* she had written: "somehow he always carried my heart and soul along with him, there is such an earnestness and meaning about everything he does, even the most trifling word or action, that carries such *truth* with it. I hear a great many talk of his faults of declamation, pauses, and so on, but I don't know how it is, he never gives me time to see them."[88] Like many another young and impressionable spectator, she could not separate the emotions evoked by an actor *in character* from the personality of the man, and only a short time was to elapse before Macready discovered that Miss Faucit had sufficient heart, displayed in all too prominent a place.

After a brief summer tour, including a performance of *Virginius* with the amateur Cambridge Garrick Club, he reopened Covent Garden as Macbeth on October 3, 1836. His co-workers were not wholly satisfactory; Osbaldistone had refused to engage Miss Huddart, and Pritchard was cast as Macduff in place of—as he had rather hoped—Charles Kemble, who had declared he would play nothing but first parts. It was Kemble's season, at least for the first three months, as he was playing a farewell round of his characters before retiring.

In October, too, Edwin Forrest came over from America to have a try at the conquest of London at Drury Lane. Macready called on him on the fourteenth, and found him of "a noble appearance, and a manly, mild, and interesting demeanour." On the seventeenth, when Macready appeared with Helen Faucit in *King John*, Forrest came out at the other theatre in his great American success, Dr. Robert Bird's *The Gladiator*. In the light of future events, the reception of Forrest by the English critics is of importance. The *Herald* on October 18 praised Bird for the "tact" with which he had adapted his play to the actor's talents, and criticized in particular—as what Englishman does not—the American's voice:

Its general intonation is decidedly what we shall call provincial.— We fancy it should be considered so, even in New York or Philadelphia. —It has a fine flavour of the back-woods . . . His action is full of variety and gracefulness,—but, at the same time, it partakes overmuch of the athletic style . . . [His] death-scene was too literal,—the gory face, & death rattle, added the horrid and abhorrent to the fall of Spartacus, but in no way increased its high tragic effect."

At the end of the play the critic notes, "More enthusiasm . . . we scarcely ever witnessed on the part of an audience in a British theatre." *The Times* said of his Lear: "his execution was uncommonly powerful and effective," and of the second act of his Macbeth: "it is questionable whether it can be surpassed by any actor of the present day."[89] There were dissident voices, to be sure. After a vicious attack on Forrest's Lear November 6, the *Weekly Despatch* concludes:

We do not know the extent to which Mr. Willis Jones [Forrest's manager] means to be punished before he admits that he is vainly endeavouring to make a star of a very indifferent actor, but we really do think that the game has been tried long enough. . . . The American hero may possibly learn his art in England, but we do not cherish the Utopian idea of his illustrating it.

And from a unique theatrical diary left by Charles Rice, an obscure music-hall singer, we can learn something of the attitude of the "atoms in the audience." Of *The Gladiator,* Mr. Rice says, with a curious aping of the critical style of the heavy journalism of the day:

one of the worst productions pretending to that title [of tragedy], which has been brought forward at either of our metropolitan theatres for some years. . . . it is nothing more than a mere vehicle in which some idea may be conveyed to the audience of the strength of a man of Mr. Forrest's dimensions; five acts, however, is rather too much for a display of this description. . . . Mr. Forrest has been so lauded to the skys by the greater portion of our newspaper critics that I shall be, perhaps, considered presumptious in deviating from this general opinion which has literally been crammed down the throats of the playgoing public;—but in what Mr. Forrest's particular supremacy consists I am at a loss to determine.[90]

On the whole, however, Forrest's reception was favorable, and Macready went out of his way to beg John Forster, then critic for the *Examiner,* "to deal liberally and kindly" by him in his notice. Forster, angry with the attitude the other papers were taking, in particular those making invidious or implied comparisons between Forrest and his friend, was determined to follow his own course. This he did with such vigor that Bulwer-Lytton observed to him, "You have scarcely left the Forest a stump!"[91] On October 29, after reading Forster's review, Macready wrote in his *Diary:* "I thought it ill-natured and not just—omitting all mention of his merit, with the enumeration of his faults," and he made it up in his own fashion by inviting his American rival to dine with him at home, and by taking part in a public banquet in his honor. On one occasion he went so far as to visit Forrest's manager and assure him that he had used all his influence, by word of mouth, by letters, and by the mediation of friends, but that Forster had "peremptorily and repeatedly" refused to suppress or qualify his opinion. "Jones said . . . that neither he nor Mr. Forrest had ever given attention to the insinuations and assertions of the base persons that are to be found about a theatre."[92] Nonetheless, Macready was a trifle disturbed to find himself quoted in the *Globe* as declaring, "Sir, there has been nothing like him since Kemble!"

It is interesting, too, to observe the roles that Macready was playing during Forrest's engagement:

	Drury Lane Forrest	Covent Garden Macready
October 17	*The Gladiator*	*King John*
October 19	*ibid.*	*ibid.*
October 21	*ibid.*	*Othello*
October 24	*Othello*	*King John*
October 28	*Othello*	*Othello*
November 4	*Lear*	*Othello*
November 14	*Damon and Pythias*	*Julius Caesar*
November 22	*Othello*	*King John*
November 25	*Othello* (with J. B. Booth as Iago)	*Macbeth*
December 2	*Macbeth*	*Othello*

This strange parallelism in repertory seems either to have passed without remark, or was accepted as natural by the newspapers. But there can be little doubt that it was intentional. When Forrest returned to Drury for a brief season on February 6, 1837, Covent Garden immediately met him with Vandenhoff as *Richard III* (Macready was ill), and on the thirteenth, even more pointedly, matched his *Brutus* with the first London appearance of his fellow American, Hamblin, as *Hamlet*. These competing bills are an ominous foretaste of Macready's last visit to America, when Forrest pursued him about the country, deliberately playing all of Macready's best parts.

On the whole this was a happy season for Macready, "profitable and agreeable," as he described it at its end. Two new plays, neither greatly successful, were to lend flavor to his repertory; his friendships in the world of society and art were widening. Only Helen Faucit disturbed him with her attention. "Is Miss——disposed to coquette with me?" he wrote on November 4, and wondered on the thirtieth whether her "volunteered expression of admiration and partiality" was "simplicity, deceit, coquetry, or passion?"

The first of the new plays was the fruit of Macready's urging the novelist Bulwer to try his hand at the drama. On the twenty-third of February, 1836, before the fracas with Bunn, he had called on Bulwer at his chambers in the Albany, and had found him in dandiacal state: "dressed, or rather *deshabille,* in the most lamentable style of foppery—a hookah in his mouth, his hair, whiskers, tuft, etc., all grievously cared for." But his disgust vanished when the young dandy handed him a manuscript, *The Duchess of LaValliere,* dedicated to him, though "he did not know whether I might think the part intended for me worthy of my powers," particularly as the main character was a female. Macready read the manuscript with approval, and with some qualifications. Bulwer, at first disposed to cavil, finally yielded to his suggestions and set about mending his play, on which he meanwhile set such impossible terms that Bunn promptly refused to have anything to do with it. The events of the "day of wrath" effectively put an end to further negotiations; and the play waited upon the pleasure of Manager Osbaldistone. On the fourth of January, 1837, after a month of careful rehearsals, the play was presented, with the author's name plainly announced as "E. L. Bulwer, Esq. M. P." It was not successful, partly because of political opposition to Bulwer, partly because it is overlong and rather tasteless. To the end of its brief run, Macready, Forster, and Bulwer each took a hand in trying to improve the effect, Bulwer by writing a special scene and insisting on its insertion only a few days before the play was withdrawn. The reaction of Charles Rice may be taken as typical of the general spectator: "I much lament that Mr. Bulwer should have expended so much excellent writing upon a subject so totally unfit for stage representation as the seduction and abandonment of Louise de la Valliere."[93]

The other new play had also grown out of the urgings of Macready. On the night of the supper celebrating the first per-formance of *Ion,* he had turned to young Browning and begged him to write a tragedy "and save me from going to America." On the fourth of October, Forster reported that the poet had com-pleted a tragedy on the subject of Strafford, though two days later Browning denied that the play was finished, which Macready thought "a circumstance to rejoice at." On the twentieth of November, the manuscript was in a condition to be read, and Macready, having tried it on his wife and sister, offered his usual criticisms and suggestions to the author. As time progressed, the actor began to have misgivings—the action was too historical, the story was not managed skillfully—but Osbaldiston caught at it with avidity, made a generous offer for the rights and decided to strengthen his company for the production. Browning inserted some "effects" that Macready thought might be improvements, and Forster and Macready set about cutting, altering, and arrang-ing the play for production. Macready was now so apprehensive of failure that he hoped some of the actors might be "restive about their parts" and so afford a decent excuse to withdraw it. To his disappointment the cast seemed pleased, and the long period of rehearsals began.

On the first of May, at Macready's benefit, *Strafford* made its first appearance, and its brief history of five performances more than justified the earlier apprehensions. For all Osbaldiston's eagerness, the piece was penuriously mounted, and only fairly acted. In response to an inquiry, Browning recalled the performance: "Macready acted very finely, as did Miss Faucit. Pym [Vandenhoff] received tolerable treatment. The rest—for the sake of whose incompetence the play had to be reduced by at least one-third of its dialogue—*non ragioniam di lor!*"[94] Forster, in the *Examiner,* was somewhat more frank about "the rest": Vandenhoff was "positively nauseous," John Webster "whimpered," and "some one should have stepped out of the pit and thrust Mr. Dale from the stage."[95] Browning was at first distressed over the reception, and inclined to quarrel with Forster—but, as in the case with Bulwer, he soon recovered, and, with added experience, was prepared to "cut and come again."

Two failures, to Macready, would have been of greater moment in other days, but he was too preoccupied with his own schemes to indulge himself in his usual soul-searching and world-cursing. In an almost, for him, happy frame of mind, he was about to become manager of a national theatre, and to elevate his wretched profession to a level of dignity in the artistic world.

❖ ❖ ❖ 5 ❖ ❖ ❖

Actor-Manager

THE IDEA of assuming a London management had long been on Macready's mind. For several years before 1837 his *Diary* records his fitful schemes, his hopes and inevitable fears. The Bath management was clearly an experiment (did he now recall the words he so solemnly wrote at the end of that season: "If they catch me in this hateful occupation again may all its worst consequences fall on me!"), and in 1834 he had progressed so far as to talk plans with Bartley, Farren, Dowton, and Reynolds about taking the English Opera House for a season, "to relieve the Theatrical profession from its present state of oppression."[1]

On June 17, 1837, matters began to come to a head. Macready called on Robertson, who had left country matters to serve as agent for the Covent Garden Committee, and discussed a plan to take over the theatre. It was a cautious enough plan, since he had no intention of making "any venture beyond that of my own talent"; that is, he would invest no money, and the proprietors were to get their rent from a percentage of the receipts. Also, he was to stand alone, to be the sole manager, without the advice or hindrance of Bartley or Farren or any of the other actors who had participated in the abortive discussions of three years before. Five days later, Robertson reported that the proprietors had heard his plan with favor "as far as they could see into it," and Macready was encouraged to propose a division of the nightly receipts which would diminish their risk if not guarantee them a profit. First, the necessary expenses of the theatre were to be deducted, then the actors' salaries, and finally from the surplus, "if any," a sum which would go to make up the usual rent. This seems to have been a fair proposition; the managements of Bunn and Osbaldiston undertaken on the usual terms had resulted in a loss to all parties. By Macready's arrangement the theatre would at any rate be kept open and the manager would be liable for nothing beyond the actual earnings of the concern. To be sure, two years later he figured that he had sustained a considerable personal loss, but this was in terms of his possible professional earnings as a touring star.

His notes on a further discussion with Robertson and Bartley on the twenty-ninth disclose more details. The proprietors were to undertake a renovation of the wardrobe and scenery, since Macready felt he was making a sufficient contribution in risking his name, time, peace of mind, and his salary as a performer. And the whole scheme was contingent upon his ability to form a satisfactory company. The proprietors countered with a proposal to add £720 to the annual expense of the theater for the alterations, a percentage to be deducted from the nightly receipts. After some misgivings, and consultations with his financial advisor, Macready submitted, and the agreement was concluded.

That he might be at hand during the necessary negotiations and preparations for the opening, he agreed to perform during the summer for Benjamin Webster at the Haymarket. What Macready's sentiments were on playing for the first time in London a regular engagement outside the two patent theatres he does not record. Webster, for his part, was apparently determined to do the right thing by the legitimate drama. He opened on the twelfth of June with Macready as Hamlet, and engaged Miss Huddart to support him. Macready continued in *Ion, Othello, Richard III,* several comedy parts—for the Haymarket was entering upon its career as the Comédie Anglaise—and, at long last, the first London production of the Macready-Knowles version of *The Maid's Tragedy.* The play had been reshaped to focus on the character of Melantius, which became a typical Macready role, brave, frank, rough, colloquial, and heroic by turns. The actor's faith in his vehicle was completely vindicated. The piece was repeated twenty-one times in the short season, the critics were nearly unanimous in their approval, and Webster, with high hopes, offered to publish the text, with a preface by Macready, in his *Acting National Drama.* One slightly sour note was the insistence of the newspaper critics on crediting all the improvements to Knowles. Knowles confessed privately that he had attempted to draft a letter to the papers explaining the nature of the collaboration and disclaiming the entire credit, but that "he could not manage it at all," ostensibly because he felt it might be putting himself forward. Mac-

1. Macready as Romeo

2. Macready as Virginius

3. Richard III attacks The Poet Bunn

4. Actors in *Acis and Galatea*: Miss C. Novello (left), Allen and Miss C. Novello (middle), James Hudson (right)

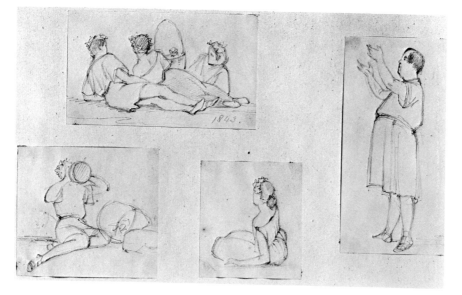

5. Members of the chorus of *Acis and Galatea*

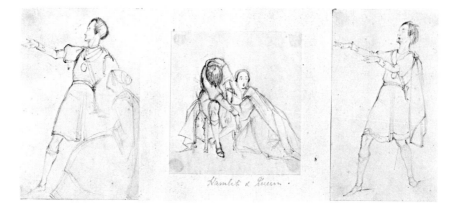

6. Macready as Hamlet: with Ophelia (left), with Gertrude (middle), seeing his father's ghost (right)

7. Macready as Macbeth: Act I, Scene iii (left), the dagger scene (right)

8. Macready and Helen Faucit in *Richelieu*, anonymous wash drawing

9. William Charles Macready, 1854

10. Catherine Atkins Macready, drawing by Daniel Maclise, 1845

11. The Macready family with W. M. Thackeray (in doorway) in front of their home in Sherborne

12. Testimonial presented to Macready in commemoration of his management of the Theatre Royal, Covent Garden, during the 1837–1839 seasons

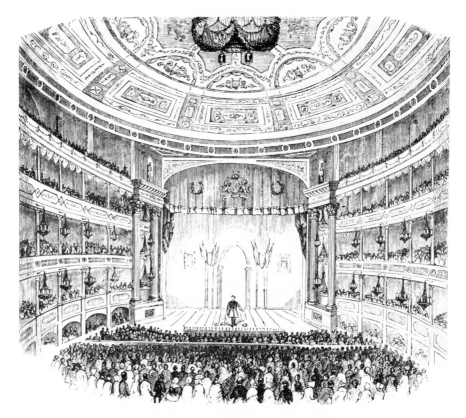

13. Macready's Farewell Address to the Audience

ready replied promptly that he would see that Knowles' share in
the work was stated in the published preface, which he did, precisely, and, no doubt, with some satisfaction. The play, certainly a
minor effort in its revised if not in its original form, was one of
the great successes of midcentury, and Miss Huddart's Evadne
proved to be unforgettable. Some years later a poetaster addressed
an acrostic to her under her married name of Warner, which concludes with a revealing tribute to Macready's part in the whole:

> M ild in your natural character, thou art
> A n able actress of the fiery mood;
> R ebundant [sic] action, frequent strut and start,
> Y our judgement wisely tells should be subdued.
>
> W ell do your death-black eyes their part fulfill,
> A nd flash to fury, or in scorn strike awe;
> R ich in *Evadne's* portraiture of ill.
> N o critic e'er condemned it; all who saw
> E steemed it noble, thrilling, awful, grand,
> R evived and cleansed by great Macready's hand![2]

During the Haymarket season, the Covent Garden company was
assembled. Macready had determined to start his management with
all things in his favor. If there was a good actor in England, he was
to be a member of the company—and at a reduced salary. He
began by hiring George Bartley as actor and stage manager, giving
him £200 for the latter position and cutting his salary to £12 a
week in the former. John Willmott, the Drury Lane prompter, was
first offered £5 weekly, under the misapprehension that his current
salary was £6. When he foolishly admitted that he was getting but
£5, he was promptly cut to £4. Helen Faucit was offered £15, Mrs.
Humby £6/10. James Warde, Edward Elton, Robert Strickland,
Tyrone Power, Frederick Vining, Mrs. Glover, Charles Diddear,
Mrs. Clifford—all the respectable and familiar work-horses of the
London stage—came willingly to his banner, and, for the most
part, without too much grumbling over the reduced salaries. Had
Macready been the sort of man to take pleasure in a vote of confi-
dence from his fellow professionals, this might have been an in-
spiriting summer. But he was not, of course.

Needing a strong actor to play second leads to his starring roles,
he offered an engagement (though disclaiming a desire to "limit"
him in any way)[3] to Charles Kean. He cannot have been surprised
at the young tragedian's refusal. He turned next to Vandenhoff,
but that gentleman was engaged for an American tour. Then he
overheard Webster speak of a provincial actor whom he was hoping

to engage for the Haymarket, one Samuel Phelps. On the eighteenth of July, with typical caution, he wrote his friend George Wightwick, theatrical critic of the Plymouth *Herald*:

Some time since I received a Plymouth paper with a criticism upon the performance of a gentleman who rejoices in the name of Phelps; other accounts that I have had represent him very favourably. As it is not improbable I may have some concern in the direction of one of the Winter Theatres next season, I should very much wish to concentrate all the talent that can be brought together, and I am very desirous of having your opinion, which I so highly value, upon the merits of this gentleman. You will perceive by the papers that I am enjoying this "warm Tragedy weather" in the oven of the Haymarket; the adaptation of Beaumont and Fletcher's tragedy has been quite a success. . . . P. S. Mr. Phelps is going to act at the Haymarket, when I shall see him but I am anxious for your opinion.[4]

On the thirtieth Macready wrote again to Wightwick, no doubt trusting that the contents of his letter might find their way to the provincial actor's ear:

I hope he is moderate in his expectations of *remuneration* for ours is now a *struggle for existence,* not for profit; and every salary on our establishment is largely, but willingly, reduced. I should like much to know what is his aim in coming to town—whether he has the 'aut Caesar aut nullus' view of young Kean, or a resolution in the love of his art to study and toil for the perfection of it.[5]

Apparently on the strength of Wightwick's reply, and without waiting for the young tragedian's debut at the Haymarket, Macready took the coach to Southhampton on the fourteenth of August where he prepared a note of invitation and went to see for himself. The play was *The Iron Chest,* which displeased him mightily with its clichés; of the new actor, who perhaps suffered from Macready's memory of Edmund Kean in the same role, he recorded his opinion very judicially in his *Diary*:

Mr. Phelps in Sir Edwin Mortimer displayed intelligence, occasionally great energy, some imagination—not much; want of finish, of experience, of logic in the working out the character—(to lay violent hands on the term)—of *depth* in all the great parts. His best scene decidedly was his death, but even there was a want of method. His level speaking is often very pleasing—always sensible. I expected from his opening more than he achieved. There was no *absorbing* feeling *through* the great scenes, no evidence of the "slow fire" "wearing his vitals"; this was particularly manifest in the last act, where he was direct and straight-forward even to commonplaceness. I think he will improve, and run both Warde and Elton hard, and very likely do much more.

Phelps had apparently been warned of the imminence of a visit from a representative of the London manager. On the fifteenth of August he wrote to his wife:

Yesterday all day I was in such a state that I scarcely knew what to do with myself. I played as well as I could, but I thought very badly. I did not know if any person was in the house from London; but at the end of The Iron Chest a note was sent round to me from *Macready* who had been there all the time *himself*. I was with him last night for upwards of an hour, and the result was I go to Covent Garden on the 16th of October. He wanted me to name my salary, which I declined doing until I have played in London; but at last I agreed to take the same salary that I may agree for at the Haymarket, which, if I succeed, I will take care shall be a good one, or I shall not go at all.[6]

Macready was likewise negotiating for a juvenile. James Anderson, then playing at Cheltenham, had applied for the post, and Macready's letters to him are a delicate combination of the disinterested elder friend and the highly interested professional manager. On August 3 he wrote to the aspirant:

You would stipulate for what *no manager with any intention to act honestly by you* can bind himself to *in the case of an untried actor*. I attempted to make the same stipulation myself, when I, a young man, first came to London; but Mr. Harris's answer showed me at once the unreasonableness of my desire, and the impossibility of granting it. . . . This is the *good sense* of the question, and is what, *if you argue & stipulate forever*, the *matter must at last resolve itself to*.

I should be very glad to see you, if you choose to trust your fortune, and my disposition to cultivate talent, wherever I can find it.—

I ought to observe, that another young man of high pretensions & provincial fame is now writing for the same situation—Therefore your answer must be prompt and definitive.

Whether through confidence in Macready's justice and judgement, or to forestall the other young man, Anderson replied promptly and definitively, for two days later Macready thanked him for the rational view which he had taken of the situation and promised to do everything in his power to bring him forward. "Many young men of very considerable promise," he wrote, "have been ruined, or ruined themselves by too ambitious an opening." Was this, too, Mr. Harris speaking? "I think you would appear under good auspices," he went on, "and under a management, whose object it is to place the plays in a becoming style before the public."[7] Anderson was to be "rated" in the salary list at £8/10 a week, which would be advantageous in bargaining with later managements, but he would be paid only £5.

Not all the actors in the new company came without stipulation of business, ready to take any part which the manager assigned them. Helen Faucit's advisor and guardian, William Farren, was able to force upon Macready a proviso that, according to her contract with the proprietors of Covent Garden, "in every Tragedy or serious play . . . Miss Faucit shall have the choice of the principal character with the privilege of refusing any and every one which she may deem detrimental to her interest to perform."[8] Macready thought it "shameful" and that she would in effect become the manager, but he realized that even the highly prized Miss Huddart was no match for Helen Faucit as the typically Victorian heroine of the typically Victorian serious plays on which he was depending for his novelties.

For, in addition to assembling a company, he was preparing his repertory. Charles Dickens, whom Forster had introduced into the Macready circle, declared his desire to write a play for him; John Hullah was at work on a comic opera. Recalling the success of *Werner* and *Sardanapalus*, Macready turned once again to the works of Byron. *The Deformed Transformed* he decided was impossible, but *The Two Foscari* looked somewhat better. Knowles promised him the first refusal on all his future productions, Bulwer-Lytton and Talfourd undertook projects. But Shakespeare was to be the backbone of the repertory, and such Shakespeare as London had not before seen, produced with all the care that a gentleman and artist and scholar could lavish upon it, produced with the same attention as a new opera or pantomime. He thought of playing the Duke in his own arrangement of *Measure for Measure* and was disappointed when Helen Faucit chose Mariana for her role rather than Isabella. But she was, after all, his Victorian heroine. Perhaps her refusal made him think twice about the Victorian nature of his audience; at any rate he never produced the play.

Miss Faucit, of course, had a contractual right to pick and refuse characters. The clause was a constant torment to the manager and he made certain that no other member of his company infringed upon his prerogatives. Republicanism, he knew, would never work in the theatre; his only alternatives were despotism or service. He was, however, more than attentive to advice and opinions from outside his company. Perhaps this reflects his conviction that his management was something more than a personal effort, was to some degree the responsibility of all men of culture. A promising manuscript would first be tried on Catherine and Letitia, and then on the varying group of friends he called his council. These included Charles Dickens, who was to be his closest and unshaken friend throughout his career and his retirement, and John Forster, the mercurial, quick-tongued, thoughtful-thoughtless critic of the *Examiner*, and, less regularly, Robert Browning, the journalists W. J. Fox and Albany Fonblanque, the painter George Cattermole, Talfourd, Procter, and Bulwer-Lytton. To be sure their advice was not always heeded, and was frequently credited to some mysterious personal interest, but a single negative comment or an affirmation hesitantly advanced could cause Macready agonies of doubt.

The numberless decisions that confronted him were his greatest burden. He was incapable of delegating authority; any of his lieu-tenants—Robertson, the box office manager; Serle, the acting manager; Wilmott, the stage director; Marshall, the scene-painter; Sloman, the head carpenter—was capable of an error which might spell disaster. For always in his mind was the image of his father, monarch of the western circuit, locked in debtor's prison; and of the father's son thrust into the world to remake what he could of the family fortunes.

In the midst of such business, he concluded his engagement at the Haymarket and, to fill up the time before the opening of Covent Garden, went to act for his stepmother in Birmingham. For the first time he made the trip by the newly opened railroad, which excited him so that he could only express the fullness of his feelings by saying his prayers; but the badness of the Birmingham actors soon restored him to his normal depression. Helen Faucit was with him on this engagement, and seems to have done her best to convince him that, were it not for Farren's disapproval, she would submit to his direction in all things. She pleased him very much by announcing that she was determined to strike out the "obnoxious clause" from her articles when she would come of age in two months, but his pleasure turned to apprehension when she insisted upon conferring with him in his dressing room, because there would be others present in her own room. And this, he wrote in his *Diary*, "After the terrible moral of the play [*The Bridal*], in which she had just been acting for the first time." She further insisted upon accompanying him back to London on the railroad, making his second trip as disturbing to his equanimity as his first, and perhaps no less prayerful.

On the thirtieth of October, 1837, Covent Garden opened under Macready's management. There had been some disappointments; the Queen had refused permission to call the company "Her Majesty's Company of Players"; the great comedian Liston could not be coaxed out of retirement; Talfourd, reminding him of the O.P. riots, had persuaded him not to require reservations for seats on the ground floor in place of the undignified rush which had hitherto preceded all popular performances. He even had to bail James Warde, an actor who spent the better part of his life avoiding bailiffs, out of debtor's prison.[9] The preparations had, in fact, left him in a state approaching desperation. His subalterns, however, did their best to anticipate his demands. Announcing the first rehearsal, Bartley asked Drinkwater Meadows to arrive several days in advance: "Macready will be in town on Saturday night—and he is in such a fidget.—I wish him to see you and the few (alas! how few!) sound ones in new parts . . . If I were in Macready's place—I would say to you to be here on Friday night and I shall be satisfied—but this is not the case with him. He will be nervous, perhaps shaken in his confidence in you, and besides we really want *Example.*"[10]

But Macready had had his way about several improvements. The playbill was a simple statement of what was to be offered, without mendacious puffing, and the ladies of the town, who had used the theatre as a booking office, were quietly eliminated from the audience. Talfourd had prepared an opening address, the principles of the new management had been explained by the manager in person to all the newspapers, and *The Winter's Tale* was to be the first bill. His determination to elevate the stage could not be misunderstood.

The first spectators in the auditorium before the performance began saw signs of the intention of the new manager to restore the house to legitimacy. "The Augean Stables" left by Osbaldiston and Bunn had been cleansed. The "festoons of richest Cobweb" on the ceiling had given way to an azure blue, the walls had been painted a light vermilion, and the box fronts done over in white and gold. Cushions with ancient stains of tobacco, porter, and "other noxious filth" had been recovered and the pit-benches equipped with back rests. The scene painter had created a new act drop with the Queen's arms in silver and gold on a blue ground, which was "exceedingly beautiful" or "paltry" depending on the spectator's politics.

Despite good intentions, despite a summer of hard work and planning, the first night was not the enthusiastic triumph he had hoped for. The audience was friendly, so friendly in fact that it unnerved him and caused him to forget part of the opening address. *The Winter's Tale* was well mounted and cast, with Helen Faucit an ideal Hermione, Bartley a good Autolycus, Miss Huddart a properly strong Paulina, and Priscilla Horton, promising great things for the future, a delight as Mopsa. But in the performance, only Anderson's Florizel seems to have made any special mark, and Macready acknowledges that his own Leontes was ineffective until the last act. In that great moment when the statue of Hermione comes to life he was at his best, utterly transported, and Helen Faucit many years later could still remember her utter terror in the face of his rapturous kisses. He was forced, in fact, to recall her to herself by whispering that she must not be frightened. But as a whole, the effect on the audience and the critics does not seem to have been inspiring. Perhaps too great care had been taken; perhaps the actors felt too strongly what hung in the balance on that fateful night. Edward Fitzgerald, Forster, Procter, and Talfourd came to his dressing room after the play, but Macready does not record, as he is usually careful to do, their approval or displeasure. Fatigue, and an increasing awareness of his managerial responsibilities, strengthened Macready's always melodramatic response to events. Irrationally he seized upon a hint of anything less than complete triumph as a promise of utter catastrophe.

Commitments had been made and the season must go on, dejected though the manager was with his prospects. On the following Monday *Hamlet* was brought forth, and the audience commented on the new staging technique by applauding several of the improvements. *The Winter's Tale* was repeated, Macready taking the occasion of rehearsal to instruct Miss Huddart in the art of acting, and then *The Bridal* was produced, during the rehearsals of which Anderson was the pupil. *Othello, Werner, The Provoked Husband, Virginius,* and *The Stranger* followed in rapid succession, carefully mounted, carefully rehearsed, and succeeding—but no more. On the tenth of October he was hard at work preparing the actors for Dimond's adaptation of *The Novice.* He took "great pains in endeavouring to infuse a spirit" into the cast. In performance "It escaped, but will do no good," largely, he thought, because of the ineffectiveness of Vining as Carolstadt.

Phelps came out in *Venice Preserved* on the twenty-seventh of October, playing Jaffeir to Macready's Pierre. The manager had tried to persuade him to play Pierre, a character "that went better with the audience," but Phelps would have none of it and made a genuine hit in the role of his choice. Three days later, Phelps made a second hit as Othello to Macready's Iago. As a result, when *Venice Preserved* was repeated on November 9, Warde played Pierre, and after that Phelps was relegated to unmistakably secondary roles. Phelps reported that Macready told him, with a frankness that makes the anecdote suspicious, "*Your* time must come but I am not going to try to hasten it. I was kept back by

Young and Kean, and you will have to wait for me."[11] As a consequence of his refusal to take lesser roles, Phelps severed his connection with the company and, since his contract forbade him to act elsewhere in London, went back to the provinces. Some years later he admitted to Thomas Latimer that, had he been in Macready's position, he would probably have done as Macready did—this after some experience as an actor-manager himself.

Before he left, however, he participated in the first of Macready's revivals to catch the public fancy, a resoundingly successful production of *Macbeth* on the thirteenth of November. The *Times* found it "almost a new play," and *John Bull* declared "The poetry of the drama is now for the first time put into motion." Approbation from *John Bull* was praise indeed, for this "apoplectic guardian of Toryism," having decided Macready's association with such men as John Forster proved him to be a radical in politics, could find little to approve in his art. The history in the contemporary press of his career as an actor, and particularly of his performance as actor-manager, is constantly shaded by political demagoguery and personal umbrage. One of the papers most constant in its abuse was the *News and Sunday Herald,* which finally got around to *Macbeth* on the seventh of January, 1838. The critic begins by declaring that the popularity of the production

is owing to the way in which the music is performed, and to the general getting up of the piece, far more than to Macready's acting of the principal character. . . . Macready has played Macbeth often enough to empty benches on former occasions, and we therefore must attribute the reputed goodness of the houses, when it is played, to some other cause than his appearance in it. The music is well performed, but the whole of the acting, from Miss Huddart's *Lady Macbeth* down to the most insignificant part in the piece is an aping of Macready in a greater or less degree, according to the ability of each to imitate his master. Gentlemen with one line to speak contrive to chop it up and interlard it with catchings of the breath, and asthematic gasps, simply because it is the *style* of the manager. Mr. Anderson is a Macready in water colours; G. Bennett is a coarse rough copy, in distemper; Diddear is an outline of the same thing on stone; but we cannot say much of the *drawing* of any one of them.

Before concluding, however, the critic of the *News* discloses the source of pique which directed his judgement.

Macready can, it seems, so little afford to hear the truth spoken, that he has had recourse to the desperate and pitiable expedient of stopping the free admissions of some of those journals that have freely criticised his acting and management. He has been heard to say, that if they will come to the theatre and find fault, they shall at least pay for coming. We can assure him that those who go in with orders, have frequently *paid for coming* and very dearly too; for to witness his assaults on Shakespeare is paying heavily for a visit to Covent-Garden.

The newspapers which had been subjected to the indignity of being removed from the free list, in addition to the *News,* were the *Satirist* and the *Weekly Despatch.* Macready thought them the most impertinent and persistent of his journalist enemies, though any unfavorable review was apt, for the moment, to make him see concerted opposition from the more respectable *Times, Herald,* or *True Sun,* not merely because it was a reflection upon his ability as an actor, but more pertinently because it might have a negative effect upon the box office. And in opposing Macready the censured papers were forced into the position of supporting Alfred Bunn, and his star at Drury Lane, Charles Kean.

For his part Poet Bunn welcomed their support and generously provided them with lies, half-truths, and pious hypocrisies as am-munition. Not that the men themselves were in want of such matériel. The reduction of the state newspaper tax in 1836 had opened the door to a crowd of mercenary and unprincipled black-guards with pens as facile as their allegiances were flexible. Their critical opinions, like their objective reporting, could be colored by a political position, by wholly personal and whimsical interests, or by the possibility of collecting blackmail. This was an era of slashing journalism at the top of the profession and of open slander and daring libel at the bottom. Politically, the weeklies tended to affect the Whigs, less because of conviction than because the Tories offered wealthier targets for blackmail. It was as a Tory, an appellation to which he did not aspire, that Macready became an automatic target; was he not seen in the company of baronets and at the dining tables of the wealthy? And, most damning of all, did he not remove the popular press from the free list, thereby at-tempting to destroy the foundations of English liberty—the free-dom of the press?

Playing fearless David, they slung their pebbles, and the pebbles hurt. Sometimes they hurt his pride, as when *The Age* attempted to put him in his artistic place: "The public knows that he is not a Shakespearean actor. His 'Richard the Third' is an impetuous bully; his 'Othello' is an ill tempered nigger; his 'Hamlet' is a snappish gentleman with one stocking down, and his 'Macbeth' done every Monday, is a political nuisance."[12] Editor Westmacott could, and did, turn this sort of thing out by the column, and, if his torch threatened to burn low, his good friend Bunn stood ready to supply fresh oil. Such attacks Macready publicly ignored, though he did not fail to record his bruises in his *Diary.* Perhaps he recalled that he had somewhat perversely played the same game on one occasion. In the *Sunday Times,* August 26, 1832, a favorable review of Knowles' *Hunchback* appeared. There is a copy of this review on which Macready has written, "By me in revenge for his [Knowles'] bad base treatment of me."[13]

What Macready could not silently ignore were attacks upon his private business. The editors were always happy to listen to the fancied wrongs of disgruntled actors and to seize their pens as heroic defenders of the helpless slaves against the ruthless, wealthy, self-seeking tyrant. On at least two occasions Macready took his tormentors into court, and on several others he was only prevented by his "council" or his attorneys. The financial satisfaction was small, in one instance £5, but he had the personal satisfaction of vindicating his right to a gentleman's privacy and thus, in spite of his necessarily public life, to the title of gentleman. There was no redress, of course, for unfavorable criticism of his performances, but there is little evidence that Macready drew his support from the "hard-headed artisans"[14] who were the principal readers of the penny weeklies.

At least once during the first months of his management Macready had no apprehensions about the health of his box office. On the seventeenth of November, Queen Victoria commanded a performance of *Werner.* Now the young Queen was, obviously, no more interested in the theatre, and her taste in dramatic entertainment was no better, than in the other arts. Trained lions and Italian opera appealed to her and Shakespeare and the classic plays were well beyond her intellectual reach. But state patronage of the arts was expected, and it is probably typical of the lady to whom the works of Martin Farquhar Tupper were so very dear that she chose to subject herself to *Werner.* She also wished to see Tyrone Power in *The Irish Ambassador* on the same bill, but, since Power was then playing at the Adelphi Theatre, Macready resisted as strongly as he could and at last carried his point.

The performance itself was very nearly a shambles. Since the manager had not had his way about reserved seats, admission to the pit was sold freely to all comers, including Alfred Bunn, who thus records the scene with envious self-righteousness:

A scene of greater blackguardism, of outrage, of the violation almost of common decency, was never known in a theater—for owing to the admission into the pit of many more people than it was calculated to hold with the slightest degree of comfort, a tumult occurred, in which the oaths of the men and the screams of the women struggled for pre-eminence; while the lessee, dressed up as *Werner,* was pacing up and down the stage in dumb-show, biting his lip and rolling his eye, amidst the internal workings of ill-concealed rage. . . .

But females were fainting, and males were fighting, and it was there-fore necessary that something should be done, and speedily. All that *could* be effected, *was* effected; and a pretty sight, to be sure, it ex-hibited. Some gentlemen seated in the public boxes, *directly opposite her* MAJESTY, with the assistance of the police, drew up a breathless set of wretches from the pit, over the front of the boxes, into the lobbies, by which operation their backs were necessarily exposed to the public gaze as well as that of their Sovereign—some fellows with half a coat left—others with a hole in the coat they had on—others with holes in their nether garments—some shoeless—some stockless—most hatless, or bonnetless;—and as these deficiencies became visible to the audience, they indulged in merriment at the expense of sympathy, and turned the whole occurance into one disgraceful scene of hooting, holloaing, hissing, and laughter. A pretty mode THIS *of advancing the drama as a branch of national literature and art.*[15]

Mr. Bunn's indignation is an affecting performance, but the Queen herself seems not to have been displeased at the eagerness of her subjects to witness her innocent intellectual diversions.

For the most part, the succeeding weeks only increased Mac-ready's depression. The houses were thin, so thin that Stanfield, who was at work on a diorama for the annual Christmas panto-mime, heard a rumor that Covent Garden was about to close. This was not true; Macready had no intention of giving up his management before the term expired, but his attitude became more and more one of grim determination. His own art was suffering from the distractions of management. In Macbeth, his favorite and perhaps his most familiar part, he suddenly felt himself far from the character. A performance of *Werner* went indifferently. "I am falling off in my art through my attention to management," he wrote; and later, on the first of the new year: "Whirled along as I now am in the current of harrassing and irritating business I have little opportunity for reflection, and am strongly impressed with the necessity of discontinuing, with the close of the present theatrical season, the extraordinary duties I have taken upon myself for my own mind's sake and for the sake of my blessed and beloved children, to whom I am anxious to devote my best energies of thought and labour."

Certainly the staging of the traditional Christmas pantomime would be distasteful to him, but he entered into the task with all his energies. For weeks he conferred with scenarist, scene painter, and machinist in an effort to outrival Bunn, whose mastery of the pantomime he had often snorted at. The subject was the old tale of Peeping Tom of Coventry, which gave him some concern as to its decency, and the main feature was a moving diorama, by Stanfield, depicting the scenes passed during a journey from the north of Italy to the British Channel. The machinist Bradwell constructed the model for an elaborate transformation scene as a grand finale, which proved, when put together on the stage, to be unworkable and caused the manager a sleepless night devising means of salvaging it. Even on the days of major performances he could not take his mind from the pantomime, spending long hours on the stage during rehearsals in the company of his cabinet, which on this occasion included Dickens, Cattermole, and Forster. Against expectation, the result was a complete success, and on the fifth of January Macready was rewarded by the repayment of nearly £1000 that he had advanced to the treasury of the theatre.

Perhaps to meet the taunts that the Shakespearean theatre had made its one success in pantomime, he resolved upon a revival of *King Lear,* from the original text, banishing Tate, and restoring— if possible—the role of the Fool. Miss Huddart, now married and billed as Mrs. Warner, "kindly undertook" Regan, but Helen Faucit, for illness or some unexplained reason, made difficulties over Cordelia. The Fool was the chief problem. Macready's conception was of a "fragile, hectic, beautiful-faced, half-idiot-looking boy," and Drinkwater Meadows, in whose "line of business" the Fool should have fallen, could hardly fit such a description. It was Bartley's hint that saved the production: he suggested a woman for the role. Macready decided immediately that Priscilla Horton, an elf-like singing comedienne, was the very person.

The production proved to be a splendid one, both in the mounting and the performance, and was probably the most effective blow in the nineteenth-century theatre's battle to restore the text of Shakespeare to the stage. The storm, said *John Bull,* beggared description, and the presence of the Fool brought out by contrast the full pathos and terror of Lear's situation as no audience had seen it for over a century. The newspapers were nearly unanimous in their praise; Macready wrote that the impression created by the production was "wide and strong"; and Bulwer's word for the performance was "gigantic."

This was all to the good, and a few weeks later, on the fifteenth of February, came a second happy event, the first production of *The Lady of Lyons.* Preparations had long been underway. Perhaps the first light that had cut through the gloom of the early months of Macready's management was the receipt of a *"Private and Confidential"* letter from Bulwer.

Do you really wish for the hazardous experiment of my assistance? I admire so much the stand you are making & I sympathize so much with your struggle, that if I really thought I could be of service, you might command me at once. I have been considering deeply the elements of Dramatic art and I think I see the secret. . . . Were you not Manager, I would not be a second time Dramatist. . . . Whatever subject I select, you may depend on domestic interest and determined concentration up to the close.[16]

Macready's reply to this "most delightful letter" has not survived, but it could not have been other than favorable. And Bulwer, a marvel of industry, went silently to work to create a drama to be ready by Christmas.

Nothing more is heard of the project until the twentieth of December, 1837, when Bulwer wrote that he had finished half of a play. On the twenty-eighth, flushed with the success of the seasonal pantomime, Macready sat down to read the completed manuscript, then entitled *The Fraudulent Marriage.* And three days later he went to call on the author to discuss the work, in particular the fifth act which seemed weaker than the rest. On the third of January, in the midst of the preparations for *Lear,* he received a note from the playwright:

I have thought of the best plan for Act 5 & think I can keep up the interest—tho' there will be no Scene quite so striking as those in the 3rd & 4th act. I have set about it in earnest & you shall have the whole play by Sunday night. Write me word where to send it. I stay in town on purpose to finish it. Now, however, for two preliminaries. In the first place I do not wish the play to be the property of the Theatre. As long as you are Manager, heaven grant that be for 5 generations, the play is yours. The instant you cease it returns to me. To prevent litigation with your possible successor—this should be an author's arrangement. Secondly, May I again press upon your mind that my object in this attempt is to give you a popular and taking play. Now unless you feel thoroughly persuaded I will not say of its *certain* success but of the great probability of its attraction, I entreat as a favour to *both of us* that you do not let any wish to compliment me, any delicate fear of wounding my amour propre, allow you to bring it on the stage. For you it would be detrimental to have your first new play either a failure, or a lukewarm success, for me it would be permanent discouragement. Far rather would I, if you entertain doubt, put aside this play & set to work at another, grudging no time, no thought, no trouble, to be really & effectively useful as an ally.

I own that I have some apprehension from the want of an actress—Miss Faucit freezes me & I have some fear also that the 5th act may be weaker than its predecessors. . . . [O]nly remember that if you do shrink from the responsibility of undertaking the play thus put to you, that I will cheerfully direct my labour to some new plot.[17]

On the fifth of January, there was another conference over the fifth act, and the next day a completed manuscript was again in Macready's hands. He thought it, "considering the time in which it has been planned and written, . . . really wonderful."

A series of letters was now exchanged over cuts in the dialogue, attempts to find a title, and various schemes for maintaining the anonymity of the author.[18] Bulwer was still stung by the attacks launched upon him in connection with *The Duchess of LaValliere.* Both he and Macready shared the opinion that they had been politically inspired and were determined that occasion should not again be given to the political-penmen to destroy a work of art. Macready suggested that a Mr. Calvert be invented to stand as author until such time as it was safe for Bulwer to appear. The author decided in favor of anonymity: "I fear the Town would be biassed," he wrote, "against the thought of any thing very good from an unknown author not heard of before in literature, whereas the anonymous at first might arouse curiosity."[19] The secret was kept, although Forster made a shrewd guess, much to Macready's annoyance, and the play was an established success before Bulwer's name was attached to it.

As for titles, Macready suggested *Nobility,* and Bulwer preferred *How Will It End,* or *Lost and Won,* or, even though this was not his favorite, *Love and Pride.* Finally, in despair, Bulwer wrote:

I think that titles are as much a plague to us as they were to Pauline & if we called it "No Title" it would hit off our own Dilemma.
    I agree with you that the adventurer is poor & bald— . . . I fear it is rather vanity than ambition that urges the womankind of the play and rather love than ambition which inspires [Melnotte]. . . .
    I suggest two more. "The Lady of Lyons—or Love and Pride"— "False courtship and true love." Of these the first is not bad I think.[20]

Bulwer was a professional writer who could ill afford to waste time and words or give control of his work into another's hands. His behavior in his series of "collaborations" with Macready is convincing testimony that his primary purpose was support of the management. In a last generous gesture, after the triumph of *Lear* he wrote Macready:

Seeing your most brilliant success in Lear, I cannot but write a line to say that no consideration for any supposed impatience of mind, and no belief in the peculiar goodness of [The Lady of Lyons] may interfere with the run of a play that has gained you such fame.—If you should therefore at all think it advantageous for the theatre or [y]ourself to postpone the "Adventurer" for a week or two longer pray do not have any scruples as far as I am concerned.[21]

But Macready was determined, rather quixotically, since the times were for consolidation and exploitation in all things, to adhere to the old repertory system, rather than exhaust the attraction of a play when he chanced to make a lucky hit. Preparations for The Lady of Lyons continued, with Helen Faucit (who froze the author) as Pauline, the proud merchant's daughter, humbled by the devotion of Claude Melnotte, her youthful lover. Melnotte was a role for which Macready was as ill-suited as for Ion, a young, handsome lover. "I wish I was younger," he wrote Bulwer during rehearsals, "and that my chere ami and myself had put our heads out of the window, when it was raining beauty—but as Falstaff says 'That's past praying for.' "[22] But, since the scene is laid in France in the days after the revolution, there were frequent opportunities for bravura statements about the worth of the individual and paeans in praise of liberty for the actor to make the most of. The real success belonged to the frigid Miss Faucit, who was so carried away by her performance that Macready had once to remind her that she was up-staging him.[23]

Successful enough when it was first performed on February fifteenth, The Lady of Lyons was not immediately the hit that the author and manager had hoped, and it was decided that Bulwer's name should be concealed for a week. During the performance on the twenty-first, the author came to consult with his star and found him in the company of his dresser. Sensing the ambiguity of the situation, and fearful lest the carefully kept secret be made public, Macready addressed his visitor in French, declaring that he wished to postpone the announcement a little longer. To this Bulwer agreed, and at the curtain call, the actor made a little speech declaring that none of the allusions in the play was "political," but that they grew out of the plot and the scene. "If I may associate such a name with an existing author's," he concluded, "our divine Shakespeare is liable to similar imputations, and I trust I shall receive credit for the assertion of the principle upon which I conduct this theatre—that art and literature have no politics." By the twenty-fourth there was no question as to the play's success with the audience, and Bulwer's name appeared in the bills. *The Times,* which had been favorable on the opening night, promptly justified the precautions of secrecy by launching an attack on both the author and the play. But it was too late to do much harm. *The Lady of Lyons,* the first original play of Macready's management, became one of the stock successes of the nineteenth-century theatre and, in the words of Bartley, "as great a draw as *The Stranger.*"

While Bulwer had been so earnestly at work in his service, Macready was having troubles with another of his writing stable, an author of somewhat greater sensitivity, Talfourd. On the seventh of January, Talfourd came to the manager's house, drew him secretively into the drawing room and confided that he had completed a play, *The Athenian Captive,* which he would like to read for him that afternoon. Macready very promptly declined to judge the work from an author's reading, particularly since Talfourd confessed he thought it was not a very good play. Talfourd left, only to return after a short ride to say that he had been thinking the matter over and perhaps his tragedy was better than he had at first believed. The upshot was that the play was sent to Macready, who read it and agreed with the author's earlier opinion, though he scarcely knew how he might convey his judgement to his friend. There was nothing for it but frankness, however. He declared that Talfourd should dictate its performance, that he would act it if he wished, but as a friend he advised him on every account to abandon the play. Talfourd's disappointment was so obvious that Macready promised to look the piece over again, though he feared, whatever his opinion, Talfourd would insist on a production. He did not know, nor did any of the cabinet, that Talfourd's own vanity was being whipped on by what Douglas Jerrold was to immortalize as "curtain lectures."

On the eighteenth came a letter which affirmed the rightness of Macready's intuition. Talfourd was annoyed at his disapproval, and declared that *The Athenian Captive* "having been written for the most disinterested purpose of serving the cause" of the revival of the English stage, he could not "consent to let his labour perish," and insisted on its performance. It is unfortunate for Talfourd that such a letter should have arrived cheek by jowl with Bulwer's completely disinterested one, but then Bulwer was not married to Mrs. Talfourd.

Macready was able to delay the production of *The Athenian Captive* by the success of *The Lady of Lyons* and the preparations for a scheduled revival of *Coriolanus* which proved to be one of his major contributions to the stagecraft of his era. By the sixteenth

of March, however, the evil had to be faced, and he received a
letter from Talfourd with a proposed casting of the play, which
left him in very low spirits. But the author had been tinkering
with his work, and had wrought some improvements. On the
twenty-first Macready began reading the play to the company in
the greenroom, but gave up after the third act, the task being
completed by Serle. Helen Faucit promptly came to refuse her
part. Macready advised her to play the part under protest and to
so inform Talfourd, which she did. Under such circumstances,
Talfourd declined her services.

The play's progress was next interrupted while the annual
Easter pantomime was devised and staged, and while the manager
produced *The Two Foscari* for his benefit. The pantomime,
Sinbad the Sailor, was irrevocably damned; the benefit was successful, though *Foscari* did not become one of Macready's more
popular plays. By the twentieth of April he was at work on Talfourd's play again, learning his role of Thoas, "a bitter drug"
and "a more difficult task than any of the same kind I have ever
in my life had to encounter. . . . It is so overloaded, and so
roundabout the subject." On the twenty-third the play was in
rehearsal upon the stage, with Dickens and Forster as cabinet
members overseeing and advising. With their approval ("for
Talfourd") Macready undertook to omit two scenes and make
certain cuts, and they later informed him that Talfourd had
undergone the amputation very manfully.

On the twenty-sixth Mrs. Warner, who had assumed the part
Helen Faucit had wished to reject, reported "a sudden indisposition"—in the ancient stage tradition she had acted during a
pregnancy until the imminent arrival of her child forced her into
the wings—and Talfourd made one last attempt to inveigle Helen
Faucit into the role. Next day, she arrived at the theatre willing to
take the part, but almost at the same moment a message came from
Mrs. Talfourd rejecting "in a less courteous strain than I would
write to any servant" Miss Faucit's performance of Ismene. Bartley
was sent off to Talfourd's chambers to fetch him, and Dickens and
Forster joined Macready for a cabinet meeting. After a long
interval Bartley returned with the dejected author, who tried to
get Macready to express a wish that the play should be done: then
"Mrs. Talfourd might perhaps be worked upon to consent to its
performance." Macready made a mighty speech upon Mrs. Talfourd's note, and declared that he had acted toward Talfourd as
he should have toward his own brother. And that for the moment
was the end of *The Athenian Captive.* The two men shook hands,

and three days later, a package arrived for the manager containing two printed copies of the play inscribed with the author's "regards, thanks, and regrets."

The business of the theatre, meanwhile, had been going on, and not happily. The failure of the Easter pantomime and a policy which forbade exploiting the Shakespearean revivals had brought the treasury low. Macready thought seriously of giving up the direction of the theatre at the end of the season instead of continuing for another year as he had intended. In the nick of time, however, another of his standard authors, Sheridan Knowles, appeared with a comedy which Forster titled *Woman's Wit, or Love's Disguises*. It was promptly put into rehearsal, although the manager had little hope for it. Knowles himself was vastly pleased with the carefully planned rehearsals, but Macready had his usual difficulties memorizing a distasteful part. It is certainly not a good play, and Macready's misgivings were judicious. But audiences are unpredictable. The production was received with great enthusiasm and was repeated 31 times during the remainder of the season. As Knowles may be credited with having first won for Macready the acclaim of a London audience, of setting him apart from his fellows, so he may be credited with having renewed his determination to rescue the drama. Theatrical memories are short, and one success can sweeten a whole year of failure.

This renewed determination was strengthened by a solemn event which took place after the performance on May 31. Summoned into the greenroom, Macready found his company assembled. Bartley, as their spokesman, delivered an address and presented a salver on which all their names were inscribed, informing the manager of their high appreciation of his noble conduct, of his uniform deportment towards them, and "of the various acts that together had brought back to them a season equal in its effects to them to the best days of the drama within the memory of the oldest actor."[24] This was indeed true. Salaries had been regularly paid, rehearsals and business matters had been conducted with equal despatch, 55 of the playing nights had been devoted to Shakespeare, 154 to other "legitimate" dramas, including the 31 nights of *Woman's Wit* and the 33 of *The Lady of Lyons,* and 138 to opera and pantomime, leaving a balance for the first time in many years in favor of the legitimate. Macready pointed this out in his reply to Bartley, defending himself from hostile accusations of those who declared he had taken the theatre only to put money into his pocket—an irony this—and asking credit for good intentions if he had been momentarily betrayed into injustice toward any of them. Shaking hands with those about him, he departed, leaving the greenroom filled with an aura of disinterested good feeling which that ancient institution had rarely experienced in all its long history.

His determination to continue as manager was announced to the public by Bartley in the customary concluding address on the last night of the season, July 6. It was a gracious performance, and betrayed the hand of its author:

An opinion has gone abroad that our standard English plays are no longer attractive to an English public. You will, I am sure, learn with pleasure that the plays of Shakespeare produced at this theatre, genuine and unalloyed, have been the most profitable performances of the season. We have further to acknowledge our obligations for the liberality and zeal with which the pens of Bulwer and Talfourd, and the pencil of Stanfield, have been engaged in our cause; and to add to the happy recollections of our season a new piece by Sheridan Knowles, together with the introduction of the name of Rooke among those which adorn the English opera.[25]

And when Bartley announced that the management would continue for another season, the cheering was so loud and long that Macready thought it time to decamp and slipped out of the theatre.

It was a fitting close to a season of triumph and disappointment when Talfourd wrote to him on the fifteenth of July and disclosed that the coals which had been heaped upon his head in the farewell address had not been heaped in vain. Ingenuously, he declared,

I was more affected & gratified than I can express to you by the noble mention made of me in the address delivered at the close of your theatre;—I rejoice to be able still to call it yours—for otherwise it will never be ours, nor will a hope for the glorious cause of the Drama remain. I cannot believe—notwithstanding all the instances of ill-requited energy—that next season will not make you and yours some amends for the generous sacrifices of the last. If not, the setting time of the great English drama has arrived, and we must be contented to catch the last gleams of its departed glory.[26]

A handsome *amende.*

It may not have been wholly disinterested. Macready had signed with Benjamin Webster to play at the Haymarket for five weeks during the summer recess of Covent Garden. He suspected that Webster was after Knowles' successful play, since he had declared that he would not act Shakespeare at the Haymarket. But what Webster really seems to have had in mind was a production of *The Athenian Captive.* The play was staged on August 4, 1838, with no pother whatsoever; Webster was a man who got things done, though willing to put up with makeshift, which accounts for Macready's reluctance to play Shakespeare for him. The result of Webster's business-like determination in the present instance was that Macready and Mrs. Warner were recalled by a cordial audience, Talfourd could scarcely remain in his box from excitement, delight, and surprise, and the cabinet convened for congratulations. Macready played seventeen performances of *The Captive,* together with several of his comedy parts and one performance of Melantius for Elton's benefit. Elton had hoped that his former manager might be persuaded to act for him gratuitously, but Macready had dashed his hopes by saying that it was a matter of professional conduct with him to be paid for acting. Elton swallowed his disappointment and was prompt, on the day after the benefit, to bring Macready £25. Macready immediately sat down and wrote him a check for £30, as a benefit donation.

During the Haymarket performances he was working on the plans for his second Covent Garden season. His principles of management were to be unchanged. Shakespeare revived would be the backbone of the repertory, the legitimate drama was to predominate, and virtually the same company was to be assembled. From a letter to Colonel Smith,[27] an antiquarian to whom Macready frequently turned for information about historical costume, it is evident that he contemplated a revival of *Richard II*—his interest in that play seems never to have waned—and for many weeks his mind was occupied with *The Tempest,* his first great effort of the season.

This production of *The Tempest,* October 13, 1838, is one of the evidences of the anomalous attitude which he took towards the restoration of Shakespeare. The text was purged of the additions of Dryden and Davenant, of the secondary pair of lovers and such matter, but a great deal was made of machinery: the first scene was played totally in pantomime with a huge ship foundering upon the stage ocean, and with Ariel (Priscilla Horton) floating above in a flying harness. These details sound like Bunn at his worst, and indeed Macready was to complain about the introduction of a ship and the elimination of poetry at Covent Garden in 1842.[28] Yet the other details suggest the good taste of the manager: Prospero's Isle was covered with trees and rocks in fantastic shapes, "as though the sylphs that dwelt there had gambolled and twisted them into sylph-like meanings,"[29] the music was chosen largely from Purcell and so performed that it seemed to come, magically, from every part of space. Yet this seemingly ideal setting was, as *The Spectator* observed, principally made up of scenery from the

unfortunate Easter pantomime, *Sinbad the Sailor,* and some of
Dryden's text was retained to provide additional songs for Priscilla
Horton.[30] There were, however, no complaints from the audiences
who came in huge numbers for 55 nights to see the play and
would have come for many more had not Macready persisted in
his stubborn refusal to put it on for a run. *The Tempest* was
another experiment in the development of a new theory of production, and it was not yet clear (until Charles Kean exploited it to
the ultimate absurdity) where the line should be drawn. Macready's intention is plain, to give stage realization to the images
which Shakespeare's poetry called to his mind, and John Forster's
description of the result, though not unprejudiced, is probably
accurate as far as the majority of the audience was concerned. "It
is a daydream," he wrote, "realised for all eyes and hearts."[31]

The repertory was established, with *Hamlet* (October 15) every
Monday until further notice, *The Lady of Lyons* (October 17)
every Wednesday until further notice, and *Othello* (October 18)
every Thursday until further notice. Old plays were revived on off
nights to give Vandenhoff and Phelps, who had rejoined the company, chances to star. *Cato* appeared, once only, on November 2;
Anderson was permitted to try the lead in *Ion; Venice Preserved*
and *Jane Shore* made brief appearances. But *The Tempest* carried
all with it until the approaching Christmas holidays demanded a
new pantomime.

Success eliminated a good many of the frictions of management,
but a little unpleasantness managed to arise. To forestall Bunn's
production of Rossini's *William Tell* at Drury Lane, Macready
decided to revive Knowles' old play, of which he was thoroughly
tired. The preparation was a hard and dull task for him. Knowles
made some few changes in the script and all had to be rehearsed
anew. It had a reasonable run of fourteen performances, but
Knowles saw fit to demand a portion of the nightly receipts.
Macready recalled that Knowles had given him the gratuitous
rights of performing the play at the time of its first production
and rejected the suggestion, paying the author instead £20 out-
right "for the work he had done—which was *very little!*"

The pantomime, *Harlequin and Fair Rosamond,* was another
distasteful task. Preparations did not go well. A diorama that he
had counted on was disappointing when exhibited. Intended to
duplicate the success of Stanfield's *Journey to England* of last
Christmas, the subject chosen was the events of the years 1837–8,
including the coronation of the Emperor of Austria and a view
of the smoking ruins of the Royal Exchange. Forster, Dickens,

Browning, and Fonblanque were the advisors, attending rehearsals diligently and with greater interest than Macready was able to muster. The day before Christmas was spent in a final rehearsal that lasted from eight in the morning until nearly eight-thirty in the evening. At the conclusion Macready was in his usual state of despair. He summoned the stagehands together and began running over possible changes and simplifications in the production, discovering in the process that much of the difficulty lay in poor organization, that they had not been properly instructed. His early years backstage on the Birmingham circuit came to his aid. The Eminent Tragedian showed the blundering stagehands how they might perform their tasks with greater despatch, and, as a result, at the technical rehearsal on Christmas day all went smoothly. But he was still displeased with the work of his scene painter Charles Marshall, and felt that the anticipated failure of the pantomime would be due to his "shameful inefficiency," and to his vanity and presumption in undertaking a diorama. The manager's worst fears were realized. On December 26 *Harlequin and Fair Rosamond* went down, he declared, to utter defeat, and ruin, like the ghost of his imprisoned father, stared him in the face. But in some manner unexplained, for Macready rarely mentions such works once they have reached performance, the pantomime was saved, ran 41 nights, and immediate ruin was postponed.

New plays had been arriving regularly since the commencement of the season. The manager welcomed them, read them, and turned them over to the advisors for consideration. Dickens wrote a farce at the instigation of Forster, but it proved flat in the reading. Fanny Kemble Butler sent him, from America, her play, *An English Tragedy*. Reading it, Macready was enthralled; "one of the most powerful of the modern plays I have seen," he wrote, "most painful, most shocking, but full of power, poetry, and pathos. She is one of the most remarkable women of the present day." He sent it to Bulwer for his opinion, and then called on Mrs. Butler's friend, the Reverend William Harness, for an opinion. Harness was disposed to hedge. The first three acts he felt were hazardous (the subject of the play was seduction), but he proposed consulting Henry Hart Milman and Harriet Martineau. Bulwer was apprehensive—it was too gross, he felt; and Harness reported that his sister would not let him continue reading the play. That was enough for Macready. Much as he liked the work, he wrote Mrs. Butler a polite note of rejection, and looked elsewhere.

On one of his friends, Bulwer, he could depend absolutely. With great delight he heard on the twenty-fourth of October that a rough sketch of a play, an historical comedy on the subject of Richelieu, had been completed. Nor, knowing Bulwer's rate of composition, could he have been greatly surprised when the manuscript arrived on the twelfth of November. The process which gave final form to *The Lady of Lyons* was repeated. Macready at first found the new play deficient in dramatic interest. Bulwer had intended for Macready the role of the Chevalier de Marillac (later called DeMauprat) "the wittiest and bravest gentleman" at the court of Louis XIII. The plot was to be his struggle against the enmity of Richelieu, who was to involve him in a marriage reminiscent of *The Maid's Tragedy*. But Macready was quick to see that Richelieu was the most interesting figure of the play and he convinced Bulwer, against his wishes, that the plot must be recast. On the seventeenth of November, the actor laid his plans before the author for building Richelieu into the dominant character, and Bulwer's reluctance was overcome. He was in "ecstacies" over the proposed alterations, agreed to have them in a week, and appeared the next day with two good scenes already finished. Macready meanwhile was reading up in the history of the period. He consulted Alfred De Vigny's *Cinq Mars* and found it good enough to send to Bulwer with a note pointing out its significance. But the revised version of the play, when it was finally put into his hands, was too long. He set about cutting it, act by act, with the assistance of Robertson. Then, on the twenty-fifth of November he read the play to Bulwer, Forster, and his wife and sister, after dinner. The hour was perhaps unfortunate. Forster went to sleep.

Bulwer was of course disappointed and angry, but Forster could offer no other explanation than that the play did not hold his interest. Macready commented that his critic-friend had warmth of feeling, but not much judgement, and lacked the fine tact of good breeding. Nonetheless, he wrote Bulwer that *Richelieu* would not serve his interest as an author or a politician.

But Bulwer was not a man to give up. He came at once to Macready, they discussed the play, and determined to go on with it. For two weeks they exchanged notes, Macready always planning, suggesting alterations, and making decisions as to plot and incidents, and Bulwer acting upon them. On the sixteenth of December a special meeting of the cabinet—enlarged to include Henry Smith, Serle, Browning, Fox, Blanchard, and Lane—was called for a reading of the play. Each was given paper and pencil and cautioned to speak no word during the process. The comments were nearly all encouraging, Fox and Serle were both enthusiastic, and Browning contented himself with a Browningesque, "The play's the thing." On January 5, 1839, the manuscript was read to the company in the greenroom, and the manager was "most agreeably surprised to find it excite them in a very extraordinary manner." The next month it was put into rehearsal.

Author and manager were still at work making changes. Characters were strengthened, lines which failed of effect in rehearsal were improved or omitted. In the final version, it was discovered that Macready had cut over eight hundred lines, both in places where action could be more effectively substituted, and in places where the plot line needed simplification. Macready himself studied his character not solely from the revised script but, as in his preparation for a Shakespearean role, from the histories of the period. The whole production was planned with careful attention to historical accuracy in plot, character, costume, and setting.

On March 7 *Michelieu* was performed with unequivocal success. In his old age, the playwright Westland Marston related the story of the first night and gave at the same time a vivid picture of playgoing in the midyears of the century:

In March, 1839, I fought my way with another young enthusiast to the pit door of old Covent Garden, on the first night of Bulwer's "Richelieu." What a human sea it was, and how lit up by expectation, that surged and roared for two hours against that grim, all-ignoring barrier! But its stubborn resistance, and the dense pressure which, at last, almost wedged out the breath of every unit in the crowd, gave an almost stern delight, a zest of contest for a prize, of which the lounger into a reserved box or seat has no conception. The interest connected with a new play was increased by the fact that Bulwer was the author, for with us young critics his epigrams, his rhetorical flashes, and, let it be said, a vein of aspiration and generous feeling, rarely absent from his later works, had made him a favourite. . . .

Suppose, then, the thronged house hushed, the curtain raised, the gay scene of the conspirators and gamesters going forward beneath the roof of Marion de L'Orme. Even amidst the interest of this opening scene, the thought of the house escapes to Macready. Will he be discovered with all the insignia of his rank and power? Will he be closeted with Louis, or giving audience to a spy? Will his manner have the pride of the churchman, or the smoothness of the diplomatist? The first scene is over, and we have our answer.

Macready, as the Cardinal, enters, followed by the Capuchin Joseph, and the coming revelation—signal, and in some respects new—of the actor's powers, is at once foreshadowed by his appearance. How full of individuality are the whitening hair, the face sharpened to the utmost expression of subtlety and keenness, the gait somewhat loose with age, but now quick and impulsive, now slow or suddenly arrested, which seems to give a rhythm to the workings of his brain.

The description continues, recording the successive revelation of Richelieu's character through colloquialism, sly wit, and power, until the final scene where the Cardinal, on the verge of death, attends the King to submit his resignation:

How touching was the proud humility of the weak old man as he relinquished, seemingly forever, the splendid cares of State; how arresting the sight of him as, supported in his chair, his face now grew vacant, as if through the feebleness of nature, now resumed a gleam of intelligence, which at times contracted into pain, as he gathered the policy of his rivals—a policy fatal to France! One noted the uneasy movements of the head, the restless play of the wan fingers, though the lips were silent, till at last the mind fairly struggled awhile through its eclipse, as, in a loud whisper, he warned the King his succours would be wasted upon England. Then came the moment when, recovering the despatch which convicted his foes of treason, he caused it to be handed to the King, and sank supine with the effort. Slowly and intermittently consciousness returned, as Louis thrice implored him to resume his sway over France. So naturally marked were the fluctuations between life and death, so subtly graduated (though comprised within a few moments) were the signs of his recovery, that the house utterly forgot its almost incredible quickness when, in answer to the King's apprehensive cry as to the traitors—
"Where will they be next week?"
Richelieu springs up resuscitated, and exclaims—
"There, at my feet!"

And finally, as the curtain fell,

it was an audience dazzled, almost bewildered by the brilliancy of the achievement, that, on the instant fall of the curtain, burst into a roar of admiration that, wild, craving, unappeasable, pursued, like a sea, the retreating actor, and swept him back to the front.[32]

The *Times*, knowing the author, could not like it, of course. It was "Clever," nothing more. But the *Chronicle* was approving and there could be no doubt of the feelings of the audiences. *Richelieu* was performed 37 times in the remainder of the season, became the *rôle à faire* for every succeeding star, and the one play of its period which has survived on the contemporary stage. DeVigny, who had been consulted on the characterization, saw an early performance, and wrote a graceful note to Macready: "Vos gestes mêlés d'habitudes ecclésiastiques et d'infirmités et d'énergie extérieur combinés parfaitment et tous le rôle composé avec un art sûr et profond."[33] Bulwer himself felt that full justice had not been done to some of his points—he missed a comic scene (a "coarse and vulgar attempt at a low farcical point" is the way Macready describes it),[34] and felt that at one point the dismissal of Baradas was too colloquial. "[T]he thought of your conception," he wrote, "is almost too subtle for the gigantic audiences you have."[35] Macready thought this an invitation to substitute "melodramatic rant . . . for the more delicate shadings of character that I endeavour to give," and dismissed the letter with a few private observations about Bulwer's taste.

There could be no question about the success of the second season at Covent Garden. *The Tempest* and *Richelieu* alone assured full houses and the standard plays filled in the gaps reasonably well. But Macready had almost from the start determined that this would be his last term in the post. He felt that he was deteriorating as an actor. His experiences with *Richelieu,* where the daily cares of management had prevented him, he said, from realizing his ambitions for the character, further convinced him that it was time to retire. When Webster came to him on the twenty-first of March with an offer of £100 a week to act four nights for a full season, he promised to sign with him as soon as the proprietors of Covent Garden had refused his offer. What the offer was, we do not know, but it was made presumably more as a matter of form than with any expectation or desire of its acceptance. On the sixth of April the contract with Webster was signed, and Macready began making plans to exit from Covent Garden in glory.

The final play of his management could only be one of Shakespeare's, and the staging must be a kind of summary of all his ideals and ambitions. He had long thought of a revival of *Henry V* and now he set to work with Stanfield to create an unforgettable production. The cabinet was summoned to attend rehearsals—Bulwer, Dickens, Forster, Daniel Maclise, Fox—all of whom offered suggestions freely. Forster was particularly obstreperous, directing and suggesting until some of the actors were able to convince Mrs. Humby (originally cast for Mrs. Quickly) that he was the author of the play. He finally so upset her with his cries of "Put her through it again, Mac!" that she gave up the part to Mrs. Jones. The spectacular production opened on June 10, and was performed 21 times to the end of the season. It was thoroughly satisfactory to Macready, the grand gesture at his exit, though some of the critics questioned the taste of Stanfield's pictorial illustrations of the speeches of the Chorus. The result was, to judge from the descriptions, a near approach to the brilliant motion picture version by Sir Laurence Olivier a century later. *Henry V* lends itself to this sort of treatment, the author himself seems to have longed for it, and, at the very worst, no great harm was done. The first night spectators stood up and cheered as it was announced for repetition four nights weekly, and on the sixteenth of July assembled in an almost riotous mob to see it for the last time and hear Macready's farewell speech as manager.

A summary of the season shows how closely Macready had clung to his original purpose. There had been 118 nights of Shakespeare, 144 of other legitimate plays, and only 79 of opera and pantomime. He had accomplished his intention of restoring the drama to its ancient dignity, and without loss to himself (except by his own peculiar method of calculation). And there was awaiting him an honor in which he took great satisfaction.

The Victorians, liking both ceremony and food, liked nothing so much as the two in combination. Theirs was an era of vast public dinners in honor of this or that hero, or in support of this or that charity. In the Macready circle the tradition was for dinners upon any commemorable occasion. The literary historian could establish with some certainty the dates of the completion of each of Dickens' novels by the successive dinners that were held to solemnize the occasions. The retirement of the great John Kemble from the stage had been marked by a famous banquet during the course of which Macready had met the even greater Talma. It is not surprising, therefore, that Macready's friends and cabinet members should hit upon the idea of a great feast in the Freemason's Tavern, to commemorate his management, to honor his name, and to have a reasonable excuse, through toast-drinking, for an evening of jollification. Macready, of course, took the event very seriously, spending many laborious hours over the speech with which he would reply to his toast. "This honour," he wrote, "is a business of much, very much solicitude and, like most honours, carries with it its full share of trouble." But it was also gratifying and he recorded the whole event in his *Diary* in detail.

Arriving in the reception-room of the Tavern on the twentieth of July, he was greeted by Martin Archer Shee, president of the Royal Academy, and Richard Monckton Milnes, M. P. Later came Samuel Lover, the editor William Jerdan, several noblemen, Dickens, Bulwer, and his friendly rival of old, Charles Young.

With the appearance of the Duke of Sussex, who was to preside, the group moved into the main dining room where Macready was cheered and applauded as he passed to his seat, embarrassed by those who rose up to stare at him, and moved by sight of his wife seated in the gallery, "perhaps the sweetest moment of the night to me." He was placed on the right of the Duke. Somewhat unnerved by his highness' volubility, he looked so grave and pale that Bulwer afterwards declared he resembled a "baffled tyrant." At length the musical program was completed and the Duke arose and proposed Macready's health in a flowery speech, which he had quite probably not composed. As the guest of honor prepared to reply, the whole assembly got to its feet, shouting and waving handkerchiefs, both the men on the floor and the ladies in the gallery. Macready looked about him with pleasure and some apprehension. "It was not like an English assembly," was his proud thought.

His speech was a lengthy and solemn one, perhaps too solemn for the occasion, but these people had assembled to honor his achievement, and he was determined that they should at least know what he had set out to do. He had noticed, he said, that of all the branches of art or science of the day only the drama had been in a course of decline. The staging of the plays of Shakespeare was but a barbarous burlesque of the poet's conceptions. His purpose had been to make what improvements he could in the existing system, to make the arts of decoration serve the purposes of the playwright; to the success of this plan he attributed the success of his management. He had hoped to leave in the theatre "the complete series of Shakespeare's acting plays," the text restored and the staging so directed that the productions would have been "one of the best illustrated editions of the poet's works." In relinquishing his task unfinished, he yet hoped that the theatre might remain the temple of Shakespeare, no longer a place of demoralizing and licentious resort. In conclusion he paid tribute to Bulwer, to Stanfield, Dickens, Talfourd, and Serle. He sat down in another burst of rapture from his hearers.

There were other toasts, some eight, and Macready arose the next morning with an aching head. But he had had his day, a memory which he could never forget. Others were determined that it should not be forgotten also. His newspaper tormentors went to work with a will: but with such a will that he felt secure against self-betraying malignity. Only one prompter could have inspired such a performance as the following:

THE MACREADY MUMMERY

A most farcical exhibition took place on the 20th of this month, at the Freemason's Tavern, the hero of which was "the great tragedian." The public had been already sufficiently nauseated by the bouncible efforts made by Macready to unseat Garrick, Kemble, and Kean, from their pedestals, and to exalt his own rueful figure in their place. But a treble-distilled dose of buffoonery must be crammed down the stomach of the town, like the compound antibilious pills, under the immediate patronage of his Royal Highness the Duke of Sussex. . . . The weakness of the Duke of Sussex, in reference to [testimonial dinners], is too notorious for us to dwell upon at any length, and we shall therefore only state that he was enthroned as chairman, on the important occasion of giving a public dinner—a public dinner! to the "only representative of Shakespeare's heroes!" To Macready alone! then, it has been allotted to give an embodiment to the imaginative creations of the poet; he alone has had his spirit purely warmed by the "muse of fire"; he alone has climbed "the heaven of invention," and felt the genius of the immortal bard! Oh! what a mighty virtue there is in a paint brush! Shakespeare conceived, Macready delineated, and Stanfield executed! . . . Henceforth the performance of Shakespeare's divine writings will be dioramic, and every penny peep show in the kingdom will carry out to a glorious consummation the sublime labours and intelligence of Macready. . . .

Let us proceed. The health of the Queen was drunk, and considering how much she has done for British performers, and the legitimate drama, it was a very appropriate commencement of the toasts. . . . But now came the great business of the day—the health of Mr. Macready.

"Gentlemen," said his Royal Highness, "I rejoice in proposing the health of our extraordinary Roscius, whose intellectual and moral efforts have restored the theatre to an unparalleled pinnacle of glory. He has revived ten of Shakespeare's plays, and has erased from them every passage that could wound the sensitive-feelings of a vestal virgin; but what is more, this distinguished member of the Vice Society has cleansed the saloon of all its impurities! He has regulated the breadth of Shakespeare's language, and the length of the petticoats of the frail."

We cannot pretend to describe the ecstatic burst of feeling led on by Sir Lytton Bulwer, which was elicited by this announcement; it was a magnificent tribute to moral greatness, from a band of the purest worshippers of morality, who "hold the mirror up to nature," by endeavouring on the public stage "to show virtue her own feature," and who in private life give to "vice her own image." There is nothing like precept and example. The toast was responded to "with unbounded applause," as they say in the bills, and Mr. Macready rose to acknowledge the compliment. His countenance assumed the genuine tragic fierceness and importance, such as it wore on the eventful night, when after exclaiming

> More lives must yet be drained;
> Crowns got by blood must be by blood maintained,

he rushed upon the defenceless manager, and cracked *his* crown. He, however, essayed to look more like William the Conqueror this night, than Richard the Third, as he gazed upon his audience in the infinitude of his satisfaction.

There follows a burlesque speech, patterned on the Third Richard's first soliloquy, with "Macready" revealing himself as money-mad, ranting, dictatorial, and envious. After further slurs upon Bulwer and the assembled company, the report concludes,

Every man was either a Garrick, or a Shakespeare, in his own opinion, while in the opinion of the judicious, each was the ass in the lion's skin.[36]

Nor was this all. Shortly after the dinner, a pamphlet was put on sale in the form of *A Letter to His Royal Highness the Duke of Sussex on the Late Management of Covent Garden Theatre,* from "A Proprietor of Covent Garden Theatre." The anonymous scribe wishes to warn the Duke that he has been taken in, that all the presiding officers of the banquet were notorious radicals or reformers, and the Duke has, quite innocently, given his authority to those "favorite tenets of despoliation"—referring presumably to the current agitation for the abolition of the monopoly of the two patent theatres. As for Macready's services to the drama, the "proprietor" is willing to grant him a few revivals of Shakespeare and the introduction of the melodramas of Bulwer—but what has he done for Sheridan Knowles, "our modern Shakespeare?" He has given him nothing but a few pounds to induce him to turn *Tell* into an opera as opposition for the production of Rossini's version at Drury Lane. Macready's acting, further, depends wholly on scenic exhibition, gorgeous apparel, and glittering paraphernalia for its effect, and he is scandalized to record that Macready once suggested to Stephen Price that the music in *Macbeth* be omitted.

The managerial efforts of this pretender to the throne of Kean and Young, continues the pamphlet, were based upon a belief that playgoers would make no distinction between the preparation of a play and its performance. And although his management has done nothing whatsoever for the drama, it has considerably advanced Macready. Cannot he—who not long ago was paid £320 by Price to break his contract—command £100 at the Haymarket, and even more in the provinces? And has not every other performer in the company been employed to fill up the gaps in those plays wherein he thought proper to allot himself a principal character? And have not his best receipts, in consequence, been solely attributable to his pantomimes?

Taken as a whole, it might be a pretty damning attack, particularly since it purports to come from one of the proprietors of Macready's theatre who should be in a position to know. But there seems to be enough evidence to show—certain anecdotes which appear only in *The Stage Before and Behind the Curtain*, the reference to *William Tell*, the sneers at Bulwer, and the comments on actors' salaries—that this summary of Macready's first period of management was merely a further show of malignity on the part of a former *manager* of Covent Garden. It was active and undying malignity and it pursued him nearly to the end of his career. The Poet Bunn had a long memory.

✧ ✧ ✧ **6** ✧ ✧ ✧

Regisseur

INTERLUDE AT THE HAYMARKET

THE UNRELENTING enmity of Macready's former manager, Alfred Bunn, contrasts strikingly with the friendship,
or perhaps the forebearance, and the reasonably businesslike attitude of Benjamin Webster, who was to be his manager intermittently until his retirement. Webster had a temper and he was the
most casual of producers, but he was determined to provide at
least an attractive playbill, and to make it attractive, insofar as
he could, in legitimate terms. He hired the best actors he could
get; he readily agreed to Macready's demand of £100 a week; he
was even persuaded to hire, somewhat reluctantly, some of the
members of the Macready Stock Company, those players who were
most constantly associated with his name: Mrs. Warner, Miss
Faucit, Samuel Phelps, and Priscilla Horton. These things he did
because he realized that Macready had a value which none of the
other stars could lay claim to: he was, in a manner of speaking,
the "proprietor" of the plays of Bulwer-Lytton, and Webster, who
had no antiquated notions about repertory, saw an opportunity
to profit handsomely from the public's demonstrated appetite for
his lordship's work. Indeed, he admitted to one of Macready's
lieutenants that he expected the actor to bring plays to him. And
he had barely signed a contract with Macready before he was in
correspondence with Bulwer-Lytton for the performing rights to
his plays. On May 28, 1839, the author replied, granting him permission, for 50 guineas, to act *The Lady of Lyons* until the end of
the year, and continuing,

With regard to Richelieu—I should advise you to consider well whether
you would find it answer to get up so xpensive a play—, I fear that

the xperiment wd disappoint you—The splendour of detail at Covent Garden—would throw into shade less elaborate preparations—& yet for a play that has lost the gloss of novelty you would find equal expense a hazardous adventure.

Ever the business man of letters, he is quick to add:

I have written a play of very strong domestic interest that I think will suit the Haymarket well—It was written with that view—But before I say more of it—or propose the terms, I shall wait for Mr. Macready's opinion—And till Henry 5th is out—He is not at leisure to read it critically—It is an English subject—cost. about the time of Elizabeth & would not require much cost in getting up—The principal parts by Macready, Mrs. Warner, & O. Smith.[1]

Macready's first opinion of Bulwer's new play, *Norman,* rendered to his *Diary* on the sixteenth of June was succinct, *"I do not like it,"* but his second thoughts upon rereading were somewhat more favorable. No doubt he recalled that Bulwer was still his hope among authors and realized (with a sigh?) that the same kind of collaboration that had produced *The Lady of Lyons* and *Richelieu* might produce a third success. There were other plays to be considered also: T. J. Serle's new hack-piece, which overemphasized the female lead, and Browning's *Victor, King of Sardinia* ("a great mistake"). Bulwer-Lytton, having discussed his play, preferred to work on it by himself and rewrote it in a characteristically short time, retitling it *The Sea Captain, or The Birthright.* Macready liked this version less than the original, but Webster had signed for the rights, and there was nothing for it but to "cut and come again" (the rueful phrase is Bulwer's).

After the partial realization of his ideal theatre during the two seasons of his management of Covent Garden, Macready found acting at the Haymarket a depressing experience. The audiences, he felt, were not of the same intellectual quality as those at the patent house, and the theatre itself was a doghole—"dirt, slovenliness, and puffery make up the sum of its character."[2] Though these sound like the terms which he so often applied to Bunn's management, there was the difference that Webster treated him on the whole very fairly, respecting his value as an artist and an attraction. Although the manager was intent on making money from Bulwer, Macready was permitted to open as Othello, and the performances of *The Lady of Lyons* were interpersed with sixteen performances of Shylock, a role which he found rather uncongenial.

Rehearsals for *The Sea Captain* began in the latter part of August, and proceeded in the characteristic agonies of doubt. Bulwer was inclined to withdraw the play and pressed Macready for a decision, but the actor refused to take the responsibility. Forster and Willmott were both confident of its success. Helen Faucit fell ill; Mrs. Warner and Robert Strickland were not, Macready thought, up to their parts. The author came almost daily with new lines to be inserted, and Macready went to the first performance suffering from misgiving and apprehension. His taste did not betray him, though the audience seems to have been partially fooled.

The Sea Captain is inferior to its two predecessors, accentuating all the faults of Bulwer's style: his easy resort to melodrama to escape from plotting difficulties, his insistence upon poetic speech, and his utter lack of the poetic faculty. According to the *Times'* report of the first night, the three first acts went off in a dangerous silence, even the "complimentary applause" at the fall of each curtain waxing faint. But in the fourth act came the climactic scene in which proud Lady Arundel is forced to recognize a humble sea captain, Norman, as the son she had abandoned in his infancy, and the evening was saved. Mrs. Warner, by the strength of her acting of Lady Arundel, carried the audience with her in spite of the fact that their "republican" sympathies were naturally against her. The critic praises her "stifled by-play, her curbing every natural feeling, with the greatest and most apparent effort." This was obviously Macreadyism, the all-powerful domestic emotion manifesting itself in spite of every effort to remain heroic—or in this instance, inhumane. As for Macready's character, which he did well, it was "a mere phantom who can be made to talk against Mammon and gold in one part, and wish to be 'Captain Croesus' in another—a prodigy of heroism and disinterestedness of the melodramatic stamp." (Nov. 1, 1839)

Other papers were less kind and Bulwer was so ill-advised as to take issue with them in the preface to the published play. His defense of himself was surely the weakest that could be made. He was, he says, but a novice in the art of playwriting; he was in uncertain health and broken spirits (he was indeed having domestic difficulties); and adverse criticism had checked his inspiration and damped his ardor. And although the critics, like the *Times* reviewer just quoted, had complained that the characterization was flimsy, "I do not think my faults as a dramatic author are to be found in the study and delineation of character." Thackeray, in a merciless parody of the play in *Fraser's Magazine* for January 1840, reminded Bulwer of his distinguished predecessor in the same line of argument, Sir Fretful Plagiary. Under the heading "Epistles to the Literati," Thackeray, masquerading behind his

pseudonymous butler, Charles Jeames Yellowplush, annihilated
first the preface and then the play, pointing out the ridiculousness
of the plot, the sketchiness of the characters, the religious clap-
traps and false poetics of the dialogue. Cries the bluff sea captain
at the conclusion of the climactic scene:

> Hark? she has blessed her son! I bid ye witness,
> Ye listening heavens—thou circumambient air:
> The ocean sighs it back—and with the murmur
> Rustle the happy leaves. All nature breathes
> Aloud—aloft—to the Great Parent's ear,
> The blessing of the mother on her child.

Some measure of the excellence of the acting can be gained
from the fact that, in spite of such passages, in spite of a plot
hastily botched-up from Alexandre Dumas, and a denouement
which derived its inspiration from the least savory incident in
Much Ado about Nothing, The Sea Captain was performed 38
times. It is a testimony of the author's honesty that he gives due
credit to the actors in his preface.

The run of this play saw concurrently the development of an
incident which caused great unhappiness to Macready and confirmed his opinion of his profession. It will not seem strange to
anyone acquainted with greenroom gossip that Helen Faucit's
illness, which began early in October and became increasingly
worse until she was obliged to withdraw from the theatre, was
diagnosed by Mrs. Warner, Ellen Tree, and Miss Lacy as pregnancy and that, offended by Macready's concern for her professional fortunes, they credited him with being the other interested
party. The effect of such a story on the Eminent is not difficult to
anticipate. He hastened to announce that all his interviews with
his young leading lady had been conducted with the utmost propriety. He told his wife the whole story and she agreed that Miss
Faucit should be invited to their home, so Miss Faucit came, once
to a dinner party and once for a private conference on acting,
during which Catherine was careful to "look in" several times for
respectability's sake. Suggestive paragraphs crept into some of the
unfriendly papers and Macready questioned his dresser very
closely: had he ever said anything reflecting on the lady? Lunn,
the dresser, replied stoutly that he had spoken of her most respectfully and had answered all light and jesting comments with an
assertion that she had seen Macready only on business. The story
assumed ridiculous proportions—which would have persuaded a
less serious man to laugh it away—when Lunn disclosed that not

only Helen Faucit's but Priscilla Horton's name had been linked with Macready's, and even Emmeline Montague's, a young actress whom Macready had scarcely seen.

The gossip became public knowledge. The *Theatrical Journal* reported it: "A cruel and utterly unfounded report respecting the cause of Miss Helen Faucit's temporary retirement, has obtained currency, which could only have originated with some creature of the most depraved imagination. The truly excellent actress is . . . worn down with exertion." A later notice, remarking that Miss Faucit had six slanderers, including two prominent on the stage, is more precise: two physicians testify that she is not pregnant but suffering from "a morbid sensibility of the nerves."[3] Mrs. Warner, meanwhile, became colder and colder towards her erstwhile mentor, and Helen Faucit was sent off to a resort to recover her health. It was not until she had parted from him that Macready realized that the unfortunate girl actually was in love with him.

This, of course, did not help matters any. When she returned from the spa, improved in health but unchanged in her devotion, he tried to reason with her. He suggested a serious study of her profession as a kind of allopathic dose, recommended marriage, anything to prevent her from "widowing her heart" by fixing it "upon one object, whose rare opportunities of enjoying her society afforded him no power of recompensing her tenderness."[4] He would, for his part, always be her friend. At another meeting she confessed to have discovered during her illness her love was all she had to live for, but that she was trying to wrench her heart from him. *"It was a most distressing interview,"* wrote Macready, *"It was a bitter, a most afflicting scene* . . . I took one little remembrance from her, which will always be precious to me. I kissed her forehead—and no more. Our parting was really terrible."[5]

There were other interviews, other partings. Macready tried to persuade her to give up her agonies of self-reproach, lectured her for two hours on the characters of Rosalind and Lady Townley, wrote verses for her album, autographed pictures, composed an essay on acting for her study.[6] She in her turn sent him nosegays to wear "in his characters," alternated between resolutions to make the best of her situation and moments of pathetic backsliding. Once she wrote him a note which set him to thinking upon the temptations of his profession: "the wonder is that, with the provocation of so much excitement and so much opportunity, the tendency of our nature is repressed even as it is." At another time, she sent him a letter "nicely written," but signed with a word which is left blank in the published *Diary*, and which haunted him all through an evening's performance. "God bless her," he wrote, "and make her, and keep her a good girl."

In the end, it all blew over. Miss Faucit was married, happily and prosperously, to Theodore Martin, a barrister and literary man who was doubtless everything Macready would have liked to be. The friendship between Macready and Miss Faucit remained warm and sincere to the end of his life, and he could, looking back on the unhappy months of 1840, comfort himself with the thought that he had behaved rather like a kindly old character man in a play, and as in a play the curtain had fallen on a satisfactory solution and the prospect of a happy future for all the actors.

For all the actors except one, perhaps. Mrs. Warner, whose jealousy seems to have started the whole business, grew less and less reasonable until Webster was finally forced to refuse to re-engage her at the expiration of her contract. Leaving the Haymarket, she played for a time with Samuel Phelps during his famous management of Sadler's Wells, and then tried her hand at the management of the equally shabby Marylebone Theatre. When she at last failed and was left destitute at her husband's death, Macready was one of the first to go to her assistance.[7] That was many years later, but it proves that Macready was capable of forgetting and forgiving, characteristics which are somewhat surprising in the light of his unrelenting hatred of Bunn, and Thesiger, and the others who had, in his eyes, wronged him. It is perhaps ungenerous and untrue to suggest that the difference lay in the damage that Bunn and Thesiger had done to his pocketbook. For Mrs. Warner, when she had been Mary Huddart, had loved him too.

The Haymarket season terminated on January 15, 1840, with a final appearance of *The Sea Captain,* and Macready, after agreeing to rejoin Webster after Easter, undertook a brief engagement at Drury Lane. It was his first appearance at that theatre since the Bunn fracas, and as he entered it for a rehearsal of *Macbeth* he could not but contrast his present situation with that on the dreadful night when he and his friends fled from the manager's retainers. He returned to a splendid salary "and with homage universally rendered" from the people around him. It was a rare moment of optimism for him, completely unjustified by the outcome.

The new manager of Drury Lane was W. J. Hammond, a dealer in music who apparently hoped by a combination of Macready and a new tragedy to succeed where all his predecessors had failed in restoring the theatre to the legitimate. The enterprise had been undertaken hastily and little attention had been paid to the actual management. Lesser performers (but never the star) absented themselves from rehearsals; Thomas Archer became so insolent that Macready took his hat and umbrella and left the stage. The Lord Chamberlain made last-minute cuts in the text of the new play, awakening suspicions that he was engaged on the side of the proprietors of Covent Garden. "It looks very ugly," Macready wrote in his *Diary*, "but my province is endurance, and to 'do nothing,' or say nothing, 'from strife.' " The ghosts of past events, still in the corridors of Drury Lane, warned him to follow his oft-repeated motto, *in nocte consilium*.

January 22 was the first night of the new play, James Haynes' *Mary Stuart*. Macready had considered the piece earlier, under the title of *Ruthven*, during his own management of Covent Garden, but Mrs. Warner's indisposition at that time had caused him to abandon it. It is a rather dull play, but in the Macready manner, constructed around a stern Scots aristocrat whose predominant passions of hatred and zeal are modified by his love for his daughter. The audience was receptive, the *Times* reporting a "complete tumult of applause"[8] at the end, and the piece went on for some twenty performances, interrupted only by seven performances of *Macbeth*. On the twenty-eighth of February, Willmott repeated to Macready a rumor that Hammond, not having been seen for two days, was believed to have made off with the receipts. At the moment they both thought this unlikely, but after the performance the rumor was confirmed. Hammond had decamped, but had been arrested and a fiat of bankruptcy issued against him. Hammond complained, in a letter to the *Times*,[9] that a friend who had promised to invest in his concern had defaulted, but this did not make the actors' lot any easier.

On the twenty-ninth a committee of actors waited upon Macready and agreed to guarantee his full salary if he would act for them for a week, they having taken over the theatre in an endeavor to save what they could from the wreck. Macready would hear neither of salary or sharing, but would play out the week gratuitously if they would promise to pay the author's share. The grateful actors announced his generosity to the public in the playbill of March 6:

☞ The Public is respectfully informed that this Theatre is OPEN under the Direction of a Committee of the Performers; Mr. Macready has in the kindest manner (under the peculiar circumstances) given the aid of his valuable services for three nights more!

The act was further celebrated in a long poem by W. C. D. which appeared as a pamphlet under the title of *The Lament; or the Fall of Drury Lane*. It is a sufficiently amateur performance, and a few stanzas will give an ample taste of its quality. After discussing Hammond's various efforts to keep the theatre open, the Sweet Singer of Drury Lane continues:

> Thus he pursued the tenor of his way,
>   But unsuccessfully—the man was reedy—
> And falling fast, his losses to repay
>   Became the task of William Charles Macready.

> "Macbeth" drew crowds (quite strangers) to the door,
>   And "Mary Stuart" wonders did achieve,
> The house was crammed, till it would hold no more,
>   And how it held those, I really can't conceive;

> For each appeared to sit upon the head
>   Of his next neighbor—comfortable cushion—
> Some hard as stone, and some as soft as lead,
>   Yet better off than those that stood the pushing.

Macready may well have felt this poor payment for his generosity.

On the sixteenth of March he opened an engagement at the Haymarket which continued for an entire year, until a new scheme for management took possession of him. Although this was to be another Bulwer-Lytton season, *Richelieu* and *The Lady of Lyons* occupying the major portion of the repertory, the first new play that was brought out had come into Macready's hands in a "romantic" fashion. In December of the preceding year, Dickens had given him a Mr. Collinson's play, *Glencoe,* to consider. He found much to praise in it, and discussed it along with other plays at a dinner a few nights later with Talfourd and Forster. He was frank in declaring to Talfourd that it was written in imitation of his style, but that it lacked Talfourd's ability to point a speech. It was not melodramatic, however; it was a striking treatment of a popular subject and he had determined to act it. At this point Talfourd pulled two printed copies from his pocket and confessed to being its author. Encouraged by his cabinet, Macready persuaded Webster to put the play into rehearsal and it made a successful debut on the twenty-third of May. Compared to *Richelieu,* the play made a mediocre showing with 22 performances, but Dickens was enthusiastic about Macready's interpretation. "I have seen you play ever since I was that   high," he wrote, "but I never saw you make such a gallant stand as you did last night, or carry anything through so triumphantly and manfully by the force of your own great gifts."[10]

The next new play, Serle's *Master Clarke,* was not brought forward until September 26, and it proved a dismal failure. Macready had trouble memorizing his part, a fault which was becoming increasingly frequent. A revival of Mrs. Inchbald's antiquated *To Marry or Not to Marry* was no more successful than it had a right to be, and Macready was out of place in the midst of a company of experienced comic actors, led by Mrs. Glover. He fumed over and over about her "vulgar buffoonery," and was quite unsettled and thrown out of his character by her style. But in this case, the offender was in the right. Mrs. Glover knew her comic business and Macready quite plainly did not.

To rescue the season from complete dullness, however, there was the ever-ready Bulwer, this time with *Money,* a prose comedy of contemporary life. By mid-September Macready was busy on it, reading and cutting, and consulting Forster about its possibilities. Suggestions were sent to the author in the customary manner, and suggestions advanced to Webster as to the casting and production. Somewhat to his chagrin, Macready discovered that Webster himself wished to act Graves, a fine low-comedy role, instead of Lord Glossmore, a minor caricature in which Macready had visualized him. Webster spoke at some length upon the subject of his own talents, but Macready was not convinced. Bulwer settled the matter by nominating Webster for the part. To fill up certain other roles, Macready suggested the hiring of special actors, going so far as to announce his willingness to play extra nights gratuitously to make up their salaries.

In staging the play, Macready determined that it should be done as carefully as his Shakespearean revivals at Drury Lane. Since one of the scenes turned upon a game of piquet, he conscientiously took up the study of card playing. Count D'Orsay was sent for to supervise the costumes and give information about the operation of gentlemen's clubs. Bulwer brought his manservant to rehearsals to teach the supernumeraries the art of handing letters to their masters. Great pains were taken with the star's "pantaloons" that no wrinkle might show, and with his shoes which were especially made to "sit" to perfection. All this was bewildering and upsetting to Webster, who was content to let the acting alone carry the play. He protested somewhat querulously about the added expense and about Macready's high-handed behavior, and Macready, sensing a storm, replied that he had a duty to the author, as well as to himself; if Webster was dissatisfied the play could be turned over to Covent Garden where the Vestris-Mathews management would be certain to do it justice. This brought an indignant letter of protest from the manager. It is undated, but Macready records its receipt in his *Diary* on October first. Aside from its documentary value in relating the history of the production of very nearly the last successful comedy of the old school, before the reform of the genre by Tom Robertson, it reveals the character of a man whose temper and temperament were very much like Macready's. He had, at least, a sense of his own dignity and ability, and with this justification, that he was one of the few consistently successful managers over an extended period in the nineteenth century. The letter, like Webster, is determined and honest:

My dear Sir—

In addressing you I beg you distinctly to understand that I have not the slightest wish to offend you but really (independent of your threat of last evening) your contempt of me as an actor and manager is made so painfully apparent by your words & manner that I must give vent to my feelings on the subject, and as we are both of an irritable temperament, have thought it best to write rather than speak my feelings on the subject. Every man is more or less an egoist, especially in the profession we have adopted, and I am vain enough to suppose that I have some judgement founded upon the strength of the number of attractive pieces I have produced, in which you have not acted, or otherwise I have been a most successful imposter, which latter opinion my egotism will not incline me to. The pieces introduced by you are always attended with great expence and in five act matters I have not had one attractive novelty since the first season. First as regards authors, no allowance is ever made to me for previous failures and you always appear to me to be the last to urge any consideration of the kind indeed rather to encourage a contrary feeling. Secondly, an increase of actors, witness Mr. George Bennet's engagement which will entail upon me an extra item in the expenditure of nearly one hundred pounds[;] then there are extra scene painters, dresses, &c. I know you will say you do not compel me to this, but you also say, you will not act with such & such actors and unless such effects are produced by such scenery & such dresses it is of no use to attempt to bring out such & such pieces. Now all these points as far as my means will allow & even beyond I have most cheerfully acceded to, & endeavoured to study your every wish till at last my patience is literally exhausted as my pocket will soon be if I do not make a stand against these continued unproductive outlays. Last Evening you thought proper upon my merely making an observation upon the cast of Sir E. L. Bulwer's new comedy to threaten to send it to Covent Garden Theatre a Theatre directly opposed to the one in which you are receiving one hundred pounds per week at the least for ten months in the year but if you feel justified in doing so I beg to repeat what I then said that you are at perfect liberty to act as you please; for however I might regret such a proceeding no threats shall scare me from giving an opinion where my own interests are vitally concerned. Now, my dear Sir, I wish you to clearly understand me upon another point—In admiration of your talent I will give in to no man and your great merits I have advocated both in public & in private but unless we can work amicably and zealously together with perfect confidence in each other and I must reluctantly confess my faith in your friendship to me is shaken by last night's threats I feel that it would be far better for me to jog on comfortably in my old & humble but profitable way, than to endure this continued scene of splendid misery which will probably end in loss. Again assuring you I mean nothing offensive in what I have written leaving you perfectly free to act either for or against me, I am,

    My dear Sir,
      Yours most respectfully,
       B. Webster.[11]

To this, Macready returned a quiet reply, and their differences were temporarily healed.

As *Money* moved toward its premiere, rehearsals were interrupted by the first appearance of a domestic enemy that would hound Macready for many years and would evoke from him demonstrations of patience, courage, and deep emotion in striking contrast to his intemperate outbursts against his real or suspected professional adversaries. In spite of occasional upsets, a long life of grueling work is sufficient evidence that Macready himself had an iron constitution, but it was his fate to see his beloved children one after another fall victims to the wracking pain, the withering, emaciating decay of what the century called "consumption." He would not or could not admit it to himself, but the disease was the fatal dowry that Catherine Atkins brought him, and it was to put an end to her life only a year after the event which both so earnestly anticipated, his retirement from the stage.

In late September 1840, two-year old Henry was the first to be stricken. Month after month he lay in his bed, growing thin and pale, one day better, the next worse, while Macready went from sleepless nights of anxiety to his daytime duties in the theatre. If he left the house encouraged that Henry seemed brighter, he could be assured of a gloomy report on his return. The doctor might tell him that there was "no reason" why Henry should not recover, but the actor's ear was sensitive to the ambiguous uncertainty in his voice. He became nervous and unwell himself from lack of sleep and the ceaseless sound of coughing from the child's room. There was nothing to do but pray, as he did from the depths of his heart, and work, which he did with desperate earnestness.

On November 22, three-year old Harriet Joanna fell ill and Macready's anxiety doubled, but for two days he drove himself through his professional obligations, rehearsing *Money* and performing *The Lady of Lyons*. On the twenty-fifth he returned from the theatre so exhausted that he fell asleep while studying a new scene that Bulwer wished to insert. He awaked to find Henry worse and Harriet in a coma. The doctor arrived with leeches and medicine and the less than comforting opinion that her case was alarming "but not quite desperate." Driven to action by his helplessness, Macready went to Henry's sickroom but the doctor would not permit him to kiss his son. He next tried to see Harriet, but Catherine forced him from the room. In utter misery he flung himself on his own bed and, wrapping the coverlid about his face, lay in a kind of stupor until his sister came in tears to tell him that his daughter was dead. Without conscious purpose, he ran upstairs to the child's room, felt her heart beat—did he cry with Lear, "Look there, look there"?—but the doctor immediately entered to pronounce her dead.

The Eminent Tragedian discovered, at what a cost, the true experience of tragedy: he was unable to weep, he was quite tranquil, he wished only to remain with his dear child. But the doctor sent him to his study where he sat in meditation and prayer until, well after midnight, he was permitted to visit her once more and pray, alone, over her body, that her brother might be spared.

There was no thought of work, of course, for the five days before Harriet's funeral. In spite of prayers and anguished optimism, Henry did not improve, and Macready moved with increasing despair between the bedside of his apparently dying boy and the tiny coffin. His only distraction was to hear the other children in their lessons and prayers and to instruct them—and to remind himself—that death was to be borne, not feared. From his friends, from Dickens and Fox, he received letters which brought him comfort, and even John Forster, whose intended condolences went unspoken when he was overcome by passionate grief, may have inspired him to greater patience.

On the thirtieth of November, Harriet was laid in her grave and Henry, miraculously, began a slow but certain recovery. Two days later Macready had returned to the study of his role and on the next day he was directing rehearsals of *Money* at the Haymarket. On December 8 it finally made its appearance with complete success. Macready felt that Helen Faucit as the heroine had the advantage over him in the last scene, but he could find little else to complain of. Bulwer had consulted his talents closely in designing a comedy role for his favorite star. There is nothing very funny in the part of Alfred Evelyn; it is serious, sentimental, and its wit is grim and sardonic. The humor in the play—and some of its scenes are very funny indeed—was entrusted to the experienced comedians of the company: Webster's Graves was a droll original, the widower who constantly laments his departed wife "the sainted Maria," ("That's his wife," explains Sir John Vesey, "she made him a martyr, and now he makes her a saint"); and Mrs. Glover had a fine, outspoken, and liberal character part in Lady Franklin who finally captures the widower—"Sainted Maria," he exclaims as they go off together, "thank Heaven you are spared this affliction!" Sir Frederick Blount, the fashionable lisping coxcomb, was almost a burlesque of Bulwer himself. Lord Glossmore and Stout illustrated very shrewdly the current struggle between the aristocracy and the manufacturing magnates for political power.

In form, the play is an old comedy; it belongs to the school of Sheridan and Douglas Jerrold. Its five acts cover time and space with freedom, though the structure is somewhat tidier than usual. It begins with one of those distressingly blunt expository scenes in which one character informs the other of past events well known to both. The characters are types, almost humours, as their names indicate, and the sentimental love story of the poverty-stricken scholar, Alfred Evelyn, and his poverty-stricken cousin, Clara Douglas, is about as convincing as the corresponding situations in Dickens, which it much resembles. Macready was not happy as Evelyn, though he played the part 80 times in the season. "A damned walking gentleman!" he called it.[12] But much of himself was written into the role, his detestation of the press, his highly moral attitude towards money, his sarcastic disapproval of the existence of an aristocracy. And for all its faults, the play has a genuine charm, artificial though it may be, ending in the standard half-circle in which each character, in his particular *humour,* addresses the audience in the delightful conclusion which was a convention of the form.

Graves.	But for the truth and the love, when found, to make us tolerably happy, we should not be without—
Lady Franklin.	Good health.
Graves.	Good spirits.
Clara.	A good heart.

Smooth. [the gambler]	An innocent rubber.
Georgina.	Congenial tempers.
Blount.	A pwoper degwee of pwudence.
Stout. [the radical M. P.]	Enlightened opinions.
Glossmore. [the aristocrat]	Constitutional principles.
Sir John.	A little humbug.
Evelyn.	And—plenty of MONEY.

The company was well designed to do justice to such a comedy. The *Theatrical Journal* on November 14, 1840, celebrated the Haymarket ensemble in glowing terms:

This theatre has been lately called the actor's theatre, nor is the term inapplicable at the present moment, when we consider the varied and first-rate talent engaged. With Macready, the first tragedian of the present day, is joined J. Wallack, the first and last of the old school of genteel comedy; each of these is a host in himself; Macready fraught with honour lately gained in his own country, and Wallack, as the only man who was able to uphold the spirit and independence of the American stage; when we add to these such assistants as Phelps and Bennett in tragedy, and Rees and Strickland in comedy, with others too numerous to mention, we have, what is justly termed, the Actor's Theatre.

In addition, when Helen Faucit fell ill, her part was taken over by Fanny Stirling. This was Macready's first contact with the rising young actress who was the forerunner of the modern school of realistic acting. "She speaks with freshness and truth of tone," he noted, "that *no other* actress on the stage now can do."[18] It was not, perhaps, a wholly disinterested judgement. He was becoming considerably annoyed with Helen Faucit, whose demands as to billing and salary seemed to him increasingly pretentious.

A spiteful prank of Charles Mathews, co-manager of Covent Garden, brought him into contact, also for the first time, with another of the rising young men of the early Victorian theatre. Mathews and his charming wife, Madame Vestris, were the principal light comedians of the day and, with something like Macready's own determination, they had set out to reform the staging of comedy as he had set out to reform the staging of serious drama. Like Macready, too, they had developed a stable of playwrights and were most receptive to the work of young unknowns. In March of 1841 they brought forward *London Assurance* by "Lee Moreton," and, filled with the comic spirit, Charles Mathews allowed (if he did not encourage) the story to get round that this genius had been rejected by Macready, with the implied question, "Who is *really* the sponsor of untried playwrights, the great tragedian or the (greater) comedian?" When the rumor reached Macready by way of Helen Faucit, it had acquired some circumstantial details. "Moreton" had submitted a comedy, *Woman,* to Macready during the period of Covent Garden management, Macready had read it and agreed to produce it, "if he would take the good speeches out of the woman's part" and put them into the manager's. It was typical of the slander that was always being invented about the tragedian's selfish refusal to give anyone else a chance. At the moment, he affected great unconcern, but afterwards he sent for John Webster, a member of his company who had lived with "Moreton" during the supposed time of the rejection of *Woman.* Webster admitted knowing the man and disclosed that his name was Dion Boucicault; that the play had indeed been written and that he had tried to persuade Boucicault to submit it to Macready but that he had refused.

Armed with proof sufficient, Macready wrote Mathews to brand the tale a lie, sending copies to other performers who had managed to become involved. The letter was apparently composed in his most formal third-person style, as Mathews' reply began with the assertion that he assumed the "anonymous" note was from Macready. Mathews' next note was returned unopened, with the frigid accompanying declaration: "having already intimated, upon his admission of facts and his threat of publication, that I should decline further correspondence with him, I begged to be excused opening the enclosed." This, of course, was just the sort of reply to delight the heart of a practical joker, but Mathews must have wondered whether his joke had not gone far enough. His next move was to hedge, to protest that he had only repeated what he had been told.

Macready was not satisfied. He now sought out Mr. Lee Moreton in his lair (having offered five guineas to the man who could find where he lived) taking with him Forster and a lawyer. Boucicault, an almost-innocent tool in the affair, had a well-prepared story. He had given the play to a Mr. Ronyon Jones. Mr. Jones reported without substantiation that he had submitted it to Macready, who had chosen a part in it and directed certain alterations. At Forster's suggestion, Boucicault wrote the whole story out and signed it, and Macready read it to the performers in his dressing room at night. That was the end of the affair, although Mr. Ronyon Jones's identity remained a mystery. Boucicault made one attempt to heal the breach, but Macready sent him packing with some salutary advice. This was, perhaps, unfortunate. Macready's stiff-necked attitude cost him the labors of a capable playwright and, as he was shortly to discover, playwrights who could give him what he needed were no longer as plentiful as blackberries, and new plays were desperately needed.

DRURY LANE

At the beginning of his *Diary* for 1841, Macready had written, "It is my business to endeavour to accumulate." For the last few years he had constantly worried about his financial position; every new expense was a cause for apprehension. He was made miserable by the thought of the effect of a possible illness upon his resources and the condition of his family. One night, during his engagement at the Haymarket, the audience failed to applaud him on his entrance and the next day he wrote, "My thoughts have been uneasy and I have suffered much from them. The position in which I find myself professionally has much distressed me. The house last night was humiliating—the charm of my name, as an attraction, seems broken up; my Haymarket income is trembling." Normally, he could have expected to build up his funds by a provincial tour, but a commercial depression was spreading over the country. The Bath theatre had closed. On the sixth of March, 1841, he wrote his stepmother in Bristol: "I cannot see that a week's performances would benefit you & certainly does not seem likely to repay me."[14] To other managers he returned similar replies. Writing to the manager at Lyme Regis, he informed him that he had very little inclination to play in the country during the Haymarket recess. "Nothing," he said, "but the certainty of money overcomes my aversion to labour there. I fear you will scarcely be able to tempt me from my humour, but it is only fair that I should hear your proposals."[15]

Despite his aversion he did undertake a short tour, with the anticipated results. To his friend Wightwick at Plymouth he wrote from Exeter on April 21:

Your letter met me on my return from a martyrdom at the Theatre, which I underwent in performing with a Mr—and Mr—and Mrs—and Miss—and oh!—I MUST go to heaven after this—all my sins are atoned for in my nightly suffering. Well; your pale letter—it looks quite livid with its fears—greeted me on release from the "iron scourge and torturing h—" and its agonies of apprehension were quite luxurious to me after my excruciating realities.—The real fact is this, I have come too *late*—an earlier date would have made much difference. Last night I acted Macbeth in my *very best manner* to £26!!!— To night Werner to about the same amount. . . . *Friday morning*. . . .

Well;—if I am obliged as an actor, called Eaverly, did to put a lanthorn on a pitchfork, and poke it into the boxes to *"look for the audience"*—if there should be, in Nickleby language, a "rush of two" to the gallery—and only one forlorn wretch of a man in the vast ocean of the Pit—still—non *omnis* moriar!—My journey is not without its recompence: I have the gratification—*which I would not sell for good receipts*—of witnessing the fervour of your friendship and the hearty interest you take in my well-being. . . . Exeter and Plymouth are not the world—and Caesar was beaten in a skirmish.[16]

He could see at the moment but one way out of his dilemma, to accumulate a fortune before his attraction was lost.

Upon the conclusion of his Covent Garden management, he had written in his *Diary*, "If it were ever proposed to me to undertake the management of a theatre again, I should give no answer *until I had read carefully over the diaries of the two years now past."* If he did not follow his declared intention when T. J. Serle urged once again that the legitimate drama could only be saved by his hands, it may have been due to the nature of the proposer and the manner of his proposition. Serle had served him well as acting manager at Covent Garden and had done his best—which was never more than second-best—to provide him with new plays. But he was by temperament a dependable wheel-horse, with the determination if not the sanguineness of a provincial manager, and with an altogether correct, and foresighted, understanding of the present plight of the legitimate stage. His understanding was a good deal better than his plays, but both came to him with equal ease, and it must often have bewildered him to observe the agonies of his chief over a decision, a slovenly rehearsal, or an ill-natured item in the newspaper. Macready realized the phlegmatic nature of his aide, and perhaps sensed its value to himself. In a letter about a play which Serle was in the midst of writing, Macready has occasion to cite a current situation in which the notorious Lord Cardigan demonstrated the privileges of Class in a most abusive manner:

I only hope you will not be too philosophic—I mean in your characters —transferring your own calmly-judging philosophic temperament to them.—I would lay a wager, you have merely said, after sufficient pause, I think Cardigan was to blame—whilst I have been fizzing worse than the tea-urn before me every morning at breakfast. . . . Passions are bad, but they are the instruments, with which providence works out great events.—*Vide history passim!* The state of the stage wants that passion—the passion of enthusiasm—*now*—I am too old and too encumbered to give way to it, or—: but it must look for me, or I must remain what Wordsworth calls a "Selfish man."[17]

For Serle, as for all the playwrights of the time, Shakespeare was bard, prophet, and ready reference. Perhaps he recognized the echo of Othello addressing the senate behind Macready's letter; at any rate, upon that hint he spoke, to find as Othello did that his auditor willingly anticipated him. On December 28, 1840, Macready invited Serle to "have a good long confidential talk," to decide whether to "pull together, or . . . to pull different ways in perfect harmony of mind."[18] Of course, Macready informed Forster and other members of his cabinet of what was in his thoughts, but Serle, the phlegmatic, practical man of the theatre, was chosen as agent in the complex business of renting a playhouse and assembling a company and a repertory while the tragedian attempted to accumulate resources on a brief provincial tour.

It was to Serle that Macready confided, with the most solemn adjurations of secrecy, that, since opera seemed to be attractive to audiences, he was going to try his hand at legitimizing it. "I should like," he wrote, "to do for music what we have begun to do for the drama, i.e., bring back, extend, or create a taste for the classic and pure in style and expression. . . . I should like to carry out DRAMATICALLY the views of the *Directors of the Ancient Concerts* with regard to music—presenting classical and approved styles as a means of encouraging in COMPOSERS the taste for the true in sentiment & feeling. I think you go with me in my blind gropings."[19] Serle, groping to the same purpose, confided to Macready a modification of the scene-system that he had worked out with Stanfield and an improvement in stage lighting which was to be universally adopted; this, by "Throwing the light from the top, [would] give the natural expression to the human face, a thing devoutly to be wished for tragediennes in particular."[20] Macready's reaction to these suggestions cannot be recovered, but he had always been intensely interested in stagecraft and he was accustomed to listen closely to Mr. Serle.

On March 23, 1841, they went together for a conference with representatives of Drury Lane to present Macready's conditions: he should have liberty to close at a day's notice, "no compulsion to pay any rent," his salary to be included among the working expenses of the theatre. The terms were favorable to Macready and apparently agreeable to the proprietors. Serle was deputized to begin negotiations with actors, and the old guard began to assemble.

Although the theatre was not to be opened until Christmas, Macready began detailed preparations at once. It was in the main a repetition of the prelude to the Covent Garden management.

Young, the pantomimist, was engaged to prepare the opening
entertainment, the tragic ranks were filled with familiar names,
including a somewhat chastened Mrs. Warner, who agreed to come
to him, as Serle wrote on April 12, "on your own proposed understanding that you would do what you consider right and in the
spirit of the concern." In an attempt to remedy the chief deficiency
of his Covent Garden days, Macready instructed Serle to build up
the comic ranks. Mrs. Nisbett, a brilliant actress of high comedy,
declined to join him, preferring to stay with Mathews and Vestris
at Covent Garden—whose forces Macready was intending to raid.
Serle had a somewhat delicate task in stealing away from Covent
Garden the two Keeleys, Robert and his wife Mary Ann. "[A]
scene at the Theatre yesterday," his report reads. "[Mme. Vestris
& her husband] stating that their taking the Theatre next season wd. depend on [Keeley's] answer. Evidently they are fixing
the best comic company they can exclusively—and probably the
Proprietors may make their tenancy depend on their showing a
good one. . . . Vestris of course has *acted* to a great extent but in
the main, Keeley is a bad audience."[21] Macready himself called
on Fanny Kelly in hopes that she might be persuaded to join him
as character woman. An actress cut to his pattern, she had retired
from the stage to establish a theatre school for the training of
young actors and for the production of plays according to her own
notions. These were very like Macready's, she having been one
of the first members of the profession to scoff at Tate's version of
Lear and recognize the importance of the Fool to the play. However, her "friend," John Hamilton Reynolds, would not hear of
her undertaking the Old Woman, and consequently she was not
engaged. Next Macready began the training of Miss Fortescue,
a new aspirant for leading females, working with her at his home
(with Catherine in the next room) and in the theatre, where he
went into the farthest seats of the gallery to test her voice. He
found Miss Fortescue a sweet little girl, but he found her mother
a counterpart of Mrs. Nickleby.

Plays, too, were his concern. He read industriously all the new
manuscripts that came his way. The Reverend C. F. Darley submitted *Plighted Troth*, which he found quaintly written, but
possessing the qualities of intense passion and happy imagination.
The Reverend Mr. Darley further delighted him by giving him
a free hand as to alterations. Serle suggested a version of *Faust*
with the music selected from the works of Beethoven. To this
he would not listen. In a musical work, he felt, "the design must

be one and complete, a whole made up of harmonising parts, one character and purpose visible throughout."[22] He read industriously in English history to find a new subject for Bulwer, went through the works of Shelley to find additional lines for a contemplated revival of the Gay-Handel *Acis and Galatea,* and selected *Two Gentlemen of Verona* as his first Shakespearean novelty.

Efficient as Serle might be, Macready found himself, of course, his only deputy. Everything must be overseen in person. The designs for *Acis and Galatea* had to be examined and corrected, rehearsals conducted, the ladies' wardrobe carefully checked, the manipulation of the pantomime scenery replanned. In the front of the house he was determined to have his own way as to the reserved seats in the pit; checking facilities were provided, and programs with a description of the scenes. The free list was drawn up, including all members of the recently founded Shakespeare Society, of whose council Macready was a leading member. At the other extreme, the ladies of the town were to be excluded, as they had been at Covent Garden.

This last was a delicate proceeding, since the management had no legal right to refuse money at the door. The method of circumventing the law was described in a letter, signed by Macready but written by Forster, published in the *Times* for January 15, 1842. Prostitutes were barred from every place except the gallery, "which they could only reach by a separate pay-office, and by passing through a dismantled lobby, where the walls were purposely left unpainted and unpapered, in which no seat of any kind was placed, and which was constantly patrolled by a policeman." There was, the letter admitted, a bar in this lobby, but it had been leased years ago from the proprietors, not from the new manager.

The reason for this public explanation was an unfriendly paragraph in *John Bull* which described the arrangements in somewhat different terms. *John Bull* reported that "a staircase had been provided for the accomodation of those unfortunate women whom we had supposed to be excluded from this theatre, . . . a refreshment room had been set apart for their use, and for that of such of the public as might choose to resort to it, and . . . they were admitted into the house along with the respectable portion of the audience from the second circle upwards."[23]

To this attack by *John Bull* and letter from Macready, the *Times,* so unfriendly in the past, replied with an editorial which was a gratifying *volte face:*

Those who, for the most part, have had the control over the representations [in our patent theatres] have been neither very competent to give a right tone to the public taste, nor very scrupulous about the means which they employed to make their speculations answer. There was a great need of a reformation, and the public owes a debt of gratitude to the individual by whom that reformation has been attempted, by whom it has been to a large degree achieved.

It is not our custom to interfere in matters of a commercial nature, where there are competitors for the public favour, and private interests involved; but we cannot pass over the opportunity afforded us by the letter of MR. MACREADY . . . without expressing the opinion which we (in common, we believe, with the public generally) entertain of the exertions of that gentleman for the restoration of genuine English drama, and for the purification of our national theatres from every just cause of offense to a virtuous or religious mind. We cannot but express our indignation at the attacks made upon him for this good work, not merely by ribald publications, whose censure is praise, and the writers of which are naturally led to resent every discouragement given to immorality as a blow at themselves, but in quarters from which more generous conduct might have been expected. The man who has done more than any other individual to make SHAKESPEARE popular deserves the thanks of every one who wishes to educate the people, and raise the national character. The man who has driven *Jack Sheppards* and *Jim Crows*, and exhibitions fit only for Roman amphitheatres, from the stage, has a right to the good word of all who would not see the popular mind brutalized and demoralized. The man who has enabled us to tell the Puritans that there is a theatre in which every effort is made to exclude vice, and in which no modest person is likely to meet with contamination or insult, is entitled to the co-operation of every lover of the fine arts, and (what is more) of all who delight in rational and innocent enjoyments. (Feb. 1, 1842)

The Drury Lane management commenced in a blaze of enthusiasm. The newspapers in general now looked to Macready as the last hope of the British Theatre. Where they had before caviled at some of his proceedings, they now seemed to feel that if Shakespeare were to be kept alive on the stage, if the great tradition were to be maintained, Macready's was the way to do it. The opening revival was *The Merchant of Venice*, newly staged from studies of Venetian courts of justice, and with a program directing the attention of the audience to the significance of the settings. Friendly journalists lost no time in explaining to their readers the effect of Macready's reformations. The *Theatrical Journal*, contrasting the revived *Merchant* with the traditional performance recalls the older theatre's focus on the star player, specifically on Edmund Kean:

It was a Jew wheedling, a Jew storming, a Jew affronting the whole
state of Venice, but a Jew always triumphing some way or other,
even to the last look at Gratiano. But here, though the actor of Shylock
might still tower over the rest, as by the writer's intention it was fit
he should, there were matters to preclude the absorption of interest
in him. There was the gay Christian world as well as the dark Jewish;
there was the power and majesty of Venice to hold in awe and suspense
even the terrors of the bond.[24]

Macready's Shylock was universally approved, even though he
performed nervously, his tremendous reception at the rise of the
curtain having made him self-conscious. The theatre, according
to the *Times* reporter, was "filled to suffocation" and the receipts
were £450.[25]

The next night Macready appeared in the secondary role of
Harmony in a revival of Mrs. Inchbald's *Everyone has His Fault*.
He felt considerable apprehension about this, the first comedy
produced under his new determination to beat Charles Mathews
and Mme. Vestris at their own game. He felt afterwards that the
play had made an "agreeable impression," and the receipts of
£264 were well above average, but Macready was thoroughly out
of place in a role designed for the great eccentric comedian, Joseph
Munden, and Mrs. Inchbald's comedy ran its course in eight
performances.

The actor-manager was certainly not much better suited to the
role of Valentine in *Two Gentlemen of Verona* which followed.
The newspapers again were cordial and Miss Fortescue, his
newest protege, made a considerable hit, though she fell short
of Macready's expectations. The play was chosen, somewhat to
his chagrin, for performance on the night of January 31, 1842,
when the King of Prussia made a state visit to Drury. This was a
great occasion, and the *Times* reporter was gratified at the intelligent interest the monarch took in the performance. Like the
modern schoolboy, he had come armed with a playbook, to which
he glued his eyes and followed the actors line by line. The play
itself was repeated thirteen times.

Although nothing as attractive as *The Tempest* had been
found to open the season, something of Macready's industriousness
as a manager can be discovered from the list of plays produced
within the first month. There were two Shakespearean revivals,
The Merchant and *The Two "Walking Gentlemen"* (as a greenroom wit christened them): there was Mrs. Inchbald's comedy:
there was *The Gamester* with Macready as Beverley and Mrs.
Warner in the role which was in his mind nearly sacred to Mrs.

Siddons; there was Charles Kemble's *The Point of Honour* and a
new farce, *The Windmill* by Thomas Morton, Jr.; all in addition
to the pantomime, *Harlequin and Duke Humphrey's Dinner,*
which was given some forty-two times.

As if the labor necessary to sustain such a dramatic program
were not enough, Macready was hard at work on his venture in
improving opera, the revival of *Acis and Galatea.* Again he felt
the necessity of supervising every detail in person. He attended
conferences on the score and supervised the cutting of the music.
He rehearsed the singers in their airs and undertook to rearrange
the ballets. He climbed up into the flies to instruct the stagehands
in their business. He reduced the chorus ladies to despair by
refusing to allow them to wear "shapes" under their Grecian robes.
He took on himself the designing of the head for Polyphemus.
And he rehearsed tirelessly. He was the first man in the theatre in
the morning and the last man out at night. Finally, on February 5,
1842, the curtain was lowered after the last rehearsal and the stage
swept only five minutes before the house was opened to the
audience.

It was not merely a spectacular production. Poet Bunn and his
fellow mountebanks had made easy use of masses of supers, gaudy
costumes, and technical (and on occasion, pyrotechnical) displays
in the scenery. The staging of a Macready opera must illustrate the
music, as his staging of Shakespeare illuminated the poet's text.
The London *Times,* while suggesting that Stanfield provided more
of the attraction than Handel, acclaimed *Acis and Galatea* as an
epoch in the art of stage decoration. Not only the critics but the
general audiences were enraptured, and there were those who
recognized that the production demonstrated something more than
the art of decorating the stage, that the visual images created were
careful analogues of the style of the composer and the matter of
the librettist. And, though few commented on the fact, *Acis and
Galatea* was English born and bred, an appropriate choice for a
national theatre.

Audiences must not be blamed for applauding beauty without
testifying to its meaning. And the production gave them plenty
to look at and applaud. The curtain rose with the overture, revealing a drop synopsizing the story of the opera: on the right and left
were "subjects from Annibal Carraci," in the center a copy of
Poussin's Galatea rising from the sea, with Polyphemus on a grey
rock. The first scene displayed the most memorable of the manager's scenic innovations; the stage represented the Sicilian coast
in the moonlight with Mt. Aetna in the distance. By a complex

device the ocean was made to seem in movement towards the audience, "the waves breaking as they come; the last billow actually tumbling over and over with spray and foam upon the shore, and then receding with the noise of water over stones and shells to show the hard wet sand, and in due time roll and break again."[26] In the transformation scene, water gushed from the rock at Galatea's command and came coursing down the valley; a river god, entwined with reeds, rose slowly above. Through the watery blue shadow of the god appeared at the end the features of Acis. Up the rock rushed Galatea, and the curtain fell on a joyous dance by the peasantry as the lovers smiled upon each other.

Even the operatic chorus was disciplined into action. The shepherds and shepherdesses entered "bounding with a sense of life, and reeling with drunkenness. They flung themselves in heaps on the ground, or joined in the Bacchic games, or simply ate grapes"—but always playing an intimate part in the action. Since *Acis and Galatea* is practically without action, this may have been considerable strain upon Macready's inventive faculty, but his classical training no doubt provided him with ample materials for a superimposed reconstruction of pastoral life in ancient Greece. At any rate, "Everything was done which our stage has never seen done before; never even seen attempted."[27]

The revival of *Acis and Galatea* completely captivated theatre-going London and swept all before it for forty-three performances. Whenever it appeared on the bills the nightly receipts were certain to be above £250, and on one occasion reached £437. James Anderson declared it might have run two hundred nights had not Macready clung to his determination to maintain the repertory system. But Macready had promised variety and he intended to live up to his promises. While still excited by the realization of his ambitions for the opera, he set to work on the production of a new play by Douglas Jerrold, and Dickens, writing from America, was but echoing the sentiments of his London friends when he cautioned him to have a care for his health, pointing out that a mutton chop eaten in the fingers in his office was no substitute for a proper meal consumed at a dining-table.[28] Ludwig Schneider, a Berlin theatre manager, has left a vivid impression of just how recklessly Macready was expending his energies. After a performance of *Macbeth* which left him "stunned and overwhelmed [betäubt and überwältigt]," he went by appointment to the stage door where Macready's dresser led him to the chamber which was both office and dressing-room. It was sparsely furnished, the walls plastered with current playbills of the other London theatres. On the table was a manuscript play tentatively marked for acting in the manager's hand.

Completely exhausted, Macready, wrapped in a woolen robe, was lying on a sofa and greeted his guest with a silent handshake. Herr Schneider begged him to spare his voice so strained by the fifth act as to have nearly vanished. He then tried to convey to Macready his reaction to the performance, particularly stressing the innovations in production techniques which he intended to take back to Germany with him. But constant interruptions made communication impossible. The treasurer appeared with the box-office account, the acting manager needed instructions for the next day's rehearsals. The wardrobe master reported on costumes damaged during the performance. The printer's devil brought proofs for a forthcoming program to be read and approved. To everyone Macready listened attentively, examining closely the problem each man presented, and arrived at a decision with a brief word or gesture. This after a day of rehearsals and business, and a production of *Macbeth* which Schneider described as the most perfect tragedy he had ever seen in the English theatre.[29] Worn out as he was, Macready still could not delegate any of his responsibilities.

Dickens must have anticipated that his caution would go unheeded. After the successful production of Jerrold's *The Prisoner of War*, Macready turned his full attention at once to Gerald Griffin's *Gisippus*. It was a play in which he and his cabinet had complete faith. Past experience had showed the attractiveness of classical scenes and the struggle of love and friendship in the bosom of a great-hearted man. Since *Gisippus* had both, its success seemed to be foreordained. Doubtless, a further incitement to Macready was the knowledge that Charles Kean had turned it down. He worked hard at it, revising, rewriting (the author was dead and the whole task fell upon Macready), even splitting a character in two to provide roles for his entire company. The result was an intelligent, even scholarly production, received as such by the critics, the *Times* filling its review with tags of Greek. But scholarship is infrequently associated with theatrical success, and *Gisippus* was not greeted with any rapture by the general audience. It is a good play, and Macready showed his confidence in it by maintaining it in the repertory for twenty performances, but it never drew £150 into the theatre, except on the eighteenth of March when it grossed £257; on that night it was teamed with *Acis and Galatea*.

One other new play proved an even greater error in judgement on the manager's part. The Reverend Mr. Darley's *Plighted Troth* was next in line for presentation. Macready had a "feeling like hope—perhaps akin to trust—in the massive language and fine thought properly spread over this play." He could hardly have been more completely misguided. *Plighted Troth* is a murky, pseudo-Elizabethan melodrama, and the principal character is named, in the easiest Adelphi manner, Gabriel Grimwood. The play might have seen a second performance, but not many more, had not an unfortunate actor stepped upon Macready's hand as he lay dead, stabbed with a bread knife, beneath a table. The corpse sat up and delivered a lecture in no delicate language on the other actor's professional shortcomings. Instead of hisses and catcalls the theatre rang with shouts of laughter; Macready was thoroughly humiliated, not so much by his mishap as by his misjudgement. "Surely," he wrote in his *Diary*. "I could not believe that to be poetry, thought, energy, imagination, and melody of rhythm which was totally devoid of all these!" He commiserated with the author, who "deserved to succeed," but there was no alternative but to withdraw the play.

The rest of the short season was made up of Shakespearean revivals, *Othello, Macbeth*, and *Hamlet*, and other stock pieces. The spectacular *Acis and Galatea* had saved the treasury, and there was no longer any question about the general respect in which his efforts were held. *Gisippus* and *Plighted Troth* were best forgotten and the new season approached with courage and hope. The proprietors of Drury went so far as to hint to the papers that Macready had told them, "if he met with the degree of public support which he anticipated he would pass the remainder of his professional career within the walls of Drury Lane theatre."[30]

The new season, scheduled to commence on October 1, 1842, was to be full length, a major effort, and in preparation Macready spent a part of the summer vacationing. Much of his time, however, was given to the arrangements for the fall. Mathews and Vestris, having yielded the management of Covent Garden once more into the hands of the Poet Bunn, were promptly engaged to strengthen the comic company, as was Mrs. Nisbett. The great success of *Acis and Galatea* was to be followed up by a revival of the Dryden-Purcell *King Arthur*. Every effort was to be extended on the Shakespearean revivals, of which the first were *As You Like It* and *King John*. The editors of *Punch* submitted a pantomime, which was rejected, and Westland Marston a tragedy, *The Patrician's Daughter*, which was accepted. As the opening day approached, Macready went over every item personally, examining the costumes for *As You Like It* one by one, selecting the music, and criticizing the settings.

The first night, despite a thoroughly bad performance of Rosalind by Mrs. Nisbett and a hurried interpretation of Jaques by the overworked manager, was a good omen for the future. The play lent itself to the kind of treatment Macready delighted in: the wrestling scene was developed with painstaking attention to reality, the hunter's horn and the shepherd's pipe were used like musical themes, and in the final scene,

a fine Maypole rears its flowered crest in proud superiority in the centre of the stage, the groves and trees echo the chirruping of the feathered songsters of the adjoining woods, the rippling of the babbling streams, the flowing dash of the spraying waterfall, meet the ear, and the hunter with his living brace of bloodhounds hieing to the chase, with groupings of joyous peasants and fresh nymphs chorussing the hymns of pastoral joy, in every variety of rich costume, greet Hymen with his love-lit torch.[31]

Not all the papers were enthusiastic. Macready was chilled by the reaction of the press in general, though he was cheered somewhat by the fairly good houses the first play attracted. The *Morning Post,* usually an enemy, found plenty to criticize in Macready's own performance. "[S]o far from pourtraying [Jaques]," it pontificated, "he did not even seem to conceive it."[32] It further attacked him for having usurped to Jaques' use the First Lord's speech, but this—as the *Post* very well knew—was stage tradition. There is just a possibility that the critic of the *Post* was elsewhere during the performance—it had been known to occur—since Macready himself told Lady Pollock some years later that he had restored the original text of *As You Like It* and abandoned the preposterous convention of giving the First Lord's speech to Jaques. He further told her that Mrs. Nisbett's performance was the only shortcoming in a production which was his favorite of all the revivals.[33] It was certainly successful within the limits of the repertory system, being presented twenty-two times during the season.

Charles Mathews and his wife did not appear in the play, and Macready quite plainly did not know what to do with them. He expected Mathews to be contented with such roles as Roderigo in *Othello* and a servant in *The Rivals,* and, when the comedian remonstrated, he thought him "very silly," and forced a public admission from him that "nothing could be more kind or courteous than my conduct had been to him." During the preparations for *King Arthur,* Madame Vestris became so irritated at her assigned role that she attacked the manager with much "Billingsgate" and threw down the part and her engagement. In his desire to collect all the available talent in every line, Macready had acquired more riches than he could use. The severance of the contract was of benefit to both parties.

King John was the second Shakespearean revival of the season, making its bow on October twenty-fourth. It was produced with the same care, the same attention to historical detail, and the same concern for the disposition of the minor characters, the mobs, and soldiers, that had marked his previous efforts at restoration. It was, said the *Times,*

an animated picture of those Gothic times which are so splendidly illustrated by the drama. The stage is thronged with the stalwart form of the middle ages, the clang of battle sounds behind the scenes, massive fortresses bound the horizon. The grouping is admirably managed. The mailed figures now sink into stern tranquility; now, when the martial fire touches them, they rouse from their lethargy and thirst for action. The sudden interruption in the third act to the temporary peace between John and Philip Augustus was a fine instance of the power of making the stage a living picture. (Oct. 25, 1842)

The *Theatrical Journal* reporter thought that he had counted as many as three hundred supers at one time on the stage,[34] and Macready and Phelps were both acclaimed as John and Hubert. Performed twenty-six times, it combined with *As You Like It* to provide a good Shakespearean backbone to the season. On its twenty-fourth night it was still able to gross £306.

King Arthur, intended to repeat the success of last season's *Acis and Galatea,* was produced on the sixteenth of November and was well received by the audience, but did not prove the artistic triumph that Macready had hoped for. Stanfield had merely been an adviser to the scene painter instead of designing the production himself, and the costumes seem to have been patched together instead of being as carefully designed as those for the earlier revival. True, *Acis* was laid in classical times and the designer could turn to historical authority for a guide. This was impossible for *King Arthur,* and the effect must have been more the gaudiness of a pantomime than an aesthetically satisfying whole. Still it had been a considerable exertion—it employed seventy-nine members of the regular company, a chorus of a hundred, with a hundred and sixteen supers and twenty-five extra dancers[35]—and it was rewarded with thirty-one good houses.

On the nineteenth of November Macready made a short-lived attempt to reintroduce another kind of classic to the Victorian stage. He revived Congreve's *Love for Love* with Anderson as

Valentine and Helen Faucit as Angelica. It is difficult to say what
could have been his motive in the effort. When Planché told him
later of arranging *The Way of the World* for Mathews at the Haymarket, he was horrified at the thought and completely at sea as
to what might have been done with the character of Mrs.
Marwood.[36] His own treatment of *Love for Love* was, perforce,
butchery. Congreve's sophisticated wit was changed into heavy-
handed sententiousness. Such a remark as "She is chaste, who was
never asked the question," becomes "She has never yielded to the
temptation of a man's addresses, to whom they were never offered,"
and Sailor Ben's speeches were liberally modified, according to
this typical pattern: "I should like to have such a handsome gentlewoman for a bedfellow [*Macready:* messmate] . . . a tight vessel,
and well rigged, an you were but as well manned [*Macready:*
commanded]." Sir Sampson's delightful and thoroughly continental demands that his son should kiss him are embarrassingly
altered to requests to shake his hand, in turn blunting Ben's reply,
"I'd rather have a turn with these gentlewomen."[37]

On December tenth came the first new play of the season, Westland Marston's *The Patrician's Daughter.* Marston was an eager
young poet whose stage-struck memoirs of *Our Recent Actors*
provide vivid portraits of nineteenth-century actors, Macready in
particular, in action. He was totally unknown when his play was
accepted at Drury Lane, but it was at once evident that he was
an earnest and thoughtful dramatist with an original notion. In
The Patrician's Daughter he undertook to cast the contemporary
scene into blank verse, the first of several such attempts in the
history of the modern drama, all apparently foredoomed. The
apprehension with which the production was approached may
be seen from the prologue, spoken by Macready and supplied by
Charles Dickens, who took a close interest in the experiment:

> No tale of streaming plumes and harness bright
> Dwells on the poet's maiden harp tonight;
> No trumpet's clamor and no battle's fire
> Breathes in the trembling accents of his lyre;
> Enough for him, if in his lowly strain
> He wakes our household echo not in vain;
> Enough for him, if in his boldest word
> The beating heart of MAN be dimly heard. . . .
> Awake the Present! Shall no scene display
> The tragic passion of the passing day?
> Awake the Present! What the past has sown
> Be in its harvest garner'd, reap'd, and grown!

How pride breeds pride, and wrong engenders wrong,
Read in the volume Truth has held so long,
Assured that where life's freshest flowers blow,
The sharpest thorns and keenest briars grow,
How social usage has the pow'r to change
Good thoughts to evil; in its highest range
To cramp the noble soul, and turn to ruth
The kindling impulse of our glorious youth,
Crushing the spirit in its house of clay,
Learn from the lessons of the present day.
Not light its import and not poor its mien;
Yourselves the actors, and your homes the scene.

The play which followed those threatening couplets was a considerable relief to an audience which might have expected a severe thrashing from the author. As the title suggests, the plot is concerned with the wooing of a noble lady by a commoner, a problem of lively contemporary interest, if somewhat threadbare today. The development of the plot, as might be expected from a "maiden harp," is not handled with much skill, progressing by the easy way of the forged letter and a misunderstanding arising therefrom. The death of the heroine is awkwardly handled: the play is not a tragedy because she dies; she dies because the play is to be a tragedy. But the virtues of the play are greater than its shortcomings. The rise of Mordaunt, the plebeian politician whose love is scorned by Lady Mabel, until he is the equal of her father, the old-school aristocrat, is a reflection of the midcentury scene, and Mordaunt's jilting of her leads to an interesting apologia. He says, by way of extenuation:

I have not sought for vengeance in this act.
My life, my energies, my talents, all
Did I task for the deed! Such apparatus
Was meant for nobler uses than belong
To a mere private feud; but I have fought
A battle for high principles, and taught
Convention, when it dares to tread down *man,*
Man shall arise in turn and tread it down!

It is easy to imagine with what satisfaction these words came to Macready's lips and, although *John Bull* declared that Macready's concept of an English gentleman would have "emptied any modern drawing room in five minutes,"[38] the play was much applauded, Dickens and Forster were pleased, and Marston was called on for a curtain bow by the audience. But the measure of its attraction is the box office record; £252 on its first night, £83 on its sixth.

The season was somewhat enlivened by the customary entangle-
ments with the press. The *Satirist,* the *Despatch,* and the *Sunday
Times* heaped vituperation upon Macready with unbridled exu-
berance. He followed his usual practice of striking them off the
free list, which of course only led them to redouble their efforts.
"A. B. C." came to his defense in a pamphlet entitled *The Drama,
The Press, and Mr. Macready,* deducing the opposition of those
papers from the influence of Bunn, or to Macready's refusal to
engage Ellen Tree, the sister-in-law of one of the editors.[39] Benjamin Webster added his bit by first complaining that Macready
had taken all his good performers away from the Haymarket,
ignoring the fact that these players were "in the Macready sphere,"
and that he had hired them reluctantly in the first place, and then
taking offense because a Mr. Webster had been listed as a Sicilian
shepherd in the chorus of *Acis and Galatea.* His retaliation was
to announce in large letters on his bills for a minor comedy,
A Cure for Love, "Second waiter, Mr. MACREADY." The *Herald*
next day reviewed the performance with a full appreciation of
the joke: "Among the minor parts, that of a waiter, by Macready,
deserves special praise for the correctness displayed by the actor
by seizing the servile points of the character."[40]

The search for a new play continued, but it is not to be wondered after the disaster of *Plighted Troth* and the relative failure
of *The Patrician's Daughter* that Macready began "to doubt the
success of any play now," and wrote rather plaintively in his *Diary*
that Bulwer-Lytton alone was his "hope among authors." He had
constantly urged Browning to write him another play, and the
poet after a number of attempts at last submitted a manuscript
with the note, "There is *action* in it, drabbing, stabbing et autres
gentillesses,—who knows but the Gods may make me good even
yet?"[41] Macready could not take the leading role until after Easter,
but the author, perhaps irritated by constant inquiries from his
friends about the opening date, insisted upon an immediate production with Phelps in the lead. He did not realize, as he later
informed Archer, how impossible it was that "a serious play of
any pretension should appear under Macready's management with
any other protagonist than himself."[42] The play, *A Blot in the
'Scutcheon,* was given by the manager to Anderson to read to the
players in the greenroom, but he refused ("I fear this young man's
head is gone") and the task devolved upon the prompter, Willmott. He was hardly the man for the work, and Browning blames
the failure of the play to evoke anything but ill-placed laughter
from the actors upon the reading of the heroine's part by a "red-

nosed, one-legged, elderly gentleman." Rehearsals commenced, but Macready took little interest in the proceedings until Phelps fell ill and he decided to understudy the part. On the day before the performance, Phelps appeared at rehearsal determined to do the part if he "died for it," and Macready was forced to withdraw, offering to give both the author and the star the benefit of his consideration and study in the cuts. One suggested alteration with which he was especially pleased was a milder ending, with Tresham going into a monastery instead of committing suicide, with the lines,

> Within a monastery's solitude
> Penance and Prayer shall wear my life away.[43]

Browning rejected his suggestion, he notes, "in the worst taste, manner, and spirit."

The first night was successful. Phelps was highly praised— Macready declares him to have been bad, but this may be the judgement of too high standards or too high dudgeon—as were Helen Faucit, Anderson, and Mrs. Stirling. Bulwer-Lytton was in the audience and wrote the next day to Forster:

I saw Macready in all the pomp of an overflowing house, a most successful afterpiece, a most triumphant opera, and a most gorgeous private box. But in his pomps was sadness! He sighed at the congratulations and complained of the harrassments of greatness, and the uncertainty of success. Unhappy man! When he gets a million, he will have arrived at the summit of his sorrows.

I had thought at one time of a comic subject for him, but I feel that it would be almost an insult to talk comedy while his melancholy overflows with his houses.[44]

Alas, the houses ceased to overflow after the first night (receipts: £176), and with the third performance (receipts: £88) the play dropped from the bills forever. The incident justified Macready's conviction that, whatever his ideals for the restoration of the legitimate drama, as far as the public was concerned he was the main attraction. A serious play, no matter how well acted, would not attract if his name were not in the cast.

A subject much closer to his heart, a Shakespearean revival, was next to receive his attention. It was, curiously, *Much Ado About Nothing,* in which he elected to play the role of Benedick, and it was first performed for his benefit on February 24, together with *Comus,* in which he played the title role. Of his Benedick little need be said. Macready was a serious actor, not a comedian, and of the graceful-witty side of the character he could convey no conception. He concentrated on the ridiculous, and produced loud shouts of laughter from the audience, beginning at the scene following his overhearing of the canard that Beatrice was in love with him. "He marched from the arbour," reported the *Times,*

and he took a chair, and there he sat for some minutes with the oddest expression of countenance in the world. Benedick did not know what to make of the new dawnings of love in his bosom, so he fidgetted, and he crossed his legs in some new fashion at the end of every three words, and he looked at one moment so lugubrious, and at the next, when he chuckled over the beauty of Beatrice, so self-satisfied, that he was perfectly irresistible. (Feb. 25, 1843)

His fellow player, Anderson, was able to resist so far as to describe him as melancholy as a hearse in a snowstorm.[45] But the benefit produced £419 and the performance was repeated eleven times, a fairly good showing in a season which was beginning to run downhill.

In an attempt to rival Bunn, who was resorting to opera and VanAmberg's trained lions to keep Covent Garden open, Macready now determined upon an all-out effort in Italian opera. His choice was *Sappho,* by Pacini, starring Clara Novello fresh from continental triumphs. Here his depressed spirits were further assaulted by the temperamental demands of the artists, La Novello shocking him with a demand that her full name and all her titles appear in the bills; by the inefficiency of his musical director, who would neither study the score himself nor call in the aid of an experienced hand with Italian opera. A feud began to rage between the principal female singers, and *"Interdum feminas componere lites"* was added to the managerial burden. The opera finally was brought forward, without much benefit to the treasury. Yet, in spite of the gloom which spreads over his *Diary* during these months, when it came to the getting up of the Easter pantomime, Planché's *Fortunio,* he went to work with his accustomed vigor, directing, instructing, knowing everyone's part and acting each in turn, and delighting the author and the actors with his high spirits. The piece went splendidly and was played forty times to the end of the season.

Aside from revivals of *Macbeth, Cymbeline, Julius Caesar, The Winter's Tale,* and the "Macready plays," *The Lady of Lyons, Werner,* and *Virginius,* the remainder of the season was devoted to two new plays, both failures. The first of these was Knowles' *The Secretary,* hastily written, hastily produced, and quickly damned, and *Athelwold* by William Smith, chosen by Helen

Faucit for her benefit, and abandoned after two nights. The manager's discontent grew with each day's passing, and early in March he was discussing with his wife the possibility of another American tour to recoup the season's losses in his personal income. By the middle of April his resolution had been taken, and, although the proprietors of the theatre made some attempt to get him to re-engage for another season, he set such ridiculous terms that he was certain in advance they would be rejected. On the fifth of June the playbills announced that the season would be extended to June twelfth, on which occasion Macready would "make HIS LAST APPEARANCE *in a* LONDON THEATRE for a very considerable period."

The Queen (like a good sportswoman, said *Punch*, wishing to be in at the death) commanded a performance on that night of *As You Like It* and the season's successful farce, *A Thumping Legacy*, which choice somewhat tempered Macready's pleasure at her condescension. The selection, as he said, did him no good. But the Queen came and attracted a bumper audience (£606), and, as she departed after the performance, sent for Macready and thanked him. Prince Albert, demonstrating his knowledge of Shakespeare, inquired whether "this was not the original play." He was doubtless comforted to learn that it was.

Two nights later, in a special performance of *Macbeth* announced in enormous red letters in the playbills, Macready took his leave of the London audience "for a very considerable time." As he went on the stage he was in the lowest state of depression, but the audience (£477) soon fired him to a major exertion. On his appearance, they rose to their feet shouting and waving hats and handkerchiefs and, when wearied of that expression of their devotion, took up stamping their feet until the sound was of thunder. When they finally quieted down, Macready gave what he felt was his best interpretation of the character, delivered a farewell speech and withdrew with the audience still shouting its approval behind him. On the nineteenth, he attended the customary ceremonial dinner. It was in a way but a repetition of the ceremonies attendant upon the conclusion of the Covent Garden management, with the addition of a fearful piece of silver-plated statuary designed in his honor by an anonymous craftsman who must be the master gadgeteer of all time. This *chef d'oeuvre* was described by the *Times* with painstaking detail:

The group . . . represents Shakespeare standing on a pedestal, at the base of which, Mr. Macready, habited in the costume of the early stage, is seated, having in his hands a volume. He is attended by the muse of comedy, Thalia, and the muse of tragedy, Melpomene, and as con-

nected with the subject on which the actor is supposed to be employed—the restoration of the original text of the plays of Shakespeare,
the muse Clio is also introduced. On the other side of the pedestal is
Apollo with an attendant group of subordinate figures. Masks, &c.,
are seen on the ground on which the figures are placed. The whole
of this portion of the testimonial stands on a base of triangular form,
on one side of which, within a metope, is represented the senate scene
in 'Othello'; in a metope on another side of the base is a representation
of the prologue scene in 'Henry V'; and in the third metope, on the
remaining side of the base, the senate scene in 'Coriolanus.' At the
angles of the base three boys hold tablets on which are represented
the storm scene in 'Lear,' the meeting of the witches in 'Macbeth,' and
a scene from the 'Tempest.'[46]

In a speech of thanks, Macready rehearsed briefly his managerial
career, alluded to the assertions of the newspapers that his actions
were not altogether disinterested, and repeated that his purpose
was "elevating everything represented on the stage." He had
sought to bring all the arts and the artists together to illustrate the
text. "It was my object," he said, "to carry upwards all parts of
the drama, the poet being the first consideration, but that no
actor, however subordinate, might not help to elevate his art with
himself."[47] It was a defensive rather than a happy speech, but its
author, despite the mad acclaim of the audience and the imposing
tribute of statuary, was not a happy man. His second period of
management had convinced him that he would never succeed in
elevating the standards of the drama or in revitalizing the old
repertory system. In his own eyes his profession, always degraded,
was now hopeless, and nothing he might do would raise it. He
renewed his determination to "accumulate" and retire; to seek
out an honorable existence as a gentleman as soon as he might rid
himself of the shackles of his odious life of acting.

THE BEGINNINGS OF MODERN THEATRE PRACTICE

Reckoned in terms of variety and legitimacy, the concluding
season at Drury Lane was not the failure that Macready's account-
ing showed. Ninety-six performances were given of Shakespeare,
177 of other plays, and 148 of opera and pantomime. There were
183 nights of performing and Macready himself had played 133
times, in addition to directing and managing all the business of the
theatre; fatigue as well as his bank statement may have contributed
to his discouraged tone. Yet the experiments of his two periods of
management, the theory of stagecraft which he developed and

demonstrated, became part of the heritage of the English theatre. Indeed, the renewed consciousness of the power of every element of the production of a play to contribute to the essential unity of a work of art made possible the advances which define and distinguish the modern theatre.

Although he left behind him no published lectures or essays on the "Theatre Advancing" and no record of his Life in Art beyond a few chapters of *Reminiscences* there is sufficient evidence that Macready's stagecraft was neither haphazard nor pragmatic. It was the outgrowth, to be sure, of his years of theatrical experience, beginning with the management of his father's company, but it was modified and directed by his reading and thinking in aesthetics and philosophy and his consciousness of the world outside the theatres, the revolutionary world of nineteenth-century scientific and artistic advance. When he came to assume the management of a national theatre in 1837, it was with the determination of exemplifying a fully-formed theory. What this theory had been he outlined at the great banquet given in his honor in 1839. In reply to the toast, he rose, spoke a few sentences of dignified gratification, and formulated a creed for his successors:

It had struck me, among the many causes adduced for the drama's decline, that, whilst every other branch of art or pursuit of science was in a course of rapid advance, the drama—except in regard to a valuable change in its costume by that great artist whose name I can never mention without admiration and respect, John Kemble—the drama was stationary, its stage arrangements remained traditional, defended from innovation in each succeeding age by the name and authority of the leading actor who had gone before. . . . It had long been my ambition, and has been my endeavour . . . to present the works of our dramatic poets, and chiefly Shakespeare's, with the truth of illustration they merit. . . . What my own imagination has presented to me, in turning over the pages of our great poet, I have endeavoured to make palpable to the senses of my audience. . . . In following out an observation of Sir Thomas Lawrence, that 'every part of a picture required equal care and pains,' we have sought, by giving purpose and passion to the various figures of our group, to spread over the entire scene some portion of that energy and interest which, heretofore, the leading actor exclusively and jealously appropriated. . . . [we have sought] to transfer his picture from the poet's mind to the stage, complete in its parts and harmoniously arranged as to figure, scene, and action.[48]

The controlling idea of the theory is *unity:* the transfer of the poet's image to the stage "complete in its parts and harmoniously arranged" in every detail. It was an idea that possessed him from the days of his apprenticeship. "Those who knew him in his youth," declared the New York *Sunday Times,* "have observed that he then exhibited the same dogged determination and zeal for having things done properly as he did in the very last years of his professional life."[49] Possibly this was part of a heritage from his father, who was something of a drill sergeant with his actors; more probably it came from his education at Rugby. In the copy of Blair's *Lectures on Rhetoric,* interleaved for the instruction of his bride, Macready wrote, "I wish you to understand clearly what is meant by 'just proportion of parts'—it is a metaphor taken from material things—from bodies, and applied to literary compositions . . . as in a building . . . any single part being out of proportion with the rest, the *whole* must be faulty—(because that cannot be *perfect,* wherein a part is defective.)"[50] So in his production of *King John* a critic found "a completeness of design, a faithful adherence to the customs and manners of Gothic times, a harmony and entire finish preserved throughout, that caused the scene to be enjoyed as one of actual reality, of present, living, real existence, a history in which we feel that we ourselves are actors and participators."[51] And one of Macready's few entries in his *Diary* expressing satisfaction at a rehearsal, made after a morning of "superintendence" of *King Lear,* declares his conviction that it is "harmoniously arranged."

As may be inferred from Macready's declaration of principles, unity, or harmonious arrangement of every part within the whole, had been the least of the theatrical concerns before his day. Of his major predecessors as actor-managers, Garrick had been content with any interior, or any exterior, and any set of wings whether or not they matched the backdrop; Kemble, for all his concern with "historical" costumes and spectacular processions, had been content with the generalized antique—in both instances the leading actor was the focus of interest for the manager and thus, perforce, for the spectators. Of the commodity-minded managers, the chaos that marked the day-to-day productions of the Bunns, the Osbaldistons, and the Calcrafts may be indicated by the scene-plot for a midcentury performance of *Julius Caesar.* This totally ununified patchwork of Shakespearean backdrops and Roman street-wings, of scenes from *Virginius* and a pantomime version of *Faustus,* and of set-pieces identified only by the name of the painter, was drawn up for the guidance of the stage-carpenters who were responsible for assembling the shambles from the store rooms.

JULIUS CAESAR

Wings	No. [of Scene]	Scenes	Gro[oves]
		ACT 1ST	
Roman Street	1	Faustus Street	1
Roman Street	2	Roman Arch back'd by	4
		Roman Street	6
		ACT 2ND	
Roman Street	1	Faustus Street	1
Garden	2	Tomkin's Garden	4
		Side arch 2 E. O. P.	
Andrew's 2 door	3	Modern Anti-Chamber	2
		ACT 3RD	
Roman Street	1	Faustus Street	1
to match	2	Shakespeare Hall and back	4
Roman Street	3	Faustus Street	3
Roman Street Vestibule	4	Marshall's Set Forum	5
		back'd by	
		Moonlight Street	6
		Forum set level with 2 W[ing] Centre	
		ACT 4TH	
Wood	1	Virginius Camp	1
Proscenium and [wings] to match	2	Pizarro's Tent back'd by	3
		Back of Portia's Chamber	4
		Cauldron trap [for *Macbeth*] used	
		ACT 5TH	
Wood	1	Marshall's Wood	3
Wood	2	Tomkin's Wood	3
Wood	3	Depths of Forest	1
Woods	4	Pine Tree Flats	4

CURTAIN[52]

It is perhaps true, as James Boaden declared, that with such an actress as Mrs. Siddons before him his attention was directed to the "vehement and commanding sweep of her action" rather than to the "order or disorder of the picture . . . behind her," and the most influential literary critics of the drama in the period were mainly concerned with close analysis of the central characters. But however jealous he may have been of his status as first actor in the company and however necessarily dedicated to the study of his own characters, Macready displays a concern at once more modern and more classical in considering a Shakespearean play as a total performed action rather than a vehicle for personal display. In striking contrast with the scissors-and-paste operation of the producer of *Julius Caesar* is the carefully unified scene-plot for Macready's revival of *Two Gentlemen of Verona,* specially designed and painted under his close supervision by Tomkins and Marshall:

THEATRE-ROYAL, DRURY LANE.

In accordance with the wish, that has been frequently expressed, for some account of the local scenery and usages attempted in the revivals and novelties produced, a bill, referring to any particular views or customs, will be circulated, gratuitously, within the Theatre, and may be had on application to the servants in attendance.

December 29th, 1841.

THE TWO GENTLEMEN OF VERONA

    The Costume of this revival is that of the 15th century.

  Act. I.—Scene 1—Verona. The Tombs of the Scaligeri, the former Princes of Verona. *Tomkins.*
        Scene 2—Verona. Garden of Julia's House, with a View of the Citadel. *Marshall.*
        Scene 3—Verona. Interior of Antonio's House, looking on the City. *Marshall.*

  Act. II.—Scene 1—Milan. Vestibule in the Duke's Palace—opening on the Garden, with part of the Duomo, or Cathedral, in the Distance. *Marshall.*
        Scene 2—Milan. Garden of the Duke's Palace, with the Duomo in the back-ground. *Tomkins.*

  Act IV.—Scene 1—Milan. Duke's Palace, with the Gate of the City in the distance. *Tomkins.*
    The Escutcheons are those of the Sforza and Visconti

Supporters of the actors of the old school, the latter-day Boadens who cared nothing for the setting in front of which their idols performed, were quick enough to grumble about gilding the lily and upholstering the drama. "W. R.," in a poem to Charles Young provoked by the Macready banquet, can find only this to say of the hero of the evening:

> He overguilds the play
> That needs no decking, and he dresses well
> The Shakespeare character he cannot act.[53]

These attacks continued throughout his second period of management, and Bulwer-Lytton in 1851 begged another group of men, assembled to honor Macready on his retirement, to recall "that brief but glorious time when the drama of England appeared suddenly to revive and to promise a future that should be worthy of its past; when, by a union of all kindred arts, and the exercise of a taste that was at once gorgeous and severe, we saw the genius of Shakespeare properly embodied upon our stage, though I maintain that the ornament was never superior to the work."[54] Macready, at any rate, was perfectly conscious of the risk he was running, for after his retirement he wrote his impression of Charles Kean's revivals at the Princess Theatre: "the text allowed to be spoken was more like a running commentary upon the spectacles exhibited, than the scenic arrangements an illustration of the text."[55] At least once in one of his own revivals (*The Tempest*), this charge could in all honesty be leveled at Macready himself, and was, but Charles Kean could no nothing right.

Macready was neither a pedant nor a showman; he used his scholarly habit of mind and his inherited sense of theatrical effect to serve the ends of the poet. In searching through illustrated travel books or consulting antiquarians about costume, he never neglected dramatic propriety. As a result, for the first time in the modern theatre, audiences were made aware that a play was something to be experienced as a whole, as a work of art, rather than as a series of theatrical strokes and actor's points held together by "cementing lines" and necessary but dull "plot scenes."

Of the modern plays which Macready produced, none was closer to his heart than Gerald Griffin's *Gisippus*. After much maneuvering, cutting, rewriting, and laboring, he finally brought it out at Drury Lane on February 23, 1842. The cold reception it met with from audiences was a shock and surprise to him—the day of the Graeco-Roman drama was dead—but there was no denying the effectiveness of the production as an illustration of his theories of stagecraft. The London *Times* thus described it:

The Greek and Roman scenery was superb. The principal buildings of ancient Athens, the Parthenon, the Temple of the Winds, the Areopagus, the gardens of Academus, were presented, some from different points of view, beneath a deep blue sky; a Greek apartment glittered with the gorgeousness of Pompeii, a Roman cemetery slumbered under a dark gray heaven, through which countless stars were sparkling. Nor was this all. The decorative part of the production had been made to bear most skillfully on the dramatic interest. The desolate condition of Gisippus was greatly heightened by placing him among the tombs; there was a tranquil misery in the whole scene,— the effect of Macready's figure reclining on a sepulchre was that of a symbol of the inanity of human happiness. The gayness of the wedding procession in the first act,—the artistical arrangement of the colours in which the different members of the chorus were dressed, produced a joyous image to the eye, which symbolized the happiness of which Gisippus was so soon to be deprived; and that none of the effect of this chorus might be lost in exciting the feelings of the audience, it was judiciously contrived, that after Gisippus had resigned Sophronia, the air (from one of Beethoven's fantasias) should be heard in the distance, as a contrast to his present situation. (Feb. 25, 1842)

The same combination of historical accuracy (realism) and dramatic propriety (symbolism) Macready applied to the standard works of the theatrical repertory, principally the plays of Shakespeare. Twentieth-century scholarship and the economics of the theatre have led contemporary producers to return to an approximation of the non-representational stage of Shakespeare's day, so that Macready's staging would no doubt seem unnecessarily elaborate and overstuffed, yet there was right reason in his rejection of the meaningless clutter exemplified in the *Julius Caesar* scene-plot and his resort to history. In 1835 an enormous painting, *The Panorama of Thebes,* was exhibited in Leicester Square. Based on sketches made in Egypt, it exhibited the ruins of the temple of Karnak, with the hieroglyphics carefully reproduced. The army of the Pasha was halted in the midst of the ruins and in the distance could be seen the Nile, the Statue of Memnon, the mountains of Arabia and the tombs of the Kings "thrown back with great attention to perspective."[56] After visiting the *Panorama,* Macready wrote that he "Was struck with the advantage, in this refined age, that we possess in the exact images of those remote objects of which we read with so much interest; our imagination is enriched with precise ideas of things and places, on which our untravelled forefathers could have had but very vague and uncertain conjectures from description."[57]

With the purpose of presenting exact images to enrich the imagination of his audiences, he worked with his scene painters, Telbin, Marshall, Tomkins, and Stanfield, planning, suggesting, authenticating, exactly as he had with his playwrights in developing stageworthy texts. When Telbin submitted a plan and estimates for the production of *King John,* the manager devoted his morning to studying and revising, finally sending the painter £250 and "directions for several scenes." On another occasion, Stanfield patiently sketched the manager's ideas for him, only to have them cast aside; and Bradwell, the machinist of the theatre, had to construct a working model of the complicated opening scene for the revival of *The Tempest,* a labor hitherto reserved for pantomime.

The "exact image" that he sought as an illustration of the text must first of all explain itself. Thus, Byron's simple direction for the first scene of *Werner, "The Hall of a decayed Palace . . ."* becomes in the prompt copy Macready prepared for the use of provincial managers: "N. B. All the apartments in the Old Palace, particularly this Scene, should convey the idea of long desertion & extreme wretchedness, the rotting tapestry hanging in tatters from the walls, the cornices & ornaments crumbling with damp and decay."[58] In addition to localizing the action and instantly establishing the condition of the characters, Macready's setting enabled him to eliminate a good many passages of excessive awkward exposition and drive the action forward where the original often is forced to take the longest way about.

In a Shakespearean revival, of course, the exact image was not intended to mask inexpert playwrighting but to "make palpable to the senses" of the audience what the pages of the poet had presented to Macready's imagination. The third scene of the first act of *Othello,* in which the Moor relates the story of his love to the Venetian Senate was, according to the *Examiner,* "Perhaps the finest scene Mr. Macready has exhibited in his management." The stage direction in the first quarto is simple enough: "Enter *Duke* and *Senators,* set at a table, with lights and *Attendants."* The diagram of the scene in the promptbook indicates at once the grandeur and dignity with which the scene was to be invested.

That the effect intended was far more than dignity or grandeur can be gathered from the *Examiner's* description of it as realized upon the stage:

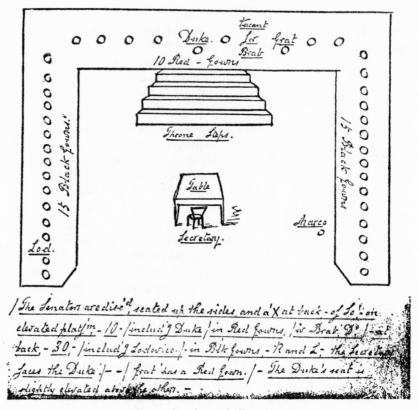

Stage plan for *Othello*, 1843

The Council of Forty are discovered in the Hall of Doges surrounded by Titians and Tintorettos—the "ten" on a raised dais extending through the whole breadth of the Hall and the Doge elevated in the midst with the ominous panel of Marino Faliero frowning over him—on the one side the trusting and manly Moor recounting his loves and perils, on the other the subtle Ancient plotting his revenge, while on the lower seats that line the two sides of the apartment sit rows of black-gowned Venetian nobles interested or careless—if anything were wanted to complete this, surely it is that most picturesque little touch in the centre, where sits the secretary of that grave and potent Signiory with his blue-gowned back to the audience, and his face intent on the enormous book before him which holds the terrible mysteries of the state of Venice! (Oct. 22, 1837)

It was a scene of dignity, to be sure, but with an added sense of power and danger, a contribution to the dramatic situation in making plain not just the position of the leading characters, but the kind of community, the code by which it lived. The manager

Othello, Act I, Scene iii, from Scharf's *Recollections*

was vastly pleased with it, "a scene of beautiful effect, one of the
most real things I ever saw."[59]

Othello was a classic, *Werner* was a "tragedy"; it is not surprising to find scenic devotion lavished upon them by the Eminent
Tragedian. The same care was bestowed upon lesser plays, upon
comedies, and romantic comedies at that. Sheridan Knowles'
Woman's Wit opens with a grand ball which "with the arrival
and departure of the numerous and superbly dressed company,
showing the dancing in an inner salon is one of the most dazzling
realities ever seen on the stage."[60] This was in 1838, three years
before Boucicault and Mme. Vestris excited playgoers with their
thoroughly representational setting for *London Assurance* (1841).

A further contribution of the exact image to dramatic propriety
is revealed in the staging of *Coriolanus.* Historical monuments
and archaeological remains were of little help in recreating the
vanished city of Antium, yet scholarship was called upon to make
palpable the community in which the exiled Coriolanus found
asylum. In this instance, also, imagination was at greater liberty
to create a setting which in lines, object, and color would symbo-
lize the position of a hero who by the slippery turns of the world
was forced to seek service in an enemy town. Act IV, scene 3,

disclosed a view of the city of Antium by starlight—a truly grand and imaginative—yet real scene—and in the centre of the stage Macready stood alone, the muffled, disguised, *banished Coriolanus*. This realized Shakespeare and Plutarch. Behind him were the moles running out into the sea, and at the back of the scene the horison drawn beyond the sea in one long level line, interrupted only by a tall solitary tower, the pharos, or watch-tower of Antium. The strict truth, and lofty moral effect, of this scene, are surpassingly beautiful. Its wide and barren aspect presents the simplicity and large-minded poverty of those old times, and the tower looks like *Coriolanus* himself in a less mortal shape, rising in lonely grandeur, but with still unextinguished light, above the melancholy of his exile and the level sternness of his contemporaries. The pathetic effect is suddenly and startlingly increased by the intrusion of music on the air, as the door of *Aufidius'* house, where the General feasts his nobles, opens on the left of the stage.[61]

To discover "moral effect" in a stage arrangement might be damning praise from a modern critic. But the critic of Macready's production is clearly using the phrase as the equivalent of symbolic or emblematic truth; in the words of Gordon Craig, it was a setting or "place which harmonizes with the thoughts of the poet."

In the matter of costume, Macready declared that he followed the innovations of Kemble and Planché. When he first came to the London stage, to be sure, he wore the conventional habits prescribed for repertory actors, including the Order of the Elephant which brought down the wrath of Planché upon John Kemble's Hamlet. In his copy of the standard Covent Garden promptbook, Macready noted down the items required to costume Henry V:

Dress
  Russet shoes & roses
  Russet Boots and spurs
  White Cotton Pantaloons
  White Julians shirt
  Blue sash—Rich Julians Belt
  White Cloak
  Hat and Feathers
  Large Gloves
  Sword
  Half Shirt
  George
  Garter

Properties
  White Button Gloves
  Large Hamlets Mantle
  Truncheon
  Ring[62]

The costuming of the character in the old days with hand-me-downs from *Julian* and *Hamlet* thrust upon *Henry V*, was in the

same spirit as the patchwork staging of scenes. And when Macready, in 1819, attempted to reform the Othello costume by
purchasing out of his own pocket a Venetian uniform, the manager
made him give it up for reasons not stated but perhaps easily
guessed.[63] Far from being discouraged, the young actor purchased
his own costumes for *Virginius,* "to be correct."[64]

Under his own management he was free to indulge his scholarly
taste for correctness. He wrote, or his wife wrote for him, a series
of letters to Colonel Hamilton Smith, the antiquary, requesting
correct details of costume for *The Merchant of Venice,* date about
1300, *Two Gentlemen of Verona,* date about 1500, and *Romeo
and Juliet,* date about 1200.[65] Nor was it merely the historical
productions which received accurate costuming. When the time
came to present Bulwer-Lytton's modern comedy *Money,* Macready turned to the dapper Count D'Orsay for the name of his
hatter, as well as other details. In later years, under other and less
scrupulous managers, the actor would "loan his clothes sooner
than have the character misrepresented."[66]

Accuracy in costuming was not enough. There must be familiarity, the costumes must be properly worn. Armor was particularly troublesome to Macready, as it is to most actors. In
preparation for his revival of *Henry V,* he not only rehearsed in
costume, but wore his armor about the theatre and at his house
and to meals to accustom himself to it. And one entire day of the
rehearsals of *King John* was devoted to teaching the actors to wear
their armor correctly. The actor must be as much at home in his
costume as in the particular setting.

This insistence on accuracy of costume was considered by his
various managers one of Macready's most trying whims. What can
have been the feelings of Alfred Bunn when his stage manager
reported a letter from the actor, then in Dublin, about *Sardanapalus,* scheduled for production over Macready's protests. But if
it is to be done, then Macready will be as demanding as possible:

As a matter of course my dress will be provided, and *ready to try on*
upon my arrival on Easter Monday morning. Having no opportunity
of consulting authority, nor giving directions here, I am obliged to
leave these matters to other tastes. I only beg I may not be *bespangled.*
—White or light blue, or pink satin or silk, embroidered with dead
gold braiding and jewels is the style of ornament. It should be noted,
that *mine* should be the *only* long dress, particularly distinguished in
that from all the other men in the play: the skirt or tunic nearly to
the ancles, but open from the middle with trowsers underneath, similar
to those in Hope's Costume.[67]

It must be assumed that the costume was satisfactory. His *Diary* is full of discontent about the production of *Sardanapalus,* but the complaints are against the play, which proved a great weariness to him.

It was inescapably, however, one of the hits of the season, full of spectacular effects, and the country managers immediately wished to include it in his repertory. To one he yielded, to his stepmother, but with such orders and demands for new scenery and costumes that the poor woman might well have been dis-couraged. Peremptory though his letter may be, it demonstrates his desire that what is done should be well done, even in a country theatre:

With regard to the dresses, a long skirt, half way down between the knees and ancles, and square at the neck, with a round high cap of [*sketch*] this form, is all that is necessary to mark the costume:—the sleeves should be full, and open at the wrist.—These of different colours with merely bands of gold & silver lace will be quite suffi-cient.—The banquet ought to be handsome—and the couch, which is used through the play, should be without back or head—a plain broad couch well stuffed [*sketch*] with two *large* deeply stuffed cushions —Two scenes would be enough for the whole play—The Hall of Nimrod with the Throne to stand from beginning to the end, which would save an immense deal of trouble.—The throne may be a *square platform,* on which is a small couch—and in front *practicable steps*— on either side merely painted ones, with fantastic massive pillars for each corner.—It should seem as if of solid gold, richly ornamented.— Now—to make it easy, and diminish expense,—instead of the bungling manner it was done in London—it will be better to adopt this method. —Observe *the scene in the 2d act* may be in the 2d or 3d grooves, so as to dispense with the necessity of *striking the Throne,* till it is entirely done with.—Let there be a sort of Persian or Egyptian style of arch at the 2d Wing—in the hall of Nimrod, from which a curtain is festooned so as to fall & meet in the centre, and shut in the Banquet &c. By this means, as I will show, the erection of the pile takes place *behind it, out of sight of the audience,* which allows the use of *one painted piece* with trick flats to fall, and shew itself on fire.—The advantage & superior effect of this is incalculable. Indeed in London the thing was *always laughed at,* & must be much worse in the country. This pile of faggots, logs of wood, and vases & rich ornaments *com-pletely hides* the Throne, which therefore may be entirely removed, & merely double steps, [*sketch*] which can be let down, placed behind the piece for Myrrha & Sardanapalus to stand upon.—It should reach nearly to the top of the stage.—I hope the Scene Painter & Carpenter will understand this, for it will save money, time, trouble & add greatly

to the effect.—If the pile of wood can sink down to discover the palace
& city in flames, of course the effect will be so much greater. . . .

8 Guards will be enough—as many women as can be mustered—and
ALL the company will be wanted.—About the fireworks . . . They
should be attached to the Pile at the sides, & upon a low ground piece
before it—also when lighted, fire may come from the top, and present
the appearance of one blaze of fire.[68]

Did Mrs. McCready suspect, knowing the flimsiness of her scenery
and theatre alike, that the ending of Sardanapalus might present
more than the appearance of one blaze of fire? It was almost a
tradition of the English theatre that the search for realism should
end with the combustion of the premises.

The electric light was to eliminate many of the dangers attendant upon spectacular production as well as to multiply infinitely
the possibilities for realism and effect on the stage. By the time
Macready appeared on the London stage, gas had replaced the
candelabra of Garrick's day, and a limited range of lighting effects
were available to him. It was possible, for example, to alternate
dim and full lights for the alternate witch and battle scenes which
open Macbeth. Beyond this simple realism, it was possible also to
use gas for atmospheric effect. In the third act of Werner, as the
first scene draws to its close, the lights gradually dim; the second
scene, following without pause, is played in increasing darkness
as the doomed Stralenheim retires, with some forebodings; the
third scene, the secret passage, is headed "ALL LIGHTS DOWN Stage
quite dark," with the added emphasis, "The Stage should be
literally quite dark." For the next scene, where Ulric confronts
his father, the lights are brought up one-half, and moonlight
added for an eerie effect. That the prompter felt it necessary to
repeat his injunctions about darkening the stage shows how
revolutionary were even these modest attempts at the manipulation of lighting.[69]

The moonlight effect in the garden scene suggests that there
were other sources of light than the floats, or footlights. One of
these was doubtless the eidophusikon invented by Loutherbourg
in the eighteenth century, a device for projecting moving objects,
such as clouds, on a drop. Some such device must have been
employed for the rolling surf in Acis and Galatea and for the
shadows on the waterfall of Stanfield's diorama. From the promptbook of the Two Gentlemen of Verona, finally, comes the direction "Green float up—and the white down,"[70] which can only
mean that the footlights were divided in color series, as in the

modern theatre, and that there was an attempt to use color in light for atmospheric effect.

The lighting equipment at Macready's disposal was of the simplest sort. There is a report that he employed the newly discovered limelight during his Covent Garden season of 1837–38, but abandoned it because of the cost. But in the same year he ordered an expensive alteration of the gas system, "In justice, as I thought, to Stanfield and the work he is engaged on for me."[71]

Whatever the means, the results which he obtained were remarkable. The storm scenes of *Lear* are probably the greatest challenge to the stage manager of any in Shakespeare. Audiences will no longer be content (nor were they in the early nineteenth century) with a formal representation, such as satisfied the Elizabethans. On the other hand, there is very real danger that the artificial tempests of the machinist will swallow up the inward tempest of the mad king. Macready's achievement in staging these scenes was memorable, particularly since it roused the plaudits of *John Bull*, a journal generally to be found among the opposition:

Forked lightnings, now vividly illumine the broad horizon, now faintly corruscating in small and serpent folds, play in the distance; the sheeted element sweeps over the foreground and then leaves it in pitchy darkness; the wind and rain howl and rush in 'tyranny of the open night.' Had such scenic imitation been introduced in some wretched melodrame, it would have been lauded to the very echo; it shall not want our eulogy at least, now that it forms the setting to a priceless diamond.[72]

Macready's interest in unity went far beyond scenic arrangement to the actual performances of the actors themselves. Thinking back over his periods of management, he concluded that the main difference between his productions and those of other managers lay in the directing of the actors. "I thought for and acted to myself every character and supernumerary figure, and taught them to act as I would have done had I been cast in their places. There was thus the mind of a first actor moving and harmonizing the action of the mass."[73] The term *first actor* no doubt suggested to Macready's classical mind the protagonist of the Greeks, the original actor who wrote, staged, and played the sole role in the earliest tragedies and thus achieved a unity impossible on stages crowded with dramatis personae. But to the modern reader, "first actor moving and harmonizing the action of the mass" can only suggest the *regisseur* of the contemporary stage.

Stage history is full of anecdotes which derive from actors' resentment, or simply bewilderment, at this Victorian prototype of the *regisseur*. Chiefly this difficulty occurred on the road, but even in London Macready's insistence upon accuracy of detail led him to chalk out movements for his leading lady, and Ellen Tree contracted "a serious disease of the knee-joint"[74] by falling repeatedly on her knees during the rehearsals of *Ion*. Mrs. Kean could probably thank the delightful comedienne Dorothy Jordan for her sore knee, since it seems to have been Macready's first playing with her in the provinces in 1812 that impressed upon him the necessity of repetition for perfection.

There was occasional objection, too, from the other side of the footlights to Macready's careful training of his actors. Reviewing Helen Faucit and James Anderson in *The Novice*, the *Spectator* wrote, "in some of the passages they delivered, we observed traces of the mannerisms of the presiding genius of the spot; and the thought occurred to us, that when the master shall come in juxtaposition with his pupils, the effect will be somewhat similar to that produced by the sight of a group of family portraits."[75] But the training of his actors—and how else but in his own image?—Macready clearly took to be part of his function as manager. "I must be a *despot*, or *serve*," he declared.[76] The habit of instruction came easy to him; after all, his introduction to the theatre had been by way of the managerial chair.

If the habit of instruction comes easily, it departs with the greatest reluctance. Throughout his life, the Eminent was forced to direct actors, even during performances. Sometimes they resisted; sometimes they were puzzled, like Mrs. John Drew, whom he instructed to stand up, the while pressing his hand firmly on her head; sometimes they obeyed: at Bristol "by dint of urging on the company and giving them proper directions all went smoothly" in an insufficiently rehearsed performance of *Sardanapalus*.[77] And in the midst of the cares of management, and in the teeth of a scandal which rankled his Victorian soul, Macready still found time to devote an entire morning to Helen Faucit, telling her all the faults he could recollect in her style, and demonstrating the cure for them.

It was a tenet of his managerial creed that every part worth acting was worth acting well; that all actors should play their best, whether as second leads (there was only *one* star) or spear carriers. To this end, he abandoned his practice of insisting that his own name appear in large letters on the bills, persuaded his actors to take roles that were not in their "line of business," and once tried to set an example himself. It is true that not many of his fellow-players are recognized today as among the great English actors:

Bartley, Elton, Bennett, Huddart, Warde, Cooper. They were first-rate players of second-rate roles, as Macready said of Charles Kemble. But they were the best available to him, and some, like Samuel Phelps and Helen Faucit, achieved distinction. And the Bartleys and Bennetts and Wardes were as proud as the Bettertons and Garricks and Kembles.

Each part, however, must be perfect if the whole is to be perfect. In the older theatre every actor had clung jealously to his contracted "business" as juvenile hero, character woman, or first heavy. The first gesture in establishing the modern system of "casting to strength," according to the demands of the text rather than the protocol of the greenroom, was made when Macready persuaded Bartley to play the Duke in *Othello* "as an example to the other actors, and to show the public that there would be no impediments to the best possible disposition of the characters in a play."[78] As a result, the *Spectator* noted that good casting in the secondary roles brought out latent points in the play. "For example, in the parental agony of Brabantio . . . we are in some sort prepared for the poetical justice of the catastrophe which overtakes [Desdemona and Othello]; and in the girlish, half-teasing solicitations of Desdemona when Othello is busy, the great disparity of the match, and the seeds of difference it contained, are seen."[79]

It is perhaps difficult for the modern theatregoer to realize that many secondary roles in Shakespeare were formerly considered merely good enough for walking gentlemen, the players who could be trusted to learn the lines and fill up the stage without detracting attention from the star or falling over the scenery, but little more. Banquo was such a role, and Macready entrusted it to, or perhaps thrust it upon, James Warde. The wholehearted approval of the critics must have somewhat salved Warde's injured feelings:

The latter part is perhaps hardly so important as those which are generally performed by Mr. Warde, but the excellent manner in which he plays it, and the finish which was given to the general effect of the drama by intrusting the character to him, show how good is the system by which all the chief actors of a company are made to participate in the performance, and insure the success of a play. In the foreign theatres it is a plan which has been long and generally adopted, and it is no small credit to the present manager of Covent Garden that he has been enabled to overcome the vanity of the chief English actors upon this point and induce them all to contribute to the general effect of the piece.[80]

There was occasional recalcitrance. Phelps was convinced that he had been "held back," Compton was inclined to quarrel when Dogberry was assigned to Keeley, Staudigl refused Hecate, Helen Faucit was in an ill humor because Mrs. Warner played Lady Macbeth; but each rebellion was put down.

All that is, except one. On April 30, 1838, *Romeo and Juliet* was revived with Macready in the role of Friar Lawrence. Anderson was the Romeo, Helen Faucit the Juliet, and Vining the Mercutio. After the performance, the manager sputtered to his *Diary:*

I find playing a part of this sort, with no direct character to sustain, no effort to make, no power of perceiving an impression made, to be a very disagreeable and unprofitable task. Having required many of the actors to do what they considered beneath them, perhaps it was only a just sacrifice to their opinions to conclude so far—but it is for the first and last time.

It was perhaps unfortunate that Macready could not give himself the lessons he gave the protesting actors; he might have cast light upon the lesser characters as he did upon the greater. James Hudson, assigned the role of LeBeau in *As You Like It,* complained that it was insignificant. So the manager read it to him in such a way that Hudson was in convulsions of laughter before he had finished. "Excellent, sir! excellent!" he said. "I had no idea what it was."[81]

Casting to strength, like propriety in designing scenery and costume, and careful planning of effects and stage business, was the first step in achieving the unity of a work of art. The second step was full rehearsal, the careful development of the plan. Until the management of Macready, rehearsal had been generally a tentative affair, little more than a walk-through to refresh the actors' recollections of their stage positions. There was almost no attempt to fit the characterizations together, to concentrate on the development of *scenes*—after all, the older plays were star vehicles, and the audience had been taught to look only at the leading personages, to listen to their impassioned speeches and wait for their big moments, their "points." It was a good deal like going to the opera.

The rehearsals, too, were somewhat operatic. Lesser players moved listlessly according to the instructions of the stage manager; major players, if present at all, spent most of their energy in seeing that they remained always "in focus," that attention was concentrated on them. Even actors who intended sensational new effects for one reason or another did not think it necessary to acquaint their fellows of their intentions. But not Macready, of course.

In his first days in London he had been laughed at for acting at rehearsal. But that did not alter his purpose. He continued to act at rehearsal, and to fume (privately and publicly) when the other members of the company were inattentive. On tour his rages were all public, giving rise to most of the unpleasant stories about his ill-temper. Although he despised these men and women who would not take their work seriously, and who contributed so largely to the bad name of his profession, Macready made a conscious effort to teach them to act with him, and to restrain his temper, though neither endeavor was very successful. It is rare indeed to find him writing in his *Diary:* "Rehearsed with civility; had occasion to observe how much country practise is likely to induce slovenly habits unless caution is constantly used."[82] Far more common is this sort of entry, dealing with the staging of a revival of *Virginius:* "At rehearsal I gave much trouble in putting the play on the stage, as it was originally got up by me. I fear I incurred much remark and ill will. I am very sorry for it."[83]

Under his own management Macready did not have to tolerate such haphazard behavior. Nothing was left to chance, even in the revival of the oldest, most frequently performed plays. Where other managers were accustomed to call special rehearsals only for the new pantomimes and operas, and fitfully for new plays, Macready rehearsed endlessly the standard plays of the repertory, Shakespeare and *Venice Preserved, The Gamester* and *The Stranger.* And the supernumeraries were directed with as painstaking care as the principals.

Some of the results have already been noted. Familiar scenes came to life in a new way. The audience, accustomed to wait for the star's points, suddenly were stirred out of themselves by a scene in which the leading character did not appear. The masses of soldiers or courtiers demanded by so many of Shakespeare's plays were no longer a band of pitiful rascals, but a contributory part of the whole action. An entire morning of precious rehearsal time would be devoted to the supers in the first two acts of *King John,* and to the other plays in like degree, but the results were such that even Alfred Bunn was startled into admitting that "Coriolanus was put upon the Covent Garden stage in a manner worthy of any theatre and any manager."[84]

Supers were used in the older theatre primarily for spectacular and pictorial effect. But the handling of mobs was so haphazard— collected from the streets, costumed in any old rags, and sent on, bewildered, to plug up gaps in the stage picture—that they were often spectacular in a sense hardly intended by the playwright. W. S. Gilbert's reference to the supers at the Adelphi theatre as "Adelphi guests" suggests strangers at a feast, bumblingly moving to their belated understanding of directions, and obviously not at home on the stage. With Macready the pictorial mob was a feast for the eye.

But the use of supers for spectacle and atmosphere was customary. Macready had more to offer the modern theatre than this.

His staging of *As You Like It,* described by an enthusiastic prompter in his copy of the Drury Lane master-text as "the most wonderfully perfect representation of court and pastoral life ever witnessed on the English stage,"[85] directed the attention of his successors in England and his disciples in Germany to the dramatic potential of the theatrical mob. In the wrestling scene, for example, Macready found certain hints of courtly behavior, and certain suggestions for excitement in the defeat of Charles. It was, further, the scene which set the plot in motion. Therefore he worked to realize it, to give it its true largeness, to make it explain itself, mainly through his handling of the supers.

The full stage was used, with a palace on the right, and with steps leading from it to the stage floor. At the back was a raised walk, with steps on both sides leading to a terrace and grounds below. After the preliminaries, and the scene with LeBeau, there is a flourish of trumpets. The promptbook directs the action:

Groups of Courtiers and Ladies, enter up terrace steps, L and move upon the scene, as if awaiting the wrestling. Attendts enter, and begin to place chairs, and prepare the ring, with ropes and pillars. As the Courtiers catch sight of Celia, or Rosalind, they salute them respectfully. As the Duke and Suite enter—Rosalind, Celia &c retire towards R 2 E, where attendts are placing seats, many of the Courtiers and Ladies, are crowding round Charles, as if congratulating him,— he is, apparently, full of confidence,—other courtiers are talking together, all in high glee, in regarding Charles, and, occasionally, glancing sneeringly at Orlando, who stands, modestly apart at back L 3 E—speaking to Dennis;—The Ring is formed as rapidly as possible, but the L entrances are not closed—the Court are grouped without and within—the Duke, LeBeau, and 2 or 3 of the Courtiers have Merlins on their wrists.
[Orlando: "When I have made it empty."] Duke and Court move to leave the ring.

[Rosalind: "Pray heaven, I be deceived in you."] As the Duke moves down to his seat, R—the Attendants clear and close the ring.—All are arranged, without, around.

[Orlando: "Ready, sir."] takes off cloak—gives it to Dennis, at back R
[Orlando: "But come your ways."] Great anxiety and interest among the bystanders, with cries of encouragement, fear &c commencing in a whisper, and as the parties close to struggle, become most vehement. [*Charles is thrown*] Gen¹ shout and applause, from all on the stage— As the Duke rises, the Attend^ts on his signal take up the ropes &c. and exit down terrace—the Courtiers &c crowd round in eager congratulations to Orl:—the Duke adv^s to Orl, Courtiers giving way.

[As the Duke speaks] Courtiers, &c, become grave, and look with timid distrustful glances at Duke and Orl. They exeunt diversely—some foll'g Duke R U E—others L U E Others, the terrace steps—All as if speak'g of Orlando.

The supers were employed to create the dignity and elegance of the court and the tension preceding the match. During the wrestling, their carefully controlled reactions built to a climax of excitement which must have communicated itself to the audience and enabled them to share the emotional values of the scene.

Macready's revival of *Julius Caesar* affords a second instance of the use of supers for "lifelikeness." Although Brutus and Mark Antony had been accustomed to deliver their orations to a handful of half-costumed, half-attentive gentlemen of the ballet, Macready provided thirty "plebians," and made them a functioning part of the scene. At the beginning of the scene (III,1) Brutus and all the conspirators are discovered on the steps of the Rostrum, with the citizens ranged to their right and left. Brutus ascends to speak, accompanied by a "low murmuring among the citizens." They move about freely during the speech—on cue—and as Brutus asks if they would not prefer to live all free men, "The Citizens turn to one another, as though quietly obtaining each other's sentiments." The body of Caesar is next brought in, by guards, and placed at the foot of the Rostrum: "This is timed so as to be done, at Brutus' exit." During Antony's oration, however, the mob comes to life. If the words themselves were not sufficient to inflame the audience, the carefully planned business ascending to a thundering climax would surely register even on the deafest spectator in the farthest reaches of the top gallery:

Antony. . . . But here's a parchment with the seal of Caesar;
　　　　I found it in his closet; 'tis his will:
　　　　Let but the commons hear this testament—
　　　　　*Several of the Citizens extend their hands to Antony & press
　　　　　forward towards him.*

Which, pardon me, I do not mean to read—
And they would go and kiss dead Caesar's wounds

. . .

'Tis good you know not that you are his heirs;
A movement of surprise and joy by all.

. . .

You will compel me then to read the will?
Then make a ring about the corpse of Caesar,
And let me show you him that made the will.
Shall I descend? and will you give me leave?
They all gather round the rostrum.

. . .

O, what a fall was there, my countrymen!
Then, I, and you, and all of us fell down,
*Some of the Cit[ize]ns here incline their heads
sorrowfully, others put their hands to their eyes, &c.*

. . .

      Look you here,
Here is himself, marr'd, as you see, with traitors.
First Citizen. O piteous spectacle!
The Mob break up and cross the Stage R & L—as going off.

. . .

Antony. Stay, country men
     The Cit[ize]ns stop suddenly, and return

. . .

       but were I Brutus,
And Brutus Antony, there were an Antony
Would ruffle up your spirits, and put a tongue
In every wound of Caesar, that should move
The stones of Rome to rise and mutiny.
All.   We'll mutiny.
     All turn as if going R & L and move a pace or two.
First Citizen. We'll burn the house of Brutus.
Third Citizen. Away then! come seek the conspirators.
Antony. Yet hear me countrymen; yet hear me speak.
     [Citizens] resuming their positions.

. . .

All.   Most true, the will! Let's stay and hear the will.
     They return to Antony.
Antony. Here is the will, and under Caesar's seal.
    To every Roman citizen he gives,
    To every several man, seventy-five drachmas.
     A general movement of surprise.

. . .

Antony. Here was a Caesar! When comes such another?
     Great excitement shewn here by all the Cit[ize]ns.

First Citizen. Never, never! Come, away, away, &c.
> *All vociferating together, as they cross R & L—Exit at*
> *the diff[eren]t ent[rance]s, as rapidly as possible. The*
> *Tumult is heard dying away in the distance until the Act*
> *drop falls.*

And, lest the effect of the moment be lost, the few following lines between the servant and Antony are "All spoken very quickly!"[86]

There can be no doubt that the skillful use of supernumeraries affected the audience as perhaps mere words in the vast reaches of the national theatres might fail to do. The reviewers, who were not always pleased with Macready as an actor, testify to his successful manipulation of the audience by means of his stage mobs. Thus, the *Spectator* on the beginning of *Coriolanus:*

The opening scene, where the multitudinous rabble rush in, mad with excitement, brandishing axes, mallets, and staves, prepares the audience for what is to follow. . . . We hear the roar of the many-headed monster, like the surging murmurs of the sea, swelling onward, rivalling in numbers and violence probably the actual Roman mob that thronged to the Capitol.[87]

In the business of smaller scenes, not involving masses of supers, Macready was also inventive. He seems to have been continually working them over in his mind, introducing improvements and experiments to make clearer the meaning or surer the effect of the situations. A promptbook of *Hamlet* which must date from very early in his career contains the standard Drury Lane business with certain additions in Macready's hand. The scene with his father's ghost (I,5) is played in a "cut wood," and the Queen in her closet wears about her neck a miniature of Claudius. At the end of this scene is a typical Macready addition, intended to amplify Hamlet's decision to be cruel only to be kind. "The Queen goes to the R wing—stops, looks back at Hamlet, clasps her hands and raises her eyes to Heaven, and rushes back to throw herself round Hamlet's neck—he repels her, and she exit sorrowfully R. H."[88] In 1837, the interview with the ghost was staged with the ghost standing on the edge of a turret, Hamlet climbing up the steep wall towards it, an effect which was, said the *Spectator,* "striking, but a little too melodramatic." In the closet scene, the Ghost rose up through a trap door and stepped between the Queen and her son just as Hamlet was about to be overpowered by his passions.[89] In 1840, the closet was hung with arras and decorated with three portraits, of Old Hamlet, Claudius, and Gertrude, and the Ghost made his appearance by stepping out of his own picture. This

Macready thought was "a very great improvement on the old stupid custom" of the pair of miniatures. The final pantomime of this scene had also been elaborated:

having bid his mother sorrowful 'good-night,' she retires towards the door, but on gaining it stops, bursts into tears, and retraces her steps to take a last embrace; but Macready raises his hand, and motions her to stop, clearly implying by his action and melancholy countenance, that the memory of his dead parent was a sacred thought, and would not allow him to enfold in his embrace her who, *even now*, held communion with his murderer.[90]

Perhaps the limit of "interpretive staging" was reached in the revival of *Henry V* which Macready chose as the last production of his first period of management. The standard stage version of the play had been greatly cut, the choruses omitted, and the usual production was ragged and casual. He thought first of restoring the Chorus, with Vandenhoff in the role, and suggested as much to Serle, his manager. Serle "observed that the choruses would admit of illustration, a hint which I instantly caught at, and determined upon doing it."[91] He commissioned the painting of a diorama to "illustrate" the choruses. The muse of Stanfield ascended to heights of invention to convey the vasty fields of France within Covent Garden's great wooden O: Macready plainly did not trust Vandenhoff's ability to hold an audience, or an audience's willingness to be recited at. He explained his purpose in a note on the playbill:

To impress more strongly on the auditor, and render more palpable these portions of the story which have not the advantage of action, and still are requisite to the Drama's completeness, the narrative and descriptive poetry spoken by the Chorus is accompanied with PICTORIAL ILLUSTRATIONS from the pencil of MR. STANFIELD.

Two things are worth emphasizing in that note. First, the wholly commendable desire for the "Drama's completeness" which was the guiding principle of Macready's career; and second, the perplexity about scenes which "have not the advantage of action." There is certainly a very real problem in *Henry V;* the dramatic interest is "light," to use N. P. Willis' epithet; both in plotting and execution it has much of the old Marlovian bluster and shapelessness, but it may reasonably be questioned whether in this revival Macready's celebrated "taste" did not play him false. Since he had restored the choruses, that is, should he not have read them?

> let us, ciphers to this great accompt,
> On your *imaginary* forces work. . . .

Contemporary opinion, however, was strongly in his favor. The revival of *Henry V* hit the taste of the public and most of the critics, and achieved twenty-one performances between June 10 and July 16, 1839.

The rising curtain displayed an act drop with the arms of France and England emblazoned on either side, the initials of the reigning monarchs being worked into the ornamental border. This drawn up, Vandenhoff in robes of russet, with Time's scythe and hour glass, is revealed standing on a pedestal at one side of a vast framework of clouds, which roll away on the line "pardon gentles all." Behind the clouds is the first illustration, an historical painting of the sort the Victorians were coming to praise so highly, an allegorical representation of Henry with the daemons of war in his train ("and at his heels/ Leashed in like hounds, should famine, sword and fire/ Crouch for employment."). Lest the audience be made too conscious of what is being done, the lines about the cockpit and the wooden O are artfully omitted. The clouds gather, the picture is shut out from sight, Vandenhoff—on his pedestal—is drawn off stage and the play proceeds. For the second chorus, the clouds part to show a painting of three conspirators receiving the bribes of the French. All this was modest enough. With the third chorus, the pyrotechnics begin:

Curtain up, & then open and move on. MUSIC,—as the Drop rises.—It continues, as the scene opens, presenting the embarkation of the King, and the sailing of the Fleet; it gradually dies away, as the night appears to come on, and the single ship is left on the scene. Chorus then speaks. ("Thus with imagined wing our swift scene flies.")

According to the *Atheneum,* in this scene, "the sunset at sea glows with light, and the distance is aërial; there is a moonlight effect, too, which is as little 'theatrical' as possible."[92] The Chorus, omitting to mention that Henry has left England's defense in the hands of grandsires, babies, and old women, adjures the spectator to follow the King to France. As he does so, the diorama commences to roll past, bringing the French coast into view, then to the accompaniment of backstage shouts, crashes, and cannonfire moves on to present the landing and assault of Harfleur. Although these are still pictures, arranged in a series, there is some attempt, not too successful, "to give continuity to unconnected views." A further attempt at continuity is the "melting" of the painted siege into reality. As the Chorus finishes his speech, the frame is drawn off; "it discloses on the stage the walls L H and gate of Harfleur manned with combatants, the English on scaling ladders attacking

Henry V, Act III, Scene i, from Scharf's *Recollections*

them—other with cannon—some behind their pavisors with the long and cross bows. The English repulsed come rushing on from 1st E L—the assailants on the stage leave their attack, when the King enters—last." The *Spectator*, while praising the diorama and the ingenuity of the melting scene, snorts at the staging of the siege. "[T]he French are quietly looking over the walls while the English King is urging his soldiers on to the breach, and when they rush forward the stage is left clear for the buffoonery of Pistol and his brother cowards—with only an uncouth piece of ordnance, which on being fired, once and no more, had made a most abortive explosion."[93] Macready had perhaps anticipated an objection to the meek co-operation of the enemy by cutting Henry's famous oration nearly in half.

The fourth Chorus finds the clouds once more in place. At the words "dreadful note of preparation" the diorama moves, displaying the hostile camps, and the opposite condition of the two armies: first the French with "distant bells heard, and the noises of the . . . camp." Vandenhoff then falls silent as the diorama turns to the English watch-fires, accompanied by music. The final chorus, at the beginning of Act Five, opens with a picture of the citizens of London, and follows with a series of scenes depicting the triumphal entry of Henry into the city. "It was wonderful," wrote Willis, "how this double representation, this scenic presentment to the eye, added to the interest and meaning of the play."[94]

The *Spectator* had a further, and rather curious, objection to the staging. The first scene, showing Henry surrounded by his courtiers, it admitted to be a gorgeous picture of regal pomp, "the stone niches and statues in the upper part of the walls massing the glitter below." Only, the *Spectator* felt that the supers might have been grouped more by color, "to prevent the confusion of splendour, that wearies the eye for want of a mass to repose on." This is curious because grouping by color was one of Macready's individual techniques. The senators in *Othello*, for instance, were ranged in red and black, and their movements were so governed that the red and black masses would always provide effective contrast. The same device was employed in *Coriolanus* where, in V,3, the scene was filled with a glittering mass of Volscian soldiers in red, suddenly parted by the appearance of Virgilia and the mourning women from Rome as by a black thread, stretching across the entire stage.[95]

With the means at his command, Macready was a master of effective staging on the grand scale required by his theatre. Feeling the necessity of presenting to the audience realizations of the time and place of a play's actions, he enlisted the techniques of the painter and mechanic with, for the most part, the restraint of the severest taste. There were times when the desire to illustrate overcame him, as in *Henry V*, where very little harm was done, to be sure. Perhaps equally harmless was his turning the first scene of *The Tempest* wholly to pantomime, with a miniature ship going down in a hurly-burly of sound effects, music, prompter's cries, and cardboard waves. Less venial is the pantomimic ending attached to the closet scene in *Hamlet*.

But pantomime, like the diorama, was one of his chief tools, and one to which less objection would be taken as the century progressed. In 1823, his staging of *Caius Gracchus* was criticized as melodramatic clap-trap for dropping the curtain on a scene full of actors. But in his handling of Byron, at which there seem to be no protests, he regularly substitutes a pantomime ending for the author's. In *Marino Faliero*, V,3, Byron ends with the Executioner raising his sword over the Doge. At this point Macready adds:

the voice of Angiolina is heard. She pushes on exclaiming:
Angiolina. I will not be with-held; my lord, my husb—:
The Senators throw themselves before the Doge as the sword of the Executioner descends,—the bell tolls—and Angiolina shrieks and falls.
THE CURTAIN DESCENDS RAPIDLY.[96]

The London *Times* dissented mildly. The new ending, it said, was no improvement, was commonplace, and interrupted the solemnity of the execution.[97] But the same device had worked very well in *Werner* and in *Sardanapalus* (with the addition of a holocaust) and, in extenuation, it should again be recalled that action speaks more plainly than words over vast space.

At any rate there was purpose behind every one of Macready's innovations. And that purpose was not merely to excite the audience with spectacle—leave that to Bunn—or with meaningless violence—leave that to the minor theatres. It *was* spectacular, to be sure, to cast Priscilla Horton as Ariel, costume her in green weeds and a wreath of coral, and then put her in a flying harness and float her about the stage. "Our aim," said Macready at his banquet, "has been fidelity of illustration. The 'delicate Ariel' is now no longer in representation a thing of earth, but either 'a wandering voice' or a visible spirit of air, flitting in his own element amid the strange and sweet noises of the enchanted island." *As You Like It,* he once said, was his favorite production: "it was a beautiful pastoral, and every minor part was well filled."[98] Yet in it he freely introduced hunting hounds to accompany the foresters, while condemning Bunn for bringing animals upon the sacred boards of a national theatre. The difference, as he no doubt saw it, was that while Bunn had produced a play to fit the animals, he had provided animals to fit the play.

Macready further clearly gave the cue to his successors. Phelps, in a modest way, Anderson, Charles Kean, Henry Irving, and Beerbohm Tree more wholeheartedly seized upon the idea of making the drama, and Shakespeare in particular, more "palpable" to the spectators. Once started, and given the assistance of greatly improved stage mechanics and lighting, there was no stopping the vicious movement which threatened to turn Shakespeare into a series of gaudy tableaux. Macready, himself, after his retirement, seems to have realized what he had done. After reading a description of Kean's revival of *The Winter's Tale*—in which every detail of setting, decoration, costuming, grouping, and color was reported, with almost no mention of any acting—he concluded with a sigh that the accessories had swallowed the poetry and action. Lady Pollock tried to comfort him by pointing out that it no longer concerned him.

'Do you know,' said he, 'why I take it so much to heart? It is because I feel myself in some measure responsible. I, in my endeavor to give Shakespeare all his attributes, to enrich his poetry with scenes worthy of its interpretation, to give to his tragedies their due magnificence, and to his comedies their entire brilliancy, have set an example which is accompanied with great peril, for the public is willing to have the magnificence without the tragedy, and the poet is swallowed up in display. When I read such a description as this of the production of a great drama, I am touched with a feeling something like remorse. Is it possible, I ask myself. Did *I* hold the torch? Did *I* point out the path?'[99]

It was a good deal for a man like Macready to have on his conscience. And, in a sense, his responsibility is clear. The costumes of "Verona c. 1200" and the architecture of republican Rome were not what the situation of *Romeo and Juliet* or *Coriolanus* brought to Shakespeare's mind; in effect Macready was upholstering rather than interpreting the images of Shakespeare. Yet his purpose was consistency and propriety, from whatever source; to achieve a harmony of setting, costume, lighting, and action, an accuracy in every detail which would build to a greater perfection of the whole, realized *plastically* in the elements of production and movement.

The Eminent Tragedian was a scholar and a poet: he created, to the extent that the resources of his theatre permitted, artistic unities developed and restricted by intelligence and taste. In another sense, then, it was not his responsibility that those who followed him in London were pedants or megalomanic showmen. But it was his fate to die without knowing that from the devoted work of his protégé Samuel Phelps, and even from the excesses of Charles Kean, the young Duke of Saxe-Meiningen derived his first notions of the possibilities of a new kind of production. The Duke's experiments with an acting company were to be a major influence on those who have been most widely credited with the foundation of modern theatre practice.

"Our aim," said Macready, "has been fidelity of illustration," to transfer his picture from the poet's mind, complete in all its parts and harmoniously arranged as to figure, scene, and action. If Stanislavsky or Gordon Craig or Adolf Appia might quarrel with that statement because of its directness and perspicuity, they could hardly differ with it as a statement of their principles.

The Rival Stars, or,
A Tragedy Rehears'd

THE EMINENT TRAGEDIAN IN AMERICA

MACREADY WAS in his fiftieth year when he concluded his management of Drury Lane in 1843. He was secure in his odious eminence as first actor, he had given the impetus to a revolution in stagecraft, and he was welcome in social circles of his own choosing. But the bodily fatigue and mental distress of the last two years recalled more frequently and vividly the two images that had haunted his career: a bankrupt father leaving his family without resources, and an actor making himself a motley to the view when age had drained him of strength and talent. Consequently he was over-quick to assign an occasional failure in a stage effect to advancing years, and to fret in his diary and his letters to his family that he was losing his power to attract audiences and accumulate resources for their future.

His family had continued to grow. There were now seven small Macreadys to be clothed and fed and educated and kept from all contact with the stage.[1] By his own standards, he was not a wealthy man and his earnings from management had been considerably smaller than he might have gained from a comparable period as an actor. It was thus with the immediate intention of restoring his income that he undertook a second American tour. He always began every new venture with grim forebodings and with supplications for divine aid, but his second departure for America was an especially solemn event. A feeling of bitterness was rapidly growing between the two nations on either side of the Atlantic.

The West had been outraged by the widely published revelations of its deficiencies by such English travelers as Dickens, Mrs. Trollope, and Captain Basil Hall; the English, on the other hand, felt that their pockets had been picked by the so-called "Pennsylvania Repudiators." And, only a little over a year before, the popular Irish comedian Tyrone Power had been lost at sea in the sinking of the *President*. Small wonder that Macready kissed and blessed his children and his wife and parted from Forster as if he were never to see them again.

Yet he went to America with great hopes. There had been prosperous hunting in the States for a constant stream of English players; Vandenhoff, Wallack, and Charles Kean had returned without scars; and he had many friends who were eager to welcome him back. In addition he carried in his luggage a letter from Carlyle to his disciple Emerson, which should guarantee his entrance into the circles of the Boston intelligentsia. Carlyle had written:

Mr. Macready's deserts to the English Drama are notable here to all the world; but his dignified, generous, and every-way honorable deportment in private life is known fully, I believe, only to a few friends. I have often said, looking at him as a manager of great London theatres, "This Man, presiding over the unstablest, most chaotic province of English things, is the one public man among us who has dared to take his stand on what he understood to be *the truth*, and expect victory from that.[2]

This was, indeed, a solemn character for an actor to bear with him as he went into a new theatre, but Macready had a secondary purpose in going to America. He was beginning to consider "dear Yankeeland" (he had other names for it at other times) as a possible place of retirement when that happy moment should arrive.

His first sight of Boston, September 20, 1843, affirmed his hopes. As the ship moved into the harbor, past the thriving little villages dotted along the shore, he could see the State House dome and the Bunker Hill Monument reflecting the light of the rising sun. Perhaps it was a happy omen. He thought of the Pilgrim Fathers, "the fervent, stern, resolute, and trusting men," who had created out of their faith in God all the "glorious and happy life" he saw on every hand. In a burst of democratic euphoria, he almost shook the hand of the kind-hearted customs officer who examined his luggage. But the glitter of the land of hope was somewhat rubbed when he arrived at the Tremont House and had to wait half an

T. R. B.

~~For the Benefit of~~ Mr. Macready, ~~he speaks~~ ~~at this service~~, ~~who~~ has the gratification of announcing to the Ladies and Gentlemen of B. and its vicinity, that he has been able to procure, positively

This Night Only

the valuable services of the Eminent Tragedian

Mr. Macready

conjointly with the distinguished Talent of

Mrs. Warner

of the Theatre Royal, Covent Garden, England.

As this is the

Last Time

previous to his departure for America, that Mr. Macready can have the honor

Portion of a Bristol Playbill in Macready's handwriting heralding the Appearance of the Eminent Tragedian hour for his private room in a bustling crowd of democrats who chattered and smoked and stared and, of course, spat in all directions.

Next day he was in New York, preparing for his first appearance. Forrest came round to see him at his hotel and was both cordial and civil. Henry Wadsworth Longfellow, whom he had met in England, came to call. He visited with Fanny Kemble, and tactfully made no inquiries about the rumored separation from her husband, the American planter Pierce Butler, though he confessed to an ungentlemanly temptation to do so. He found the actors at the early rehearsals attentive and well-behaved. And some of the cares of rehearsing and performing were borne by John Ryder, from the Drury Lane Company, who was to accompany him throughout his tour.

His first role was Macbeth on September 25 at the Park Theatre. Ryder was the Macduff and Mrs. Sloman the Lady. In spite of the hottest weather of the summer, a great house turned out to greet him, and on his entrance repeated the demonstration that had sweetened his farewell in London. An eyewitness reported:

Hats, hands, and caps applauded to the skies—I thought he would never be able to proceed. At length the tragedy commenced, and in a few minutes Macready rivetted the attention of his auditors, so much so during the progress of the play, that scarcely a sound was heard. . . . For myself, I thought Macready rather nervous, as if his style of playing was a new attempt in America; but nothing could have been more decided and brilliant than his success when he fell dead in the last scene.[3]

Diarist Philip Hone declared it a great performance,[4] but Macready was rather dissatisfied. The heat was almost too much for him, and the audience—as he should have remembered—was not disposed to applaud "points." Nonetheless he decided that they had been held by the performance, and he was in any event glad that he had brought along Ryder.

The presence of Mrs. Sloman in the cast of the opening bill was hardly a good augury. After her failure to take London by storm, she had come to America and made a "triumphant" debut at the Chestnut Street Theatre in Philadelphia, December 7, 1827. She played leads in the principal cities along the coast, "correct and ladylike . . . but too cold to suit the multitude."[5] She seems to have committed no special offense on Macready's first night, but at some time during the engagement she displayed her unhappy faculty for irritating the Eminent Tragedian. Louisa Drew remembered the event:

Mrs. Sloman, an old-fashioned actress, dressed *Lady Macbeth* in the manner which prevailed in her early life—in black velvet, point lace and pearl beads. In the murder scene part of Macready's dress caught on the tassels of her pearl girdle; the string broke, the beads fell on the floor, softly, with a pretty rhythmic sound, distinctly heard through the intense silence of the scene. This so exasperated Mr. Macready that he was almost frantic, until, with the final line of the scene, "Wake, Duncan, with th[y] knocking, Oh! would thou couldst," he threw Mrs. Sloman off the stage, with words which I hope were unheard by the public, and were certainly unfit for publication.[6]

The season proceeded, much as in his former American tour. He ran through his Shakespearean roles, gave occasional performances of *Virginius,* and of other "Macready plays" in which he had not been seen in America. The edge had been somewhat taken from these by earlier visitors and by Forrest. Hone, speaking of his Claude Melnotte, was inclined to prefer Charles Kean's interpretation. Macready should stick to Lear, Macbeth, Richard, and Hamlet, he said: "When age is in, love ought to be out."

Forrest continued to treat him with great civility, entertaining him at dinner, introducing him to his literary friends, Bryant and Halleck, and taking him off to a daguerreotyper to pose with him. "I like all I see of Forrest very much," he wrote on October 4. "He appears a clear-headed, honest, kind man; what can be better?" That was Forrest the man. Of Forrest the actor he had not changed his earlier opinion. Transferring to Philadelphia on October 21, he was in time to see Forrest's Lear at the National Theatre. He found him still of great physical powers but with no imagination, no original thought, no poetry, in his acting. Misled by the extravagant applause of his countrymen, he was willing to speak "the trash of Tate," and he was "only an actor for the less intelligent of the Americans." Critical comparisons in the newspapers unfavorable to the English visitor were later to lead Macready to more dogmatic judgements: *"He is not an artist. Let him be an American actor—and a great American actor—but keep on this side of the Atlantic, and no one will gainsay his comparative excellence."* This was a most unfortunate prediction of the event, though it is due less to the gift of prophecy than to the fact that Forrest, on the twenty-eighth, was appearing in Cardinal Richelieu at the National when Macready was appearing in the same role at the Chestnut.

Indeed, the American Tragedian seems to have been deliberately appealing to nationalistic sentiments to increase his draw at the box office. Macready was inclined to blame Forrest's advisers rather than the actor himself for this stratagem. He wrote to Letitia:

since my appearance, they have announced him in *American* letters, as "Mr. E. Forrest, *The National Tragedian!*"—and put him up in my parts the nights after I have played them—It would (except that he is not estimated highly by the *leading* people) do him disservice with the intelligent and better sort, but I believe it has an effect of making a sort of factious rush to the Theatre—as his houses were very *bad* before this device was practiced.—I do not grumble nor concern myself at all about it.—I feel almost confident my visit must lessen his consideration as an artist, when I am gone away.—I do not wish any notice to be taken of this—which was perhaps a desperate resort on the part of the managers.[7]

On the thirtieth, an editorial in James Gordon Bennet's *Herald,* relating the attack of a "subterranean" Tammany paper on Forrest's private affairs, remarked that "It is very easy to get up an excitement against any popular actor, such as Mr. Forrest. A band of forty or fifty individuals, well arranged, are sufficient to drive any actor off the stage." Macready immediately interpreted this as taking sides against *him*. The press here was as venial as that at home. The whole nation was semi-civilized. Could any civilized nation put Forrest above Macready?

On the twenty-third he had played Macbeth with Charlotte Cushman, a rising young American actress who attracted him by showing "mind and sympathy" with him, a refreshing novelty. When it came time to make preparations for his Boston season, he spoke to her about accompanying him. She was willing to chance her acceptability to the Boston manager if her expenses were paid, which Macready was glad to do to fend off a possible Bostonian Mrs. Sloman. Charlotte was not in any sense of the word a womanly woman: she was no Helen Faucit, but she had force and intelligence and she looked amazingly like Macready. But the Boston manager would have nothing to do with her, preferring quite naturally to cast his own daughter in the leading roles. Miss Cushman, however, seemed well satisfied with her bargain—perhaps she was flattered at the interest of the great tragedian—sent him flowers and verses, and kissed his hand at parting.

He opened in Boston on November 23, suffering from a bad cast and a Lady Macbeth who neither understood the part nor spoke the words set down for her. But Cambridge offered some escape from these "Daggerwoods" and he lost no time in seeking out Longfellow, who introduced him anew to Cornelius Felton and Charles Sumner. He met the historians Prescott and Bancroft, and Jared Sparks and Daniel Webster, Abbott Lawrence, Ticknor, Curtis, Grattan, and Judge Story; and Waldo Emerson impressed him with the simplicity and kindness of his manner. This was the world to which he aspired, and there were no condescending baronets to make him conscious of the indignity of his profession. Nightly, however, he must return to his fatiguing and degrading work, though thanking the inspiration that had made him bring Ryder. "What should I have done without him?" he wrote. "I could not have got through."

Back in New York for a second engagement at the Park, he made his first American appearance as Melantius, distressed because his prized Charlotte Cushman, who had been long scheduled for Evadne, had not so much as learned the words of her part. Forrest came to report the receipt of a letter from Catherine in reply to his gift of the daguerreotypes. It is a note full of the spirit to be expected from a feminine mind that had been shaped by Macready:

Having this moment looked upon what The Sun is pleased to call a likeness, but, what I should declare, the most unpardonable libel any poor human being had ever to contend against, I cannot refrain from asking you, whether it was a friendly act to persuade, that disobedient husband to sit to so unkind, so untrue a limner, as the one you have chosen for him? Will not that sweet lady your wife have some sympathy with me, when she reflects, what my sensations must have been in opening that case, which contains the horror?—I pray her, as a true woman, to give you a very good scolding, and to ask her how you should like *her,* to receive such a remembrance of you, were she three thousand long miles away from you? When she has fulfilled this wish of mine, and you are justly penetrated with the crime, of which you are guilty—I shall forgive you—like a true philosopher—and tell you, nothing has given me greater pleasure from America, than that, which the relation of the hospitality, and kindness Mr. Macready has received from you, my dear sir, and Mrs. Forrest, during his sojourn in New York, has communicated.—I only wish I had any means here of testifying my gratitude to you for your great attention to him; which has gratified him very much, and which is one of the delightful things, among the many he will have to reflect upon in remembering his visit to your great country—A country you must be aware, he has taught his whole family to reverence, and from the tone of his letters now, one that will not disappoint—his previous high estimation of it.[8]

Next day, the Philadelphia manager proposed—to his indignation —that during his Spring engagement there he should act on alternate nights the same plays as Forrest. This, together with the nightly reception that Miss Cushman was getting from the audience in *The Bridal* and *Richelieu,* doubtless changed the tone of Macready's reports to his wife. On the surface, however, and perhaps for a short distance beneath it, all was well between the English and American tragedians.

After a short return season in Boston, Macready set out to experiment with new territory. He was to make a Southern and Western tour, commencing in Baltimore on Christmas Day. It was his first venture away from the cities where firmly established traditions and strong competition had forced some regularity upon theatrical managers. Now he was moving into the regions of ambulatory stock companies and ephemeral managements. If he had been unhappy in the English provinces where reasonably well-established circuits and frequent visits from metropolitan stars had kept up some standard of public taste, what might he expect from the American provinces, with their hastily built and haphazardly run theatres, and with their barnstorming actors and speculating managers? This was the era of experiment when Caldwell and Ludlow and Smith and Forbes were beginning to establish themselves, distances were great, travel was difficult, and audiences were uneducated. To add to his trials two continental violin virtuosi, Ole Bull and Vieuxtemps, were exploiting the same territory, and their novelty would take precedence over a mere Shakespearean tragedian, however Eminent.

Baltimore was a bad beginning. The citizens were, as Forrest once declared, anti-theatrical;[9] the rehearsals for *Macbeth* were conducted without scenery, properties, or even the trap doors so necessary for the witches. The actors were incredibly bad and, at the last moment, the management failed to provide supernumeraries. What the banquet scene must have been like can only be guessed at, though Macready was satisfied that his own performance had aroused the intelligent among the audience. The next night the house was miserably thin—even Ole Bull could not attract in this "priest-ridden" town—Polonius appeared wearing a Restoration bag-wig, and Horatio spent the evening speaking Hamlet's lines. He was glad to escape to Charleston.

His intention had been to continue directly to New Orleans, but rumors of cholera led him to postpone his arrival. He was therefore willing to listen to the proposal of Forbes, the Charleston manager, that his appearance in that city should be put off until after Ole Bull had departed. During the week of freedom thus obtained, he did the town, commenting with delight on the climate and on the flowers blooming in January, but fretting at the never-ceasing rain. He was shown about by Dr. John Irving, an old schoolmate of Rugby days, and he took especial interest in the condition of the negroes. He was pained at their show of deference, amused by the servant whose task it was to brush flies from the dining table, heart-sickened over a fatal beating administered to a runaway slave. He was particularly horrified at the sight of negroes kept in jail until they might be sold. "Good God!" he wrote, "is this right? They are an inferior class of man, but still they are *man*."

On January 8 he finally appeared, as Hamlet, and felt the unresponsiveness of the audience. He worked hard, however, and "died game." When the play was repeated, on the last night of the engagement, the catastrophic inefficiency of these provincial theatres was demonstrated. Ryder, about to make his disappearance as the Ghost, had barely got out his speech when the trap opened and he descended with such rapidity that both Hamlet and his father were struck dumb with consternation. Once again the supporting actors were poor, acting with bad taste, but the audience seems to have liked him, and on the final night the house overflowed. But he continued to notice a great weariness overcoming him as he labored with his fellows at rehearsals. Was it "the coming on of time?"

On the twentieth the whole theatre, actors, scenery, orchestra, costumes, and all, packed up and took ship for Savannah where a worse theatre, worse rains, and uncomfortable lodgings awaited the star. Yet he was able to take some satisfaction in the response of his audiences. "The warm blood of these southerners," he reported to Catherine, "has been kindled into a state of unusual fervor and I was quite a means of strong excitement to them. Some women in the dress circle shrieked in the last scene and the play [*Werner*] ended with the house in a state of ferment."[10] On the other hand, the occasional obligation of appearing as Claude Melnotte now filled him with shame. But, he wrote, "I have the consolation of a Grandmother in Pauline so that at heart we are well matched as to years and I do not know which can claim seniority."[11] Five days later he was preparing for his journey to New Orleans, a ten-day excursion through shambling towns and across a wilderness. He went well prepared, with a bag full of books and a spirit full of resignation, ready to observe and to be delighted or repelled by what he saw.

The scenery was delightful, his fellow humans repellent. The first part of the rail journey lay through great swamps and pine forests, but in the next car was a miserable mass of slaves from whom he could scarcely keep his thoughts. After the first overnight stop his coach was more crowded and the democrat-at-heart protested to his *Diary,* "the dirty and ragged neighborhood that one is forced to endure is very distasteful, to say the least." This day's trip was painfully slow, progressing through the morning at about four miles an hour, with all hands turning out at one time to push, at another to chop wood to keep a head of steam in the engine. He spent the night in an inn with unplastered walls, lockless doors, ceilingless rooms, and a temperance menu. This was at the end of the railroad line, and he and the faithful Ryder were forced to hire a two-horse wagon to the beginning of the next line, four days away. The roads over which they passed were atrocious, and the going was frequently so difficult that the passengers had to get out and walk. Sometimes the driver resorted to an open field to get round bad spots in the road, sometimes they made their way through woods by blazings on the trees. They half-floated across rivers at fords, and once they were thrown into a fearful tangle by the overturning of the coach.

On January 31 they arrived at the railroad which was to convey them to Montgomery, and while their speed improved their discontent with their surroundings deepened. The scenery remained beautiful, but the men who shared their coach were a nondescript crew who spat continually. One of the passengers was a judge who, upon invitation from the train crew, "took a spell of chopping" when the engine needed wood. When they finally reached the river and could continue their journey by the long-established boat, he found himself somewhat more comfortably off, though he was still disturbed by the spitters and by the common hairbrush and comb in the washroom.

On February 3 he arrived in New Orleans and was greeted by Sol Smith, the vagabond comedian and itinerant manager who was at the moment, with his partner Noah Ludlow, conducting the affairs of the St. Charles Theatre. A rehearsal was called at once and though many actors were present who were later to be writ large in American theatrical history—Tom Placide, Sol Smith, J. M. Field—Macready did not like them. He did not like the theatre either, although the bills announced the latest in improvements for the comfort of the audience, Beebe's Patent Furnaces. But Sol Smith was a wise man as well as a funny one, and he learned after the third tirade that Macready merely needed someone to explode at, and that a servant would do as well as the manager. He became a generous admirer of Macready's work and records with some satisfaction that their nightly receipts were unexpectedly good (even Ludlow admits this with an unexpected glance outside the walls of the playhouse, "considering the depressed condition of the public mind and the public purse").[12]

The usual round of parts succeeded the opening, mingled with sightseeing trips, and visits to such celebrities as Henry Clay. By the end of the month he was again depressed in spirit and weary in body from his daily routine of rehearsal and performance and, since this exacting schedule had not tired him on previous provincial tours, he was again wondering about the "coming on of age." On the twenty-ninth, after rehearsal, he received a visit from Edwin Forrest, who was to follow him as star at the St. Charles, and on March 2, with great joy at the ending of his New Orleans engagement, he embarked for Mobile, where Smith's partner Ludlow was looking after the firm's interests.

Ludlow's opinion of Macready was very different from Smith's. He thought him inferior to Cook and J. B. Booth, thought him affected, devoid of grace, spirit, or naturalness. His judgement may have been warped by an early encounter with the Macready temper. Calling on him at his hotel to inquire after his comfort, he was met with a stern demand to know why the bills of the evening announced in large letters immediately after the actor's name that Mr. Clay would appear at the theatre. Ludlow says that he explained to Macready who Clay was, though this was patently uncalled for since the actor had visited the politician only a few days before, and pointed out that it was the custom even in England to announce the visits of distinguished persons to the theatres. The opening performance was a great success, steamboat departures having been delayed until after its finish to allow the passengers to attend, but Ludlow openly hints that Clay was the attraction. At the end of the first act, of which Macready writes that he had never performed the Ghost scene so well, Ludlow received a summons to the actor's dressing room. Not having been informed of his partner's method of handling such matters, Ludlow responded in person. The ensuing scene as Ludlow describes it must have been often repeated on tour:

he commenced a tirade on the inadequacy of the company, and their neglect of the business of the play as laid down in his [prompt] book. I told him that the play had been rehearsed three times, that I had attended to these rehearsals myself, and had been careful in pointing out to all performers in it the business as set down in the marked books that had been given to me by him for that purpose. But he was not satisfied, and at the end of the second act he sent his man, Thompson, to summon me again to his presence. Not having been educated to that kind of managerial servility which perhaps Mr. Macready had found accorded him in his own country, I declined going to his room, and requested Thompson to say that I had business in my office to attend to, and that if Mr. Macready had any matter of importance to communicate, and could send it in writing, I would give it all due consideration. I never heard any more complaints from Mr. Macready that night, nor any night thereafter.[13]

Although Ludlow was satisfied of his triumph in this skirmish, he never yielded his dislike of the vanquished. If Macready had ever held the mirror up to nature, he suggests, it must have been cracked, possibly by the ocean voyage which had brought him to "a higher temperature and a clearer atmosphere."[14]

After a brief return visit to New Orleans, where a company was assembled from the St. Charles and Mobile troupes to support him, Macready set off up the river to St. Louis. The financial depression and Vieuxtemps had preceded him and his houses, though profitable, were small. For nine nights he wrestled with the badness of the company, the primitiveness of the accommodations, and the vulgarity of the audiences. In the last scene of a performance of Iago he became so disgusted with the comments of the second gallery that he walked off the stage, though by the end of his stay he felt that he had taught them to understand him. With whatever implication, an admirer presented him with pairs of buffalo and elk horns, and he embarked on the *West Wind* for Cincinnati somewhat happier in spirit.

The southern and western tour was drawing to a close. It had been a trying and not very profitable experience. In Cincinnati, for instance, the nightly receipts of the theatre averaged only a little over $400, of which he received half. If this was considerably better than Forrest's average, it was small consolation. Forrest was trailing him around the circuit and getting so much the worst of it that he suggested to Ludlow that he alternate nights with Macready. The suggestion does not seem to have reached the Eminent's ears, but his reply would not be difficult to imagine.

In the meantime, his English friends had been after him with letters proposing to reopen one of the national theatres. Bunn's Covent Garden management was putting the legitimate on the rocks again, and the Licensing Act of 1843 had given the minor theatres freedom to perform any plays they chose. Macready had had enough of management at the large theatres except on terms more favorable than any committee of proprietors was disposed to offer. Instead, he seems to have been thinking of one of the "minors" to which the public voice might summon him. And as a means to that end he proposed a season in Paris after the close of his American tour. To Serle he wrote:

I am for holding on to the Paris scheme—letting Mr. Bunn's incompetency & the Committee's ignorance manifest themselves to the world in the UTTER ruin of the Theatre—WHAT could Mr. Bunn do next winter?—If any *accident* should give him success, that very accident would prove to us the folly of our precipitation.—I wish Willmott would be quiet—You might say so to him—I think all looks well—& I think Paris is likely to *urge on* the desired completion.— I do not like the English Opera House—it would be all the expences of a new Theatre—& Mr. Arnold [the proprietor] ought to be *out of* it. . . . I think I see a glorious end, if I can only have steady and prudent co-operation. . . .

If there be a demand for the drama, I think it may be established on actually SOLID grounds, but this cannot be done *hastily*—I do not see HOW it could be done next winter.[15]

On the thirtieth of April he left Cincinnati for New York, passing through Pittsburgh, where he was no doubt flattered to learn that the citizens were offended because he had not been engaged to appear there. In New York for his third appearance, he found himself with competition from the company at the Bowery, where Hamblin and J. R. Scott appeared in *Hamlet* on his opening night in the same character, and anticipated by one night his appearance as Macbeth. By the end of the month, he was happy to note that his company was the chief, in fact the only, attraction in New York, and Charlotte Cushman and Mrs. Hunt (later Mrs. John Drew) were giving him support which was a great relief after his provincial trials. On the third of June he took a bumper benefit with *The Bridal,* and later in the week attended a picnic dinner in his honor on Long Island. Hone, who was present, found Macready delighting the guests with his conversation as well as by recitations and dramatic readings.[16]

After this brief return to higher civilization, Macready undertook a northern tour, on the advice of a New York theatrical agent. His precise route is rather difficult to follow. With his friend David Colden he set out to explore the Hudson and the Adirondacks, to retrace his steps of seventeen years before and to try his luck in the theatres of upstate New York and Canada. Somewhere above Albany they left their transport behind them and took to the woods with several guides and, at Macready's side, a bowie knife. The wilderness impressed him even more than the Georgia swamps and pine barrens, inspiring awe and profound emotions in his breast. Camping for the night in a lean-to, he dined on slices of fat bacon roasted over a fire of green logs. "Our fare," he wrote to his wife, "was scarcely eatable *out* of camp, but did it not relish there?—and the brandy—and the tea—and the cigars!—Oh, Fawns, Dryads, bears, panthers, and moose-deer—did you ever see such a set of cosey fellows in the woods before?"[17] Leaving the camp, they made the thirty-mile trip to Lake George on a buck-board, which was a soretrial to his patience. With an allusion to *Twelfth Night* he describes patience on a buckboard and adds, "They talk a great deal in the West (where they have very rich lands) of the excellence of the "American Bottom':—I was never aware of its extraordinary properties till I saw David Colden and our driver bumping, like Stoics, on the buckboard." The Lake George steamer took them downriver to Albany where Macready set out alone on the western turnpike, passing through Utica, observing with disapproval the alterations in the Auburn prison system, visiting friends in Canandaigua. From there he went by rail to Rochester, where he at last heard the celebrated violinist who had been skimming the cream from his audiences:

Ole Bull is a *quack.* I have now fairly heard him. I heard Vieuxtemps at St. Louis, & thought the performance dull—I am disposed to think the composition was so.—But with him I listened to the *music*—with this man it was a succession of clever tricks with no reference to air, or subject; all the thought was, "that was clever"—"that was extra-ordi-nary"—but not like Paganini—not like Liszt—not like Droczmecsh. He is a humbug—he draws very sweet tones from his instrument, but it is like a manufacture of *tones*—Alas! for American taste—at the mercy, as it is, of such creatures as Mr. [James Gordon] Bennett, Mr. [N. P.] Willis, &c, &c.[18]

Buffalo, where he played *Hamlet* on the twenty-fourth, was a disappointment. As his agent had promised, there was both a large theatre and a large population, but the latter was "new, and un-educated and straggling," and his name was quite unknown. The box office receipts for the night were just over $200, and he was forced to solace himself with thoughts of home, and with a lonely celebration of his wedding anniversary. After three more nights of bad houses he went on to Montreal where he spent the month of July playing through his standard repertory, thinking long thoughts of home, and fretting over the report that a testimonial had been given to Alfred Bunn.

He was concerned, too, with his own future, in particular with the projected Paris engagement. He had written Serle in May to conclude arrangements with John Mitchell, the sponsor of the season, suggesting that Helen Faucit might be engaged to play with him. Serle's reply startled him. The Helen Faucit whom he had trained and who had hitherto been amenable to his wishes set a high value on her services and would come for only part of the season. Macready replied:

Of course she is beyond all compare the best English actress—and her co-operation in the *effect* of the plays—would be most valuable—but I do not see, how you can make a *partial* engagement with her. If she is not at the opening, the general impression may be weakened—if expected, the early attraction may be affected:—if she is of the company at the beginning, her retirement may diminish materially your strength. . . . If Miss Helen Faucit be your Desdemona [in the opening play], it would not answer to announce the play afterwards with an actress of less talent.[19]

His attitude toward America, in spite of his animadversions against American taste and the American press, is shown in the conclusion of this letter. Were it not for his home and family, he declared, he would leave America with almost painful regret. It was plainly his hope among nations.

When he arrived in New York, the Park manager filled him with theatrical gossip. Bunn was resolved that Drury Lane would be devoted to opera and spectacle; this was small surprise. Helen Faucit had been engaged for Paris; this was some satisfaction. Edwin Forrest was determined to try to get a Paris engagement too: "I could not be concerned about it in any way." Next day, he was in Philadelphia watching Forrest in one of his favorite roles, Damon, but it was of course distasteful to Macready. Somewhat more distasteful was the news that Forrest was acting Hamlet on the following Monday in opposition to him.

Forrest made a good try. The opposition of Hamlets was not successful, so he turned to roles which were "his" as much as Richelieu was Macready's. On Tuesday he appeared in *Jack Cade* and on Wednesday in *Metamora*. There may have been less dishonesty in his tactics than Macready supposed. Many years later Forrest wrote to a friend that an engagement in Boston while Edwin Booth was acting there "would create some excitement among the playgoers—and serve the pecuniary interests of the management."[20] To Macready, it was ungentlemanly conduct.

For his last night in Philadelphia, September 14, the scheduled play was the favorite *Werner* (Forrest was meeting this with a double bill of *Macbeth* and *The Gladiator*). During the rehearsal it became apparent that Edmund Connor, who was to play Ulric, had not committed the words of his part to memory. Manager Burton was for letting the event take its course, to think of something to do when the emergency arose. Macready suggested that an apology be made, and Connor permitted to read the part. But Connor would not hear of such a blot being put upon his professional reputation, and Burton's suggestion was adopted. Charlotte Cushman made matters worse by hinting that Connor would play a trick of some sort to save his face. At night, the first act went well, but as the scene with Ulric commenced, Connor gave a reel (not a very good or convincing one, Macready declared) and "sported a *fit.*" The play was stopped, an apology was made to the audience, and *The Stranger* substituted.

In spite of such a performance, representing nothing that Macready had come to represent in the theatre, the audience called for him, and he went forward to speak a few words of farewell. Hinting that this was in all probability the last time he would appear in Philadelphia, he thanked them for the warmth of their reception, most especially because of "some unworthy attempts, that have been made to excite a prejudice against me and my countrymen engaged in this profession on the plea of being foreigners." At this point, he notes, there was some "excitement" among his hearers, and he hastened to add: "But such influences I know could not reach you:—in reciprocating with my own country the welcome that is there readily & liberally extended to the artist."[21] This, of course, was a public performance, a curtain speech, and it was hardly an occasion for the actor to reveal his true sentiments about the liberality with which his profession was received. The importance of the speech lies in Macready's public acknowledgement of the political nature of the conflict into which he was being drawn.

It is ironic that the American rabble-rousers chose him as the symbol of the aristocratic oppressor of the humble. Politically Macready had always been a radical, had consistently expressed his contempt for hereditary position and for the monarchy which it maintained. Had he been an American he would have rejoiced to concur, in principle, with the common workman. During a short social trip into New England he attended a prize-giving ceremony at a local school and shook his head in distaste when the speaker pointed out that a classical education made a man a fit companion for princes and emperors. "Very bad republicanism," Macready thought, "bad philosophy—bad humanity."[22] Yet he was delighted by the system of public education as he observed it, and felt that it should be a cause for rejoicing to America and all mankind, and that England should blush at her failure to follow the American lead. But these sentiments of the private gentleman could not with propriety be made known to the audiences of the public actor. Only once, in a curtain-speech in Boston, did he venture to speak other than professionally, referring to his approval of the American public schools.[23] Boston, however, had become a special place to Macready; he had a wide circle of friends and supporters among the intellectual and professional New Englanders, and here he felt entitled to speak as a gentleman.

To a more limited extent this was true of New York. His farewell to the metropolis was somewhat happier than his farewell to Philadelphia. The heat was oppressive but the audiences responsive. He repeated his plays for the fourth time in that city, competing with a democratic convention whose shouting was plainly audible as a background for Hamlet's soliloquies. For his benefit he gave a triumphant performance of Lear to a house full in every part and highly pleased, realizing a profit of $660.[24] On the twenty-fifth, the anniversary of his American tour's beginning, he discovered that, after all expenses were paid, his total profits would be about £5,500. In that respect, at least, America had not disappointed him. He was further gratified when Mrs. Colden assembled sixty clergymen, whose scruples would not permit them to enter a theatre, for a tea, at which he gave readings from poetry and the drama.[25]

His American tour, scheduled to close in Boston, threatened to come to an earlier finish since the National Theatre, the only playhouse in the city, had been destroyed by fire. However, a committee of Bostonians, whose names read like a bluebook of American literature and politics, petitioned the Handel and Haydn Society for the use of their music hall "to enable the friends of Mr. Macready to enjoy his representations of Shakespeare."[26] The manager did his best to set up the auditorium as a theatre, but there could be no pit since it was filled with pew-like seats, which limited the attendance. Enthusiasm over his reappearance ran high. His popularity in Boston was great and his American reputation had increased steadily with the passing months. Even the clergy deigned to attend, absolved from sin by the non-theatrical locale and the ambiguous announcement that Hamlet would be "read and represented." Because of the primitiveness of the appointments, performances were given on alternate nights and his receipts were thus cut in half. However, he was in the society he loved best, home was but two weeks away, and there had been a spirited contest among the citizens for available seats. His final appearance was in Macbeth on the fourteenth of October. He acted well before a house crowded with friends, but the company cut him up and he lashed out at the faithful Ryder—with the usual instant and passionate regrets.

In a few days he was on board ship bound for home after a year's absence. It had been a hard year of constant labor, but he left behind him many warm friends, and what was equally important, he took with him a considerable addition to the funds which were to ensure his retirement. What the future held he did not know; he knew only that he could have stayed and profited greatly for another year in America. Although he did not say it, his mind was clearly made up to return for another harvest if not for a permanent residence. "If there is no bread in Israel," he wrote to Catherine, "there is plenty of corn in Egypt."[27]

THE AMERICAN TRAGEDIAN IN ENGLAND

He reached home early in November and took a brief month of rest from his professional duties. It was hardly a month of relaxation, since a project which he had instituted and had sponsored for many years in the face of massive indifference was at last nearing completion. Out of his reverence for Mrs. Siddons had grown his idea of erecting a memorial to her in Westminster Abbey. The original idea, first mentioned in the *Diary* for December 10, 1833, was that a bust should be placed in the Abbey by the Garrick Club, but time dragged on with nothing accomplished and Macready was forced to take the entire responsibility. During the last days of his management at Drury Lane, he had persuaded his company to donate their services for a benefit to raise funds and now, eleven years after the birth of the notion, he was still doggedly devoting his spare moments to its realization. It is reasonable to suppose that there was more than respect for Mrs. Siddons in his determination. To be memorialized in the Abbey was the due of every artist, every politician of note in England, but the actors who had been admitted were few. The project was thus a part of his persistent wish to elevate the profession into which he had been thrust. When the memorial was finally installed in 1849, Macready calculated that he had personally paid nearly the entire expense.

In addition to arranging the final details of the memorial, he spent his month in calling on old friends, and the parade of names in his *Diary* is an indication of the circles into which he had moved. There were business acquaintances, of course, Mitchell, the manager of the English theater at Paris, and Serle, Macready's faithful lieutenant, to settle details of the engagement. But there were others, far from the theater: the Carlyles, Samuel Rogers, Horace Twiss; Stanfield and Maclise, the artists, and, rather strangely, considering his moral and democratic scruples, Lady Blessington and Count D'Orsay.

In Paris, he was greeted by an even more distinguished circle of friends, those artists who had been inspired by his performances two decades before, and a younger group who had grown up under their influence. Alexandre Dumas, Jules Janin, Eugène Sue, these were the first callers. To them were added the actors Regnier, Bouffé, Defresne. He called on Victor Hugo, and received tributes from George Sand. Sue took him to the opening night of Legouvé's new play *Guerrero*. At the end of the third act, Sue went backstage to speak with the playwright, and Macready, supposing the play to have ended, went home. He was greatly distressed when a friend informed him of his faux pas, and could only hope that his host would think him stupid rather than rude.

He opened at the Italian Opera on the sixteenth of December in *Othello* with Helen Faucit as his Desdemona. The auditorium, large and not well adapted to the legitimate drama, was crowded and the audience (in the spirit of the place) came armed with *libretti,* from which they followed the action. Consequently Macready found them hard to play against. He could not rouse them to the enthusiasm, to the bursts of applause which helped him through a part. He could not, he says, establish *"electric contact,* to coin an expression." However, the appearance of the faithful *Virginius* on the twenty-third very nearly caused a riot of enthusiasm, the spectators loudly demanding a curtain bow after the scene in the Forum. To this he would not submit, as a sacrifice of the dignity of his poor art, but the impossible demand was to be preferred to the interested silence which had greeted the earlier performances.

The raptures which had met his appearances in 1828 were now bestowed on Helen Faucit, whose interpretation and style were as fresh and original as Macready's had once been. The critics found her very English, with the kind of grace peculiar to the drawings in the keepsakes and magazines of beauty and fashion. Macready, sensing this, was instantly disturbed. In *Macbeth* the sleepwalking scene was more applauded than the rest, but when it was repeated two days later, the account was evened by a wreath of laurel flung on the stage during the banquet scene. But it must have been plain to Macready that this Helen Faucit who had been his pupil, whom he had protected from her own emotions, and whose interests he had guarded, was now a star in her own right.

This was their last engagement together, although, in spite of the busy tongues which endeavoured to drive them apart, they remained on friendly, even affectionate, terms to the end of Macready's life.

The highlight of the brief Paris season was a command performance of *Hamlet* at the Palais des Tuileries on January 16, 1845, before Louis Philippe and his Queen. It was an especial trial, for court etiquette forbade applause of any sort, although Victor Hugo forgot himself so far as to make a slight disturbance—quickly hushed from embarrassment—during the first scene. Louis Philippe made a suitable expression of his gratitude by presenting Helen Faucit with a bracelet and Macready with a jeweled poignard. This later was discovered to be silver-gilt, and Macready's full democratic temper was aroused by the further disclosure that the very jewels were paste. "That *shabby dog*," he wrote, and later upon news of the King's abdication, "*Fagin.*"

Before returning to England, Macready, with some reluctance and some curiosity, attended an amateur theatrical performance at the English embassy. The players were all persons of wealth or social position who had, to while away an idle moment, got up three scenes from *The School for Scandal* and the Washington Irving-Howard Payne *Charles the Second*. To Macready the whole proceeding was amusing, not simply from its badness, but "to see how these persons, who so undervalue the theatrical art, expose themselves to ridicule and contempt when they essay it." He also visited the Conservatoire, where young actors were trained for the stage. His observations are interesting: "I . . . saw the inefficiency of the system clearly; it was teaching *conventionalism*—it was perpetuating the mannerism of the French stage, which is all mannerism." The free-born Englishman would not see the individual cramped, or forced into a mold. His own experience, in which he had imitated first one actor then another until he had developed his own personal style, gave a kind of justification from history to his national prejudice.

Yet the French actors, mannered though they were, were competent, even in the lower ranks. Back in England, thrust once more into the British theatre, he fretted and fumed over the quality of the acting there, and on different grounds from his objection to the French. The English were not mannered, they were simply incompetent. John Vandenhoff and his daughter were giving special performances of *Antigone*, translated from a German version of Sophocles, with music by Mendelssohn. Macready described their action as "low, provincial rant and extravagant pantomime." Going almost at once into the provinces to act, he may have realized that he had done the Vandenhoffs an injustice. During no part of his career was he so frequently "cut up, root and branch" by his fellow players. Nine hours a day he spent at his profession in rehearsing and performing with "utter blackguards or most ignorant empirics." In a letter from Manchester he gives some evidence that the faults of his fellow players were not imaginary:

I am drudging on in the not very delightful occupation of provincial acting, but as il faut manger, I must be content to work for the means. If you want specimens of the various lectiones you should attend our provincial Theatres:—ex. gr.—as was delivered some time since in that, where I am now acting

>Hamlet.—And fixed his eye upon you?
>Horatio.—Most constantly.
>Hamlet.—I would I had been there!
>Horatio.—It would have much amused you.
>Hamlet.—Very like-very like.[28]

In spite of the players this first provincial tour since his return from America went well. He played Robertson's circuit and then headed north into Scotland. At Manchester he received £50 a night (which might have repaid a less conscientious man for the abuse to which his art was subjected) and his attraction seemed not to have diminished except in *Virginius*. It "has ceased to number among my most attractive plays," he wrote to the Manchester manager,[29] but it was performed once during the engagement, nonetheless. At Sheffield, the most was made of the new honors which had recently come upon him. The playbill announced *Hamlet* "(As recently represented by him, at the TUILLERIES, PARIS, before His MAJESTY LOUIS PHILLIPE the Court of France, and the Various Potentates and Ambassadors of Europe.)" Robertson, the manager, put the responsibility for such a monster attraction squarely up to his customers. In a footnote to the bill he points out "nothing short of the most liberal patronage can by possibility remunerate him, and he trusts to the good taste of the Public of Sheffield, for such an amount of support as will at all events secure him against loss."

Macready had not given up the idea of establishing in London a new home for the national drama. His letters and diaries of this period are full of schemes. The abrogation of the patents, allowing any theatre in the city to perform the "legitimate" drama, and the abandonment of both Drury Lane and Covent Garden to the uses of opera raised new problems as well as new opportunities. Willmott, his former prompter, advanced the possibility of constructing a new theatre, and inquired whether he intended to take a London engagement during the season. To this Macready replied:

The matter of the building is a thing only to talk about, and I must be in London for that.—Mr. Maddox [manager of the Princess] has been applying to me—and Mr. C. Bass, who has stepped into the shoes of Mr. Lamont [former manager of Covent Garden]—I do not fancy either, and imagine the season is now too far advanced for Shakespeare's plays:—the Princess will not, I should suppose, hold enough to make my terms easy to the manager, and Covent Garden I think in its dirt and bad character could scarcely bring audiences.[30]

Later in the same month, he made some further observations to Willmott on the nature of an ideal theatre. Willmott seems to have suggested a structure somewhat smaller than the two national playhouses. Perhaps the comfort of the audience and the relaxation of strain on the performers evident in the erstwhile "minor" theatres had proved instructive. Macready replied:

I think your general ideas on the subject extremely good and practicable, and in my opinion it is only in a Theatre, so economized in point of space, and of fair and reasonable dimensions, that the drama has now (with so much Opposition) a chance of existence. The more I think of Drury Lane or Covent Garden, the more I am disposed to believe, that no permanent interest will ever attach to them—their day is gone—they have had their chance, and abused it.—If the happy mean of size, between too large and too small, could be obtained, and such a locality as the one we look at, I think there could not be a doubt on the subject.[31]

The scheme remained alive for some time and the cabinet was reassembled to confer upon it. In May Fox and Forster proposed an investigation of the St. James, and Mitchell, the manager, expressed his willingness to talk business. In July this venture was abandoned as requiring too great a financial outlay. Macready looked at the Lyceum, formerly the English Opera House, where he witnessed a burlesque of *The Lady of Lyons*. "It is disgraceful to taste," he wrote, not altogether unexpectedly, "and in the exposure made of the legs of a great number of women it is indecent and immoral. Oh—England's drama!" In August, despite his letter to Willmott, he considered another attempt at Covent Garden, but a series of prosperous London and provincial engagements put the matter out of his head for two years. On the second of January, 1847, Forster had a new suggestion involving public subscription, which resulted in Macready's hinting to that effect at a public dinner. Nothing came of it and when Forster was so misguided as to suggest the Lyceum (late home of the bare-limbed women) Macready was horrified and seems to have abandoned forever the idea of resuming management. "The Patents," he wrote to Horace Twiss, "lasted just long enough to kill the drama out-right . . . and then, like the Kilkenny cats, we of the drama killed them—so being all dead now, as Voltaire says, the play is over."[32]

As he had intimated in his first letter to Willmott, the London managers were negotiating with him for an engagement. Forster conveyed an invitation from Webster, who wanted to know Macready's terms and what actors he would require for support. Macready replied that he would engage for eight weeks at £100 and *required* no especial support, but would recommend Charlotte Cushman, who was then in England. On second thought, not wishing to "seem unkind" to Helen Faucit, he withdrew his official recommendation of Miss Cushman. Webster's receipt of this information was couched in such terms that Forster rejected it on the spot. Maddox, proprietor of the Princess, was more amenable. He reported that Miss Cushman, new-risen to stardom, had refused to engage at his theatre if it were to act with Macready, and that Helen Faucit demanded whatever terms were to be given to him. However, Maddox promised to try to get Miss Cushman, and the agreement was concluded for Macready's first regular engagement in a minor theatre.[33]

It is possible that his decision to go to the Princess was governed in some part by the recent appearance there of Edwin Forrest. The American actor had returned to England, full of hope of repeating the popular success of his previous appearance. But he had chosen a poor time for his effort. The United States was in exceedingly bad odor with the English public at the moment, as a glance at the political cartoons in *Punch* will indicate. The Oregon dispute, the non-payment of state's debts, and the failure of the United States Bank were all subjects for attack. In addition, Forrest had not improved as an actor through the years. His old peculiarities of rant and physical exertion had been intensified, and the British public and the critics were not slow to point this out. Catherine relayed to her husband, who was playing in the provinces, the impression of an eyewitness that "Mrs. Sterling when she left the stage must have been covered with foam as Mr. Forrest had it all around his mouth till it was disgusting."[34] Macready's absence prevented him from showing professional courtesies to his rival, as he had during the earlier visit, and made it impossible for him to restrain the exuberant virulence of John Forster's pen. Reviewing *Macbeth,* Forster wrote:

Our old friend, Mr. Forrest, afforded great amusement to the public by his performance of Macbeth on Friday evening at the Princess's. Indeed, our best comic actors do not often excite so great a quantity of mirth. The change from an inaudible murmur to a thunder of sound was enormous; but the grand feature was the combat, in which he stood scraping his sword against that of Macduff. We were at a loss to know what this gesture meant, till an enlightened critic in the gallery shouted out, 'That's right! sharpen it.'[35]

Bulwer-Lytton, too, had been unfriendly, though without intention. Forrest wrote to request permission to perform *Richelieu* and *The Lady of Lyons* at a nightly rate, and received a cold reply that "having invariably declined to allow the representation of my plays nightly at any metropolitan Theatre, I cannot comply with your request."[36] Bulwer intended to say that he leased his plays only for a stated number of performances at a time, but Forrest took him to mean that no one but Macready should be permitted to perform those roles in London.

Forrest left London with bitterness in his heart, convinced that he had been the victim of a conspiracy organized by the friends of Macready to drive him from the stage. Actually, the London critics, with the exception of Forster, were no more severe than some of his own American commentators. Reviewing a performance of his Claude Melnotte in New York, Stuart of the *Tribune* had heaped him with ridicule:

Mr. Forrest, in the dress of the Prince of Como, with his spotless white kids sticking uneasily to his hands, and a sly bit of white embroidered pockethandkerchief jutting with a wild, romantic elegance, out of his pocket, looks exactly like a consequential footman, who avails himself of the absence of his master, to go gallivanting in his clothes. But it is in the love scene where Mr. Forrest's total unfitness to play the enthusiastic gallant is most painfully conspicuous. What with Pauline's silly love-prattle, and Mr. Forrest's rhapsodical gurgles, the scene is a perfect picture of absurdity. Pauline is not a gentle cooing dove, and we would not wish to compare Mr. Forrest to an affably sighing rhinoceros.[37]

The same kind of treatment was administered to his *Hamlet,* Stuart remarking on the maudlin sentimentality of the nunnery scene and describing his performance during the play before the King as having "the air of some huge gipsy, watching with roguish glance an opportunity to rob the hen-roost."[38]

Macready was of several minds about Forrest's failure. Liking the man and his wife, he could be "truly sorry for him," but he could not wish him *great* success. He was, however, surprised at the report of the disastrous failure of Forrest's *Macbeth*. He had found him, he wrote in his *Diary* on February 23, "dull . . . but not otherwise offensive." It is clear, both from the tone of this entry and from the fact that he was then performing in Newcastle, that he could have had nothing to do personally with the general disapprobation which the London audience manifested for the "American Tragedian," as Forrest was now billing himself. Nor could Forster, with his single pen, however envenomed, in the weekly *Examiner* have organized and directed a claque. But Forrest had been hurt, and it was not his to reason why. The revenge which he took on his elected enemy was to lead to one of the most melodramatic chapters in the history of the theatre.

Before opening at the Princess, Macready had a second distasteful experience with amateur actors, this time a company which Dickens and his friends had organized. Charles Dickens, who was certainly an actor manqué, and Forster, and a group of *Punch* editors, Leech, Jerrold, Lemon, and others, had joined forces to present *Everyman in his Humour* at Fanny Kelley's little theatre. There was, of course, a supper in celebration afterwards, in the midst of which Macready was taken ill and forced to leave. Someone rather unkindly suggested that the success of the amateurs was the real cause of his illness, and indeed Catherine was heard to remark a day or so later that the review in the London *Times* was "more kind really than ever the *Times* showed itself towards William."[39] After the group appeared in another play at the St. James's, Macready agreed that their performance was exceedingly good for amateurs, but that the actors wanted to be judged as if they were members of "the profession," of which "they do not know what may be called the very rudiments." Nonetheless he carefully instructed Dickens and Forster in the management of their fight in *The Elder Brother* and, fuming over the nuisance, helped them with their costumes. After the performance, he wrote in his *Diary*, "As Macbeth says—*No more sights!*"

Macready's feeling about amateurs goes deeper than a mere professional's contempt for those who play at his profession. It is rooted in his conviction, which was well grounded, that the profession to which he was allied was a despised one, and despised by the very people who played at it. This was not true of Dickens and Forster, nor perhaps of the *Punch* circle (though they certainly disported themselves editorially at the actors' expense); it was an entirely accurate interpretation of the sentiments of the literary coteries and of the upper circles of society. It is only necessary to glance at the collected letters or the published diaries of a dozen eminent Victorians to catch the odor of condescension whenever a theatre person crosses the page, the air of startled surprise when the actor turns out to be intelligent or modest. The highest commendation that several memorialists can find to make of Macready is that no one would ever guess him an actor. And Macready, while resenting these opinions, shared them.

The first of six short engagements at the Princess' began on October 13, 1845. Maddox, the manager, was a speculator in the best theatrical tradition. The plays were mounted as casually as possible, casts were assembled in a hit-or-miss fashion, and the discipline was lax. After the rehearsal on October 30, Macready complained, "These little theatres hold so many great men and such very bad actors." Yet it was the greater tribute to his popularity that on the opening night the Princess was jammed to suffocation and he could only compare the rapture of the audience to that manifested on his last night at Drury Lane. Indeed, the editor of the *Times* informed him that the paper had received an average of a dozen letters a day throughout the preceding fortnight inquiring about his return to London.

During the engagement he played only Hamlet, Lear, and Othello, repeating the same roles during his second season (January and February, 1846) and adding Richelieu. In the intervening month he played all his standard roles in Dublin where he was supported, if that be the word, by the manager Calcraft in the second male leads, and by Mrs. Ternan in principal females. During this engagement he met for the first time Mrs. Ternan's celebrated and talented daughter Fanny, whose sister Ellen was later to cut rather a wide swath through the marital life of Charles Dickens. At the moment she was appearing in an afterpiece, *The Young Actress,* in which she played the following "hangers about a country theatre": Fanny (The Prompter's Daughter), Hector (A Stage-Struck Yankee), Effie Heatherbloom (with a National Pas Seul), Victoire (A French Itinerant Musician), Margery (a Country Gawkey), and Goody Stubbins (an antiquated picture, with the song "O Cupid God of Love."). Macready says of her only that she is a very sweet child and does not mention her prodigious display of talent. This, in a way, is a commendation of her skill, since he finds room during this engagement only to execrate the acting of all the members of the company. Echoing an unnamed poet he agrees that Ireland is the *"base posterior of the world."*

In March he undertook a similar junket to Edinburgh where a startling incident in the audience drove resentment against his fellow actors out of his mind. The opening play on March 2 was *Hamlet* and, although the audience was somewhat cooler than he had anticipated, he was determined to extend himself, and afterwards was convinced that it was among the best readings he had ever given the role. One of his unique pieces of business, and one which he had been using for years, occurred just before the play-scene. At the announcement of the King's approach, he cries, "I must be idle," with a "quick and salient walk up and down the front of the stage, waving his handkerchief as if in idle and gay indifference, but ill concealing, at that instant, the sense of an approaching triumph."[40] During this tense moment, and at this piece of business always acknowledged as one of his best points, out of the dead silence of the house there came a resounding hiss. John Coleman, who claims to have been standing in the wings, reports that Macready first turned pale at the sound and then livid, "absolutely hysterical with rage." He turned towards the hisser, bowed derisively and staggered back to sink into a chair. Someone in the gallery yelled, "Throw him out," and the critic rose solemnly in his box and faced the gallery, then in dead silence walked slowly from the theatre. "Then Macready," Coleman goes on, "like a man possessed, leaped into the breach and took the audience by storm. Surely he must have been inspired by the ordeal through which he had passed. Such a delirium of excitement for actors and audience as followed that play scene and the closet scene I have rarely, if ever, witnessed."[41]

At first, the greenroom rumor was that the hisser had been a newspaperman who had come in the company of Edwin Forrest. But Murray, the manager, and John Ryder preferred to think that it was Forrest himself. For a week or more the identity of the blackguard in the boxes was quizzed over. Calcraft wrote from Dublin that Charlotte Cushman, when she heard the story, had declared at once, "It is Forrest." The policeman on duty further supported the Murray-Ryder hypothesis. But that one actor could so far forget himself as to abuse a fellow actor publicly was not made certain until Forrest identified himself and defended his action in a letter to the *Times* and observed that he "would do the same again." It was the right, he contended, of every man to hiss, and as he had already led the applause at points which he considered good he was justified in ridiculing the famous *"pas de mouchoir."* The right of a critic to praise or blame is immemorial, but there should be surer proof of his disinterestedness than could be produced for Forrest. Had the matter stopped there, he could have been convicted of nothing worse than inexcusably bad taste. But Forrest neither forgot nor forgave his London failure, Forster's criticism, nor what he conceived to be Macready's hostility. The echo of that unfortunate hiss was to be magnified a thousand times on May 10, 1849, and the end was to be bitterness and bloodshed that would have driven a more sensitive man than the "American Tragedian" from the profession.

Macready, his art vindicated by a successful repetition of *Hamlet* on his closing night in Edinburgh, returned to London for his third series of appearances at the Princess. Here he repeated his previous roles and added a new one, his first in several years. He had been considering, in frequent consultations with his cabinet, *The King of the Commons* by the Reverend James White. On the fifth of February he read the play (White himself reading one of the Scots characters) to Thackeray, Dickens, Forster, Fox, and Maddox. Thackeray said it was "Safe," the others were enthusiastic, and only Fox abstained. Next day Thackeray wrote to explain what he meant by his "unsatisfactory kind of praise."

What I meant by 'Safe' is the best word to be applied to a play I think: safe of a real agreeable—of course I don't know how permanent— success. The play seems to me to be better than the Lady of Lyons with the exception of the admirable climax of the latter—always pleasing, tender, jovial—interesting in a word, the main character a capital hearty *rôle* to go to the ["country" crossed out] public with. I have brought away the most pleasant impression of it. What more is requisite? A work of supreme genius? I don't think this is or pretends to be one but it pleases exceedingly though it does not astonish: and, I take it, this is as valuable a quality as any in a play. I speak here the truth, the whole truth & nothing but the truth. But then who am I to be a critic?[42]

Thackeray in this instance was a very good critic indeed. *The King of the Commons* pleased without astonishing. The leading part was a typical Macready character. The other roles, filled by such old hands as Ryder and Cooper, and such rising members of the younger school as Fanny Stirling, Leigh Murray, Henry Compton, and Augustus Harris were well-fitted and attractive. First presented on May twentieth, it received thirteen performances before Macready's engagement came to an end. It was his last successful new part and he never revived it in London.

After a summer provincial tour, he came back to London to appear at another minor theatre, this time the Surrey. This was a genuine descent into the minors, for the Surrey had long been the home of melodrama, of Newgate and nautical pieces, and its audiences were the roughest in London. Edward Stirling, the manager, had determined to try to duplicate the success of Phelps' Shakespearean revivals at the equally "illegitimate" Sadler's Wells and led off with Macready. Perhaps to everyone's surprise, the Surrey audiences took to him at once. On the opening day, they began assembling at two o'clock in the afternoon, and on the closing night the entrance doors were broken down by the rush of spectators.[43] The *Theatrical Journal* uses this as evidence that the "*Lower* orders (we use the term fashionably) have *souls* rather above than below the higher classes," with an obvious sneer at the aristocrats who patronized Italian opera rather than Shakespeare at the fashionable theatres.

During the engagement, Richard Bedingfield of the newly founded *Theatrical Times* gave a definitive analysis of "Macreadyism": he is more critic than actor, wanting the "flashes of fire and enthusiasm to raise and warm the heart and fancy."[44] It was only natural that an actor whose style was so peculiarly his own should become more hardened and mannered as the years passed, and should fail to respond to new styles and tastes. Yet the audiences of the Surrey, who might be expected to resent coldness or a critical approach in an actor, were thoroughly pleased with his performances. He gave at this time, also, the first of a series of readings from Shakespeare at the various Workingmen's Institutes which were springing up in an attempt to improve the conditions of the lower classes. Here too his success was signal. Whatever his occasional misgivings about the failure of his powers or the ability of his plays to attract, the broadening public was loyal to him.

After another provincial excursion, he returned to Maddox at the Princess', first in the late spring of 1847 and then, after a summer hiatus, in October. During the first of these engagements he confined himself to his established parts, and Matthew Arnold, who was a frequent spectator, found it a somewhat drab experience. Many years later, he wrote:

I remember it as if it were yesterday. In spite of his faults and his mannerism, Macready brought to his work so much intellect, study, energy, and power, that one admired him when he was living, and remembers him now he is dead. During the engagement I speak of, Macready acted, I think, all of his great Shakespearean parts. But he was ill-supported, the house was shabby and dingy, and by no means full; there was something melancholy about the whole thing. You had before you great pieces and a powerful actor; the theatre needs the glow of public and popular interest to brighten it, and in England the theatre was at that time not in fashion.[45]

The dinginess of the production—to a generation that Macready had taught to expect something better—is best illustrated by a criticism which appeared in *Punch*:

SHAKESPEARE—though sophisticated SHAKESPEARE—is mighty at the Princess's. In *Macbeth*—especially in the fifth act—MACREADY has delighted even "Our Fast Man." After seeing the actor, the "Fast Man" (he confessed as much to a friend) did not visit a Casino for a single week, and had some notion of going so far as Islington to behold *Macbeth's* head upon a pole. The "Fast Man," moreover, thinks MISS CUSHMAN's *Mrs. Macbeth* first-rate. MISS MONTAGUE—the new *Desdemona*—is a charming actress, with a dove-like manner, and a voice of magical sweetness—a voice that would draw a suit out of Chancery. "Will it draw houses?" asks MR. MADDOX; and *Punch* answers—*"Mr. Maddox, it will."*

Punch, however, must not quit MR. M. without expressing his intensest admiration of his scenery—it is so primitive, so perfect. For instance here is a faint shadow of the external and internal architectural glory of Dunsinane Castle: [a cut showing two actors upon a bare stage backed with a large curtain bearing the words "This is supposed to represent Dunsinane Castle"] The scenery of *Othello* is equally true; and then so domestic!—though the bed of *Desdemona,* from its yellow tint, did excite in our mind a somewhat unpleasant recollection of "The Industrious Fleas."[46]

During the second of these engagements, Macready appeared in his last new role. The company was a strong one, with Charlotte Cushman (who appeared as Romeo to her sister's Juliet on the off-nights) in the principal supporting parts. The new play, an instantaneous and complete failure, was *Philip van Artevelde* by Henry Taylor. The original work was a monstrous two-part poem, "never designed for the stage," but Macready had been taken by the libertarian sentiments of the leading character and by the occasionally vigorous poetical passages. With the author's consent he pasted up an acting version. Those who had read the play were utterly confused by the stage version, since it involved a reconstitution of the events of the narrative, and the critics were harsh in their condemnation. Taylor himself was pleased, both with the arrangement and with Macready's performance, and Dickens—either the loyal friend or responsive spectator—declared that he had never seen him "more gallant and free." Macready blamed the failure on the rest of the cast, and the critics were inclined to agree with him. Maddox had not extended himself, certainly, in bringing the play out to best advantage. For the opening the parsimonious manager provided a respectable number of supers for the starving men and women of Ghent. When the play failed to attract, these supers were the first to go, half the second night, half of the remainder the next night. At length there were fewer than a dozen in the crowd, at which Macready groaned, "Down to ten, eh? I see famine has done its worst."[47] But from whatever cause *Philip van Artevelde* was a failure and, though he continued to study manuscripts, Macready never again appeared in a new play.

On December 7, 1847, he played one scene of *2 Henry IV* at Covent Garden for the benefit of the fund to purchase Shakespeare's house as a national shrine, and then indefatigably took to the road once more. "A splendid stroller," was Maclise's name for him,[48] but in his own eyes he was ever the martyr to his profession, driven by the necessity of accumulating for his dear children's sake. Almost without pause he was back at the Princess' for the sixth time on February 28, 1848, with a new leading lady.

Fanny Kemble having proved reasonably attractive during an earlier engagement at the theatre, Maddox determined to try both his stars together as a novelty. Macready had visited with her several times on his last American tour, but his only recorded opinion of her acting was on seeing her perform with the amateurs at the St. James's. *"She is,"* he wrote, *"ignorant of the very first rudiments of her art.* She is affected, monotonous, without one real impulse—never in the feeling of her character, never true in look, attitude, or tone." He seems at some time to have conveyed this opinion to her, for she repeats it twice (in modified form) in the *Records of a Girlhood.*[49] In her second volume, *Records of Later Life,* she gives some details of their engagement together, and it is interesting to find for the first time the other side of Macready's complaints about his fellows. In general, her opinion of him was a ladylike counterpart of his opinion of her. She is rather startlingly in agreement with his notion that Charles Kemble, Young, and Charles Kean were inferior to him, but she considered his major Shakespearean impersonations good only in part, his comic power nil, and his voice unmusical in the extreme. Werner, Virginius, and Rob Roy were his great roles, in her opinion, and he was vain and selfish in his practice of his art.[50]

Macready was understandably annoyed when he saw the bills announcing "Mr. Macready's and Mrs. Butler's First Night," with their names in equally large type, but he was determined to assert his primacy back of the curtain. Without waiting to be asked he took the star dressing room, and Fanny, who had occupied it very comfortably during her earlier season at the Princess' was forced to mount a steep flight of stairs to one of lesser dignity. Her chief complaint about this was that she might not hear her summons when given by the call-boy and so miss an entrance—for she was determined not to go into the greenroom with the secondary players and await her call with them. Was she not Fanny and a Kemble? There was something of the Macready about Mrs. Butler.

Further evidence of this appeared during the rehearsals for *Macbeth*, the opening play. The arrangement of the setting for the banquet scene had been "from time immemorial"[51] two thrones at the center back and two long tables on either side for the guests, leaving the center of the stage free for the interplay with the ghost of Banquo and Lady Macbeth's startled comings and goings. Fanny came on the stage prepared to rush rapidly from throne to stage and to sweep back in the grand manner which she had inherited from Mrs. Siddons. To her surprise she found that Macready staged the scene with a long table directly at the foot of the throne which she could get around only at peril to her balance. She protested and Macready firmly replied that his business depended upon such an arrangement of the setting. She remonstrated, but the table remained. She finally gave in and took a woman's revenge by remarking to the company that "since it was evident Mr. Macready's Macbeth depended upon where a table stood, I must contrive that my Lady Macbeth should not do so."[52] That her sharp tongue found its mark is indicated by the entry in Macready's *Diary* under the date of February 19:

Rehearsed Macbeth, Mrs. Butler the Lady Macbeth. I have never seen anyone so bad, so unnatural, so affected, so conceited. She alters the stage arrangements without the slightest ceremony, and, in fact, proceeds not only *en grande artiste,* but *en grande reine.* She is *disagreeable,* but her pride will have a yet deeper fall, I feel confident. I must strive, and be careful, and hope in God for myself.

In the performance, he felt he acted with strength, care, and effect, although occasionally disconcerted by "this monstrous pretender to theatrical art." Fanny was somewhat disconcerted herself. She had heard of his violence in action, but had congratulated herself that there would be no opportunity for it in the scenes between Macbeth and his wife. But when he came to the line "Bring forth men children only," she was astonished and dismayed to be seized ferociously by the wrist and compelled "to make a demivolte, or pirouette, such as I think that lady did surely never perform before, under the influence of her husband's admiration."[53]

The engagement which began with such manifestations of temper on both sides went fairly well. Macready was partially won over to Fanny's acting, praising her Desdemona as a "very correct and forcible conception," while maintaining his opinion of her inability to carry it out. Critics who had come expecting a struggle for supremacy between the "Kemble school" and the "Macready school" of acting were disappointed. "The distinctions between the various styles of acting," concluded the *Theatrical Journal,* "adopted by the different players are in fact not in reality so striking as on reflection they appear to the memory to be; the rules and laws of genuine acting are laid more deeply than in the mere outward manner."[54] Audiences were warm in their approval, though Macready felt that old Charles Kemble made a spectacle out of himself by pounding the floor with his cane in solitary approval of his daughter's good "points." Only the London *Sunday Times* maintained unrelenting opposition, declaring "the whole performance went off as tamely, as coldly, as a consultation of physicians upon a hypochondriac patient."[55]

During his tour of the provinces just before his engagement with Fanny Kemble, Macready had played at Newcastle. Called before the curtain on his last night, he had spoken of the city (in the actors' fashion, but with some truth) as an old home, and announced that his next visit there "would in all probability, be his last." He declared his wish to retire "because of the present deplorable state of the national drama." On the thirteenth of April he wrote a long letter to an American friend who had apparently suggested that he come to New England to live. He proclaims himself one of "liberal sentiments," with hopes for a "solid constitutional government which would have an influence in its peaceful and merited success upon the world's progress." As for the invitation to retire to America, it is constantly and fretfully agitating his mind. The coarse language of the American press on the Oregon affair, the attitude toward credit, the Mexican war, and other matters of "taste" had made him alter his plans for settling there, although his family had taken it as decided. But now, "a slave of circumstance," he must reconsider. His English friends assure him he is too old, uprooting will make him wither at the top, but that is nothing to the prospects of his "precious tribe." How much, he would like to know, would it cost for a family of eleven—for there were now eight children in addition to his sister and his wife to be supported—to live in Cambridge?

Is there any prejudice among native Americans against the nat-
uralized? Would his "calling" be against him among the more
serious and consequently damage the prospects of his sons in business, and his daughters in society?[56]

The nature of the questions indicate how seriously he was considering the move, and this is confirmed by the entries in his
Diary. He alternates between partial commitment and wholehearted rejection, urged on by financial considerations and dis-
couraged by press reports. John Quincy Adams speaks in the
House of Representatives and is christened a doting old ruffian—
"No more America for me!"[57] At the news of a dinner in Forrest's
honor in 1846, he declares that he prefers a "crust in England,"
but by the fourteenth of March, 1847, he at last sees his way clear
for making preparations to settle abroad. *"America* appears our
only *certain* dependence! I do not *like* it, but must make the best
of it, if we cannot live here." Three days later he had a scheme
to play two seasons of "subscription nights" in England, two
seasons in America, and then retire to Cambridge, Massachusetts.
By the twelfth of June his mind was fully made up. America was
to be his refuge. He began negotiations immediately for a professional tour, and wrote once again to his New England correspondent, who seems to have called to his attention certain
differences in the American way of life which might cause friction:

It would be no violence to our customary mode to address servants in
the most courteous manner, for our children have been brought up
strictly in the observance of this duty, and it has caused me to have
met with no single instance of incivility during my two years sojourn
in the United States.—Then in regard to our relations with those
about us, I do not *think* (and it is a subject on which my thoughts are
almost constantly at work) that we should be likely to undervalue
what is sterling in intelligence or valuable in acquirement because the
manner might differ a little or much from what we have been accustomed to observe in English society.—In short, the whole tendency
of our ruminations and our conferences appears to gradually confirm
us, Mrs. Macready and myself, in the belief, that to exchange our dear
old England for the new country, which her sturdy sons have made
for themselves, will be the best for our children. . . .

My present plan is, to reach the States in September, and making
my farewell (professional) visits to the different cities return to England
in the Spring /49: make my last tour through the principal towns here,
and, after acting my round of characters during the season, take my
leave of the stage before a London audience in the Spring 1850. This
would enable me to return to the States, if I hold to my purpose,
which will be *fixed* one way or the other before I see you. . . .

England will right herself yet, I think, and the abuses of the aristocratic class will be swept away:—the question with me is, can I afford
for my children's sake to wait the chances of the struggle, that must
precede it?—I think not.—[58]

Before his departure for this crucial American tour, Macready
played a short engagement at still another minor theatre, the
Marylebone, and embroiled himself in a professional argument.
Drury Lane had been during the past year under the management
of Jullien, "the eminent musico," who had tried various schemes
to keep it open. "It began," records *Punch's* theatrical historian,
"as a Turkish Tent in October, it became a grand Opera House
before Christmas, and ere March had found its ides, it had lost
its identity by conversion into an arena for horsemanship. . . .
Horses pranced where VEDY had capered, and grooms occupied
the ground once filled with a happy dramatic peasantry at
eighteen-pence per night." All these schemes were doomed to
failure and Jullien entered into negotiations with Alexandre
Dumas for the importation of the troupe of the Parisian Théâtre
Historique. "We had heard," says *Punch,* "that there was to be
an opposition from the British dramatists; but, as we knew that
compact little body could not by possibility spread itself into
anything beyond a single private box, we did not apprehend much
disturbance from that quarter." Nor would they, he supposed, be
so ungrateful as to quarrel with their bread and butter, alluding
to the dependence of the English stage upon translations from the
French. *Punch* is then forced to relate the story of his misjudg-
ment:

No sooner had the doors opened, and the French musicians taken
their places in the orchestra, than those great engines of public
opinion, the catcall and the whistle, began to exert their influence.
That astounding reasoner, the street-door key, acted upon as it was
by all the force of fervid flatulence, silenced everything in the shape
of argument on the other side, and, if AEOLUS had taken the first row
of the pit for himself and friends, he could not have dealt out heavier
blows than were puffed forth from the lungs of a generous British
audience. In vain did the band attempt to abate the storm by throwing the oil of *God Save the Queen* on the troubled waters.

At length, after a dumb overture, of which "not a drum was heard,"
the curtain rose upon the deck of the *Pharaoh,* and the vessel encountered such a storm as its crew had not looked for. There was
pantomime on the stage met by opposition pantomime among the
audience; fists were shaken from box to box; hands were laid upon
hearts; umbrellas were hoisted, handkerchiefs and shawls were waved;
orange-peel was hurled upon the stage; and amidst all this din, the

actors were going through their parts as if they had been playing to a perfectly attentive audience. . . .

In the course of the evening Jullien came forwards and went through a series of contortions of the most extraordinary character. He pulled half-a-crown out of his pocket, rammed his finger down his throat, pointed up to the chandelier, cast his eyes down the hole through which the footlights are drawn up, and set his lips in motion at a fearful rate for five minutes together. What he meant by all these displays of physical force, it is impossible to tell; but we could see that emotion shook his whiskers to their very roots, and that passion gave fearful activity to his eye-balls. . . . but not a single syllable was heard, nor would there have been had he possessed the power of one of his own monster ophycleides. (XIV, 263)

Macready was horrified at the proceeding and hastened to the theatre to offer his sympathy to the manager. In addition he composed a letter of apology in the name of his profession, promptly published as a broadside by M. Jullien. In it he declared his grateful recollection of the kindness that had been shown him on all sides in Paris, and expressed his pain and surprise at the "disreputable proceedings" of the members of his profession at Drury Lane, for it was common knowledge that the riot had been instigated, not by the dramatists as *Punch* hinted, but by "players and fellows connected with the theatres." That night he went himself to the theatre where the tumult was so long repeated that he left in disgust. The result of the publication of his letter was a communication from a law firm, in the names of Webster, Charles Kean, Mathews, Farren, Harley, Buckstone, Meadows, Paul Bedford, Leigh Murray, and half a dozen others dissociating themselves from his professional protest. It was later rumored that Mathews and Webster had themselves paid the rioters and had hastened to give bail for those who were arrested. The whole trivial affair blew over and was soon forgotten, but less than a year later Macready was to find himself in the same position as the unfortunate French players.

At the moment, however, he was involved in plans for his farewell benefit which had been "commanded" by the Queen.[59] The program which the Queen selected was the first three acts of *Henry VIII* and *The Jealous Wife,* with Charlotte Cushman, Mrs. Warner, and Phelps lending their talents for the occasion. A tremendous crush resulted, with the disturbances in the audience which were *de rigeur* at one of his benefit nights. And *Punch,* which had been twitting the Queen for several years about her neglect of the art of the theater—and with complete justification—treated the situation with fine irony, describing the imaginary knighting of the player by the Queen while Albert bestowed upon him the insignia of the Fleece, Bath, and Garter.[60]

Perhaps had it been brought to their attention, Queen and Consort would have better understood and appreciated another of Macready's contributions to the improvement of their subjects. As part of his preparations for going to America he had undertaken an edition of the poetical works of Alexander Pope "revised and arranged expressly for the use of Young People." There is some irony in the manager who had rescued one after another of the texts of Shakespeare from a century and a half of corruption and improvement affiliating himself with the Reverend Thomas Bowdler, editor of the Family Shakespeare. But he was acting in the dual capacity of father and mentor: his first intention was to leave his own children something "better worth your grateful remembrance than the ordinary memorials of leave-taking"; his second, to acquaint the young with the excellences of Pope while shielding them from passages "which if comprehended would shock the delicacy of an uncorrupted taste without imparting any benefit to the understanding." Nor, as a life-long student of Byron, would he commit the folly of the scholarly censors of Martial and group the indecencies in an easily consulted appendix. Omission and alteration are silently made and Pope emerges as a poet of strictest morality, "exquisite fancy, refined wit, accompanied with peculiar felicity of diction and a versification the most melodious under the regulation of a judgement scrupulously severe."[61]

Granted that it was a task of supererogation, Macready was well equipped for it by his years of collaboration with playwrights living and dead. Fecal imagery disappears without trace, and references to pox and warm desires are disguised by verbal antimacassars. Elaborate annotations, particularly of references to classical authors are carried over from earlier editors with the intention of stimulating rather than satisfying curiosity, but Macready may have betrayed his own purpose of not stimulating an improper curiosity when he blacked out with his pen the note to *Dunciad I*, 167 in the copy presented to his daughter Lydia. Turning to the copy of one of her elder brothers she could readily have discovered a quotation from Cibber: "In a word, he made his attack upon his Periwig, as your young fellows generally do upon a lady of pleasure, first by a few familiar praises of her person, and then a civil inquiry into the price of it." However, since Lydia received her copy at the age of seven, it would have doubtless taken her some years to work through to the forbidden information.

In his introduction, Macready uses one aspect of the poet's character for a moral lesson. He points to Pope's "over-sensitiveness to the abuse flung on him by the envy of unworthy and incapable writers" and laments his weakness in resenting it. The poet should have had the practical philosophy to ignore their "impotent malice" like Edmund Burke, who declared, "Loose libels ought always to be passed by in silence. . . . If I can live down these contemptible calumnies, I shall never deign to contradict them in any other manner." As Macready himself shared the weakness of his admired poet, so he might himself have often consulted Burke's principle. At no time in his career would it have served him to better purpose than in the months immediately to follow. But the book was "intended only for the young," and while few parents "will not approve at least of its design" the Editor's intentions were the creation of a pedagogical and literary exercise for his children rather than a practical philosophy for himself.

At the beginning of September, after a round of final visits to friends, and a last performance at Birmingham, he embarked for America for the first series of his farewell appearances. At last the retirement toward which he had been working for so long was in sight. His old competitor Charles Young had written to Catherine to warn him against committing himself: "don't let him publicly and formally *announce* and *take his leave*, because then he will not have committed himself (happen what may, in the shape of altered times and change of circumstances) *irrevocably*, never to *return*, if he should wish to do so."[62] But the emphasized words, meant as solemn warnings, were the very ones Macready wanted most to hear. He was about to shake off the chains that had bound his spirit, and he had no intention of assuming them again.

FORREST *VS.* MACREADY

On the twenty-fourth of September, 1848, Macready arrived in Boston, where he found waiting for him his old acquaintances— Charles Sumner, Cornelius Felton, Longfellow, Edward Everett, Josiah Quincy, Charles Eliot Norton, and the rest. He had little time for social amenities, however, being in a quandary about his first appearance in New York. Normally he would have gone to Hamblin's Park Theatre, where he had acted before, but James Hackett had taken the lease of Niblo's Astor Place Opera House

and was most anxious to secure the services of the Eminent
Tragedian. His case was persuasive; he could offer an immediate
opening and he could charge a dollar a seat. Accumulation determined the decision. Macready began his final American tour
at the Astor Place on October 4 in *Macbeth*.

It was a good beginning. The *Albion* reporter, Professor Howe,
was delighted to find the auditorium "densely packed," and the
Herald was most flattering, describing the overcrowded omnibuses
which began arriving at the theatre an hour and a half before
the performance commenced.[63] Macready himself felt that it was
"one of his nights," and extended himself to the uttermost. But
there was a canker in the rose. A Boston "penny paper" had
greeted his arrival with a scurrilous attack, and two of the minor
theatres were entertaining their audiences with burlesques: *Who's
Got Macready* at Mitchell's Olympic, *Mr. McGreedy, or a Star
at the Opera House* at Chanfrau's New National. Neither of these
pieces seems to have been printed, and the first soon vanished
from the bills. But *Mr. McGreedy* continued to be played throughout his New York engagement. It was a kind of vaudeville sketch
giving Frank Chanfrau, the popular comedian, an opportunity
to mimic the styles of various prominent actors, involving a
burlesque of *Hamlet,* and presenting its author, Charles Burke,
in the title role. That some sport was made of Macready's supposedly grasping nature is evident from the *Herald* reviews: "The
offering of 'security' to the tragedian is most excellently done,"
it comments, concluding that the satire is a little too sharp, but
that the reviewer is not equipped to pass judgement on Burke's
imitation. (Oct. 12–13, 1848)

Macready does not seem to have noticed the efforts of his
brethren to make a theatrical analysis of his character, but he
chose in a curtain speech on the opening night to comment on the
attentions of the Boston press. The speech was taken as a challenge,
though he no doubt intended it for a justification. James Oakes, a
devoted friend of Forrest's, seized the gauntlet and published on
October 30 a lengthy article in the *Boston Mail* setting forth all
his hero's grievances, and all Macready's villainy. The English
tragedian, it declared, had treated his American rival with indignity during his visit to London in 1845; he, or his "toady"
Forster, had undertaken to pack the Princess' Theatre with a hired
claque; he had prevented Forrest's getting an engagement in Paris;
he had suborned the press against him.[64] The article was obviously
intended to interfere with the success of Macready's Boston engagement, but the dear Yankees were unmoved. He played two weeks

at the Howard Atheneum with considerable success, though tormented by the inattentive company, and then moved into Forrest's stronghold, Philadelphia.

With careful calculation, Forrest played his round of characters during the same engagement, duplicating wherever possible Macready's roles. The bills ran as follows:

		Macready (Arch Street)	Forrest (Walnut)
Nov. 20	(opening)	Macbeth	Macbeth
21		Stranger	Metamora
22		Othello	Othello
23		Werner	Damon
24		Shylock	Gladiator
25		Richelieu	Richelieu
27		Lear	Lear
28		Stranger	Gladiator
29		Virginius	Virginius
30		Henry VIII	Jack Cade
Dec. 1		Lady of Lyons	Richelieu
2		Hamlet	Hamlet

But Forrest was not content to stop with such a fairly common though hardly ingenuous professional opposition.

Just before the performance on the opening night, Ryder reported that there would be a disturbance from an organized claque in the theatre. Macready determined to brave it out, but he must have quailed a little at the shouting which went up from the audience on Ryder's first entrance—the signal for attack having been given too soon. On Macready's entrance the storm broke again, but the hisses were nearly drowned by the cheers of his supporters. Forrest's claque did their best, persisting throughout the performance, attempting at a prearranged signal to interfere with the actor's best points, but sometimes by the interest of the scene betrayed into silence despite themselves. Macready was singularly in possession of himself. Apposite lines,—"I dare do all that doth become a man,"—were flung at the conspirators, who responded by tossing a penny and a rotten egg on the stage. Recalled after the final curtain, he was greeted by an uproar of applause and hisses, "Nine cheers for Macready," being answered with "Four cheers for Forrest." When something like silence was obtained, Macready thanked his friends for their support and, in a direct allusion to the article in the *Boston Mail,* declared on his sacred honor that the circumstances there set forth were "false in the aggregate" and that there "was not for a single one the smallest shadow of foundation." He then commented on Forrest's accusations and denied them one by one. The speech was received with warm approval by the majority of the house, but he took the precaution of obtaining an escort to his lodgings, in case the minority wished to continue the argument further.[65]

The wisdom of bringing the quarrel before the audience may be questioned, and it would undoubtedly have been better to follow the advice of Edmund Burke and suffer the opposition of Forrest—insofar as Forrest would permit—in private. But Forrest was determined to work out his grudge in the market place. His next move was to publish a lengthy "Card" in the *Public Ledger* on November 22:

Mr. Macready, in his speech last night to the audience assembled at the Arch street Theatre, made an allusion, I understand, to "an American actor" who had the temerity on one occasion, *"openly* to hiss him." This is true, and by the way, the *only* truth which I have been enabled to gather from the whole scope of his address. But why say "an American actor?" Why not openly charge me with the act? for I *did* it, and publicly avowed it in the *Times* newspaper of London, and at the same time asserted my right to do so. . . .

Mr. Macready is stated to have said last night that up to the time of this act on my part, he "had never entertained toward me a feeling of unkindness." I unhesitatingly pronounce this to be a wilful and unblushing falsehood. I most solemnly aver and do believe that Mr. Macready, instigated by his narrow, envious mind, and his selfish fears, did *secretly*—not openly—suborn several writers for the English press to write me down. Among them was one Foster [*sic*], a "toady" of this *Eminent tragedian*—one who is ever ready to do his dirty work; and this Foster, at the bidding of his patron, attacked me in print even before I had appeared upon the London boards, and continued his abuse of me at every opportunity afterwards.

I assert also, and do solemnly believe, that Mr. Macready connived when his friends went to the theatre in London to hiss me, and did hiss me, with the purpose of driving me from the stage—and all this happened many months before the affair at Edinburgh, to which Mr. Macready refers, and in relation to which he jesuitically remarks that "until that act he never entertained towards me a feeling of unkindness." Pah! Mr. Macready has no feeling of kindness for any actor who is likely, by his talent, to stand in his way. His whole course as manager and as actor proves this—there is no thing in him but self—self—self— and his own countrymen, the English actors, know this well. . . .

Many of my friends called upon me when Mr. Macready was announced to perform [in New York], and proposed to drive him from the stage for his conduct towards me in London. My advice was, do nothing—let the superannuated driveller alone—to oppose him would be but to make him of some importance. . . .

EDWIN FORREST

It is difficult to conceive the state of mental derangement that could have tricked Forrest into so displaying himself. The blow to his ego in the failure of his London engagement must have been crushing indeed. But he was the very apotheosis of the frontier "rip-tail-roarer"; with a body like an elephant, he had also some of that monster's fabled memory.

Macready instantly drafted a reply denying that he was "wanting in self-respect so far as to bandy words upon the subject" but pleading that his professional interests were bound to suffer if he did not state that he would bring the whole matter into the courts to "place the truth beyond doubt." The announcement continues:

Reluctant as he is to notice further Mr. Forrest's Card, Mr. Macready has to observe, that when Mr. Forrest appeared at the Princess' Theatre in London, he himself was absent some hundred miles from that city, and was ignorant of his engagement, until after it had begun;—that not ONE SINGLE NOTICE of Mr. Forrest's acting appeared in the Examiner during that engagement, (as its files will prove,) that Mr. Forster, the distinguished editor, whom Mr. Macready has the honor to call his friend, having been confined to his bed with a rheumatic fever during the whole period, and some weeks both before and after.

For the other aspersions upon Mr. Macready published in the Boston Mail, and now, it is understood, avowed by Mr. Forrest, Mr. Macready will without delay apply for legal redress.[66]

Macready went to the theatre that night fully prepared for a physical assault. He emptied his purse at the hotel, commended himself to God, and pursued his course bravely, planning to obtain and publish sworn statements from England to support his claims and to play out his tour to the bitter end—he could not know how bitter. But the Philadelphia audience had cooled overnight, presenting no opposition during the performance of *Othello* and, on the night of his benefit, even bursting into applause at the "fancy dance" in *Hamlet*. Macready thanked them for the way in which they had defended him, "a stranger, from the grossest outrage, the grossest injustice," and moved south.

Their paths parting for the moment, the quarrel between the two tragedians went into hibernation. But the lines were clearly drawn between them. In Forrest's card and Macready's answer the points at dispute and the interpretation of them by each side were made clear. Through the long winter, while Macready was prospering in the south and his evidence was arriving from England, Forrest nursed his mood. The victory was to be his, and the shame.

Macready's southern and western tour followed the route of his earlier venture—Baltimore, Washington, Richmond. His opening in New Orleans was again delayed by an outbreak of cholera; he consequently lengthened his stay in Charleston until February 1849. New Orleans was worth waiting for. Ludlow and Smith had been industriously developing the theatrical interests of the community; their theatre, the St. Charles, had been enlarged and such modern improvements as reserved seats introduced. And Macready's reception there was all that anyone, even Macready, could have wished for. The house was crowded for the first time since its enlargement, and Sol Smith records, with the comment of an exclamation point, receipts of $1300.[67] "When the scene in the first act shifted," reported the *New Orleans Commercial Bulletin,* "and discovered *Hamlet* near the throne, this prince of actors was greeted with the most enthusiastic and prolonged applause."[68] Smith notes, happily, that the engagement continued to be prosperous even though Macready played every night. New Orleans could not get enough of him. The *Picayune* declared of his Othello, "We have never yet seen anything so brilliant; such acting would redeem the vices of the stage, were they tenfold what they are." *Punch,* which was conducting a personal feud with the United States at the moment, seized upon this review for a sermon, pointing out that it was impolitic for the paper to praise Othello on the stage and advertise negroes for sale in its columns.[69] On the twentieth of March the citizens assembled to pay tribute to the Eminent at a banquet.

The wit and talent of the town were requisitioned to do him sufficient honor. "Behind the chairman was hung an admirably executed portrait of the tragedian, and in front of him, when the dessert was spread, were placed a facsimile of Shakespeare's house at Stratford-upon-Avon, and a temple of Thespis, both in confectionery, the latter inscribed with the principal characters of the drama, in the personation of which Mr. Macready excels."[70] A toast was drunk to *Shakespeare and Macready,* "The greatest dead poet; the greatest living actor; the former the diamond; the latter, the golden setting in which the brilliant shines."[71] Macready's contribution was a "splendid democratic speech" which quite enraptured the banqueters and may have stolen a little of Forrest's thunder, since democratic orations were his avocation.

For, in spite of this pleasant and prosperous interlude, Forrest was still in the play. As the scene of Macready's performances shifted from New Orleans to St. Louis, Forrest's re-entrance became more and more inevitable, like the *scene à faire* of the well-made play. A foreshadowing of the climax of the American tour appeared in Cincinnati. Here, during the scene after the play in *Hamlet,* half the carcass of a sheep was tossed from the gallery to Hamlet's feet. Analogous gestures seem to have been not uncommon expressions of critical disapproval among American galleryites. A disgusted spectator in Saco, Maine, managed to hit one of the actors in a Thanksgiving performance with a dead turkey, while a fellow critic expressed his disapproval with a package of beans. An actor named Dempsey, who offended the gallery critics of Pittsburg, received a bag of coal dust; which he promptly hurled back, declaiming, "Dust to Dust and Sweets to the Sweet."[72] Whether the Cincinnati sheep-flinger was objecting to Macready's acting or his nationality is not clear. Archer thinks it a "mere ebullition of amiable vivacity."[73] Macready called it "disgusting brutality, indecent outrage, and malevolent barbarism." It is certainly not to be blamed on Forrest; he was busy entertaining and inflaming his Bowery b'hoys.

As Macready drew nearer New York, excitement in the city began to run high. For some weeks before his opening on May 7, the New York *Herald* had been running a series of editorials and news items, reporting the situation and urging the two players to make up. On the thirteenth of April Macready heard that Forrest intended to open against him at the Broadway Theatre. His comment in his *Diary* is curiously unapprehensive: "So that it is now apparent all this villainous proceeding on his part has been to get up an excitement in the hope it will draw money to him." The *Herald* next reported that a coalition of the Friends of Forrest was formed, like the Wolves of Edmund Kean three decades earlier, to hiss the eminent English tragedian from the stage, and that the supporters of the latter were rallying to protect their favorite. The *Herald* then suggested editorially that each actor play six nights to see who got the most money dollar for dollar, the loser to be set down as nobody, "or if Forrest likes it better, a 'liar'."[74] Macready fretted about the continual linking of his name with Forrest's in the press, but he seems to have anticipated no serious trouble. Having decided that the "opposition" was wholly a scheme to draw money, he refused to see the intensity with which Forrest and his supporters hated.

To a great mass of Americans, chiefly urban laborers, Macready had become not merely the English actor who contested the superiority of their idol, but The Foreigner, symbol of the constant threat to what was even then described as the American Way of Life. The philosophy of Nativism which began to emerge in the early years of the nineteenth century was reaching its first climax in the 'forties. Inspired by Colonel James Watson Webb, proprietor of the *New York Courier and Inquirer,* secret societies and a formal political party, The Native Americans, had been formed in New York, Philadelphia, and other cities and villages in the east, vowing "hostility to every non-American influence that could clash with the settled habits of the American community,"[75] principally aliens and Roman Catholics. Though earnest and honest men could be found both in the party and in such secret societies as The Native Sons of America and The Order of United Americans, the movement naturally appealed most strongly to the prejudices and convictions of the ignorant and the poor. As it increased in size, Nativism turned as such movements do from platforms and resolutions to action, mob action. Its history is peppered with riots: on election night in 1842 the windows of the home of the Catholic Bishop of New York were shattered by stones and the militia called out to protect the church buildings; in 1844 a bloodier battle in Philadelphia between the Irish and the Native Americans caused widespread death and destruction and threatened to invade other cities. And unscrupulous politicians, ward heelers and their ilk, were not slow to turn the popular philosophy to their own uses. To precipitate a riot they needed only a catalyst, and such was to be Macready's role in the most violent drama of his career.

On the seventh of May Macready was in New York, rehearsing Macbeth for the evening's performance at the Astor Place Opera House. The cast was a good one, Mrs. Coleman Pope as the Lady, Wemyss as Duncan, C. W. Clarke as Macduff, William Chippendale as one of the witches, and the faithful Ryder as Banquo. But the roles might as well have been filled from the company at Madame Tussaud's. The story of the night is vividly reported in the *Herald,* which had followed the whole contest with considerable impartiality, and some good sense:

As soon as the doors were opened, a very large number of persons, altogether of the male sex, entered the theatre, and took their seats in different parts of the house. They were followed by many others, among whom were probably fifty or sixty ladies. . . . It now began to be whispered about that the reception of Mr. Macready would not be favorable on the part of a portion of the auditory; and the appearance of Mr. Matsell, the chief of police, and a very strong body of the force under his orders, seemed to strengthen the rumors which were circulated throughout the theatre. The house was, however, perfectly quiet until the curtain rose upon the first scene, when the appearance of Mr. Clark, who personated the character of Malcolm [*sic*] elicited three loud and enthusiastic cheers from the parquette and gallery. From this moment, the cheering, hissing, whistling, and other expressions of feeling began, and not a syllable was heard, the remainder of the scene, and the succeeding, till the entrance of Macbeth, passing in dumb show. When Macbeth and Banquo entered in the third scene, the uproar was deafening. A perfect torrent of groans and hisses assailed Mr. Macready, and a deluge of assafoedita was discharged upon him from the gallery, filling the whole house with its pungent and not particularly fragrant odor. A rotten egg *à la Montreal,* was projected against him, but missing the face of the eminent tragedian, bespattered the stage at his feet. The friends of Mr. Macready, who appeared rather to outnumber those opposed to him, now manifested their feelings by cries of "shame!" "shame!" cheers and wawing [*sic*] of handkerchieves, provoking a response in the form of renewed groans, hisses, and half a dozen rotten potatoes on the part of the others. . . . The scene which followed beggars description. Hisses, groans, cheers, yells, screams, all sorts of noises, in the midst of which Mr. Macready still maintained his position in the centre of the stage. "Off!" "off!" shouted one party. "Go on!" "go on" screamed the other. Mr. Macready approached the lights. He was greeted by roars of ironical laughter, and reiterated hisses and groans.

Macready declared in his *Diary* that his intention at this moment was to address the audience, and announce that he would instantly resign his engagement rather than endure such disgraceful conduct. For fifteen minutes, he says, he stood quietly on the stage waiting for an opportunity to speak; at last he gave the order to proceed with the play. The *Herald* report continues:

A banner was at this moment exhibited in front of the amphitheatre, bearing on its side, "No apologies—it is too late!" and on the other, "You have ever proved yourself a liar!" The appearance of this banner was the signal for a perfect tornado of uproarious applause, laughter, cheers, and groans, in the midst of which an old shoe, and a cent piece were hurled at Mr. Macready, who picked up the copper coin, and with a kingly air, put it in his bosom, bowing, at the same time, with mock humility, to the quarter of the gallery from which the visitation had descended. . . . [There were further cries:] "Three groans for the codfish aristocracy!" which were responded to with marked enthusiasm. . . . "Down with the English hog!"—"take off the Devonshire bull!"—"remember how Edwin Forrest was used in London!". . . . When the curtain fell in the second act, the tumult was fiercer than ever, and it was quite apparent that something still more serious was approaching. Yet the greater portion of the auditory opposed to Mr. Macready seemed in excellent humor. They chaunted snatches of the witches' choruses. . . . One gentleman in the parquette, amongst those who were hostile to Mr. Macready, ogled the house through a stupendous glass eye, large enough for a horse collar; and others threw themselves into a variety of attitudes more picturesque than becoming. . . . [In the third act] Smash came a chair from the gallery, nearly grazing the head of one of the members of the orchestra, and strewing the stage with fragments, within a few feet of Mr. Macready. Macready bowed and smiled. Another chair falls at his feet, with a crash, which resounds all over the house. . . . Mr. Macready stands quite unmoved—not the slightest tremor visible—not the least bravado either, in his manner. Another chair is hurled on the stage, and the curtain suddenly falls. The ladies hurry from the boxes; all but a few, who betray not the slightest alarm. Still the uproar continues. There is loud talking in the lobbies. A great crowd outside thunders at the doors, and threatens to break into the theatre. Mr. Matsell and a strong party of his police-men barricade the entrances. The ladies are hurried out by one of the doors that open in Eighth street. (May 8, 1849)

Backstage, Macready was declaring that he had fulfilled his obliga-tion to the managers and would remain no longer. He undressed, thought some of taking the dagger which he had worn in his role for protection, decided that it was unworthy of him, and walked calmly out the back door with his friend David Colden. The *Herald* reporter concludes his record of the evening with the conviction that the effort to drive Macready from the stage had been organized and pre-concerted, but that no personal injury had been intended. The missiles, he points out, were not aimed directly at the actor but were calculated to miss him. The attack certainly had its effect. Macready, in his lodgings, feeling the contumely that had been visited upon him, was determined not to appear on the New York stage again.

Next day he arose, not surprisingly, with a headache. He was soon presented with a problem. A committee of prominent New Yorkers called on him with a public document demanding that he appear once more, assuring him "that the good sense and respect for order prevailing in this community"[76] would sustain him on the subsequent nights. They were not entirely motivated by esthetic considerations. For them, as for the mob, the Macready-Forrest quarrel had become a symbol of a larger political and social issue. "The respectable part of our citizens," wrote Philip Hone, "will never consent to be put down by a mob raised to serve the purposes of such a fellow as Forrest."[77] With such an appeal and such assurances of protection and support, the English player could not well resist. His second appearance was announced for Thursday, May 10.

But if the "codfish aristocracy" was not to be put down, neither were the Bowery b'hoys. Inflammatory notices were posted in the upper wards:

WORKINGMEN!
Shall Americans or English Rule in This City?
The crew of the British steamer have
threatened all Americans who shall offer
their opinions this night at
the English Aristocratic Opera House

Workingmen! Freemen! Stand Up to Your
LAWFUL RIGHTS.

Other handbills were circulated among English sailors urging them to "sustain their countryman." Astor Place was designated as the rendezvous for both factions[77a] and bands of ruffians, as on the first night, were supplied with free tickets of admission to the Opera House. Throughout the whole proceeding, Forrest kept an indiscreet silence. There was no necessity for him to speak; his work was ably done by two of the most precious scoundrels in the city of New York.

The first of these was "Captain" Isaiah Rynders, the Tammany boss of the Sixth Ward, the first political leader to employ gangs to great advantage. He had appeared in New York in the mid-thirties after a dark career as a Mississippi river-boat gambler and knife-fighter. About 1843 he had organized the Empire Club, a "Chowder and Marching Society," to support Democracy as conceived by the party bosses and to administer in true democratic fashion the corruption of the notorious Five-Points area. He surrounded himself with a poetically named crew of deputies: Dirty Face Jack, Country McCleester, and Ned Buntline.

The last of these, whose actual name was E. Z. C. Judson, is known to literary history as the inventor of the dime novel and of the stage-name (and much of the reputation) of "Buffalo Bill." To the social history of America, however, he is of greater importance as a riotous scoundrel, proprietor of a blackmailing weekly, and the idol of the Native Americans. Bristling with red mustachios, he was constantly spoiling for a "muss," and the melodrama of his fiction is an accurate reflection of both his biography and his philosophy. The first move in the Astor Place Riot was taken by him, as Rynder's lieutenant.

On Wednesday, May 9, an English-born theatrical agent, Warde Corbyn, met Judson on Barclay Street. Judson said he was looking for "Ned Forrest," who lived somewhere in Chelsea. He made no secret of his purpose, declaring to the agent, "You know there is going to be a muss, and I want to see Forrest to know if he is right or wrong, for I consider myself the leader of the Native American Party in this matter, and if Forrest is right I mean to see him through." Corbyn, who had seen some of the anti-Macready demonstrations organized by Rynders, suggested that, since there was likely to be some hard fighting, Judson might well keep out of it: he had been involved in more than his share of "musses." The editor was fearless and determined. "That may be," he replied, "but I mean to see it out."[78]

His plans were devious and well-laid. It was never proved at his trial that he saw Forrest, but he behaved as if the American Tragedian had persuaded him of the rightness of his cause. First he went to his newspaper office, filled with murderous weapons (later to be described as "merely souvenirs"), and wrote a most conciliatory editorial on the theatrical rivalry to be inserted, as a red-herring, in his blackmail sheet, *Ned Buntline's Own*. Then on the evening of May 10, he disguised himself in his brother-in-law's clothes, and persuaded that innocent to accompany him to the Opera House where, he suggested, there was to be "some sport." On the way they stopped for a drink in a large saloon on Broadway, and Judson revealed for the first time that he was armed with two loaded revolvers, in case he chanced to meet some of his enemies.[79]

At about eight o'clock, the two men went out into the street where they heard rumors that "the riot has commenced." Judson quickened his pace. It would not do for the Party Leader to be absent from action. This time the affront to America must be resented with complete efficiency, under competent direction. This time not even the most aristocratic citizens would dare to go against the mandate of the people.

The "aristocracy" was not unprepared for trouble. On the morning of May 10 there had been a conference in the office of Mayor Woodhull about the best means of coping with the threatened disorders. The Mayor was most earnest in his pleas to Niblo and Hackett to cancel the performance. But Hackett, who had a personal grudge with Forrest, would not hear of surrender and demanded only police protection.[80] The matter was referred to Police Chief Matsell, but since he felt the peace officers might not be able to handle a full-fledged attack on the theatre, it was decided to alert the New York Guard. The Seventh Regiment, cavalry and infantry, was ordered to assemble at Central Market at seven in the evening and await the event.

With full assurance of support and protection, then, Macready arrived at the theatre, and was immediately heartened to see a full carload of policemen deposited at the door by the Haarlem Railroad. By carefully controlled distribution of tickets, most of the *Forresters* had been turned away at the door and the house filled with Macreadyites. Nonetheless some of the opposition slipped through the guards and at Macready's entrance on stage, there was an attempt at concerted booing, quickly drowned by the enthusiastic applause of his supporters. From his vantage point behind the footlights, the actor could see the little group of "wretched creatures" in the gallery, calling out in savage fury and shaking their fists at him, and he pointed them out to the police scattered through the auditorium. A sign was placed against the proscenium: "The friends of order will remain silent," and the play continued, with the opposition now made conspicuous by silence in the other parts of the house. During four scenes they were permitted to vent their fury while the police quietly gathered near them. Then, at the end of the act, the officers descended upon them and bundled them out of the theatre in a well-planned and executed maneuver.

The "friends of order" responded with a round of cheers as the star read significantly,

> I will not be afraid of death and bane
> 'Til Birnam *forest* come to Dunsinane,

and again, as he cried triumphantly,

> our castle's strength
> Will laugh a siege to scorn.

At the Broadway, where Forrest was as usual revolting against tyranny in *The Gladiator,* his own followers were responding with similar enthusiasm. There was plenty of excitement inside both theatres—in the street something worse was about to occur.

Judson and his brother-in-law, arriving at Astor Place shortly after the commencement of the performance, found themselves in a mob variously estimated at ten to fifteen thousand persons, partly made up of the b'hoys who had been refused admittance, partly of the curious. When the gallery contingent was ejected into its midst, the mob suddenly came to life. Barred from the theatre, they were determined to batter it down. Means were readily at hand, since the Astor Place sewer was being repaired and a supply of paving bricks had been stacked on the curbing. It was but the work of a moment to smash the window panes,

The Attack upon the Astor Place Opera House

though the boarding behind them resisted for a while. As a kind
of protection the rioters managed to knock out the street lamps
also, although the lights over the exit doors of the theatre were
untouched and some illumination came from the interior through
the shattered windows. Most of the actual attackers seem to have
been young men under twenty, and one of these Judson seized as
a likely aide. The youth identified himself as "a Northern Liberty

boy" from Philadelphia. Judson declared that the riot wanted a nucleus, volunteered his services and began directing operations. He incited the mob against the police, crying, "The ground is your own; you have a right to it, and I will aid you in defending it."[81] He suggested starting a small fire to summon the hook-and-ladder company; its equipment would provide an excellent means of storming the theatre, which was to be destroyed as a sacrifice to Nativism. Mr. Judson did not believe in half measures.

Within the theatre, the tumult increased. Four men whom the police had attempted to confine under the stage busily went to work to set fire to the house; they were discovered in time. When Macready went to his dressing room to change after the banquet scene, he discovered it deep in water; the paving bricks had broken the pipes. Other bricks smashed the chandelier and the audience began taking cover near the walls. Still the play went on, with stones crashing on every side and battering rams pounding on the doors. Chippendale, who was singing one of the witches, noted that "the hero of the night behaved as cool as a cucumber, and, indeed, so did all of the *corps dramatique*."[82] In the fifth act, during the fight with Macduff which was perhaps the greatest moment in his repertory, Macready flung his whole soul into every word, "exciting the audience to a sympathy even with the glowing words of fiction, whilst these dreadful deeds of real crime and outrage were roaring at intervals in our ears and rising to madness all around us." At the fall of the curtain, the cheers of the spectators for a moment drowned the sounds of riot without, and Macready actually went on for a bow and a curtain speech, in pantomime, of farewell.

The problem, now that his duty to the public had been completed, was to get safely away, and an earnest consultation was held in his dressing room. The chances certainly appeared slim. The players did not know that, about nine o'clock, Chief Matsell had given up hope of controlling the mob with his police officers, and Mayor Woodhull had ordered the militia to the scene. Under Generals Sandford and Hall the detachment of troops, sixty horse and some three hundred men, marched up Broadway and arrived at Astor Place as the performance was finishing. The horsemen were first ordered to clear the street before the theatre, and rode boldly forward. The mob, busily carrying out one or another of Judson's schemes for destroying the resort of the kid-glove aristocracy, was too preoccupied to notice the approach of the new enemy. The horses had nearly reached the Opera House when the alarm was given. With concerted fury, and with no break in the rhythm of its attack, the mob turned against the soldiers. A hail of paving blocks disabled nearly all the riders, and their horses became unmanageable. The vanguard, clinging in pain and desperation to their mounts, managed to escape to the Bowery, driven from the field.[83]

The infantry seemed to be more successful. Forming in ranks across Eighth Street they marched through a groaning and hissing crowd to the back of the Opera House. Here they divided, forming two lines, four men deep, facing Broadway and the Bowery. The lines then marched in opposite directions, clearing the whole street which was then handed over to the police. The Broadway troop was ordered to the center of the riot on Astor Place, where the men were forced to march single file through the dense mob. At the front of the theatre, the soldiers contrived to re-form in depth and work their way almost across the street, but the crowd, rallied by Judson's war-whoops, let fly a volley of stones which succeeded in knocking out a number of the troops and in severely injuring General Hall. The order was given to fix bayonets; the result was farcical. The quarters were so close that, as the militia attempted to carry out the order, the mob began wrenching rifles from their hands. The soldiers fell back to the sidewalk in front of the theatre, re-formed. General Sandford, declaring that in thirty-five years in military service he had never seen a mob so violent,[84] asked for the order to fire. This the Sheriff and the Recorder reluctantly gave; the riot act was read twice; the mob hissed and booed it into inaudibility. The command was given to fire.

The Rioters, the Militia, and the Police

The first volley went into the air above the crowd, and Judson yelled loudly that the militia was using blank cartridges.[85] With howls of rage and delight the mob re-attacked and the militia fired again, lower. A few rioters, and an innocent bystander or two, fell, but the mob was blinded with rage. The third volley, fired low and point-blank, did "fearful execution." Cursing and vowing revenge the rioters began to withdraw towards the Bowery, still firing stones, taking with them an uncounted number of wounded, and leaving behind in the street between seventeen and twenty dead.

The Last Volley

The sound of the first volley had penetrated to Macready's dressing room and only increased the apprehension of the group gathered there. But the actor again displayed his calmness by declaring that he was ready to "meet the worst with dignity," and scoffed at suggestions that he should disguise himself. He at length consented to change cloaks with Clarke, who had played Macduff, and to wear another man's cap, which had to be split up the back to fit him. With two friends he made his way to the stage door, but the soldiers who were stationed there would not allow him to leave. With considerable aplomb, he crossed the auditorium and joined the line of spectators still escaping into Eighth Street which had been kept clear of the mob. Walking as slowly as he could persuade Judge Robert Emmett, his companion, to go, they made their way around the excited crowd, crossed Broadway and headed for Emmett's house. Here, in consultation with friends, a plan of strategy was drawn up for his escape from the city. At four the next morning a carriage and pair was ordered to drive "a doctor to some gentleman's house near New Rochelle."[86]

The time had been well chosen. At that hour of the morning, the city was normally deserted save for farmers coming to market. But the stratagem for Macready's escape was something more than a romantic gesture. During the night a furious group of men had chased an omnibus down the street thinking the actor was in it. "They've killed twenty of us, and by God we'll kill him," they cried. Another group ransacked his hotel. And before the Boston train left New York that morning, a gang of "roughs" passed through searching for him.[87] Once safely on the train at New Rochelle, he journeyed to Boston without molestation, but found that the incident went with him. He was recognized several times and forced to endure the curiosity and sympathy of his fellow-travelers.

It was with a haunted feeling that he got off the train in Boston, and took a cab to George Curtis' house. It is hardly surprising that after the events of the tenth of May he should be somewhat apprehensive of appearing in public, even at a safe distance from New York. He had some idea of proceeding at once to Halifax. The Mayor of Boston and the chief of police called to assure him that he would be protected from outrage. He spent his time bidding farewell to his New England friends, and writing letters of thanks to those in New York who had been his supporters. To Washington Irving he wrote:

I feel proud and honored in seeing your name at the head of the list of gentlemen and friends, inviting me to return to my engagement in New York. It was an act, that I should under similar circumstances (as I have proved) considered myself *bound* to do.—I am not less grateful to you for standing forward on that occasion, disastrous as it has proved to many, and painful and unfortunate to myself.—It was, I feel confident, a needful duty, and I honor and am grateful to the subscribers of the paper presented to me.[88]

Carrying the Wounded to the Hospital

Nonetheless, and with any thought of settling in America quite vanished, it was with great relief that he stepped aboard the *Hibernia* for his return to England.

As for Forrest and the rioters, secure in the possession of their victory over the eminent English tragedian, they had little else to show for it. Writing to his own "toady," James Oakes, Forrest gave a very innocent account of himself:

I most sincerely regret to say that last night, the military fired upon the people who were standing outside of the Astor house Theatre and many wounded. This blood will rest upon the heads of the Committee who insisted that Mr. Macready should perform in despite of the known wishes of the people to the contrary, and on the heads of the public authorities who were requested by many of the citizens to close the house, and thereby prevent any farther demonstration.[89]

Apparently the sounds of demolition from the crowd merely "standing" outside the Astor Place Theatre did not reach the Broadway where Forrest was holding forth. But the effect was made plain to the American tragedian in a more personal way. According to a letter of Chippendale's, the audiences for Forrest's last two appearances fell off to nothing,[90] possibly because so many of his loyal supporters were in jail.

For days after the riot, the *Tribune* printed a growing list of the men who had been arrested by the police—a savory crew of sixty-three with police records and state prison terms. When their case came to trial, however, on the thirteenth of September, only ten of the accused remained, many having slipped through the fingers of the police, but among the prisoners was E. Z. C. Judson, who attempted to turn the proceedings into a dime-novel melodrama. James Smith, his attorney, conducted a running battle with the trial judge, Charles P. Daly, playing strongly on the public sentiment in favor of the rioters. The general feeling seems to have been that riots were safety valves, and that conviction was impossible.[91]

Smith's line of defense follows a familiar pattern; he pleaded for acquittal on the grounds of free speech and a free stage. "Acting," he said, "is not a concededly useful art, protected by the law, but it is a mode or fashion which depends for its existence upon the gratification for the public in an unrestrained way." If, as was widely suspected, Mr. Forrest was paying Mr. Smith to defend his supporters, Mr. Forrest may well have wondered whether his money was well spent. Forrest himself was never proved to have been the power behind the riot, but American papers as well as English were convinced beyond doubt of his motivating influence. The *New York Courier* decided "the fact that Mr. Forrest had declared in public that Mr. Macready should never be permitted to appear again on the stage in New York warranted the inference that the disturbance on Monday night was of Mr. Forrest's procurement."[92] *Punch* was more forthright, since the riot fell in with his current campaign. His elaborate fantasy, partially supported with accounts from the American press, begins:

A few remnants of the aboriginal savage occasionally visit New York. By the last accounts from America, we learn that some of the tribes of Cur-ribs—(a most despicable and degraded specimen of the wild man) —held a war-meeting at the Astor Place Opera House, on the occasion of MACREADY's appearance as *Macbeth*.

It must be known, that the chief of this tribe of Cur-ribs is EDW INF OR REST, or WHITEFEATHER, a sinewy savage of indomitable face, who has had the advantage of several visits to Europe; but who, it seems, has returned to America, if possible, a greater savage than he quitted it. Now, it would seem that WHITEFEATHER believes in an old Indian superstition; namely, that to kill a man of genius, is to become the possessor of his departed power. To this end, WHITEFEATHER laid on the war-paint, shaved his head for the war-plume, and resolved to slay the English MACREADY.

We regret that we cannot give the speech verbatim as delivered by WHITEFEATHER to his tribe. It is, however, acknowledged to have been a marvel of eloquence in its way, calling upon the tribe (paid for the occasion) to bury the axe, but to lay in a plentiful supply of rotten eggs, wherewith to assail the pale-face MACREADY. WHITEFEATHER, moreover, dwelt with passionate earnestness upon the significant use of a bottle of assafoedita at the proper moment at the pale-face. "Even as the stench," said WHITEFEATHER, "will fill the nostrils of the pale-face, so will my name smell among the nations." (XVI, 217)

Neither the bloody end of the riot nor the conviction of some of the rioters put an end to the Native American movement. Judson, condemned to a year on Blackwell's Island, continued to publish *Ned Buntline's Own* from his cell and declaimed that "the British dogs who lapped the blood of Americans in order to appease the wrath of a few British refugees . . . [will pay] for this damnable deed of blood and murder."[93] On his release his admirers drove him in an open barouche with six white horses to his home accompanied by a brass band playing "Hail to the Chief." Rynders, his immediate superior, advanced in Tammany circles until he became a general Committeeman for the city and county of New York along with Fernando Wood and Boss Tweed.

Of these events and persons Macready seems to have been ignorant. For him and for his friends, Forrest was the only villain, and American *versus* British taste in acting the point at issue. And his resolution was final. "Nicholas or Nero," he said to W. J. Fox, "but *never* the United States."[94]

$\diamond$ $\diamond$ $\diamond$ 8 $\diamond$ $\diamond$ $\diamond$

Exit Macbeth

AFTER HIS FIRST appearance in London, Macready had chosen as his motto Seneca's "Inveniet viam aut faciet." For nearly half a century he had been trying to make a way and now, ironically, he found it thrust upon him. He returned to England a kind of national hero. Even the American press was aware of his new importance as a political symbol. The New York *Courier* concluded its account of the Astor Place riot with a fine burst of condemnation:

[Forrest] is safe forever, not only from rivalry, but from that envy from which it often springs. He succeeded last night in doing what even his bad acting and unmanly conduct never did before,—he has inflicted a thorough and lasting disgrace upon the American Character.[1]

His way found, Macready lost no time setting about his final provincial engagements. Playing Macbeth at Birmingham on June 26, he received a tremendous ovation. The English audience was showing that it could stand by its national favorites as jingoistically as the Americans; the same reception greeted him wherever he played. Benjamin Webster, past differences eclipsed by the new publicity value of Macready, lost no time in signing with him for his farewell appearances in London.

The taking of a farewell was a highly complicated maneuver. The original plan was for two seasons at the Haymarket, running from October to December and from April to July, with an additional benefit at such larger house as might be available. Since Macready intended his retirement to be final, performances must be so scheduled as to extract the last dram of oil from each role before it was abandoned. On off nights, an occasional excursion to a country theatre would assure that no resource be overlooked.

He approached the Haymarket opening, scheduled for October 8, by a leisurely route: Worcester, Brighton, Plymouth, Nottingham, Derby, Leicester, Manchester, annoyed by his fellow actors and cheered by his audiences. But once in London he became the industrious tyrant of his managerial days, endlessly rehearsing even his most familiar parts, forgetting himself in the emotional strain of performance, aware that there was no longer the "wild abandonment to a delighted feeling" that he used to sense in his audiences. Mrs. Warner suggested a consolation: the Haymarket audience had so long dieted on Charles Kean that their tastes were dulled. Further, Webster's stage management continued to be, by Macready's measure, casual. *King Lear* was "rehearsed" with several actors absent and several roles uncast. He appreciated J. R. Planché's description of the Haymarket as *The Patented Self-Acting Theatre.*[2]

The first series of performances concluded with *Macbeth* on December 8. But his gratitude that the event brought closer his release from his profession was premature. Another year and much personal sorrow was to intervene before the words "last time forever" would precede his name on the playbills. Meanwhile, Forster had an ambitious plan for the actor to turn lecturer and public reader, and he had agreed to play a special performance, by command, at Windsor Castle.

Queen Victoria had instituted a series of plays under the direction of Charles Kean with casts especially assembled from the leading players of the country. Macready was to do Brutus in *Julius Caesar,* and it must be admitted he performed with bad grace. It was not merely the occasion, and the feeling that the aristocracy was patronizing him, that brought out the worst in his personality. His despised younger rival, Kean, was in charge of the production, and Macready was not long in finding a point of disagreement. Kean had engaged a young man from Edinburgh to play Lucius. This was not at all satisfactory to the prospective Brutus, who went to Webster to inquire whether his nephew George Webster might play the role at Windsor, as he had done for Macready in the provinces. News of this got to Kean who at once addressed a temperate note to Macready pointing out that he was the manager of the Windsor theatricals and had the sole responsibility for casting, but that, had Macready spoken earlier, he would have been glad to accommodate him. This called forth a note from Macready in his most stiff-necked prose declining to correspond with Kean save through his solicitor, to which Kean replied with considerable self-restraint. Macready, in the meantime, wrote directly to an officer of the Queen's household to request permission to substitute *his* Lucius for Kean's on the grounds that his performance of Brutus required the close support of an actor familiar with his business. Whatever the merits of the argument, and the contending actors, young Webster appeared as Lucius beside Macready and before the Queen. In spite of bad temper on all sides, the performance on February 1, 1850, went off well, though Macready rejected an invitation to spend the night at Windsor, paying seven guineas to engage a special engine to return him to London.

Although Macready's contempt for the aristocracy was as great as his dislike of his theatrical rivals, he confined its expression to words rather than such expensive gestures. The singular personal indulgence of a private locomotive was induced by the illness of his eldest daughter Nina. Since early December she had been wracked with coughing, and he recognized the gradual wearing down that had preceded the death of Harriet. The consequent anguish of his mind may have accounted in part, but only in part, for his crabbed behavior during the preparation for the Windsor performance. Nina was able to sit up for an hour at her birthday ball but her decline thereafter was rapid and unchanging. Since his wife was again pregnant, Macready and his sister had to assume charge of the sick room, a task which all too clearly was another death watch. The burden largely fell on Laetitia, since the actor kept doggedly to his commitments in the provincial theatres, though his mind was on his child and each performance was an agony.

On February 20 he returned from an Irish tour and went directly to Hastings whence the sick girl had been removed. Almost without interruption for four days he sat by her bed, encouraging her, playing with her dog, praying. During her brief periods of sleep, he wrote letters, several a day, to Catherine exhorting her to patience, reminding her of her duty to God and her earthly family. His *Diary* for the period shows that he was equally in need of the same exhortations himself. Day after day he reiterates his faith as if reiteration could convince him of the necessity of the event. In the early morning of February 24, Nina died and Macready, wrestling with doubt, wrote: "But let me not, Oh God of wisdom and virtue, Creator and Parent, Almighty Power, let me not murmur at Thy decree! In the fulfillment of this, to me, *sad destiny,* I acknowledge manifold mercies, most indulgent exemptions from aggravations of my misfortune, which *apparent accident* has delivered us from. . . . Oh God, strengthen my resolves and renew a right spirit within me." But it was his strong sense of duty, to his wife, to his family, to his occupation, that came to his rescue. He permitted himself a few days of inactivity, of grief, and then went about his business.

Nina's death caused a postponement in the performances scheduled at the Haymarket, and the second series actually ran from October 1850 to February 1851. The announcements of the final performances were sufficiently complex to bewilder the most seasoned playgoer. It was important to impress upon the prospective spectator that this was the final engagement of the Eminent Tragedian, but Macready was insistent that there be no "trickery." Consequently, Webster devised a series of labels, "Last time but one," "Last Time," and "Last Time Forever," which seem to have met the letter of the law, while causing much sportive comment from the press. *Punch* eavesdropped on the bewilderment of an "Enthusiastic Playgoer" reading a Haymarket bill:

"Mr. Macready's farewell Engagement on any stage"—Ah!—"Positively the last week but three of Mr. Macready's ever performing on any stage."—H'm! That's rather rash though, considering they all come back once or twice. However, let's see. H'm—H'm—Ah—Now I like this!—(*Reads*)—"To guard against misunderstanding or disappointment, it is deemed requisite to state that these performances will not be extended, and that the public announcement of Mr. Macready's last performance of each of his characters will be most faithfully adhered to." Now, that I call strictly honourable and right. No more first last appearances, and second last appearances! These are to be real farewell performances for once.—(*Reads again*)—"Henry IV., Mr. Macready, his Last Appearance but One!" Oh! I'll wait for the last— that will be the day after tomorrow, I see—Eh? What's this?—"Previously to his final performance!" Oh! That's the last but two then!"— (*Reads again*)—"Being positively his final appearance—previously to his finally repeating his range of characters, for the last time, before his retirement from the stage, when each of his parts will be repeated for the last time forever." Eh? Let's see?—(*Making a desperate effort to collect the result*)—His last appearance but one—previously to his appearance—before finally appearing in each of his characters—previously to his concluding performances on any stage. Confound it. I've lost my reckoning—(*Tries again, counting on his fingers*)—His last —previously to his farewell—before finally—previously to his concluding—Oh! Good Gracious!—Is he ever going to go, I wonder. . . . I'd better go and see him tonight—after all. (*Exit for the Haymarket.*)[3]

Which was, no doubt, precisely what Webster intended.

During his time off from the Haymarket, Macready continued his final engagements in the provinces, playing his favorite char-

acters for the last time and bidding a dignified farewell to each
town in turn. His curtain speeches, save on his last American tour,
had always been models of restraint and these were no different.
Only in Bristol, a scene of his early triumphs, was he unable to
keep the tears from coursing down his cheeks. He was touched
by an invitation from Bulwer-Lytton to retire to a house near
his estate, and visited him for the satisfaction of seeing it, although
he had already chosen his place of retirement at Sherborne. In
October he was in Glasgow, and so mellowed by the historical
sense of the occasion that he wrote a warm-hearted letter to
Knowles, from whom he had been long estranged.

Last night ended my theatrical career in Glasgow—and Virginius
was my character! I tried to make the representation worthy of the
poet. The date of my professional life is fixed, if indeed, I carry it out
so far. In all human probability we shall never meet in this world
again, and here, where our acquaintance—and our friendship—began
in correspondence, by this same means I take leave of you, and send a
hearty God bless you to you wherever you may be. . . .
What a world of recollections intervene the present moment, and
poor John Tait's first introductory letter of Virginius from this good
old city!—How much to be thankful for—to lament, and to forgive!
—I write these hasty lines in fullness of heart to say farewell and again
God bless you.[4]

The final, "last time forever," performances at the Haymarket
commenced with *Macbeth* on October 28, 1850. He duly performed his range of characters, in the traditional manner, but
he was determined to do more than repeat. During this engagement he also appeared before a London audience for the first
time in a character new to them. On the first of December he
performed *Richard II*. Had it been surrounded with the pageantry
which he would have given it at Covent Garden it might have
caused something of a flutter. But it was put together in the
makeshift fashion typical of the Haymarket and failed utterly
to attract.

One interruption in the performances was certainly gratifying
to him. By special invitation he visited Oxford, Cambridge, Eton,
and Rugby, when he gave readings of *Hamlet* to benefit the fund
for the purchase of Shakespeare's house. At Rugby on November
12 he was filled with the memories of his youth, with bitterness
at the reminder of a career frustrated, with gratitude that he had
pursued his elected duty to its appointed end.

There was little of the usual melancholy about Macready's
final performances. He was still a powerful actor; in certain roles

he was far from the sere and yellow, and he himself felt no reluctance in giving up his profession. But there were some roles for which he was no longer physically fitted (he, at least, was not so ill-advised as to play Claude Melnotte) in which he provided some amusement for the sportive playgoer. Thackeray describes one of these in a letter to Mrs. Sartoris, November 3, 1850:

the struggling outside and the pushing and squeezing and battle at the money-hole were well enough and like the old things; even till the curtain drew up it was pretty pleasant in the pit: but when the play began and old Hamlet came on with a gnarled neck and a rich brown wig over his wrinkled old face, the youthful business disappeared altogether. . . . What a wretched humbug that old Hamlet seemed with an undertaker's tray on his head, flapping about his eternal white pocket handkerchief, and being frightened at that stupid old Ghost.[5]

Other spectators were less faultfinding. On three nights, his children were permitted for the first time to see him as an actor, and the general public continued to crowd in, undiscriminating save for *Richard II*. If there was no sentiment behind the footlights, at least there was in the pit. An anonymous poetaster caught the flavor of one such occasion perhaps more accurately than the sharper pen of Thackeray, for it is evident that a trip to the Haymarket was a sentimental—if somewhat perilous—journey undertaken as a man might play over the songs of his youth, for this Virginius, or Werner, or King John was not merely a fine theatrical performance but it carried its freightage of memories.

THE PASSAGE OF HAYMARKET PIT
A LAY OF MODERN BABYLON

The hour of six has sounded from near and distant tower,
The gas-lights glitter glaringly, the clouds of evening lour,
A thousand wagging tongues are heard two thousand ears to tell,
An eminent tragedian is taking his farewell.
The clatter of the cab horse, with iron-bounded feet,
Rings noisily and rapidly on the stone-coated street;
Right onward to the Haymarket the cabmen fiercely drive,
Where coronetted carriages continually arrive. . . .
But it is not in the carriage way the battle must be fought,
'Tis where the entrance of the pit is desperately sought;
Where voices, which by infancy or age are rendered shrill,
Raise the loud shriek of "oranges," or scream "Who'll buy a bill?"
A crowd is round the portal—tremendous is the crush—
All summoning their prowess up to bear th' expected rush;

The nimble youth, the stalwart man, the veteran bent with age,
Following their favorite actor as he quits for aye the stage.
And now the door is opening—a movement stirs the mass,
The beating heart prepares to brave the fury of the pass. . . .
How terrible the struggle, how furious the tide—
How sharply JOHNSON's elbow digs into THOMSON's side—
How vehemently TOMKINS for air and mercy calls—
How hopelessly 'neath fifty feet the hat of JENKINS falls—
How many lose their temper! SMITH, of the fiery brain,
Bids HOBSON of the overcoat "not to do that again." . . .
The outward opening is past—the struggle still is rife,
The money-taker's box is now the goal of death and life;
Once miss the small arch'd opening, and all has been in vain,
For hopeless is the effort to reach that box again. . . .
But happy are the buffeters, with all their trials past,
To take their places in the pit, and see the play at last;
While mutual urbanity is rapidly regained,
And all the little brusqueries of the pit-pas[s] explained.
JOHNSON extends to THOMSON the playbill to peruse,
And TOMKINS tells to JENKINS the last dramatic news.
SMITH, of the fiery temper, towards HOBSON blandly cools,
And volunteers the avowal that "hasty men are fools." . . .
All other sentiments are still'd, except the sad delight,
Caused by the interest that's felt in that eventful night,
When the great actor unimpair'd snatches from Time his power,
And gallantly anticipates his own departing hour. (xx, 51)

On February 3, the long series of repetitions at the Haymarket came to an end and preparations were made for his farewell benefit, his "last time forever" before a London audience.

The theatre chosen was Drury Lane and the date February 26. Phelps closed his own theatre for the night to join the company, and Mrs. Warner was on hand for Lady Macbeth.

It was not to be expected, Macready being Macready, that the occasion should be without difficulty. James Anderson, who had rather over-parted himself as the manager of Drury, informed Willmott, who was in charge of the farewell arrangements, that he intended to allow his own company to watch the performance from backstage. When Macready rejected the proposal and declared that if Anderson continued to insist he would engage a smaller theatre, Anderson was bitter in voicing his resentment: Macready was proud, dictatorial, inconsiderate.[6] Actually Macready was anticipating for the last time the stage-fright which had so often kept him from realizing his conceptions. As he wrote Willmott:

on such an occasion the strength of my nerves must naturally be more than ordinarily taxed, & it will be a night for me to go through (with every aid & attention that the kindness of my friends can offer me) most trying to my feelings & most exhausting to my powers. If therefore Mr. Anderson persists in requiring, in addition to the terms of the agreement, that a number of persons, *Strangers to me,* shall have places between the wings and behind the scenes, I have no alternative but to declare I cannot face the interruption.[7]

He was, however, willing to accommodate Anderson's company by giving them free admission to the boxes.

But this was no more than a necessary storm. The day itself passed smoothly. During every action which prepared for the performance, Macready repeated to himself, "I shall never have to do this again," and no feeling of regret intruded upon his "placid satisfaction." From his dressing room (the one he had fitted up as his office during his period as manager) he could hear the shouts and cries of the crowds waiting in the streets and remembered the time when those very sounds seemed a matter of life and death to him.

On his entrance he was for a moment overcome, though more by thinking of the presence of his children in the theatre than because of the enthusiasm which rolled over him. With whole heart he threw himself at last into the enactment of Macbeth, his favorite role and the Shakespearean hero which is historically most conspicuously his.

The orchestra strikes up Matthew Locke's reedy sinister overture, inseparable from *Macbeth* since Davenant's revival in 1672[8]; the allegorical front curtain rises to reveal a heavy green drape that fills the proscenium arch with its soft folds. This was one of Macready's managerial innovations, of which a German visitor had written with approval: "The whole spiritual life of the performance begins for the audience with the overture, and while the green drape is down the spectator is removed from the reality [of the theatre] and transported into the spirit of the play."[9] With the last minor chords of the overture, the stage lamps are dimmed and the drape is withdrawn to the sound of rain, thunder, and lightning.

The first scene is shallow, closed in by two huge flats set in the first row of grooves. Unconventionally, the two flats do not fit snugly together, but have inner edges of profile board which overlap.[10] In the center of the darkened stage, heads together, stand three horrible figures whose beards and short kirtles give them a

masculine appearance.[11] They confer inaudibly for a moment
while the thunder crashes, then rush apart, one to the left and one
to the right near the proscenium, one gliding between the flats
into the darkness at the center back. Suddenly the witch at the
back returns and cries in a full masculine voice:

> When shall we three meet again
> In thunder lightning or in rain?

The other two stop and turn,[12] replying from the sides of the stage:

> When the hurlyburly's done
> When the battle's lost and won.
> That will be ere the set of sun.

The witch at the back moves forward into the dim light, asking,
"Where the place?" The witch on the right answers, "Upon the
heath." As the witch on the left says, "There to meet with—
Macbeth" an ominous roll of thunder punctuates the line. Full
voiced, male and malevolent, they perform their incantation and
slip stealthily from the stage, the first and third witches halfway
back from the curtain on the left, the second witch alone near the
curtain on the right. In less than five minutes, the spell of absolute
and confident evil has been cast over the play by these three supernatural beings, meeting as it were for a conference, and then
going at once about their dark business.

As the stage lamps are turned up, there is a flourish of drums and
trumpets,[13] the flats are withdrawn and from a few feet above the
spot where the second witch had disappeared there enters the
first of a series of majestic processions introducing the countering
idea of royal power. Two chamberlains come first, walking backwards and bowing to King Duncan,[14] who moves to the middle of
the stage for his opening lines. He is followed by Malcolm and
Donalbain together, a physician, Ross, Lennox, three officers, and
six lords. The procession is halted by the appearance, from down-
stage left, of the Bleeding Officer, supported by two soldiers. The
Officer gasps out his report of the valorous deeds of Macbeth and
Banquo against the Norwegian invader. As he is assisted across the
stage, the physician, at a signal from the king, comes forward and
goes off with him on the right.[15] At this moment, a trumpet heralds
the approach of Macduff and the sharp-eyed Lennox comments
that his haste promises strange tidings. The six lords hasten across
the back of the scene to the left to point up the entrance of the
newcomer. Macduff[16] kneels to the king and gives his excited news
of total victory. Duncan sends Macduff, Lennox, and the six lords

off[17] left to invest Macbeth with the new title of Thane of Cawdor, and the royal procession makes its exit on the right as the lamps dim down and the green curtain falls.

It rises again on foggy darkness. The backscene of the heath is masked by a huge opaque cloud, in turn made misty by curtains of gauze clouding which hang in front of it.[18] The first witch is alone at the back staring into the blackness and listening. After a short pause the second witch enters from the right and the third from the left. The first witch advances to them at the center[19] to relate his adventures with the ship-master's wife; the opaque cloud rises slowly and the light begins to increase. As his fellow witches offer instruments for vengeance, the stage brightens still more and the gauze clouding is drawn off.[20] The first witch produces his own charm, a pilot's thumb, and a marching tune can be heard in the far distance, now clear and now faint as wafted by the winds.[21] The witches dance, the lights continue to rise, the march grows louder and the mist and clouds have dispersed to reveal the barren rocky heath stretching toward a distant sunset. Two spindling trees, one at right and one just left of center, accent the barrenness. In the distance, on the right, part of Macbeth's army can be seen. The third witch leaves his fellows and moves upstage to listen to the windborne march, then rushes down to announce the coming of Macbeth. We hear Macready's voice, "Command they make a halt upon the heath," followed by a series of "Halts," delivered by the prompter and his assistants in as many voices as they can summon. The martial music ceases. The three witches have danced their way to the left side of the stage, awaiting the entrance of Macbeth.[22]

He comes in, from the back at right, crossing a rustic bridge in the center, and striding towards the footlights, a warrior returning homeward flushed with victory,[23] glancing at the sky as he says, "So fair and foul a day I have not seen."[24] He is something under six feet in height and speaks with a quiet voice that suggests subdued power.[25] His wig is short and black, and a clipped beard and moustache outline his mouth and jaws. He is wearing a knee-length garment like a kilt, a beret with badge and feather, and a plaid scarf thrown over his left shoulder. In his right hand he bears his baton, on his left arm a small round shield.[26]

Banquo is with him, on his left, as they encounter the witches. Macbeth does not react with the conventional tragic start, but rather, like a brave soldier, turns to his companion with a look of surprise. Banquo demands their identity, but when he asks, "Are you ought that man may question," each witch lays the forefinger of his left[27] hand on his lips and with his right points at Macbeth.

Macbeth, Act I, Scene iii, from Scharf's *Recollections*

Macbeth turns to the witches, his right hand raised in surprise, his left clutching his scarf, his eyes wide and his mouth slightly open.[28] The first witch quickly takes his finger from his lips and backs away, raising both arms[29] as he hails Macbeth Thane of Glamis and points crookedly at him. With the same business, the second witch hails him as Thane of Cawdor. The third witch, with the same gesture, hails him as king hereafter, and all three kneel in unison, continuing to point as if transfixing him with their fingers. "In the name of truth," cries Banquo, meaning to continue his cross-examination, but at the word *truth,* the witches start in confusion. However, they deliver the requested prophecy, pointing their crooked fingers this time at Banquo and then turn left as if withdrawing. Macbeth crosses to them and curtly and fretfully commands them to stay.[30] While he speaks, they remain momentarily fixed, glaring at the two officers over their left shoulders.[31] They vanish into the wings, leaving Macbeth and Banquo alone for an instant of half-doubt, half-belief.

The King's messengers enter from the front on the left, the six lords remaining near the wings as Macduff and Lennox present the royal thanks and confirm the prophecy of the witches by proclaiming Macbeth Thane of Cawdor. All present bow to Macbeth,[32] except Banquo who asks, aside, whether the devil can speak true. A shaft of light from the wing has fallen on Macbeth's face[33]—perhaps to mark the brand that is upon him, perhaps to signal the beginning of his withdrawal from his companions. Somewhat abstractedly he thanks them for their pains, they bow and confer on the left, moving upstage to center as Banquo, saying "Cousins, a word, I pray you," goes up to speak with them. Macbeth is alone on the apron for his soliloquy, which he begins with an air of brooding revery, almost as sensitive as Hamlet.[34] But first he once more acknowledges the kindness of the messengers, who bow in reply.[35] As if endeavoring to deceive himself,[36] he exclaims "This supernatural soliciting cannot be ill," but then, as if a thought of indefinable evil shot through his mind, continues in a startled and hurried manner, "cannot be good." From this moment on, Macbeth is an altered man, shaken by dark emotions, the slave of fate[37]: "If chance will have me King, why, chance may crown me." Unconscious of his companions, with glassy eye and dreamlike expression, he works across the stage with an uncertain gait, until they break in upon him. The messengers join the lords at the left entrance and Banquo comes down to recall him to his senses.[38] As Macbeth speaks to his friends with overdone warmth,[39] Banquo goes once more upstage, crosses the bridge, and pantomimes orders to the army waiting off right. The martial music resumes, *forte*,[40] as Macbeth orders them towards the King, and the curtain falls on the general exeunt.[41]

Before the curtain rises again on the fourth scene, the music shifts to a royal march to re-establish the counter-idea. Once more from the right enters the royal procession: two chamberlains, Duncan who goes to the center, Malcolm and Donalbain who cross to the left, Ross and the physician who come down right, and three officers who group themselves behind the King. After Malcolm reports the execution of Cawdor, a second procession enters on the left: Macduff and Lennox who cross the stage, Macbeth, Banquo, and the six lords who advance and kneel before the King. One of the lords carries two banners rolled together[42] which he places at the King's feet as a sign of the recent victory. As Duncan salutes Macbeth, the lord withdraws with the trophies, and Macbeth crosses to the left, bowing to Malcolm and Donalbain as he passes them.[43] But when Duncan proclaims Malcolm his successor, Macbeth's manner combines bewilderment and agitation. Duncan moves upstage, speaking to Banquo, and the rest of the court follows forming a half circle in front of the King. Macbeth is left alone to reveal how deeply the witches have impressed him:

Stars hide your fires:
Let not light see my black and deep desires.

Still in revery he slips off right to announce the King's coming to his wife. The circle in front of Duncan divides as he speaks his final words of commendation and the company parades in good order after Macbeth.

The fifth scene presents the third idea of the production—the domestic situation which is to be engulfed by both the force of Evil and the ambition for royal power. Lady Macbeth enters through an opening at the left, reading her husband's report of his victory and the prophecy of the witches. Macbeth arrives from the right, and they embrace warmly. She greets him, but through her speech his restlessness is apparent, his lips moving involuntarily until at last the words burst from him: "My dearest love, Duncan comes here tonight." In reply to his lady's, "And when goes hence?" he says quickly, "Tomorrow," as if merely stating a fact, and then, as if aware that his wife guessed his thought but saw his want of resolution to do the deed, continues with a lower tone and slow and conscious manner: "as—he—purposes."[44] The significant pause is repeated by Lady Macbeth as she says

> He that's coming
> Must be provided for;—and you shall put
> This night's great business into my despatch.

Macbeth tries once more to delay. "We will speak further," he says. But Lady Macbeth has assumed command. "Leave all the rest to me," she says firmly, and taking him by the right hand, leads him off the stage.

After the curtain falls, the lights dim for the arrival of Duncan at Macbeth's castle by night, the royal march is played, and, at rise, the royal procession enters for the last time, from the left. First come a seneschal and four officers who go up to the castle gates, right of center; next, two chamberlains with torches; Duncan, Malcolm, Donalbain; then Macduff, Banquo and Fleance in a group; and six lords (gentlemen of the ballet) to fill up the gaps. During Banquo's description of the castle, a counterprocession begins to enter through the gates. This is led by Seyton, followed by eight servants with torches, eight ladies who stand at either side of the gate and curtsey to Lady Macbeth who sweeps down stage, right of center, and bows low before the King[45]— a crowded scene, made colorful and glittering by torchlight. To this is added a lively martial tune from offstage, as Duncan begs to be conducted to his host, and the doubled procession moves with pomp into the castle: seneschal, four officers, two chamberlains, Duncan and Lady Macbeth, six ladies, Malcolm and Donalbain, Macduff, Banquo and Fleance, the physician, six lords and four servants. This series of processions, each larger and statelier than the last, establishes the background of majesty against which the story unfolds, provides the spectacle demanded by the huge amphitheatres of midcentury, and at the same time makes concrete the temptation which the witches have held out to Macbeth. After the procession has disappeared, the music continues, with gradually diminishing volume, until the scene is changed.

The seventh scene is the anteroom of the castle, during the state banquet in Duncan's honor. As the great flats close across the scene of the exterior of the castle, an opening is discovered in the left-hand flat, from the top of which a lighted lamp is lowered during the scene change.[46] Behind this entrance a sewer and eight servants cross from right to left bearing alternately torches and gold and silver dishes containing boar's heads, haunches of venison. Through this rear door enters Macbeth to read the first of the great soliloquies. "If it were done when 'tis done, then 'twere well it were done quickly," with uncommon vigor and freshness. Image crowds upon image, thought suggests thought to a mind both powerful and strongly agitated.[47] It seems a moment of almost naturalistic self-analysis, rather than a formal, aria-like pause in the action of the play. Lady Macbeth enters through the opening in the flat in search of him, and when he declares that they will proceed no further in their plot, she takes his hand in anxiety. But her cue is to be scornful, hoping to make firm his purpose:

> Was the hope drunk
> Wherein you dress'd yourself? Hath it slept since?
> And wakes it now, to look so green and pale
> At what it did so freely? From this time
> Such I account thy love.

And she throws him from her. But Macbeth, preoccupied, taut, "I dared do all that may become a man. Who dares do more is none," crosses left. Lady Macbeth berates him from the right, but moves before him to the left as she speaks of destroying her child. Finally resolved to "bend up/ Each corporal agent to this terrible feat," Macbeth whirls upon her, seizes her right arm and hastens her off through the opening in the flat.[48] The music begins quietly, increasing to a crescendo as they leave the stage.

❖ ❖ ❖ ❖ ❖ ❖ ❖ ❖

The second act is played in the courtyard of Macbeth's castle, an enormous walled square filling the entire stage, with a main

arched entrance under a heavy tower at the center rear and two
smaller doorways at the front, on the left leading to Duncan's
apartment, on the right to Macbeth's. There is a gallery across
the back with stairs on either side. The curtain rises as the lamps
are dimmed. From the King's chamber enters a servant with a
torch, crossing the stage. He is followed by Banquo (carrying the
diamond ring which is Duncan's gift to his hostess), Fleance, and
another torch bearer. Macbeth enters with Seyton from the down-
stage door on the right and meets Banquo, standing a little to his
left and slightly upstage. The King's diamond changes hands and
they speak nervously of the prophecy of the witches. During this
dialogue the silent Fleance stays close to his father's left hand,
ironically centered. Macbeth bids them good night, and distant
thunder growls as Fleance and Banquo mount the right-hand stairway, preceded by the torchbearing servant, cross the gallery and
enter the first door on the left.[49] As Macbeth paces up and down
on the left, Seyton attempts to penetrate his abstraction by moving
into his field of vision. At length, Macbeth becomes aware of his
servant,[50] and with a touch of almost paternal consideration[51] sends
him off with a message to his wife, and remains alone on the
stage, silent.

Slowly he senses the presence of the dagger of the mind wavering
before him in the air. He does not start at it at once as if it were
"tangible to the eye." Rather he keeps his eye constantly on the
painting of his fear, recoiling and advancing to the dread object
of his struggling excitement, and finally drawing his own dagger.[52]
The whole soliloquy is delivered with a ghastly expression of
imaginative terror, the earlier portion at once majestic and full
of awe, climaxing with one of Macready's typical elisions: "There's
no such *thingitisthe* bloody business which informs thus to mine
eyes."[53] Now there is a shift in his tone and manner, thoughts of
night, witchcraft, and wolves crowd upon him, and he envisions
Murder moving like a ghost toward his design. This is his cue to
act, and with a stealthy, felonlike step he crosses to the King's
chamber. The small signal bell sounds twice, off left, and in an
almost imploring voice, he cries:

> Hear—hear it not Duncan, for it is a knell,
> That summons thee to heaven or to hell,

pointing upward and downward.[54] He steps to the door moving
carefully to prevent its creaking,[55] pausing when part way through
so that his left leg and foot remain tremblingly in sight for a
moment, and then disappears. For one observer of the perfor-

mance, "in contrast with the erect, martial figure that entered in the first act, this change was the moral of the play made visible."[56]

The thunder, which had been low and muttering during Macbeth's exit, now bursts with fury, and sheets of rain are heard to beat upon the castle walls. After a long pause, Lady Macbeth enters. Thunder punctuates her speech as she recalls drugging the attendant grooms, and as she reaches the end,

> death and nature so contend about them
> Whether they live or die,

the storm breaks out in fresh fury, and Macbeth's offstage cry and his Lady's speech are muffled by it. Suddenly Macbeth rushes on stage, two daggers clicking like castanets in his hands; he stops, bent backwards as if shot through the breast with an arrow.[57] His face is white, his hands and daggers stained with gore.[58] In a broken and terrifying whisper, he says, "I have done the deed. Didst thou not hear a noise?" He recalls the grooms blessing themselves in their drunken sleep and infuses additional pathos into his own need for blessing by repetition when

> "Amen"
> Stuck—stuck in my throat.[59]

Once again the wife tries to hearten the husband to complete the business, to smear the grooms with the blood that will convict them of murder, but Macbeth is horror-struck. "Look on't again I dare not," he cries and rushes to the right-hand side of the stage, as far as possible from Duncan's door.[60]

Lady Macbeth crosses strongly to him, seizes the daggers, and goes into the King's chamber, shutting the door behind her. Her stricken husband, alone, looks fearfully about, and raises his hand to his head as if to shut out the world.[61] This however is the signal for the world to intrude, there is a storm of knocking at the center gate.[62] Recalled to himself Macbeth now becomes aware of his raised hands, and his lamentations, for his lost innocence become fearfully bitter.[63] As Lady Macbeth returns, he buries his head in his arms. She looks at him aghast, tries her old stratagem of scorn. He ignores her, and shudders at the knocking. She tries to persuade him to put on his night robe and thus avoid suspicion, but he does not hear. Finally she cries,

> Be not lost
> So poorly in your thoughts,

and—touching him for the first time in the scene—seizes him by the hand and shoulder, pulls him toward their room.[64] As they reach the door, Macbeth turns toward the center gate with a savage howl:[65]

Wake Duncan with thy knocking! I would thou couldst!

They exeunt and nothing remains but darkness and the sound of knocking.

The sustained knocking continues at intervals until Seyton, yawning, enters from the right, his plaid trailing on the stage after him, hanging from his left shoulder. He pauses at the first entrance, and then goes lazily to the center door at the back which he unlocks and opens revealing another door beyond. The outer door is then unlocked and he re-enters with Macduff and Lennox.[66]

> *Macduff.* Was it so late, friend, ere you went to bed,
>   That you do lie so late?
> *Seyton.*   Faith sir, we were carousing till the second cock.
> *Macduff.* Is thy master stirring?

So much for the Porter Scene. DeQuincy to the contrary, there is to be no relaxation of the tension.

Macbeth, wrapped in an enormous nightrobe, enters from his apartments on the right. The stage grows lighter as Macduff goes left to awaken the King and Lennox remains to describe the wildness of the night to the murderer. He is interrupted by Macduff's shrill cry of "Horror," from within; and the lights come up still more as Macduff rushes in with the report of the assassination. As Macbeth and Lennox go into the King's chamber, Macduff, crying, "Ring the alarm bell!" rushes up to the center door. The bell responds, a solemn, measured tolling. Macduff's cry of "The great doom's image," is echoed by a buzz of voices off stage, and he rushes about from door to door, beating at them violently with the hilt of his sword.[67] The courtyard fills rapidly with a milling, wondering throng, panting with apprehension, their eyes darting wildly about.[68] Banquo, Fleance, and Ross enter from doors at the left of the gallery, Malcolm, Donalbain and the physician from doors at the right of the gallery. They descend to the courtyard, followed by lords who remain on the stairway. Four officers enter from under the stairs on the right, Seyton and the seneschal are at the right front entrance. Six soldiers enter from the center door and advance two paces on the stage. Behind them are eight servants, some without caps, some with their sheathed swords in their hands, some fastening on weapons, plaids, or portions of their dress.[69] The claymores drawn and glittering in the half-light add to the ominousness of the scene. Meeting Banquo, Macduff exclaims, "Our royal master's murdered!" and the crowd takes up the cry, "Murdered!" At this the officers move to the stairs, as if to confer with the lords, but stop on Macbeth's entering speech.

Macbeth, Act II, Scene i, from Scharf's *Recollections*

Macduff explains to Malcolm and Donalbain that their father is dead and Lennox adds that the guards are suspected. Malcolm and Donalbain, with the physician, exeunt left into the dead King's room.[70] At this point Macbeth reveals that he has killed the guards —there is a general expression of surprise—and that he repents his act, but he speaks so quickly that he gives the impression of hoping no one will hear him or realize the implications of what he has done. To distract attention from her over-protesting husband, Lady Macbeth faints and is carried to her room, and a moment later the situation resolves itself into a spectacular tableau. Banquo pledges to avenge the King, Macduff declares, "And so do I," and the whole mob, except the servants, flashing their claymores in the semi-darkness, echoes them, "So all!" The mob sweeps toward the center door as the quickly closing flats shut them from our view.

The lamps are once more dimmed and the flats withdraw to reveal a wood at the edge of the heath.[71] To a rumble of thunder the first witch enters, down left, singing over his shoulder, "Speak, sister, speak! Is the deed done?" The second witch replies, from offstage, "Long ago, long ago; above twelve glasses since have run," and he enters. The third witch enters from the opposite side, singing that "Many more murders must this one ensue." The fourth witch, entering left, sings "He must—," the first, "He shall," the third, "He will spill much more blood/ And become worse to make his title good." At this, all the singing witches enter from right and left and sing a lengthy, threatening chorus. The number completed, the first witch proposes a dance, to which the third and fifth reply, "Agreed." All the witches raise their wands on the last "Agreed!" and wave them at the word, "Rejoice," sung by the chorus. As the next solo commences, the witches lower their wands and listen attentively to the singer. At each chorus, the wands are brought into action. The song finished, all the witches dance, one facing the other, without making the smallest noise with their feet. The dance finishes with a loud peal of thunder, and the witches instantly turn their backs to the audience, searching the heavens to right and left. The scene concludes with an echo song, "Nimbly, nimbly," during which the entire chorus of witches makes for the wings, stopping and turning on each echo, and then resuming the exit.[72] The last echo falls on an empty stage, and the act drop is lowered.

❖ ❖ ❖ ❖ ❖ ❖ ❖ ❖ ❖

The third act commences with Shakespeare's brief "carpenter's scene," Act II, Scene 4: The Old Man is eliminated and the omens are discussed by Macduff and Ross alone.

The flats are withdrawn to reveal once more the courtyard of the castle. Banquo is alone on the stage as the second scene of the third act begins, considering the apparent fulfillment of the prophecies of the weird sisters. As he takes this as an omen that their prophecies about his future may also be fulfilled ("By the verities on thee made good"), the center doors at the back are opened by Seyton and a new royal procession enters to cut short his soliloquy: six lords, two officers, Seyton, Lennox and Ross, Macbeth and Lady Macbeth, the physician (who seems to go with the crown), and eight ladies. While Macbeth is sending Banquo and his son into the trap he is about to prepare for them, he lays his hand on Fleance's head.[73] Macbeth falls to thinking out loud about his bloody cousins who are "filling their hearers with strange invention," but he is recalled by Lady Macbeth who, fearing his unpracticed skill in such matters, touches his shoulder, and he changes the subject, dismissing Banquo and Fleance to their fate.

Expecting the murderers, he likewise dismisses Lady Macbeth and her attendants to their apartments, down right. As Seyton is about to leave through the center door, Macbeth asks, "Attend those men our pleasure?" and the servant returns down left, then crosses behind Macbeth to the right exit.[74] The murderers who return with him are the former second and third officers of Duncan's army.[75] Seyton, once more crossing behind the actors, exits left. There is no break at the end of the murderers' scene; they leave and Lady Macbeth returns with Seyton. As she enters the lights are slightly dimmed. She is wearing her queenly robes,[76] but the scene is full of pathos and remorse. The new King envies Duncan:

After life's fitful fever *he* sleeps well

is spoken in tones of hopeless yearning, his heavy sigh trembles through the theater.[77] And as Lady Macbeth questions him as to what is to be done with Banquo and Fleance, he turns from her with a furtive look—the guilty man is alone, isolated even from the partner of his crime. He gives a sinister, ill-suppressed laugh:[78]

Be innocent of the knowledge, dearest chuck,
Till thou applaud the deed.

Again there is a change of voice and manner. If in his early bewilderment at the prophecies of the witches there was some of the sensitivity of Hamlet, there is now a smack of Richard III about him. His voice is decided and firm, his manner hard, composed, and full of the terror of almost abstract Evil.[79] For the moment everything is consistent with the image of complete surrender to the weird sisters, but it will not remain constant for long.

The murder of Banquo is played as a kind of emblem of Macbeth's moral condition. The murderers are huddled at the front of the darkened stage when we hear their victim off left call for a light.[80] The murderers quickly hide behind the first wing on the left. Banquo enters with Fleance, bearing a torch, and crosses to the right, pausing at the exit to observe that "It will be rain tonight." As the two go off right, the First Murderer cries, "Let it come down," and the three rush off right. There is a clashing of swords; we hear Banquo within cry, "O, treachery," and see the shadowy form of Fleance make his escape across the stage to the left. As the sounds of the struggle cease, the murderers return, their swords smeared with blood and their leader—we must recall the assassination of Duncan—with his hands and face bloody. But, as in the case of the greater murderer, the act is not final, it

is never done when it is done, and the three grope their way off
stage to carry the news to Macbeth.

The brief, dark "carpenter's scene" of the murder of Banquo
helps to emphasize the spectacular nature of the banquet scene
to follow. After a short musical transition in the orchestra the
curtain rises to reveal a great hall. At the center of the back is a
raised dais with two throne chairs, one on the right for the Queen,
one on the left for Macbeth. A page stands beside each, and below
them, Seyton on the right, and the physician on the left. Directly
before the dais on the floor level is a table, with two chairs at
either end; two more large tables are placed obliquely at either
side of the stage, extending from the middle almost to the footlights. Lennox is seated at the right hand table, on the inside of
the front end, and various guests are distributed in other seats.
At the back, on either side, are groups of soldiers. The tables are
piled high with most splendid fruits, and gorgeous dish covers
glitter in endless perspective.[81] Servants, gathered at the center
table, move to right and left to serve the banqueters and music
adds to the high festivity of the beginning.

Macbeth, wearing a crown and a crimson tunic over a white
kerseymere shirt,[82] comes down from the throne to the center table
among his guests. As he bids them a hearty welcome, the nobles
sit, first bowing to Lady Macbeth. Observing that both sides are
even, he carelessly draws toward him a chair which had been
placed on the center trap of the stage. Before he can sit, however,
the first murderer enters on the right and slinks to the front left
corner of the stage. Macbeth crosses to him and learns of the
death of Banquo and the escape of Fleance.[83] Lady Macbeth,
speaking from her throne, reminds him of his royal duties and
he returns to the left of the center table. During the Queen's
speech, Seyton and three servants have returned from waiting on
the side tables and, at the right end of the center table, meet the
other officers who come down with cups and salvers to be filled
for further serving.[84] Behind this group the ghost of Banquo,
covered with blood, rises through a trap door and sits on the chair
at the right end of the center table. Macbeth fills a huge beaker
from a wine jug and drinks to the health of the company. Lennox
begs him to sit, and the servants draw apart and begin waiting on
the side tables. Macbeth puts down his beaker and remarks that
"The table's full." But Lennox points to the chair Macbeth had
moved at the right. As Macbeth stares at it, Banquo slowly turns
his chalky face towards the King, revealing a vermilion gash across
his throat. "Which of you have done this?" cries the King, and

instantly all the noise of festivity ceases as the company turn to look at him. Ross bids them rise, and they quickly get to their feet; but the Queen orders them to sit, and on her reassurance they slowly resume their stools, their eyes fixed on Macbeth. The King meanwhile has been shuddering and trembling before the glance of the avenging spirit and endeavoring to shield his eyes from a sight that almost seems to burn them.[85] His wife crosses down to him from her throne and, taking his right hand, asks, "Are you a man?" and endeavors to pour courage into him by pointing out, "You look but on a *chair*." At this, Banquo rises. "Prithee see there! behold! look! lo!" cries the King, and the company follows his pointing hand. Macbeth's courage begins to return, his voice hardens, his body tenses, and he gazes boldly on the ghost.[86]

> Why, what care I? If thou canst nod, speak too.
> If charnel houses and our graves must send
> Those that we bury back, our monuments
> Shall be the maws of kites.

During this scornful speech, Banquo moves slowly backward and off the stage near the proscenium on the right. Macbeth, still shaken, clutches the empty chair with his left hand, to support his slumping body.[87]

Lady Macbeth goes upstage to draw the attention of the guests from her husband. He comes forward to muse upon ghostly revengers, and the servants move, four to the right, three to the left, one staying at the center table to pour wine. Once again reminded of his duties by his wife, Macbeth seizes a goblet, which an attendant quickly advances to fill, and pledges the company a second time, with significant and apprehensive glances at the empty chair,[88]

> I drink to th' general joy o' the whole table,
> And to our dear friend Banquo, whom we miss;
> Would he were here!

Banquo reenters through the group of servants on the left, but Macbeth does not see him, and continues,

> to all and him we thirst,
> And all to all.

As the company returns the pledge, Macbeth's eyes fall upon the ghost, and he recoils in horror, adjuring with breathless agony, "Avaunt and quit my sight."

Lady Macbeth tries to calm the assembly, and at her bidding they reluctantly sit, some staring at Macbeth, some at his wife.

Shrinking, Macbeth turns away from the ghost, and as it slowly withdraws once more, sinks into the empty chair, burying his face convulsively in his mantle as if to shut out sight, sense, and recollection.[89] His lament that his cheeks are blanched with fear brings the lords once more to their feet, but Lady Macbeth now urges them to depart. They are quick to obey, bowing, of course, and looking distrustfully at the King as they go off right and left. The Queen curtseys to them while Macbeth recalls that murder will out and then lays plans for the defense of his shaky position in a new, hardened manner.[90] "We are but yet," he says firmly, "young in deed." Still musing, he exits left, leaving his wife to follow as best she may.

The whole scene has presented a vivid contrast between the rich, royal, joyful setting and situation, and the acts of madness played against it, a contrast that serves to emphasize the horror of Macbeth's position.

The flats in the first groove close over the banquet scene and are covered by a gauze clouding behind which a dark canvas cloud is lowered.[91] The flats are then withdrawn to display clouds as far as the fourth grooves. Hecate rises through the grave trap, front and center, on a set piece which is immediately lowered as she steps onto the stage. During her speech her name is called by spirits under the stage and high up in the flies. The clouding slowly ascends and at the back of the stage a practicable cloud car with four white-clad children as spirits is lowered from above. The Chorus, "Come away, come away", is hollow and unearthly, rather than pretty-grotesque, the conventional effect aimed for in the witches' music.[92] At the end of the song, Hecate steps into her car, which immediately begins a slow rise. When it is two feet from the stage floor, the cloudings that fill the stage are drawn off, displaying a bird's-eye view of the country with a transparent winding river softly glowing in the moonlight. The final chorus, farther off, fades into silence[93] and the act drop is lowered.

❖ ❖ ❖ ❖ ❖ ❖ ❖ ❖ ❖

The first scene of the fourth act reveals a dark and dreary cavern. The weird sisters are on stage, one at the mouth of the cavern, intently on watch, one cowering over the livid flame flickering beneath a caldron, and the third on the opposite side of the stage, seated on a jut of stone, his arms folded, rocking to and fro in impatience. In the expectant silence not a word is spoken. Then from offstage comes a cat-call and the first witch hisses, "Thrice the brinded cat hath mewed." The eyes of the other witches are

Macbeth, Act III, from Scharf's *Recollections*

instantly turned toward him: they listen intently, motionless. The witch at the caldron hears his familiar; he starts from his cowering attitude: "Thrice; and once the hedge-pig whines." Another pause, and silence. At length the third witch springs to his feet: "Harper cries!" and then, exulting, to his fellows: " 'Tis time! 'Tis time!"[94] They join hands and circle the caldron, speaking slowly so as to make a complete turn on each repetition of "Double",

> Double, double, toil and trouble;
> Fire burn and caldron bubble.

At these words they poke the fire under the caldron and at the end of the incantation wave their wands over it twice. Suddenly Hecate appears through an opening in the right flat. The witches turn and kneel to her, then rise, after which the whole tribe of witches appear from the right and form four concentric circles around the caldron, covering the entire stage area. As they sing, the witches circle in opposite directions:

First witch. Here's the blood of a bat. (She advances to the caldron.)
Hecate (at the back). O! put in that, put in that.
Second witch. Here's a lizard's brain. (Advances to the caldron.)
Hecate. Put in a grain.
Third witch. Here's juice of toad, here's oil of adder,
> Which will make the charm grow madder.
  (Advances to the cauldron.)

As each witch makes her individual contribution, the entire chorus turns and looks closely at the singer. Then extending their wands directly to the cauldron, still in their circles, the Chorus sings:

> Put in all these, 'twill raise the stench.

The third witch comes once more to the cauldron, bidding them hold. They draw back their wands. "Here's three ounces of a red-hair'd wench," and the Chorus resumes its circling and counter-circling of the cauldron until the second witch's thumbs announce a visitor. The witches divide to the right and left, close to the entrances. There is a series of heavy knocks, and the choral witches vanish, leaving the original three to confront Macbeth.

He enters without his kingly robes. He is dressed in a tartan skirt with a tartan scarf over a padded flannel vest, but his beret has been replaced by a coronet cap with feather.[95] He orders them to give grounds more relative for their ambiguous prophecies of the first act and they offer to let him hear the truth from the mouths of their masters. This too offers opportunity for spectacle. The stage is darkened, soft music is played in the background and, as each apparition appears to predict the future history of Scotland, there is a strong flash of light, the back of the cavern splits open, and the figure is seen, brightly lighted in billowing clouds.[96] Macbeth is at first thunderstruck by the clear meaning of the visions, then taking heart from the prediction that no man born of woman can harm him assumes the hardness that has twice enabled him to carry out his dark purposes and resolves on the slaughter of the innocents at Castle Macduff. The audience, however, is spared the horror of seeing the event.[97]

The sleep-walking scene is, by contrast, simply staged. A room in the castle, with a small table at the left to hold the taper that Lady Macbeth carries in, a convenient alcove at the right for the physician and gentlewoman to hide in. Lady Macbeth enters on the right, being careful to give the idea of sleep, not insanity, walking with a heavy and inelastic step, speaking with a muffled voice and gesturing mechanically.[98]

❖ ❖ ❖ ❖ ❖ ❖ ❖ ❖ ❖

Drums and trumpets announce the final movement, as Macbeth reading a letter enters with his attendants. "Bring me no more reports," he cries, tearing the letter and throwing it off stage. A proud expression of haughty self-complacency is implicit in his bearing, his head thrown back, his lip curling with scorn, and he asks, "What's the *boy*, Malcolm? Was he not born of woman?" But a moment later, when the cream-faced loon has brought information of the approach of the English forces, Macbeth sinks into deep and melancholy pathos, "I have lived long enough . . ." his whole body relaxing, as nerveless as his mind.[99] This mood passes, however, as Seyton brings him news that arouses his determination. "Give me mine armour!" he thunders imperiously; then, seeing the physician, suddenly alters his tone and manner to ask colloquially, "How does your patient, doctor?" The contrast is extreme, but reminds the audience that beneath the martial and imperial exterior there is a simple and loving husband, distraught about his wife. After the physician has replied that her illness is not in the body but in the mind, Macbeth strides back to Seyton to have his armour buckled on, turning in intervals of stormy chiding which suggest almost the ravings of a madman to direct inquiries in a calmer tone to the physician, and at the last, rushing off to meet the approaching foe.[100]

In his next scene, Macbeth enters with Seyton and some of his soldiers, throwing his brag at the enemy:

> Our castle's strength
> Will laugh a siege to scorn; here let them lie
> Till famine and the ague eat them up.

He has wound up his courage to the highest pitch once more, only to be shaken, first by the cry of women within, then by Seyton's report of the Queen's death. His baton falls to the stage, hinting at his grief and suggesting that his hold on his position is perilously uncertain. For a moment he stands silent, the very muscles of his face slackened,[101] and then begins,

> She should have died hereafter;
> There would have been a time for such a word.

A pause, then,

> Tomorrow,—and tomorrow,—and tomorrow

slowly and haltingly at first, conveying the agony of his mind; then as if struck with the thought which follows, he goes rapidly through the famous passage. There is no excitement in the reading, only a withering calm, a controlled agony. His voice is chill with despair, his look blank and desolate.[102]

He is interrupted by the messenger who comes to report that Birnam Wood is moving towards Dunsinane. Macbeth responds with a maddened roar, "Liar and slave," he cries, half drawing his sword over the trembling form of the terrified messenger who has fallen to his knees. But this is the second blow to the King's

determination. For a second time he wavers in irresolution, beginning "To doubt the equivocation of the fiend that lies like truth."
But he manages to recover sufficiently to end the scene with a
ringing defiance of his foes:

> Blow, wind! come, wrack!
> At least we'll die with harness on our back.

The flats withdraw and show the entire depth of the stage, at
the back a set scene of wooded hills.[103] Malcolm appears to be
alone on the stage, standing in a thicket. Four trumpets sound, one
after the other, from the front to the back of the stage. At Malcolm's command, the trees suddenly disappear, becoming five
officers and eighteen soldiers. At the same moment, the carpenters
release a series of flaps on the set piece. The painted trees vanish
and the hills are seen to be alive with (painted) soldiers.

All, however, is but preparation for the climactic moment of the
production: the death-duel between Macduff and Macbeth. The
scene is on the ramparts of the castle, with a great iron gate in
the background.[104] Macbeth enters, determining not to commit
suicide. As he crosses to the left, the gates are burst open with a
tremendous shout, and Macduff rushes in, down left, and throws
himself on guard[105] crying, "Turn, hellhound, turn!" Macbeth
tries to warn him off, but Macduff advances against him with four
blows to the head; they lock swords, reverse positions, and Macbeth
flings him away with an expression of ineffable contempt.[106] His
bearing is self-confident, he holds his sword with careless ease,
his head drawn back, his lip sneering, as he reveals that his life
is charmed and will not yield to one of woman born. Macduff
counters with the story of his nativity, that he was "Untimely
ripped" from his mother's womb, and the effect upon Macbeth
is wondrous. Struck with utter dismay, he stands gazing upon his
enemy in breathless horror as if all the sinews of his frame had
relaxed at one moment.[107] "I'll not fight with thee!" he cries, and
retreats towards the castle.

Macduff's taunts of "Coward" and "Show and gaze o' th' time"
awaken in him his martial ardor. He turns upon his fate and
stands at bay.[108] His eye kindles, his bosom swells, his head is up-
reared in defiance, and, "deserted by fate and metaphysical aid,"
he summons up his honest power to fight and die like a hero. Six
times the swordsmen rush upon each other with a cut and lunge;
closely engaged they fight round in a cartwheel six times. Macduff
cuts at Macbeth's head, misses, and the force of the blow carries
him across stage to the right. Macbeth pursues, they lunge at each

Macbeth, Act V: Macready (center) as Macbeth and Wallack as Macduff

other five times, and on the sixth lunge Macduff delivers the death stab.

Macbeth staggers back, catches himself and, with a momentary suggestion of his regal stride, returns, only to fall on Macduff's sword in yielding weakness. The spirit fights, but the body sinks in mortal faintness. Thrusting his own sword into the ground, Macbeth raises himself by its help to his knees where he stares full in the face of his vanquisher with a resolute and defiant gaze of concentrated majesty, hate, and knowledge,[109] and instantly falls dead.

Malcolm and the thanes enter with banners and accompanying trumpet flourishes. To the general cry of "hail, King of Scotland," the curtain falls.

Afterpiece

ASYLUM FOR A TRAGEDIAN—a retired Hamlet.
Dorset County Chronicle, 24 December, 1857.

ONE MORE ordeal remained after the final benefit, the public banquet on March first. Organized by Dickens, with his usual delight in such occasions, it was attended by six hundred persons and a list of "stewards" which was an artistic who's who of the day. Prince Albert had gracefully declined the chairmanship, declaring that he never appeared for private individuals but only for institutions—which Macready no doubt felt himself to be—and Bulwer-Lytton took over with his most eulogistic fervor. In proposing the name of the hero of the evening, he gave a summary and criticism of his career, printed verbatim in the Pollock edition of the *Diaries,* which is at once generous and just. Macready replied with an extension of his farewell speech at Drury Lane, urging once more that other producers take up the work of restoration that he had started, and, with special words of commendation, "establishing his estate" upon Samuel Phelps, the actor-manager who in eight years had converted Sadler's Wells from a home of melodrama to a temple of Shakespeare.

There were other toasts and speeches from W. J. Fox, Charles Kemble, Chevalier Bunsen, Dickens, and Forster. For the overcrowded hall most of the speeches seemed overlong, many were inaudible, and Thackeray ("The health of Mrs. Macready and her family") chose to exhibit a humorous turn "at least not appropriate to a festive occasion."[1] But all was borne with good will and Forster created a sensation by reciting an unscheduled but dutiful production of the muse of the Poet Laureate, Lord Tennyson:

> Farewell, Macready, since to-night we part;
>   Full-handed thunders often have confessed
>   Thy power, well-used to move the public breast.
> We thank thee with our voice, and from the heart.
> Farewell, Macready, since this night we part;

> Go, take thine honors home; rank with the best,
> Garrick and statelier Kemble, and the rest
> Who made a nation purer through their art.
> Thine is it that our drama did not die,
> Nor flicker down to brainless pantomime,
> And those gilt gauds men-children swarm to see.
> Farewell, Macready; moral, grave, sublime;
> Our Shakespeare's bland and universal eye
> Dwells pleased, through twice a hundred years, on thee.

Perhaps no less conventional as a measure of the Eminent Tragedian's status as Eminent Victorian was his appearance in wax effigy in "Madame Tussaud and Son's Great Room." Here, as Exhibit 94, Coriolanus, "in the most splendid Roman costume ever seen in this country,"[2] he was enshrined in a more popular if less permanent memorial than he had so long sought for Sarah Siddons. If he was aware of the honor, he does not seem to have commented upon it.

Indeed, he was under the impression that he had left the distasteful theatre forever. When it was suggested that he might return to the stage, his reply was firm: "A certain space of life, a certain amount of duty to be done, is apportioned to each of us, and when that space has been occupied and our obligations to duty discharged, the shelter of a quiet home has more of real respectability, I think, than the repeated returns to public life, which public characters too often make." He had never forgotten his first visits to a London theatre, when he had witnessed the decayed grandeur of John Kemble who had clung too long to his profession; he had once spent an evening of torment playing opposite Mrs. Orger when she had been coaxed out of retirement and was more concerned with the security of her wig than the consistency of her characterization;[3] most certainly he recalled the fatal weakness of his idol, Mrs. Siddons, who could not resist the temptations of flattery or avarice and displayed herself in performances which were fragmented burlesques of her most famous interpretations.

In his determination to put such temptations out of reach he had resolved to leave not only the stage but London itself. Having disposed of his costumes, his personal properties, even his promptbooks, he next undertook a symbolic casting off of his circle of acquaintances. He made farewell visits to Procter, Bulwer-Lytton, Douglas Jerrold, Samuel Rogers, and Abbott Lawrence who was then visiting in England. As he came away from the last call he acknowledged to himself that for the first time he had been meeting his fellows on common ground, without the stigma of his

degrading profession, a goal toward which his life had been
directed. The society and conversation of these men had been
one of his major pleasures, but he was about to take a step which
would sharply reduce the occasions when that society would be
available. London, like the theatre, he placed behind him—or
meant to—writing to a correspondent in 1861, "You would be
surprised to remark how entirely theatrical subjects have lost
their interest with me. The past is a dream, so little has been the
result derived from it."[4]

Macready's decision to retire to the village of Sherborne was
reached within six months of his flight from New York. The
reasons for his choice were thoroughly in character. Sherborne, he
wrote to Bulwer, was an isolated community "nestled down to
an everlasting doze in one of the valleys of Dorsetshire, where
there are, as my temptations, one of Edward 6th's endowed schools,
and some monastic remains, which are very superior specimens
of Gothic architecture, an epitaph of Pope's in a beautiful church,[5]
and certain traditions of Raleigh." The scholar, gentleman, and
responsible paterfamilias could hardly ask for more. But more
there was, a beautiful and historic mansion. He described it to
Bulwer with proper modesty: "In addition to the notabilia, there
is an old-fashioned house, large enough to be an ark for us all—
and what have I to do with more?—My large little family will
not let me want occupation there; and except in aiding and
preparing them for the world, whose evening shades will be
beginning to close around me, I may say with Pope, that there

> 'life with little else supply,
> But just to look about us, and to die.' "[6]

In spite of the passive and rather gloomy text which he had
selected for his retirement, Macready was only in his fifty-eighth
year when he left the stage. He could not know, of course, that
twenty years still remained ahead of him in which he was to look
often upon death, though not the death he anticipated, but he
should have known that he would not look long upon the "everlasting doze" of Sherborne without stirring it awake.

At first he was content to play the country gentleman. It was
the conventional behavior of the early Victorians who had made
their fortunes to retire to country homes, for the rural aristocracy
still had traditions of dignity and respectability which the city had
not yet developed. The "old-fashioned house" was a large Georgian
building erected by the Portman family as a resting place between
their country residence and London. Macready seems to have

rented it from the Digbys, the ruins of whose ancestral castle can be seen from the upper floor, together with a fine view of the Abbey which so attracted him. It is a house that must have, in every way, satisfied his tastes: the exterior is severely unostentatious, the entrance hall, high-ceilinged and with a noble fireplace, has a kind of modest elegance, and the staircase is decorated with murals in the approved state of neoclassic suspended animation by Thornhill. Always aware of its origins as a halfway house for a great county family, Macready described his new home as reduced to "the hermitage of one of the world's worn out pilgrims,"[7] but his activities belie his pose. In view of those activities, he would doubtless rejoice to find that it is now occupied by Lord Digby's School for Girls.

Seen from the twentieth century, Sherborne is inevitably colored by familiarity with Barchester. The High Street, beginning in the Vale of Blackmore, rises slowly past an almshouse which boasts an altarpiece by Van Eyck, past the King's School where a gilded statue of young Edward superintends the refectory, past the Abbey and Monk's well (what must have been thought of as the dissenting Chapel is on one of the few tributary streets), to a cluster of inns which principally accommodate the buyers and sellers at the weekly market. In Macready's day, Sherborne, like its High Street, was chiefly concerned with school, church, and market; its expected excitements were connected with the local hunt, the volunteer rifles, and the agricultural prize-giving, its unexpected thrills were provided by runaway horses, carriage accidents, and such law-breakers as might receive four years' penal servitude for stealing a piece of cheese.[8]

The Digbys were seldom in evidence, but their functions as leaders and ring-givers were eagerly assumed by Sir William Medlycott who could with equal enthusiasm organize a platoon, slaughter game, award a blue ribbon, chair a literary meeting, or invoke Jingo. Macready, from his great house overlooking the village, soon found his own place in the hierarchy. He became a warden of the Abbey Church and took a stand on tithes and the impropriety of altar candlesticks. He joined the board of the Sherborne Literary Institution and for several years arranged the dozen annual lectures which it sponsored. He displayed a proper responsibility to the poor of his community: in accord with a custom he had established at Elstree he donated funds that they might purchase coal at half price during the Christmas season, and in 1859 he willingly joined a committee to establish a Penny Bank for the working classes. To the former Hamlet, thrift was more than an ironic catchword.

For if Macready had left London society and the theatre behind
him, he had quite deliberately taken his principles with him to
Sherborne, and—perhaps to the chagrin of his new neighbors—he
lost no time in asserting them. He entered two of his sons in the
King's School then under the direction of the Reverend Hugo D.
Harper who, at 27, was experienced neither as a disciplinarian nor
diplomat. When it was discovered that a volume in the school
library had been defaced, the headmaster announced that he was
prepared to hear a confession or receive information. Since neither
was forthcoming after a reasonable time, he fined each schoolboy
a penny and ruled that each should write out a long "punishment."
To one who had been educated under the ever-present threat of
the birch rod such disciplinary action would appear mild and
rational. But a principle was a principle. Macready, in the stiff
third-person style which he had reserved for such malefactors as
Bunn and journalists out of favor, informed the young headmaster
by letter that he would not permit his boys to pay the two pennies
or to write out the punishment. Although he followed this with
a less formal note giving as his reasons that his boys had not
committed the offense, and that the Reverend Hugo's strategy
tempted the students to betray their fellows, the headmaster was
so flustered by his crusty opponent that he fled to the protection
of his board of governors. Thus, as so often in the actor's career,
a small matter became an issue and both parties passed the point
of no return. The governors had little choice but to back the
Headmaster and Macready had no alternative but to withdraw his
sons from the school and undertake their education himself.[9]

The decision was a matter of principle, to be sure, but it was
not without another kind of satisfaction for him. He had always
been fascinated by education. In Boston he had made a curtain
speech on the public school system, praising America and wishing
that England might follow her lead. He had devoted the year
before his marriage to the proper education of his wife, and he
had been something of a martinet where his children's studies were
concerned; he had been head boy at Rugby and no little Macready
was permitted to forget it. Thus, there is personal satisfaction in
his declaration to W. J. Fox: "I am very busy just now having my
house full of pupils and my head so full of languages that it is a
miniature babel."[10] His youngest son, Nevil, recollects his father's
pedagogical methods:

I can see myself now, a small, fat boy, at one end of the library, which
seemed a very big room; my father, his white head slightly bent, in
his easy chair at the other end of the room. The piece chosen was 'The

Vision of Mirza,' beautiful English, but somewhat wearisome to a small boy once he had mastered the allegory. As a start I had to open my mouth three times till the jaw cracked. Then at each syllable the jaw-cracking experience was repeated, the tongue and lips being moved to ensure the correct enunciation of each letter. Having repeated a sentence several times in this manner, syllable by syllable, I was allowed to read it through without the jaw-cracking operation, though constantly stopped by such remarks as: 'I cannot hear the "d" in "and." '[11]

Macready's principles of education, centering on the outmoded art of "elocution," must appear reactionary to the graduates of modern teacher-training schools. But they were based on conviction and experience. As he once told the audience assembled to hear him read from the poets, "The study of the art to which my life has been devoted certainly gives—sometimes at least—a clearer and deeper insight into the poet's meaning, and furnishes a more prompt and forcible expression of it than casual and unpractised readers may usually be able to command, and furnishes perhaps illustrations of the text, by tone and inflection, more distinct and satisfactory occasionally, than even the most lengthened and elaborate comment. We are often made sensible of particular habits of thought and language by hearing them from another's voice, when they would fail to affect and impress themselves on our minds by the page beneath our eyes."[12] There is not a little to be said for this defense of the now lost art of reading aloud.

Five years after his retirement Macready found an outlet for both his interest in education and his missionary zeal. On July 7, 1839, he had written in his diary, after recording his disgust with a Sunday sermon, "what a benevolent and rational man might do with the high resolve of devoting himself to the improvement of the condition, moral and intellectual, of his fellow men!" In 1846, he discovered his medium; he accepted invitations to read *Macbeth* to mechanics institutions at Warrington and Manchester.[13] Mechanics and Workingmen's "Institutes" were the nineteenth-century equivalents of adult education. Founded by public-spirited citizens and supported by private funds, they provided factory and farm workers, fathers and children together, with useful knowledge. During the early years of his retirement Macready willingly gave his services as a reader to workingmen's schools and the Literary Institutions (much like the American Lyceums of the day) which were their parents in Birmingham, Warminster, Bristol, Bridport and Sherborne. So frequent and well-received were his appearances that a London journalist was able to use them in an attack on Dickens: "MR. CHARLES DICKENS has been reading his own works in the metropolis for money, and MR. MACREADY has been delivering lectures on Shakespeare in the provinces for charity."[14]

In the year of Macready's retirement there were 610 Mechanics Institutes in England and Scotland with over 100,000 members.[15] If they sometimes, as Hazlitt suggested, confounded knowledge of useful things with useful knowledge,[16] and if they were forced to accommodate their programs to the twelve-hour working day of factory children and the seasonal employment of farmers, they at least recognized, as the state resolutely refused to do, that ignorance in the "operative classes" was a major obstacle to progress.

During the winter of 1855–56, Macready was director of the Sherborne Literary Institution. From the Rooms of that society, on April 21, he issued a proposal for establishing an Evening School for the Industrial Classes to be supported as in America by the community at large rather than by the private gifts of members of the Institution. It was, he declared, "the Christian duty" of the community to make the children "intelligent men, RESPONSIBLE FOR THEIR CONDUCT." To attract and hold scholars, he further proposed a "remuneratory plan" whereby fifty boys would study three nights a week for at least five months under a competent master, assisted by members of the Committee and the Vice President of the Literary Institution in rotation as "weekly visitors." Each scholar would pay a penny a week as a fee, but there would be rewards for punctuality, good conduct, and proficiency.

From the first, and for as long as Macready's time and energy could be devoted to it (the neighboring gentry maintained their disinterest), the school was a success. A meeting place was found in the parish rooms of the Wesleyan Methodist Chapel, a respectable hall but safely on the other side of the High Street from the King's School. At the end of the first year a deputation from the masters and pupils presented the founder with an illuminated testimonial of gratitude.[17] The state Inspector for Schools spread a different, but more gratifying, report on the record. He found the Sherborne establishment the best evening school he had visited, with more than eighty boys whose ages ranged from ten to twenty years, but averaging eighteen. Attendance was regular, cheerful, and spontaneous, but more impressive, for him, than the efficiency of the school and the docility and attainments of the pupils was the spectacle of their head teacher punctually devoting himself to teaching "the children of a few Dorsetshire labourers the humblest rudiments of that language whose sublimest creations his genius had been for many years accustomed to interpret to successive thousands of cultivated listeners." The Inspector modestly denies his own ability to expound the moral significance of the occasion, but several editors, quoting his report, were ready to extrapolate the obvious.[18]

Thus the early years which Macready had intended to devote to looking about him were full of the kind of busyness for which he thought he had yearned: governing his family, assisting his fellow men, and rigidly proclaiming his satisfaction that the theatre was a thing of the buried past. His public readings were from the poets, not the dramatists, and generally from those poets who had little contact with the stage: selections from *Paradise Lost,* Dryden's "Song for St. Cecilia's Day," the story of Le Fevre from *Tristram Shandy,* and Pope's "The Dying Christian to His Soul." An observer records that the last piece was read "with a variety of tone, inflection and modulation which placed the whole vividly before every auditor and brought tears into many eyes. The last two lines were a striking portraiture of the triumph of the spirit over the failing flesh; they were delivered in a somewhat high pitch of voice, but still not that of earthly vigor but of spiritual strength, and their jubilant tones thrilled to the heart of the hushed listeners, who seemed spellbound under the magic utterance."[19] Macready confessed to W. J. Fox that "in distrust of my own reasoning I endeavoured to bring the resources of my own art to play," and that the effect of "The Dying Christian" was "quite like one of the happy minutes of 'the old times.'" But he resolutely backed away from what he had achieved: "If I make further ventures in this way, I think, I must not step out of the 'charmed circle' of these elocutionary effects."[20] The beloved art would not be separated from the despised profession and both continued to assert their rights to his attention.

Nor could he wholly sever his connection with the London society he thought he had abandoned. As chairman of the Literary Institution he provided the members with an amazing array of lectures for so remote a village by persuading his literary friends to make the arduous trip from London. The townsfolk were thus able to hear Forster, the Rev. James White, Thackeray speaking on George III,[21] and Dickens reading one of his Christmas stories. And Macready was able for a few days' time to experience the pleasures he had once cherished almost above all others, intellectual debate and a sophisticated audience for his regular family readings. Frederick Pollock recalls one such occasion:

It is impossible to conceive anything more magnificent than the Milton reading was—such thoughts, such language, and so enunciated. The voice was like a pealing organ, with stop after stop, as it were, pulled out in succession, until the sound rolled forth in a full tide of power and beauty. The Hamlet surpassed all that I had supposed possible in that way. Much, of course, is lost by the abscence of all stage effect, but, on the other hand, much is gained by having every part finely rendered. Polonious is no longer a buffoon, Laertes becomes a gentleman, and Horatio a fit companion for Hamlet. The Ghost was very grand, and the effect was increased by the expression of the face and fixed stare of the eye, from which you will collect that the performance was not addressed to the ear alone, but within certain well-chosen limits also depended on the face of the reader being seen. It was curious how one missed the applause and movement which accompanies the entrance of Hamlet in the theatre, and how familiarly unfamiliar the well-known voice fell upon the ear during the first sentences of the part of Hamlet, in consequence of not hearing it then for the first time in the piece as one did when the play was acted; and yet how much more true it was that Hamlet not be the only gentleman and the only person of courtly bearing at the Court of Denmark, as he generally was on the stage.[22]

For these readings Macready prepared as carefully as if they were first performances in a new role and, as Pollock notices, will-he nill-he, they were not prepared for the ear alone.

He maintained a large correspondence with his old acquaintance both in and out of the theatre. To Samuel Phelps he sent praise for his production of *A Midsummer Night's Dream* and advice on preparing his son for a career as a public servant, and searched his mind for a political friend who might do the boy good.[23] When Mrs. Warner became ill and destitute, he was one of the first to come to her assistance and supervised the upbringing of her son after her death.[24] Alexander Dyce consulted him before the publication of his *Notes on Shakespeare*,[25] and Lady Pollock persuaded him into an exchange of letters on Shakespeare's characters. Dickens submitted a draft of an article for criticism and gently rallied him about his reluctance to include dramatic passages in his public readings:

My dear old Parr, I don't believe a word you write about King John. I don't believe you take into account the enormous difference between the energy summonable-up in your study at Sherborne, and the energy that will fire up in you (without so much as saying "with your leave" or "by your leave") in the Town Hall at Birmingham. I know you, you ancient codger, I know you! Therefore I will trouble you to be so good as to do an act of honesty after you have been to Birmingham, and to write to me, 'Ingenuous boy, you were correct. I find I could read 'em King John with the greatest ease'. . . .

I think of opening the next book I write, with a man of juvenile figure and strong face, who is always persuading himself that he is infirm. What do you think of the idea? . . . I should make him an impetuous passionate sort of fellow—devilish grim upon occasion—and of an iron purpose.[26]

Macready may indeed have felt like Old Parr, the almost legendary English Methuselah, who long outlived his generation. Two years after the death of Nina, his first-born, death took from him his wife and with the same dread instrument, tuberculosis, which caused him to fear (and with reason) for the rest of his family. In the next year grief and apprehension were increased by the death of his youngest son, Walter. Although his friends marveled at his patient endurance and despaired at his determination to remain in Sherborne, he was once again in the grip of a duty willingly assumed. Indeed, the determination with which he threw himself into his community responsibilities may have been in some part an escape from his personal sorrow. But when, in 1857, his son Henry fell prey to his mother's disease and in the next year his youngest daughter, Lydia, and a few months later his constant companion through life, his sister Letitia, he must have felt the urgency in a note from Dickens:

I think you *must* come to London and bring the children with you. I have said this so often to Forster that I cannot help saying it now to you. You ought to be near us, and more of us, and among us. For your own sake, because our affectionate companionship might lighten your load; for ours, because it is so sad to us to think of you away down there.[27]

Macready, however, clung to his determined course for another two years. "The dullness of Sherborne," he wrote stubbornly to Lady Pollock, "is a sort of Elysium" compared to his Covent Garden management.[28] In the spring of 1860 he gave a reading from the English poets to liquidate all existing claims on the Wesleyan Chapel and startled his acquaintances and those in the great world who remembered him by announcing his marriage on April 3 to Cecile Louise Spencer, twenty-three years old, an intimate friend of his daughter Katie. Among the bride's virtues was the fact that she had only once in her life, at the age of six, attended a theatre. John Forster lost no time in pointing out the unsuitability of the match, but as the bridegroom wrote to his devoted friend, Lady Pollock: "I am quite aware that the change I have made in my home may be subject to varieties of opinion; but I have, in deliberating upon it, satisfied myself that a judgement formed without knowledge of the conditions under which such a change has been decided upon, cannot be worth attention. . . . I hope in God you will never experience the loneliness of a widowed home."[29]

He had, in fact, chosen wisely. At Cecile's insistence the Sherborne home was abandoned and the family moved to a small house on Wellington Square in Cheltenham. The second wife was all that the first could not be, a well-educated intellectual companion, a woman of no nonsense and considerable charm. If she did not invite the romantic raptures with which Macready had surrounded his "heart's darling," the beloved Catherine, she was a patient companion and nurse. And when, in his sixty-ninth year she bore him a son, even Forster was compelled to admit his error in condemning the marriage.[30]

The public, however, had seen the last of him. Though he occasionally visited London, it was to consult with his own or his children's physicians. News of the theatre he was content to receive from Dickens or the Pollocks. In 1862 he rejected a request to read in Bath: "I have now no tones left to answer the emotions that seek expression through the voice."[31] But those who came to call were sure to involve him in a discussion of the text or the characters of Shakespeare, and, despite himself, he would find that his arguments always turned upon theatrical effectiveness. As an instance, a group was discussing Macduff's grief-stricken cry after hearing that his wife and children had been murdered by Macbeth: "He has no children." Several interpretations were suggested, each depending on "He" referring to Macbeth. But Macready held that "He" referred to Macduff himself, who was dwelling in abstraction upon his own desolation and refusing to heed what was said to him. This interpretation Macready declared was "capable of the most effect on the stage, and . . . convey[ed] the most pathetic signification."[32] Although at least one member of the group recognized the wayward grammar involved in such reasoning, pathos and stage effectiveness were accepted as overriding virtues.

Quiet though life in Cheltenham was, Macready was able to look forward to one climactic event. Of all his children, Katie had always been closest to his heart and mind. To see her happily and suitably married, and to a man who would appreciate and encourage her poetic talent, might well be the last business of his earthly career, and it was with great satisfaction that he heard her reveal her engagement to the eldest son of Bulwer-Lytton. However, since she was to winter in Madeira to try to build up strength to throw off the "colds" to which she was subject, she decided that no public announcement should be made until her return in the spring. Throughout the dreary winter months, Macready awaited her return and the marriage that would unite his family with that of his ancient collaborator. Katie's letters were bright and full of plans for the future; Madeira as a health resort was all that could be wished. For her return in April 1869 the family made extraordinary preparations. Macready, who now seldom left home, undertook the journey to Plymouth with his wife to welcome her. They were waiting on the quay as the ship put in, and as soon as the gangplank was fast, not Katie but the captain himself came down, drew Macready to one side, and told him that Miss Macready had come on board in seeming good health, that she had been a most lively and charming passenger, and then a week out from Madeira one night had a series of hemorrhages, died within a few hours, and was buried at sea.[33]

Macready never recovered from the shock and grief of this revelation. He had borne with dutiful patience the deaths of a wife and six children, he had devoted his professional life to an art that was written on the wind and his retirement to schemes that ended in defeat. He refused longer to endure, longer to persevere. Without a struggle he allowed his body to slip into senility.

As his years increased he had, without willing it, lived more and more in the theatre of his past. Priscilla Horton—now more famous as Mrs. German Reed—came to visit and sang one of Ariel's songs in *The Tempest*. The memories which it awakened, of departed friends, of "the public leaning to me, so earnest in their enthusiasm," brought tears to his eyes. He spent long hours of every day poring over the texts of his favorite plays; and experimenting with new readings and interpretations. And towards the end of his life even this was denied him. Increasing feebleness deprived him of the power of reading, or even holding, a book. One day his wife came upon him sitting alone in his study and smiling to himself. "I have been over Hamlet," he said, raising a trembling hand to his temple, "here." He could remember the whole play, every word, every pause, and he added—true to his principles of acting to the last—"the very *pauses* have eloquence."[34]

Finally even consciousness was denied him. Day after day he lay on the couch in his Cheltenham living room in sight of the few mementos of his professional past that he had permitted his wife to preserve, sleeping or staring upon vacancy. Yet when memory stirred it was the theatre that returned. In June of 1871, Helena Faucit and her husband Theodore Martin came to pay their

respects. As plain Helen her talents had been molded under Macready's direction, as impressionable Helen she had confused the
life of the play with the life of the player and offered him a fear-
some temptation, as popular Helena she had departed to star in
her own orbit. For many years they who had once shared the
intimacy peculiar to the little world of the repertory theatre had
neither met nor, apparently, thought back to the days of triumph
and distress.

Macready was asleep on his couch as Miss Faucit entered the
room. Gently she moved to a chair and sat at his feet watching him
intently. Moments passed before the old man opened his eyelids,
and slowly a look of pleased surprise shone through the aged mask.
The sentimental observer might have read this as Macready's
wordless greeting to his estranged partner; but for Helena Faucit
it was the well-remembered expression of King Lear, waking
after his torture, to find Cordelia at his side.

> You must bear with me.
> Pray you now, forget and forgive; I am old and foolish.[35]

It had been two decades since he had bid farewell to the stage.
But in the end of his life, when all those things that he had willed
to value more highly had fallen away, he found in his art the only
reality, the only true value of his experience. Perhaps this is why
his projected autobiography was never completed; until it was too
late he refused to recognize that the only true life of William
Charles Macready was the Stage Life of the Eminent Tragedian.

On April 27, 1873, he died, and the New York *Tribune* in its
obituary notice reported, "The last days of his life have been days
of deepening darkness, of gradually growing imbecility, of sorrowful decay, and immitigable gloom. Death, it is certain, came as a
relief from unbearable infirmity."[36] The newspapers in England
and America, the source of so much distress to him during his
career, united in columns of eulogy, recalling his achievements as
an actor and his innovations as a producer, recognizing him as the
standard against which all future revivals of Shakespeare must be
judged. The quarrel with Forrest and the Astor Place riot were
retold in great detail, and few papers failed to note—as if it were a
final justification for Macready—that he outlived Forrest by four
months. From the length of the obituaries and the pages of
memorabilia, it was clear that the press and the public recognized
that an eminent Victorian had departed.

What was not so apparent was that the actor had left a more
permanent memorial than is usually permitted to the Profession,

even when enshrined in Westminster Abbey. True, his personal achievement as a player lived only in the memory of his audiences and in the imperfect records of his critics. But his practice as regisseur neither retired nor died with him. It has recently been demonstrated that Charles Kean not only followed his practice but pirated his productions.[37] More important, at the farewell banquet, Macready had gone out of his way to name Samuel Phelps as heir to his principles of unity, of making the performed play an exact realization of the poet's image. Phelps, in his historic management of Sadler's Wells, had vigorously developed Macready's precepts. His performance of *King Lear* in Berlin in 1859 was seen by the impressionable young Duke of Saxe-Meiningen, and it was this performance that converted the Duke from a passionate playgoer into a serious and creative poet of the playhouse.[38] In a few years the Meininger players, with their famous slogan, *Im Ganzen, da sitzt die Macht,* would carry the gospel of unity to the theatres of the Western world, and those principles which seemed revolutionary to the departed admirers of Macready would become the common practice of producers from the Slavyansky Bazaar to Broadway.

This is the one legacy of the Victorian theatre to survive the century, whether applied to the classic drama (the Meininger), the drama of realism and naturalism (Antoine and Stanislavsky), or the symbolic and poetic drama (Lugné-Poë). Its fundamental validity is perhaps most clearly demonstrated in the stage career of Jacques Copeau, at once one of the most influential of twentieth-century directors and a determined opponent of the realist theatre of which Macready was harbinger. "The design of a dramatic action," he wrote, "is the unification of movements, of gestures and of attitudes; the harmony of faces, of voices, of silences. It is the totality [*Ganzen*] of the scenic spectacle, emanating from the one thought which conceives it, rules it, and harmonizes it. The direction creates this secret and invisible bond, and makes it control the actors—this bond . . . without which the drama, even interpreted by excellent actors, loses the greater part of its effect."[39] Copeau was born five years after Macready's death, but in spirit he was among the disciples gathered at Freemason's Tavern, July 20, 1839.

It may seem inexact to class as a Victorian an artist whose development spans the period of the Regency and the Romantic Revival, and whose public career after the accession of the Queen was relatively brief. But Thomas Carlyle, whose chronology parallels Macready's, once declared that "the man is the spirit he worked in and what he became,"[40] and Macready was born to be a Victorian. He was of the middle class; his constant concern with material acquisition was directed by his goal of independence for himself and his children. His *Diaries,* often read as a record of splenetic egoism,[41] are evidence of a continuous effort to bring himself to account for his lapses in the self-discipline necessary to adhere to his strict code of duty as head of a family and a member of society. There is something in him of Prince Albert and Herr Teufelsdroeck, something of the *persona* of *In Memoriam,* something of Mr. Gradgrind, and a touch, of course, of Mr. Pecksniff, but nothing at all of Wilkins Micawber.

As an artist, he was conscious of his response to the artistic influences of his age. His education had inculcated a respect for the authors of Greece and Rome and he continued to study them and their English imitators throughout his life. But in his winter of unhappiness, with Harris casting him as one villainous monster after another, he was an attentive auditor at Coleridge's lectures in Flower-de-Luce Court.[42] When he allowed himself to deal with his announced subject, Coleridge had contrasted Beaumont and Fletcher, whose plays are mere aggregations without unity, and Shakespeare, who "worked in the spirit of nature, by evolving the germ from within by the imaginative power according to an idea," creating a drama whose "vitality grows and evolves itself from within—a keynote which guides and controls the harmonies throughout." Specifically, Coleridge cited the "idea" of *Lear:* "It is storm and tempest—the thunder at first grumbling in the far horizon, then gathering around us, and at length bursting in fury over our heads;—succeeded by a breaking of the clouds for a while, a last flash of lightning, the closing in of night, and the single hope of darkness! . . . whilst Macbeth is deep and earthy,—composed to the subterraneous music of a troubled conscience, which converts everything into the wild and fearful!" [Lecture VII] The Coleridgean "idea" added to Sir Thomas Lawrence's principle, "Every part of a picture required equal care and pains," would evolve into that harmonious and complete arrangement of parts which was Macready's later aim as a Shakespearean actor-producer.

Wordsworth early became an object of admiration and later an influence on his style. From Liverpool in 1823 Macready wrote to his London agent, "The only grand things I have seen during the whole summer have been Borrowdale, Wordsworth, and York Minster. . . . It was an opportunity I could not resist to call on Wordsworth. I was fortunate in finding him at home and disengaged; he accompanied me to Winandermere (*sic*), and that I must certainly note as the most agreeable evening of my whole tour. I do not know whether you are fond of his poetry, but I regard him with gratitude and veneration for the good I have drawn from his writings. I must confess that when he 'nods' I turn the leaves over with a rapid finger, but where he is himself, standing out in the full expression of his deep and lofty thought, he is among the mighty."[43] With the poet, Macready believed that art should be purposeful, and as a proto-Victorian that the purpose should be inspiration to self-improvement. To *The Excursion* he responded with gratitude and reverence; the sonnets on the Duddon abounded "in moral truths that tend to direct or confirm the mind."[44] When, in "The Voluntaries of Evening," Wordsworth nodded, he was compared unfavorably with Felicia Hemans' "Sabbath Sonnet."[45]

Wordsworth's occasional descents into the prosaic stemmed from his early commitment "to imitate, and, as far as possible, adopt the very language of men," and Macready's style of acting *apud homines* was analogous both in purpose and risks. At the height of Macready's success, a critic summed up the relationship of the romantic poets and the major figures of the early nineteenth-century stage: "The spiritual tendency which was first manifested in the poetry of Wordsworth, Coleridge, and Shelley, has found its dramatic exposition in Mr. Macready's acting. If [Edmund] Kean were the Byron of actors, Macready may in many respects afford a parallel to Wordsworth . . . [in particular his] insight into the laws of nature under its varied modifications."[46]

Macready's library, the literary and social circles in which he chose to move, the guests who visited Elstree or came to dinner in London, are a measure of his participation in the growth of the Victorian idea. G. M. Young observed that Tennyson's *In Memoriam* illustrates the characteristic Victorian incapacity to follow, and at the same time unwillingness to quit, any reasoning likely to end unpleasantly.[47] Macready's *Diaries* are full of his fervent wrestlings with religion, affirmations of belief in Providence. But on his bookshelves were Chambers' *Vestiges of the Natural History of Creation* and Mantell's *Wonders of Geology,* and in his guest book the names of Lyell, Faraday, and Darwin. When William Buckland, Dean of Westminster, published his treatise on "Geology and Mineralogy" it was taken as an assault on the Mosaic account of creation. Macready immediately found himself on the side of the scientist. "*Why,*" he wrote, "should men be at such pains to defend the *ipse dixit* statement of Moses? . . . Why, then, is not man to exercise his unbiassed reason—*the reason God has given him to use*—upon this and other questions, which, as those of morality, for example, materially affect his salvation?"[48]

The movement of those sentences from the boldness of the opening question to the pious close finds its contemporaneous literary echo in Tennyson:

> Who loves not Knowledge? Who shall rail
> Against her beauty? May she mix
> With men and prosper! Who shall fix
> Her pillars? Let her work prevail. . . .
>
> Let her know her place;
> She is the second, not the first.
>
> A higher hand must make her mild,
> If all be not in vain; and guide
> Her footsteps, moving side by side
> With wisdom, like the younger child:
>
> For she is earthly of the mind,
> But Wisdom, heavenly of the soul.[49]

There are other similarities between Macready and the man who was to be the Victorian Poet Laureate. Tennyson's attempts to give reality to classical and historical figures by the use of rhetorical "colours" and his development of such a character as Mariana springs from the same spirit that inspired Macready's attempts to give reality to the works of Shakespeare by "fidelity of illustration" and precise character delineation. But he was no admirer of Tennyson's poetry and, when Tennyson published an anonymous rejoinder to Bulwer-Lytton's anonymous satire, *The New Timon*, Macready deplored the littleness of revenge which led him to react (not unreasonably) to such lines as these:

> Not mine, not mine (O muse forbid!) the boon
> Of borrowed notes, the mock-bird's modish tune,
> The jingled medley of purloined conceits
> Outbabying Wordsworth and outglittering Keats
> Where all the airs of patchwork-pastoral chime
> To drowsy ears in Tennysonian rhyme![50]

Macready's interest in the United States was partly economic, but it also epitomizes the paradox of Victorian political thinking. In principle, he was a radical; he inveighs against position and privilege in his diaries and letters; the attacks of the penny-press were as much against his political friendships as against his acting. He read Benjamin Franklin and William Ellery Channing. Part of his retirement was given to schemes to improve the lot of the humbler classes. In practice, however, he often betrayed the sense of class and precedence that was the Victorian heritage from the Regency. Doubtless his feeling of the indignity of his calling partially explains the ambiguity of his social philosophy. He was always annoyed if there were not time for him to change from his stage costume into a gentleman's evening dress before taking a curtain call. When Bulwer-Lytton and Talfourd received invitations to a court ball, he wrote: "It is not a pleasing reflection, without caring for the thing itself, that my pariah profession should entitle me to the lavish expression of public praise, and exclude me from distinctions which all my compeers enjoy."[51]

Thus, like most men, Macready was compounded of paradoxes; indeed, the years through which he lived have been called The Age of Paradox. Yet paradox is surely the mark of any vital, aspiring thing, whether it be a man, a period, or an art; it is the constant element in tragedy, the most aspiring form of the art of theatre. What gives the Victorian paradox its special importance is that it remains unresolved, untransmuted; in subsequent decades it became more firmly fixed. If some of the terms and conditions have changed, it is still the paradox of the twentieth century. And so, in his life and works, Macready acquires an interest beyond the ordinary citizens of his day and the ordinary men of the Victorian theatre. A strange and at times a perverse man, he was subject to the compulsions of his nature and his era; yet he emerges like the equally strange and perverse Antigone, the archetype of paradox in drama, not unpraised, not without a kind of honor: The tragedian who was the Victorian ideal and a commentary upon it.

NOTES

INDEX

Notes

PROLOGUE

1. George Henry Lewes, *On Actors and the Art of Acting* (London, 1875), p. 41.
2. William Charles Macready, *Reminiscences and Selections from his Diary and Letters,* ed. F. Pollock (London, 1875), II, 370. Hereafter cited as *Reminiscences.*
3. Lady Pollock, *Macready as I Knew Him* (London, 1885), p. 140.

1. THE PROFESSION

1. British Museum, 11795.k31.
2. James Winston, *The Theatrical Tourist* (London, 1805), p. 59; an illustration showing the exterior of the theatre faces p. 57.
3. John S. Cunningham, *Theatre Royal, The History of the Theatre Royal, Birmingham* (Oxford, 1950), p. 41.
4. *Dramatic Magazine,* I (1829), 90–91.
5. Cunningham, *Theatre Royal,* p. 25.
6. William Archer, *William Charles Macready* (London, 1890), p. 5.
7. "Walking Gentleman," a theatrical term for an actor whose duty was "to make himself generally useful," without studying "capacity," that is, without developing a special line of business: juvenile hero, male heavy, First Tragedy. See *The Literary Review and Stage Manager,* I, 43.
8. Kathleen Barker and Joseph Macleod, "The McCready Prompt Books at Bristol," *Theatre Notebook,* IV (1950), 76 ff.
9. John Coleman, *Fifty Years of an Actor's Life,* II (London, 1904), 146–47.
10. B. P. Bellamy, *A Letter to the Dramatic Censor of the Suffolk Chronicle* (Ipswich, 1813), p. 19.
11. T. J. Serle, *The Players* (London, 1847), II, 307.
12. *Mr and Mrs Bancroft On the Stage and Off* (London, 1888), II, 68.
13. *Liverpool Theatrical Inquisitor for the Year 1821,* I, 59.
14. Bellamy, *A Letter,* pp. 24 ff.
15. A copy is in the Theatre Collection, New York Public Library.
16. F. C. Wemyss, *Twenty-six Years in the Life of an Actor and Manager* (New York, 1847), p. 53.
17. "W. C. Macready (The Elder)," MS, Folger Shakespeare Library.
18. *Reminiscences,* I, 95.
19. *Ibid.,* I, 76.
20. *Ibid.,* I, 82–83.
21. Cunningham, *Theatre Royal,* p. 26.
22. Richard Wright Proctor, *Manchester in Holiday Dress* (London, 1866), p. 131.
23. *Ibid.,* p. 141.

24. William Smart, *Economic Annals of the Nineteenth Century* (London, 1910), I, 183.

25. Proctor, *Manchester*, p. 144.

26. The account of William Charles Macready's early years, unless otherwise indicated, is drawn from his *Reminiscences,* which break off in December 1826. The original manuscript, heavily scored by the editor, Sir Frederick Pollock, is in the Princeton University Library.

27. W. H. D. Rouse, *A History of Rugby School* (New York, 1888), pp. 138–39.

28. *Ibid.,* p. 153.

29. William Charles Macready, *Diaries,* ed. Toynbee (London, 1912), II, 292–293, *fn.* Hereafter cited as *Diaries.*

30. *Reminiscences,* I, 15.

31. *Ibid.,* I, 32.

32. James Boaden, *Memoirs of the Life of John Philip Kemble* (Philadelphia, 1825), pp. 534–35; H. Saxe Wyndham, *Annals of Covent Garden Theatre* (London, 1906), I, 332 ff.

33. Boaden, *Kemble,* pp. 316 ff.

34. Percy Fitzgerald, *The World Behind the Scenes* (London, 1881), p. 35.

35. See Herschel Baker, *John Philip Kemble* (Cambridge, Mass., 1942), chap. xii.

36. James Boaden, *Life of Sarah Siddons* (London, The Grolier Society, n.d.), II, 234.

2. STEPS TO THE TEMPLE

1. *Reminiscences,* I, 41.

2. Archer, *Macready,* p. 36.

3. *Cf.* DeWilde's painting with the description of "Sublime Admiration" in Henry Siddons, *Practical Illustrations of Rhetorical Gesture and Action* (London, 1822), pp. 72–73 and plate 13.

4. Wemyss, *Twenty-Six Years,* p. 52.

5. *Reminiscences,* I, 27.

6. James Boaden, *Memoirs of Mrs. Siddons* (London, 1827), I, 170.

7. For a complete list, see Archer, *Macready,* pp. 30–31.

8. *Reminiscences,* I, 65.

9. *Examiner,* March 15, 1818.

10. *Examiner,* Dec. 5, 1819.

11. Unidentified newsclip, dated Dec. 28, 1814, *Macreadiana* Scrapbook, Garrick Club.

12. *Reminiscences,* II, 441–42.

13. Playbill, Birmingham T. R., Sept. 7, 1812.

14. Playbill, Newcastle, Apr. 20, 1814. A MS note on the playbill for *Rokeby,* May 20, 1814, identifies the adaptation as by Macready himself; *Macreadiana* Scrapbook, Garrick Club.

15. Macready to Drinkwater Meadows, May 1 [no year], Drinkwater Meadows Collection, Garrick Club.

16. *Reminiscences,* I, 63.

17. James Boaden, *The Life of Mrs. Jordan* (London, 1831), II, 20.

18. *London Magazine,* Jan. 1820.

19. *Reminiscences,* I, 55.

20. *Ibid.,* I, 57.

21. An obituary notice, giving somewhat contradictory details of Mrs. Garrick's life, appears in *The Era,* May 21, 1881.

22. The date of Macready's debut in Bath is erroneously given in his *Reminiscences.* The corrected date is from the playbill.

23. *Reminiscences,* I, 92.

24. *Genest Ana,* Harvard Theatre Collection.

25 John Genest, *Some Account of The English Stage* (Bath, 1832), VIII, 492.

26. The negotiations for a London engagement are given in detail in Archer, *Macready,* pp. 28, *ff.*

27. *Reminiscences,* I, 101.

28. This information, communicated by his granddaughter, clarifies a number of otherwise cryptic entries in Macready's *Diaries.* On Aug. 31, 1833, he wrote to his wife from Birmingham that he would inquire after Mrs. Twamley "as a duty to humanity (for I have not very strong individual feelings)." On the covering leaf of the transcripts from Macready's *Diaries* in the Harvard Theatre Collection is the penciled note: "Louise Twamley was a child of Macready's father by Mrs. Twamley." E. Twamley was a leading dancer at Covent Garden in 1816.

29. *English Stage,* VIII, 561.

30. *Reminiscences,* I, 107.

31. Macready to James Anderson, August 3, 1837, Harvard Theatre Collection.

32. *Reminiscences,* I, 118.

33. *Ibid.,* I, 126–27.

34. *Ibid.,* I, 127.

35. Quoted by Archer, *Macready,* p. 36.

36. "Theatrical Examiner," No. 253.

37. Quoted in *Reminiscences,* I, 131. See also *Weekly Despatch,* Sept. 30, 1816, whose critic complains of Macready's "habit of appealing to his cravat, which does not accord with the tone of Italian costume."

38. Quoted in *Reminiscences,* I, 130, n.

39. *Reminiscences,* I, 132.

40. *English Stage,* VIII, 604.

41. *Reminiscences,* I, 136–37.

42. J. A. Hammerton, *The Actor's Art* (London, 1897), pp. 123–24.

43. Quoted in *Reminiscences,* I, 140, n.

44. *Reminiscences,* I, 142.

45. Ludwig Tieck, *Dramaturgische Blätter* (Breslau, 1826), II, 175–76.

46. Undated newsclipping, Harvard Theatre Collection (TS 943.6).

47. *Reminiscences,* I, 84.

48. *Ibid.,* I, 174.

49. *Dramatic Opinions and Essays* (New York, 1907), I, 271.

50. John Coleman, *Fifty Years of an Actor's Life* (London, 1904), II, 507.

51. *Theatrical Inquisitor,* XII (1818), 449.

52. *Reminiscences,* I, 167.

53. *Ibid.,* I, 173–74.

54. Unidentified, undated newsclip, Harvard Theatre Collection (TS 943.6).

55. *Reminiscences,* I, 178.

56. G. T. Watts, *Theatrical Bristol* (Bristol, 1915), pp. 96–97.

57. Original in Folger Shakespeare Library.

58. *Reminiscences,* I, 163.

59. *Ibid.,* I, 163–164.

60. Undated clipping, Harvard Theatre Collection (TS 943.6).

61. "Memoir of Macready" inserted in the extra-illustrated Matthews and Hutton, *Actors and Actresses of Great Britain and the United States,* IV, i, part 1, Harvard Theatre Collection.

62. Playbill, Oct. 25, 1819.

63. Reviews from the *Morning Chronicle,* the *Times,* the *Courier,* the *Literary Gazette,* and the *Examiner* are reproduced in *Reminiscences,* I, 197–99n. Since they also appear in the original manuscript (Princeton University Library), Macready must have followed the practice of most young actors in saving his own notices.

64. *Cf.* "The Diary of Benjamin Webster," *Theatre Annual,* 1945, p. 55.

65. *Examiner,* Oct. 31, 1819, p. 699.

66. *Theatrical Inquisitor,* XV (1819), 329.

67. *Reminiscences,* I, 203.

68. *Ibid.,* I, 206.

69. Covent Garden playbill, April 22, 1820.

3. THE EMINENT TRAGEDIAN

1. Charles Lamb, *Specimens of the English Dramatic Poets Who Lived about the Time of Shakespeare* (London, 1808).

2. *Reminiscences,* I, 208.

3. *Dublin University Magazine,* October 1852, p. 435.

4. Glasgow, April 21, 1820, Harvard Theatre Collection (TS 992. 31 7F, No. 1).

5. Macready to John Forster, Jan. 16 [1851], Victoria and Albert Museum.

6. *The Old Drama and the New* (Boston, 1923), p. 245.

7. *Theatrical Journal,* III, 147.

8. *Literary Gazette and Journal of Belles-Lettres,* Oct. 18, 1823.

9. Edward Fitzball, *Thirty-Five Years of a Dramatic Author's Life* (London, 1859), II, 104.

10. *Collected Works,* ed. Glover and Waller (London, 1903), VIII, 455.

11. *Diaries,* I, 107, 29; II, 138, 344.

12. *Ibid.,* II, 114; I, 30. In May 1841, he wrote to T. J. Serle, "That Mrs. Stirling has stuff in her:—I think I could fashion it into something much better."

13. *Examiner,* Dec. 5, 1819.

14. *The Mirror of the Stage; or, New Dramatic Censor,* Monday, Dec. 30, 1822.

15. *Diaries,* I, 23, 74.

16. *New Monthly Magazine,* July 1, 1821.

17. Unidentified newsclip, 1825, *Theatrical Cuttings,* III, Harvard Theatre Collection.

18. *Literary Gazette,* Jan. 15, 1831.

19. London *Times,* Oct. 25, 1842.

20. Westland Marston, *Our Recent Actors* (London, 1890), p. 21.

21. Jan. 25, 1838.

22. *Diaries,* I, 207, 39, 4, 58.

23. [G. Daniel], "Remarks" prefatory to *Susan Hopley* (by G. D. Pitt), Cumberland's Acting Plays (London, n.d.).

24. *Diaries*, I, 5.

25. *Theatrical Looker-On*, II (1823), 65.

26. *Weekly Freeman's Journal*, Feb. 11, 1826.

27. *Spectator*, XI (1838), 996.

28. Marston, *Our Recent Actors*, p. 45.

29. *Examiner*, Jan. 25, 1838; Marston, pp. 46, 65.

30. Lewes, *On Actors and the Art of Acting*, p. 36.

31. London *Times*, April 24, 1848.

32. *Spectator*, III (1830), 846.

33. *Theatrical Journal*, III (1842), 189.

34. *Ibid.*, XXI (1870), 180.

35. *Diaries*, I, 273.

36. *Reminiscences*, II, 154.

37. *Selected Letters of Anton Chekhov*, ed. Lillian Hellman (New York, 1955), p. 317.

38. Undated letter, or letters, Forster Collection, Victoria and Albert Museum (F 48.E24). The blanks in the transcriptions represent illegible spots caused by the pasting up of the manuscript copy.

39. III, 167.

40. *Diaries*, I, 63.

41. MS note by John Forster, Forster Collection, Victoria and Albert Museum, No. 315.

42. Lady Pollock, *Macready* (London, 1885), p. 11.

43. Marston, *Our Recent Actors*, p. 8.

44. *Diaries*, I, 2–3.

45. *Ibid.*, II, 364, 419; I, 400, 352, 348, 177, 112.

46. Lady Pollock, *Macready*, p. 29.

47. *Reminiscences*, I, 274.

48. *Ibid.*, I, 115–16.

49. *Autobiography* (Cambridge, Mass., 1964), pp. 35–36.

50. *Reminiscences*, I, 66.

51. Lady Pollock, *Macready*, p. 37.

52. Marston, *Our Recent Actors*, p. 49.

53. *Reminiscences*, II, 2.

54. H. T., "Memoir of Mr. Macready," p. 71, Harvard Theatre Collection, extra-illustrated Matthews and Hutton, IV, i, 1.

55. *Lectures on Oratory, Gesture and Poetry* (London, 1873), p. 134.

56. *Diaries*, I, 283.

57. *Reminiscences*, II, 178.

58. Feb. 1, 1821.

59. *Reminiscences*, II, 424.

60. *Ibid.*, I, 216, 219.

61. *Ibid.*, I, 217.

62. August 17, 1820. Collection of Mrs. Christopher Preston.

63. *Reminiscences*, I, 218.

64. Unidentified newsclipping, Nov. 15, 1820, Harvard Theatre Collection, extra-illustrated Matthews and Hutton, IV, i, part 1.

65. In Princeton University Library.

66. Archer, *Macready*, p. 45.

67. H. W. Edwards Bookseller, Catalogue no. 63, item 152.

68. *Personal Reminiscences of Barham, Harness, and Hodder,* R. H. Stoddard, ed., (New York, 1875), p. 246.

69. *The Life and Death of KING RICHARD III, a tragedy, restored and re-arranged from the text of Shakespeare, as performed at the Theatre Royal, Covent Garden* (London: Printed for R. and M. Stodart, 81 Strand, 1821). The Harvard copy is inscribed, in the hand of William B. Wood, "By Wm. Macready, of C. G. Theater." See Wood's *Personal Recollections of the Stage* (Philadelphia, 1855), pp. 431–32.

70. May 1, 1822, Henry E. Huntington Library.

71. A. G. L'Estrange, ed., *Life of Mary Russell Mitford,* (London, 1870), II, 149.

72. *Letters of Mary Russell Mitford,* Henry Chorley, ed., 2nd series (London, 1872), I, 120.

73. L'Estrange, *Mitford,* II, 154.

74. MS in the Henry E. Huntington Library.

75. L'Estrange, *Mitford,* II, 158.

76. *Ibid.,* II, 163.

77. MS in Folger Shakespeare Library.

78. Macready's annotated copy of Hugh Blair's *Lectures on Rhetoric and Belles-Lettres* is in the Harvard Theatre Collection. This is another instance in which Macready prefigures some of the characteristics of Victorianism. Even Albert was to observe that "every human being, including his wife, was capable of unlimited improvement if they only tried hard enough."—Longford, *Queen Victoria* (New York, 1964), p. 305.

79. Elliston Papers, Harvard Theatre Collection.

80. *Ibid.*

81. MS in Folger Shakespeare Library.

82. Short for "Daggerwood," a bad actor. Sylvester Daggerwood is a character in *New Hay at the Old Market* by George Colman the Younger (1795).

83. MS in Folger Shakespeare Library.

84. Oct. 18, 1823.

85. MS in Princeton University Library.

86. *Ibid.*

87. *Ibid.* According to an unidentified newsclipping in the Garrick Club *Macreadiana,* Vol. III, Macready had been a visitor at the Marchioness of Londonderry's "and his union with a lady of title was talked of as more than a probability." And see *Diaries,* II, 432.

88. The quotation is assigned to Byron; Harvard Theatre Collection, extra-illustrated Matthews and Hutton, IV, i, part 2.

89. *Reminiscences,* I, 304.

90. George Raymond, *Memoirs of Robert William Elliston* (London, 1846), II, 434–435.

91. *Reminiscences,* I, 304.

92. Unidentified newsclipping, May 12, 1825, Harvard Theatre Collection, *Theatrical Cuttings,* Vol. IV.

93. *Some Account of the English Stage,* IX, 294.

94. *The Drama, or Theatrical Pocket Magazine* (London, 1822), II, 247.

95. Wemyss, *Twenty-Six Years,* p. 86.

96. August 21/22, 1826, MS in Princeton University Library.

97. British Museum, Add. MS 42879.

98. Harvard Theatre Collection, *Theatrical Cuttings,* IV. If these may be presumed the sentiments of a "writer" offended by the presumption of a

player, they may be set against a more objective opinion affixed to the Covent Garden playbill, Oct. 18, 1826, in the Victoria and Albert Museum: "Mr. MACREADY has, it is true, an occasional hauteur of manner, and an unfortunate susceptibility of trifles, which renders him at times unpleasant to his brother actors, but he is neither unfeeling, heartless, nor unprincipled."

4. THE SPLENDID STROLLER

1. *Reminiscences,* I, 315.

2. *Ibid.,* I, 318.

3. George C. Odell, *Annals of the New York Stage* (New York, 1928), III, 233.

4. *Ibid.,* III, 235.

5. *Reminiscences,* I, 319.

6. *Ibid.,* I, 319-20.

7. William F. Woodeson, *A Slight Sketch of the Performances at the Theatre Royal Drury Lane, during the Season of 1827 and 1828* (London, 1828), p. 16.

8. *Ibid.,* p. 63.

9. Brunton's Diary, MS in Harvard Theatre Collection.

10. Alfred Bunn, *The Stage* (Philadelphia, 1840), II, 211.

11. *Reminiscences,* I, 74.

12. Marie-Antoinette Allevy, *La Mise-en-Scène en France dans la première moitié du dix-neuvième siècle* (Paris, 1938), pp. 91–92.

13. *Ibid.,* p. 28.

14. J-Q. Borgerhoff, *Le Théâtre anglais à Paris sous la restauration* (Paris, 1912), p. 121.

15. *Ibid.,* p. 123.

16. *Reminiscences,* II, 181.

17. Postmarked Apr. 18, 1828, Collection of Anthony Macready.

18. *Bentley's Miscellaney,* XLI (1857), 544.

19. Borgerhoff, *Le Théâtre anglais,* p. 145.

20. June 30, 1828, MS in Folger Shakespeare Library.

21. July 5, 1828, Harvard Theatre Collection, *J. S. Knowles Ana,* I.

22. *Reminiscences,* I, 331.

23. Unidentified newsclipping, dated Sept. 27, 1828, quoting from the *Revue Encyclopédique,* Harvard Theatre Collection, *Theatrical Cuttings,* V.

24. Cf. Downer, "Players and Painted Stage: Nineteenth Century Acting," *PMLA,* LXI (1946), 548ff.

25. Undated clipping, Harvard Theatre Collection, *Theatrical Cuttings,* V.

26. Macready to John L. Greaves, Feb. 1, 1830, MS in Princeton University Library.

27. *Diaries,* I, 33.

28. *Ibid.,* I, 115.

29. Macready to Catherine Macready, March 17, 1833, Collection of Mrs. Christopher Preston.

30. Macready to Catherine Macready, Feb. 12, 1835, Collection of Mrs. Christopher Preston.

31. Jane Carlyle to Macready, Aug. 11, 1853, Collection of Anthony Macready.

32. *Diaries,* I, 39.

33. Miss Macready to Mrs. Cattermole, Morgan Library, Autographs, Dramatic.

34. Macready to Catherine Macready, Aug. 21, 1833, Collection of Mrs Christopher Preston.

35. Richard Renton, *John Forster and his Friendships* (New York, 1913).

36. Macready to Greaves, April 8, 1830, Princeton University Library.

37. *Diaries*, I, 45.

38. Macready to Catherine Macready, Jan. 26, 1829, Collection of Mrs. Christopher Preston.

39. Macready to Catherine Macready, March 17, 1833, Collection of Mrs. Christopher Preston.

40. Macready to Catherine Macready, March 17/19, 1836, Collection of Mrs. Christopher Preston.

41. For Miss (Susan) Kenneth, see *Theatrical Times*, III, 68; also unidentified newsclipping (1826?) in Theatre Collection, New York Public Library.

42. Macready to Calcraft, Nov. 15, 1830, Harvard Theatre Collection, extra-illustrated *Narrative of Kemble's Retirement*, p. 50.

43. Macready to Catherine Macready, Sept. 17, 1834, Collection of Mrs. Christopher Preston.

44. Macready to Catherine Macready, June 17, 1836, Collection of Mrs. Christopher Preston.

45. Macready to Greaves, Feb. 1, 1830, Folger Shakespeare Library.

46. March 17, 1836, Collection of Mrs. Christopher Preston.

47. *Macready as I Knew Him*, p. 64.

48. *The Poetical Works of Lord Byron* (London, Oxford Standard Authors, 1939), p. 550.

49. *Spectator*, V (1832), 516.

50. Macready to Catherine Macready, Dec. 21, 1832, Collection of Mrs. Christopher Preston.

51. Bunn, *The Stage*, I, 99.

52. *Diaries*, I, 14.

53. Macready to Catherine Macready, Aug. 24, 1836, Collection of Mrs. Christopher Preston.

54. *"Appetite.* A monstrous abortion, which is stifled in the kitchen, that it may not exist during dinner."—"Dictionary for the Ladies," *Punch*, I, 264.

55. Bunn, *The Stage*, I, 33.

56. I (1846), 51–52.

57. Harvard Theatre Collection, extra-illustrated Matthews and Hutton, IV, I, part 1.

58. *Theatre Notebook*, IV, 130.

59. I, 27.

60. October 11, 1833, New York Public Library.

61. *Diaries*, I, 74.

62. *Ibid.*, I, 80.

63. *Ibid.*, I, 81.

64. Bunn, *The Stage*, I, 156.

65. Transcript from Macready's Diary, Feb. 5, 1834, Harvard Theatre Collection; *Theatrical Journal*, I, 410.

66. *Diaries*, I, 108.

67. Harvard Theatre Collection, extra-illustrated Pollock, *Macready's Reminiscences*, IV, face p. 413.

68. Bunn, *The Stage*, I, 158.

69. March 18, 1834, Folger Shakespeare Library.

70. *Henry Crabbe Robinson on Books and their Authors*, E. J. Morley, ed. (London, 1938), I, 441.

71. *Diaries*, I, 212.

72. *Ibid.*, I, 213.

73. Bunn, *The Stage*, I, 289.

74. *Diaries*, I, 250.

75. *Ibid*, I, 253.

76. Playbill, Oct. 16, 1835.

77. Quoted in Charles Rice, *The Dramatic Register of the Patent Theatres, &c. 1835–1838*, Oct. 22, 1835, Harvard Theatre Collection.

78. *Ibid.*, Nov. 16, 1835.

79. Jan. 27, 1836, Harvard Theatre Collection.

80. Jan. 30, 1836, Harvard Theatre Collection.

81. April 16, 1836, Stead Collection, New York Public Library.

82. April 22, 1836, Folger Shakespeare Library.

83. *Diaries*, I, 302.

84. Bunn, *The Stage*, I, 209.

85. *Morning Chronicle*, Apr. 30, 1836.

86. *Diaries*, I, 313.

87. Joseph Knight in *Dictionary of National Biography*.

88. Miss Faucit's diary for Feb. 16, 1836, quoted in Theodore Martin, *Helena Faucit* (Edinburgh, 1900), p. 25.

89. Dec. 1, 1836.

90. A. C. Sprague and Bertram Shuttleworth, eds., *The London Theatre in the Eighteen-Thirties* (London, 1950), p. 6.

91. Bulwer to Forster, Nov. 6, 1836, Bulwer Archives, Knebworth.

92. Diaries, I, 358–59.

93. Rice, *Dramatic Register*, VI, 21.

94. Archer, *William Charles Macready*, p. 100.

95. *Ibid.*

5 · ACTOR-MANAGER

1. Transcript of Macready's Diary, Jan. 3, 1834 (Harvard Theatre Collection).

2. *Theatrical Journal*, I (1839), 145.

3. Aug. 2, 1837, Victoria and Albert Museum.

4. W. May Phelps and John Forbes-Robertson, *Life and Life-Work of Samuel Phelps* (London, 1886), pp. 356–57.

5. Archer, *William Charles Macready*, p. 108.

6. Phelps and Forbes-Robertson, *Samuel Phelps*, p. 43.

7. The Anderson-Macready correspondence is in the Harvard Theatre Collection.

8. *Diaries*, I, 405n.

9. Warde resorted to melodramatic contrivances to continue the practice of his very public profession, while keeping his home address private. On Jan. 10, 1839, he wrote to Willmott, the prompter: "Am I in the new Play that was announced last Saturday, if I am pray send me by little John the Barber, who knows where to find me, the part, & the manuscript to read." Harvard

Theatre Collection, extra-illustrated *Macready's Reminiscences*, IV, face p. 112.

10. Sept. 19, 1837, Meadows Collection, Garrick Club.

11. Phelps and Forbes-Robertson, *Phelps*, p. 50.

12. Unidentified newsclipping, in *Macreadiana*, Garrick Club.

13. See William Archer's notes in his copy of *Reminiscences* at I, 344, British Drama League Library.

14. Charles Knight, *London* (London, 1843), pp. 350–352.

15. Bunn, *The Stage*, II, 287–288.

16. Charles H. Shattuck, *Bulwer and Macready* (Urbana, 1958), pp. 56–57.

17. *Ibid.*, pp. 59–60.

18. For a full account of the writing of *The Lady of Lyons*, see "Bulwer and his Lady," by Dewey Ganzel, *Modern Philology*, LVIII (1960), 41–52.

19. Shattuck, *Bulwer and Macready*, p. 63.

20. *Ibid.*, pp. 68–69.

21. *Ibid.*

22. *Ibid.*, p. 64.

23. *Diaries*, I, 444.

24. *Ibid.*, I, 460.

25. Unidentified newsclipping in Harvard Theatre Collection, *J. S. Knowles Ana*, II, 191.

26. Harvard Theatre Collection, extra-illustrated *Macready's Reminiscences*, II, 165.

27. Postmarked Sept. 17, 1838, Harvard Theatre Collection.

28. *Diaries*, II, 188.

29. *Examiner*, Oct. 21, 1838.

30. XI (1838), 996.

31. *Examiner*, Oct. 21, 1838.

32. Marston, *Our Recent Actors*, pp. 25–35.

33. March 10, 1839, Henry E. Huntington Library.

34. March 12, 1839, Princeton University Library.

35. *Diaries*, I, 502n.

36. Clipping from an unidentified journal, July 28, 1839, Princeton Theatre Collection.

6. REGISSEUR

1. Harvard Theatre Collection, extra-illustrated *Macready's Reminiscences*, III, face p. 461.

2. *Diaries*, II, 22.

3. I (1840), 68, 122.

4. *Diaries*, I, 67.

5. *Ibid.*, I, 69.

6. After her death the notes were preserved by her husband, Sir Theodore Martin, who read from them to Macready's granddaughter, Mrs. Lisa Puckle.

7. Lady Pollock, *Macready as I Knew him*, pp. 87–88.

8. Jan. 23, 1840.

9. The *Times* noticed Hammond in its regular column devoted to Bankrupts, but it does not seem to have printed any correspondence from him. (March 4 and 17, 1840.) Hammond, "an excellent comedian," died in New York, August 24, 1848. (Odell, *Annals of the New York Stage*, V, 386.)

10. *Diaries*, II, 62n.

11. Webster's draft of his letter is in the Harvard Theatre Collection. See *Diaries*, II, 86.

12. A "walking gentleman" is a line of theatrical business sometimes called General Utility—confidants, friends-to-the-hero, secondary roles necessary to the plot line, but in which the actor had little opportunity of making a personal impression on the audience.

13. *Diaries*, II, 114.

14. MS in Princeton University Library.

15. Macready to George Smith, March 16, 1841, Harvard Theatre Collection.

16. MS in Henry E. Huntington Library.

17. Macready to Serle, Nov. 8, 1840, Victoria and Albert Museum; *cf.* *Diaries*, II, 81–82.

18. MS in Victoria and Albert Museum.

19. May 28, 1841, Victoria and Albert Museum.

20. Postmarked Jan. 21, 1841, Victoria and Albert Museum. On March 5, 1842, the *Spectator* suggested the substitution of the Bude light (a kind of lime-light projector) for footlights.—see John W. Dodds, *The Age of Paradox* (New York, 1952), p. 60n.

21. April 12, 1841, Harvard Theatre Collection.

22. *Reminiscences*, II, 181.

23. *Ibid.*, II, 189n. *Figaro in London* had earlier suggested another complication: it would be difficult to justify the exclusion of whores from the pit, with Lady Blessington in the boxes. II, 79.

24. III, 314–15.

25. The box-office receipts cited in this chapter are from the manuscript Drury Lane Account Book in the Victoria and Albert Museum.

26. *Theatrical Journal*, III, 50.

27. *Ibid.*, III, 306.

28. *Diaries*, II, 170n.

29. L. Schneider, "Die Londoner Theater in Frühjahr 1842," *Gubitz's Gesellschafter* (1843), p. 438.

30. *Theatrical Journal*, III, 211.

31. *Ibid.*, III, 322.

32. Oct. 5, 1835.

33. Lady Pollock, *Macready*, pp. 20–22. Her account is confirmed by the promptbook for the revival, edited by Charles Shattuck (Beta Phi Mu Chapbook No. 5/6, Urbana, Ill., 1962).

34. III, 346.

35. *Theatrical Journal*, III, 382.

36. Planché changed her name to Malfort and her sex to "a treacherous male friend." See his *Recollections and Reflections* (London, 1872), II, 62.

37. A copy of the promptbook, formerly owned by Anthony Trollope, is in the Folger Shakespeare Library.

38. Archer, *William Charles Macready*, p. 135.

39. The copy in the Harvard Theatre Collection is dated Feb. 7, 1842.

40. *Theatrical Journal*, III, 398.

41. W. H. Griffin, *The Life of Robert Browning* (London, 1910), p. 113.

42. Archer, *Macready*, p. 136.

43. Griffin, *Browning*, p. 119n.

44. The Earl of Lytton, *The Life of Edward Bulwer* (London, 1913), II, 33.

45. On Macready's *Comus,* see Charles H. Shattuck, "Macready's Comus: A Prompt-Book Study," *JEGP,* LX (1961), 731–748.

46. *Reminiscences,* II, 210n.

47. *Reminiscences,* II, 210n.

48. *Diaries,* II, 17–18.

49. New York *Sunday Times,* May 4, 1873.

50. I, 70, Harvard Theatre Collection.

51. *Theatrical Journal,* III, 346.

52. Folger Shakespeare Library.

53. *Theatrical Journal,* I, 169.

54. *Reminiscences,* II, 377.

55. *Ibid.,* II, 446.

56. London *Times,* June 15, 1835.

57. *Reminiscences,* I, 46.

58. A copy of the promptbook, formerly owned by Sir Henry Irving, is in the Harvard Theatre Collection.

59. *Diaries,* I, 418.

60. *Spectator,* XI (1838), 490.

61. *Examiner,* March 18, 1838.

62. Undated copy, Folger Shakespeare Library.

63. *Theatrical Inquisitor,* IV (1819), 78.

64. *Reminiscences,* I, 209.

65. Princeton University Library.

66. New York *Star,* April 16, 1881.

67. Harvard Theatre Collection.

68. Macready to George Macready, Aug. 10, 1832, Princeton University Library.

69. Promptbook, Harvard Theatre Collection.

70. Copy marked by George Ellis, Folger Shakespeare Library.

71. *Diaries,* I, 431.

72. George C. Odell, *Shakespeare from Betterton to Irving* (New York, 1920), II, 211.

73. *Diaries,* II, 380.

74. *Atlantic Monthly,* LXVIII (1891), 859.

75. *Spectator,* X (1837), 970.

76. *Diaries,* I, 459.

77. *Ibid.,* I, 177.

78. *Ibid.,* I, 416.

79. XI (1838), 1038.

80. London *Times,* Nov. 7, 1837.

81. Lady Pollock, *Macready,* p. 21. Although the London *Times* was generally cool to the revival, criticising Macready for "overstriving for light and shade," it praised Hudson's LeBeau "the extreme absurdity of which provoked an immense deal of laughter." October 3, 1842.

82. *Reminiscences,* I, 360.

83. *Ibid.,* I, 390.

84. Bunn, *The Stage,* III, 23.

85. Copy in Folger Shakespeare Library.

86. Copy in Folger Shakespeare Library.

87. XI (1838), 253.

88. Copy in Folger Shakespeare Library. This seems to be a copy of the standard prompt in use at Drury Lane after 1822, with additions in Macready's hand. Nearly every scene bears the young actor's signature.

89. X (1837), 946.

90. *Theatrical Journal*, I, 126. The "innovations" of the portraits had been tried by T. J. Serle in his own performance of Hamlet in 1826 (*New Monthly Magazine*, Jan. 1, 1826). In the light of Serle's suggestions for the production scheme of *Henry V* (see below), it would appear that Macready was more willing to adopt other men's ideas than many of his contemporaries would admit.

91. *Diaries*, I, 484.

92. *Atheneum*, Jan. 15, 1839.

93. XIII (1839), 558.

94. H. Saxe Wyndham, *The Annals of Covent Garden Theatre* (London, 1906), II, 139.

95. *Spectator*, XI (1838), 253.

96. Macready's working copy, formerly owned by Anthony Trollope, Folger Shakespeare Library.

97. May 20, 1842.

98. Lady Pollock, *Macready*, p. 20.

99. *Ibid.*, pp. 83–84.

7. THE RIVAL STARS, OR, A TRAGEDY REHEARS'D

1. *Diaries*, II, 388. By his first wife, Macready had ten children: Christina (1830–1850); William (1832–1871); Catherine (1835–1869); Edward (1836–?); Harriet (1837–1840); Henry (1838–1857); Walter (1840–1853); Lydia (1842–1858); Cecilia (1847–1935); Jonathan (1850–1908). Macready never knew the fate of his son Edward, who is still considered "the Family Mystery." Edward had wanted to go on the stage, but his father sent him to Addiscombe for officer training. His regiment was posted to India where he proved a good officer, but got heavily in debt through gambling. Macready, in a "Roman father's letter," ordered him to return to England. He boarded a ship in Bombay, and was never seen again. In his will, Macready left him £100, "if living." The family has always believed that he swam to a nearby Australian ship and went off to that continent. (Mrs. L. Puckle). The *Theatrical Journal* (XX [1859], 399) reported that Edward made his debut at Ballarat in *The Lady of Lyons*, and that he demonstrated "attention and study, but not genius."

2. *Correspondence of Thomas Carlyle and Ralph Waldo Emerson* (Boston, 1888), II, 35–36.

3. *Theatrical Journal*, IV, 353–354.

4. *The Diary of Philip Hone*, Allan Nevins, ed. (New York, 1936), p. 671.

5. Club of Odd Volumes, *Exhibition to Illustrate the History of the Boston Stage* (1915), pp. 17–18. See also Odell, *Annals of the New York Stage*, III, 313.

6. *Autobiographical Sketch of Mrs. John Drew* (New York, 1899), pp. 96–98.

7. Oct. 27, 1843, Collection of Mrs. L. Puckle.

8. Nov. 3, 1844, Folger Shakespeare Library.

9. Forrest to Archer, Oct. 30, 1831, Harvard Theatre Collection, extra-illustrated *Macready's Reminiscences*, II, face p. 319.

10. Jan. 21, 1844, Collection of Mrs. Christopher Preston.

11. Jan. 14, 1844, Collection of Mrs. Christopher Preston.

12. Noah Ludlow, *Dramatic Life as I Found it* (St. Louis, 1880), p. 581.

13. *Ibid.*, pp. 592–93.

14. *Ibid.*, p. 597.

15. April 5, 1844, Folger Shakespeare Library.

16. Hone, *Diary*, p. 706.

17. June 20, 1844, New-York Historical Society.

18. August 20, 1844, Folger Shakespeare Library.

19. Macready to Serle, Aug. 20, 1844, Folger Shakespeare Library.

20. Forrest to Oakes, Dec. 2, 1869, Princeton University Library.

21. Transcript of Macready's Diary, Sept. 14, 1844, Collection of Mrs. L. Puckle.

22. *Ibid.*, August 14, 1844. This "transcript" may rather be his daily notes intended for later copying into his diary; they are very nearly illegible.

23. Harvard Theatre Collection, extra-illustrated Matthews and Hutton, IV, i, part 1.

24. Hone, *Diary*, p. 715.

25. Macready to Catherine Macready, Sept. 28, 1844, Folger Shakespeare Library.

26. Harvard Theatre Collection, extra-illustrated *Macready's Reminiscences*, V, following p. 248.

27. Sept. 28, 1844, Folger Shakespeare Library.

28. Macready to——, from Manchester, April 1, 1845, Harvard Theatre Collection, extra-illustrated *Macready's Reminiscences*, V, face p. 261.

29. Feb. 10, 1845, Harvard Theatre Collection. During its revival in Paris, Gérard de Nerval had described it as "oeuvre ennuyeuse mais honorable." Nerval's accounts of the English performances, highly favorable to Macready's interpretations of Hamlet and Macbeth, but still fretful about the ghosts and witches, are reprinted in *La Revue Théâtrale*, no. 29.

30. March 7, 1845, Harvard Theatre Collection.

31. March 28, 1845, Harvard Theatre Collection.

32. Macready to Horace Twiss, Sept. 24, 1844, Princeton University Library.

33. Macready had made a single appearance at a minor house as a favor to Knowles on his benefit night.

34. Undated letter, Collection of Mrs. Christopher Preston.

35. *Examiner*, March 1, 1845.

36. March 4, 1845, extra-illustrated Harrison, *Edwin Forrest*, Princeton University Library.

37. April 13, 1855. Stuart, whose real name was Edmund O'Flaherty, told Joseph Jefferson that "he was paid a stated sum of money to go to the theatre regularly every night during Forrest's engagements at the Broadway Theatre in 1856, for the purpose of writing him down." *The Autobiography of Joseph Jefferson* (Harvard University Press, 1964), p. 128.

38. March 20, 1855.

39. J. H. Froude, *Letters and Memorials of Jane Welsh Carlyle* (New York, 1883), p. 256.

40. *Examiner*, Oct. 11, 1835.

41. *Evening Telegraph*, Feb. 22, 1890.

42. Feb. 6, 1846; Henry E. Huntington Library, dated from *Diaries*, II, 321.

43. *Theatrical Journal*, VII, 292, 319.

44. I, 140.

45. *Letters of an Old Playgoer* (New York, 1919), p. 23.

46. XIII, 141. Maddox used the closing night of the season to defend his allegiance to the legitimate drama: "I think the appearances of Mr. Macready and of Mrs. Butler prove this—they are the lawful children—the true representatives of our divine bard—and in addition to them I may add that

talented lady, Miss Cushman, whom I first had the honour to introduce to the British Public. I believe she is legitimate too." *Theatrical Journal*, VIII, 261.

47. Edward Stirling, *Old Drury Lane* (London, 1881), I, 183.

48. John Forster, *Life of Charles Dickens* (London, 1872/3), II, 342.

49. New York, 1879, pp. 189, 390.

50. New York, 1882, p. 644.

51. *Ibid.*, p. 637.

52. *Ibid.*, p. 638.

53. *Ibid.*, p. 635.

54. IX, 58.

55. Quoted in *Spirit of the Times*, March 28, 1848.

56. Macready to Ruggles, April 13, 1848, Folger Shakespeare Library.

57. *Diaries*, II, 329.

58. Macready to Ruggles, June 2, 1848, Harvard Theatre Collection, extra-illustrated Clement, *Charlotte Cushman*, Vol. I, face p. 18.

59. Before announcement was made of the Queen's "bespeak," a paper was circulated "requisitioning" Macready to "appear in one of the characters of the national drama to which he has rendered such essential services." Among the signers were thirteen lords, Count Dorsay, Bulwer-Lytton, Browning, Moncton Milnes, Cobden, Carlyle, Hallam, Tennyson, the members of Macready's cabinet, Charles Young, and—Charles Kemble. *Spirit of the Times*, July 29, 1848.

60. XV, 33.

61. *The Poetical Works of Alexander Pope. Revised and Arranged Expressly for the Use of Young People*, by William Charles Macready (London, Bradbury and Evans, 1849), Preface, iv.

62. Young to Catherine Macready, May 17, 1848, Harvard Theatre Collection, extra-illustrated Macready's *Reminiscences*, Vol. VI, following p. 465.

63. Oct. 7, 1848.

64. W. T. Price, *A Life of William Charles Macready* (New York, 1894), p. 121.

65. Philadelphia *Public Ledger and Daily Transcript*, Nov. 21, 1848.

66. Handbill, dated from Jones' Hotel, Nov. 22, 1848, Harvard Theatre Collection, extra-illustrated Matthews and Hutton, Vol. IV, 1, part 1.

67. Sol Smith, *Theatrical Management in the West and South* (New York, 1868), p. 217.

68. Quoted in *Theatrical Journal*, X, 99.

69. XVI, 133.

70. *Spirit of the Times*, XIX, 77.

71. *Punch*, XVI, 168. The toast inspired Mr. Punch in his continued protests against Victoria's inattention to the theatres. He comments: "This is very pretty, but what follows is, in our opinion, very much prettier. For an English actor (name not given), one of the New Orleans company, no doubt struck by the simile of the Diamond and the setting in association with the QUEEN's Windsor diamond present to MR. CHARLES KEAN, rose and proposed—'Queen Victoria and Charles Kean—the greatest living sovereign and the deadest living actor, the former, the diamond; the latter, the *tin*.' "

72. "Carboy's Reminiscences," undated excerpt from *Philadelphia Sunday Despatch*, Harvard Theatre Collection.

73. Archer, *William Charles Macready*, p. 177.

74. *Theatrical Journal*, X, 149.

75. Louis Dow Scioso, *Political Nativism in New York State* (New York, 1901), p. 15.

76. Document dated May 8, 1849, New-York Historical Society.

77. Hone, *Diary,* p. 876.

77a. George Washington Walling, *Recollections of a New York Chief of Police* (Denver, 1890), p. 46. Walling was a young policeman at the time of the riot and took part in the defence of Astor Place. Afterwards, by studying the handbills and conferring with printers he was able to trace them to Rynders' Empire Club and the Native American Party (p. 47).

78. *National Police Gazette,* Sept. 22, 1849.

79. New York *Herald,* Sept. 20, 1849.

80. H. M. Ranney, *Account of the Terrific and Fatal Riot at the New-York Astor Place Opera House* (New York, 1849), pp. 16–17.

81. New York *Herald,* Sept. 20, 1849.

82. Sol Smith, *Theatrical Management* (New York, 1868), p. 217.

83. New York *Tribune,* May 12, 1849.

84. *Ibid.,* May 14, 1849.

85. *Ibid.,* Sept. 20, 1849.

86. Thomas Addis Emmett, *Incidents of my Life* (New York, 1911), p. 130.

87. G. T. C[urtis], "William Charles Macready," *Appleton's Journal,* May 24, 1873.

88. May 22, 1849, Harvard Theatre Collection.

89. May 11, 1849, Princeton University Library.

90. Sol Smith, *Theatrical Management,* p. 217.

91. See the article on Daly in the *Dictionary of American Biography.*

92. *Theatrical Journal,* X, 186. T. A. Emmett declared that Forrest "availed himself of the anti-Catholic, anti-foreign excitement generated by the Know Nothings" to start the riot. *Incidents,* p. 130.

93. H. E. Hammond, *A Commoner's Judge* (Boston, 1954), p. 91.

94. *Personal Reminiscences of Sir Frederick Pollock* (London, 1887), I, 282.

8. EXIT MACBETH

1. Quoted in *Punch,* XVI, 217.

2. *Diaries,* II, 433.

3. XX, 37. In a letter to "Dear Fanny [Haworth?]," Macready warns her, "Remember that February 30 is not *'The last night of all'*—It is the last night at the Haymarket, which they choose to term the last night of all." Princeton University Library.

4. Oct. 1, 1850, Harvard Theatre Collection, extra-illustrated *Life of Sheridan Knowles,* I, following p. 68.

5. *The Letters and Private Papers of William Makepeace Thackeray,* Gordon N. Ray, ed. (Cambridge, Mass., 1945), II, 703.

6. James R. Anderson, *An Actor's Life* (London, 1902) pp. 192–93.

7. Jan. 31, 1851, Collection of Mrs. Christopher Preston.

8. The following pages are intended as a running account of what a spectator might have seen at an *ideal* production of Macready's *Macbeth.* It is based upon a promptbook in the Seymour Collection of the Princeton University Library used by E. L. Davenport and inscribed: *"Haymarket, Oct. 28th. First night of Mr. Macready's farewell engagement."* Unless otherwise noted, all the business described is from this prompt copy.

9. L. Schneider, "Die Londoner Theater in Frühjahr 1842," *Gubitz's Gesellschafter* (1843), p. 437.

10. Folger Shakespeare Library promptbook, *Macbeth* 20. Transcribed for Charles Kean by George Ellis, prompter at Drury Lane, July, 1846. Hereafter cited as *Folger 20.*

11. *Spectator,* X (1837), 1072. By old theatrical custom, the "speaking witches" are played by men.

12. *Folger 20.*

13. So the Princeton promptbook. But see *Folger 20:* "No Flourish Mind!"

14. *Folger 20.*

15. *Ibid.*

16. So *Folger 20.* Princeton promptbook assigns this to Ross (who is not a member of the royal party on its entrance).

17. *Folger 20;* Ross in the Princeton promptbook.

18. *Ibid.*

19. *Ibid.*

20. *Ibid.*

21. "March—very distant—L—commencing with the Kettle Drums. This was played in the Green Room, and the Door opened and shut, occasionally, to give the idea of the wind wafting the sounds to and fro."—*Folger 20.*

22. The drawings in this chapter, from George Scharf, Jr., *Recollections of the Scenic Effects of Covent Garden Theatre during the Season 1838–1839* (London, n.d.), were made during actual performances or rehearsals with Macready's approval.

23. *Theatrical Journal,* I (1839), 277–79.

24. Arthur Colby Sprague, *Shakespeare and the Actors* (Cambridge, Mass., 1944), p. 231.

25. *Literary Gazette,* Jan. 17, 1820.

26. Scharf, *Recollections.*

27. So the Princeton promptbook; according to *Folger 20,* they use the left hand for pointing.

28. Macready, objecting to Maclise's painting of the witches as too horrible, thought that "a horror can be better conveyed by a feeling of alarm exhibited in the face that looks at it." Lady Pollock, *Macready,* p. 58.

29. *Folger 20.*

30. *Political and Literary Journal,* Oct. 13, 1849.

31. *Folger 20.*

32. *Ibid.*

33. Promptbook of *Macbeth,* Victoria and Albert Museum: "From R Lightning thrown directly on Macbeth's face." Hereafter cited by the pressmark, *Forster no. 7920.*

34. Marston, *Our Recent Actors,* p. 50.

35. *Folger 20.*

36. *New York Mirror,* IV (1826), 95.

37. *Theatrical Journal,* I (1839), 277–79.

38. *Folger 20.*

39. Marston, p. 50.

40. *Folger 20.*

41. The word βασιλευς is penciled three times in Macready's hand during this scene in *Forster no. 7920.* This would seem to be the theme, or Coleridgean "idea," for his characterization at this point. See *Diaries,* II, 480.

42. *Folger 20.*

43. *Ibid.*
44. *New York Mirror*, IV, 95.
45. *Folger 20.*
46. *Ibid.*
47. *New Monthly Magazine*, Dec. 1827.
48. *Folger 20.*
49. *Ibid.*
50. *Ibid.*
51. *Examiner*, Oct. 4, 1835.
52. Charles Durang, *The Philadelphia Stage*, Chap. 32 (originally published as a serial in the Philadelphia *Sunday Despatch*, pasted in a scrapbook, Harvard Theatre Collection). *Folger 20* adds: "Keep all quiet about the stage R & L at back!!!"
53. Harvard Theatre Collection, *Genest Ana.*
54. *Spectator*, Nov. 11, 1837; *Genest Ana*; Sprague, *Shakespeare*, p. 409.
55. Folger Shakespeare Library, *Macbeth* promptbook no. 28, made by John Moore. Cited hereafter as *Folger 28.*
56. Marston, *Our Recent Actors*, p. 51.
57. Sprague, *Shakespeare*, pp. 242, 400. The Princeton promptbook notes that offstage in Duncan's chamber shall be placed, "Looking glass—Lights. Daggers & Blood"; in Macbeth's chamber, "Wash basin—soap—towell—Glass."
58. *Theatrical Inquisitor*, XVI (1820), 402.
59. *Examiner*, May 15, 1836.
60. Shakespeare Memorial Library (Stratford-on-Avon), promptbook copied from Macready by G. Hastings for Barry Sullivan. Hereafter cited as *Stratford prompt.*
61. *Forster no. 7920.*
62. The knocking was produced by means of an iron bolt.
63. *Theatrical Inquisitor*, XVI, 402.
64. "Lady M: does not touch M: during this speech until the last word 'thoughts'—when she seizes him by the hand and shoulders and pulls him away L. H." Macready's note in *Forster no. 7920.*
65. *Political and Literary Journal*, Oct. 13, 1849.
66. *Folger 20.*
67. *Folger 20:* "Buss of voices R & L—in alarm—NOT TOO LOUD."
68. Cf., Barham, "The Witches' Frolic" in *Ingoldsby Legends*, first published in *Bentley's Miscellaney*, IV (1838), 501–11. There is one direct allusion to Macready's current (1838) revival of *Coriolanus* in the same legend, suggesting that the following lines are a poetic report on his production of *Macbeth:*

> Nay, the truth to express, as you'll easily guess,
> They have none of them time to attend much to dress;
> But He or She, as the case may be,
> He or She seizes what He or She pleases,
> Trunk-hosen or kirtles, shirts or chemises,
> And thus one & all, great & small, short & tall,
> Muster at once in the Vicarage hall,
> With upstanding locks, starting eyes, shorten'd breath,
> Like the folks in the Gallery Scene in Macbeth,
> When Macduff is announcing their Sovereign's death.

This passage was called to my attention by the late Dorothy Sayers.
69. *Folger 20.*
70. *Ibid.*

71. Details of this scene are from *Folger 20*. The "singing witches" are performed by both men and women.

72. "The 'echoes' are done by 2 Sopranos, Tenor and a Bass, close behind the Scene that is on."

73. *Folger 20*. In at least one performance, Helen Faucit as Lady Macbeth "played" her finger about Fleance's head while her husband prepared to send father and son into the prepared trap. Morley, *Journal of a London Playgoer* (London, 1891), p. 291. Whether she would have dared to usurp Macready's business in his own production is questionable.

74. *Folger 20*.

75. *Ibid.*

76. *Ibid.*

77. Marston, p. 50; *Examiner*, Oct. 9, 1836.

78. Marston, p. 52. "Very sweet and tender was the conception that a touch of human pity and regard for the weakness of his wretched sleep-walker of a wife, had entered the bosom of the royal murderer then,—but we venture to think, very misplaced and wrong." *Examiner*, Oct. 9, 1836.

79. *The New Mirror*, Dec. 9, 1843.

80. Details of this scene are from *Stratford prompt*.

81. W. M. Thackeray, *Notes for a Speech at Dinner* (Philadelphia, 1896), p. 16.

82. *Forster no. 7920*.

83. *Macbeth*, Duncombe's ed. (London, n.d.). Casts from Drury Lane, 1840; Covent Garden, 1839. Most of the stage business is taken from Oxberry's ed. of 1821, which is prefaced with a cut of Macready and gives the Covent Garden cast with Macready, Egerton, Terry, and Mrs. Faucit.

84. *Folger 20*.

85. *Literary Gazette*, Jan. 17, 1820.

86. *New Mirror*, Dec. 9, 1843.

87. "If I stand here I saw him"—unidentified engraving in Harvard Theatre Collection.

88. *Examiner*, April 13, 1823. *The Atheneum* (quoted in Sprague, pp. 263–64) records a new piece of business inserted in 1849. During the general confusion, the physician comes forward and pantomimes a medical opinion as to Macbeth's sanity to the Queen. Since the business does not appear in the later promptbooks, Macready must have agreed with the critic that it was of doubtful propriety.

89. *Literary Gazette*, Nov., 1823; *New York Mirror*, IV, 95.

90. *New Mirror*, Dec. 9, 1843.

91. Details of this scene are taken from *Folger 20*.

92. "The Chorus was sung on the bridge, at the extreme back of the flies— every person sung with his face turned to the wall, but as loudly as possible! The Chorus consisted of 8 1st Sop., 8 2nd do, 8 tenors, 8 Altos, & 8 Basses."

93. "The last Chorus was not sung on the bridge, but at a greater distance in the painting room, with door open, which closed gradually towards the end."

94. James Sheridan Knowles, *Lectures on Dramatic Literature: Macbeth* (London, 1875), pp. 64–66.

95. *Forster no. 7920*.

96. *Folger 28*.

97. The long scene in England is kept almost intact (with only rudimentary indications of business) to give Macduff his dramatic moment. A second reason for its retention is suggested by the note which introduces it in the

Princeton promptbook: "Mr. Macbeth, *you may rest yourself.*" Macbeth has been on stage almost continuously since the beginning of the play, and strenuous exertions are still to come. For Macready, an actor who normally employs great physical force in his representations, the respite of the scene in England and the ensuing "Sleep-walking Scene" is essential if he is to measure up to the expectation of the audience in the exciting duel which concludes the play.

98. Helena Faucit, *On Some of Shakespeare's Female Characters* (Edinburgh, 1891), p. 288.

99. *New York Mirror,* IV, 95.

100. Marston, *Our Recent Actors,* pp. 52–53; Sprague, *Shakespeare,* p. 273.

101. *Examiner,* May 2, 1846; Sprague, *Shakespeare,* p. 274.

102. *New York Mirror,* IV, 95; a.l.s. Macready to Gaspey (Stead Collection, New York Public Library); *Theatrical Journal,* III (1842), 106.

103. *Folger 28:* "A set scene with pieces variously arranged and all with flaps so that when the cue is given all the flaps fall down and discover troops in the foreground R & L and painted figures in the distance. . . . [At the trumpet flourishes:] each flourish more distant according to the number of flaps." The prompter who prepared the *Stratford prompt* warns at this point: "N. B. Unless there is a Scenic Effect, Scene 5 is better omitted."

104. *Illustrated London News,* XV, 235.

105. *Forster no. 7920.* The details of the duel are also to be found in this copy.

106. *New York Mirror,* IV, 95.

107. *New Monthly Magazine,* Dec. 1, 1826.

108. Marston, *Our Recent Actors,* p. 53.

109. *Examiner,* Oct. 4, 1835; *New Monthly Magazine,* Dec. 1827.

AFTERPIECE

1. *Personal Reminiscences of Sir Frederick Pollock,* I, 292.

2. Unidentified newsclipping, John Ellis scrapbook, Collection of Anthony Macready.

3. "Dyce MS notes" in Dyce Letters, pressmark 26. E. 14, Victoria and Albert Museum.

4. *Reminiscences,* II, 451.

5. "In Memory of Robert, Second Son, and Mary, Eldest Daughter of William, Lord Digby." The epitaph begins:
   Go, fair Example of untainted Youth
   Of Modest Reason and Pacifick Truth . . .

6. Shattuck, *Bulwer and Macready,* p. 238.

7. Macready to unidentified correspondent, Sept. 10, 1857 in Daly, "Bill of the Play," Henry E. Huntington Library.

8. See *Dorset County Chronicle, passim.*

9. A. B. Gourlay, *A History of Sherborne School* (Winchester, 1951), p. 110.

10. Macready to W. J. Fox, July 5, 1851, Collection of Mrs. Christopher Preston.

11. Sir Nevil Macready, *Annals of an Active Life* (London, 1924).

12. Unidentified clipping dated Nov., 1854, Ellis scrapbook, Collection of Anthony Macready.

13. Unidentified clippings dated 1846 in *Macreadiana,* Garrick Club.

14. Ellis scrapbook, Collection of Anthony Macready.

15. E. L. Woodward, *The Age of Reform* (Oxford, 1946), p. 475.

16. *Ibid.,* p. 13.

17. *Dorset County Chronicle,* May 21, 1857.

18. Ellis scrapbook, Collection of Anthony Macready.

19. *Ibid.*

20. June 7, 1852, Collection of Mrs. Christopher Preston.

21. Thackeray records that his efforts earned £25 for the benefit of the Institution. *Letters and Private Papers,* IV, 72. See also *Dorset County Chronicle,* Dec. 28, 1854, March 18, 1858, April 29, 1858.

22. *Personal Reminiscences,* I, 296–97.

23. Macready to Phelps, Feb. 13, 1857, Victoria and Albert Museum.

24. Macready to Phelps, undated fragment; also letter of Sept. 29, 1852, Folger Shakespeare Library.

25. Macready to Dyce, June 2, 1853, Victoria and Albert Museum.

26. Nov. 1, 1854, Morgan Library.

27. Oct. 2, 1858, Morgan Library.

28. *Reminiscences,* II, 446.

29. *Ibid.*

30. Dickens to Macready, Sept. 7, 1863, Morgan Library.

31. *Dorset County Chronicle,* April 24, 1862.

32. Pollock, *Personal Reminiscences,* II, 112.

33. I am indebted to Mrs. Lisa Puckle for this account.

34. Archer, *Macready,* p. 189.

35. Martin, *Helena Faucit,* pp. 316–17.

36. April 30, 1873.

37. Charles Shattuck, *William Charles Macready's King John* (Urbana, 1962), p. 7. See also Professor Shattuck's Introduction to his promptbook study, *Mr. Macready Produces As You Like It* (Urbana, 1962).

38. Ernest Leopold Stahl, *Shakespeare und das Deutsche Theater* (Stuttgart, 1947), p. 486.

39. Marcel Doisy, *Jacques Copeau, ou l'absolu dans l'art* (Paris, 1954), p. 60.

40. *Sartor Resartus* (New York, Modern Student's Library), p. 180.

41. Victoria's own *Journals* are full of what a recent biographer has called "operatic" outbursts and exploding epithets conferred upon enemies or opponents; cf. Elizabeth Longford, *Queen Victoria* (New York, Harper & Row, 1964), p. 31.

42. Note, *hors du texte,* in the manuscript of his *Reminiscences,* Princeton University Library. Macready also owned a copy of Coleridge's *Notes and Lectures on Shakespeare; cf., The Library and Collection of Works of Art of William Charles Macready, Esq.* (London, Christie, Manson and Woods, July 8, 1873).

43. Macready to Maywood, Sept. 30, 1823, Harvard Theatre Collection.

44. *Diaries,* I, 242, *Reminiscences,* I, 358.

45. *Diaries,* I, 246.

46. *Theatrical Times,* II (1847), 164.

47. *Victorian England* (London, 1936), p. 75.

48. *Diaries,* I, 345.

49. *In Memoriam,* cxiv.

50. *Diaries,* II, 322–25.

51. *Ibid.,* II, 9.

Index